Paula Ferraz

WORLD PROSPECTS
A Contemporary Study

WORLD PROSPECTS
A Contemporary Study

John Molyneux

Vice-Principal
Bloor Collegiate
Toronto, Ontario

Marilyn Olsen

Head of Geography
Harbord Collegiate
Toronto, Ontario

Prentice-Hall of Canada, Ltd., Scarborough, Ontario

Canadian Cataloguing in Publication Data

Molyneux, John, date.
  World prospects

Includes index.
ISBN 0-13-968826-9

1. Social history – 20th century.
2. Economic history – 20th century.
3. World politics – 20th century.
4. Industrialization. I. Olsen, Marilyn. II. Title.

HN16.M64   309.1'04   C78-001402-2

Prentice-Hall, Inc., Englewood Cliffs, New Jersey
Prentice-Hall of Australia, Pty., Ltd., Sydney
Prentice-Hall of India Pvt., Ltd., New Delhi
Prentice-Hall International, Inc., London
Prentice-Hall of Japan, Inc., Tokyo
Prentice-Hall of Southeast Asia (Pte.) Ltd., Singapore

ISBN 0-13-968826-9

Design: Julian Cleva/Gail Ferreira
Illustrations: James Loates
Cover photograph: A view of the earth taken from the Apollo
8 spacecraft as it orbited the moon. (*Courtesy NASA*)
Composition: Webcom Limited
Printed and bound in Canada by The Bryant Press Limited

4 5   83

Contents

Preface

World Prospects: A Contemporary Study has several aims, and we feel that all are of equal importance. The book attempts to provide you with information about some of the world's major concerns, such as economic growth, birth control, and political systems. Newspaper and magazine articles present a wide range of views on these issues. For example, some articles emphasize the advantages of continued economic growth, while others stress the disadvantages. In the Discussion and Research sections of the text, we ask you to examine the values underlying these contrasting points of view, and therefore to develop your critical thinking skills.

Analytical skills will also be developed in the Statistical Interpretation sections of the book. You are required not only to draw maps and graphs and to perform calculations, but also to comment on your results.

A further aim of the text is to create in you an awareness of the dynamic aspects of any given situation. In the book, then, issues are often analyzed on the basis of established trends and possible changes. We encourage you to do the same, through the various discussion questions and statistical assignments. We also hope that in addition to becoming aware of changing trends within a certain area, you will perceive the great differences that exist from one part of the world to another.

Apart from the aims of *World Prospects*, a few words should be said about its format. The book contains numerous discussion questions, calculations, and cartographic analyses, far more material than can be handled in a single year's course. While we think that the intellectual stimulation you gain from the book will increase with the number of assignments done, we realize that total completion is impossible.

We also want to point out that you do not have to study the themes in the order set down in the text. It is quite possible, for instance, to justify *Change* as the first theme for study, and to examine the course material from that standpoint. The chapter conclusions that we have provided throughout the text are not intended to lock the themes in a specific order. Rather, their purpose is to show that all the issues studied are interrelated, and to propose several specific relationships. Should you investigate the themes in a different order, we suggest that you write your own conclusions; in this way, you will have the chance to link themes yourself, and to consider relationships that we have not discussed.

We would sincerely like to thank Rob Greenaway and MaryLynne Meschino, whose help and encouragement in the preparation of the text have been tremendous.

John Molyneux/Marilyn Olsen
Toronto, 1978

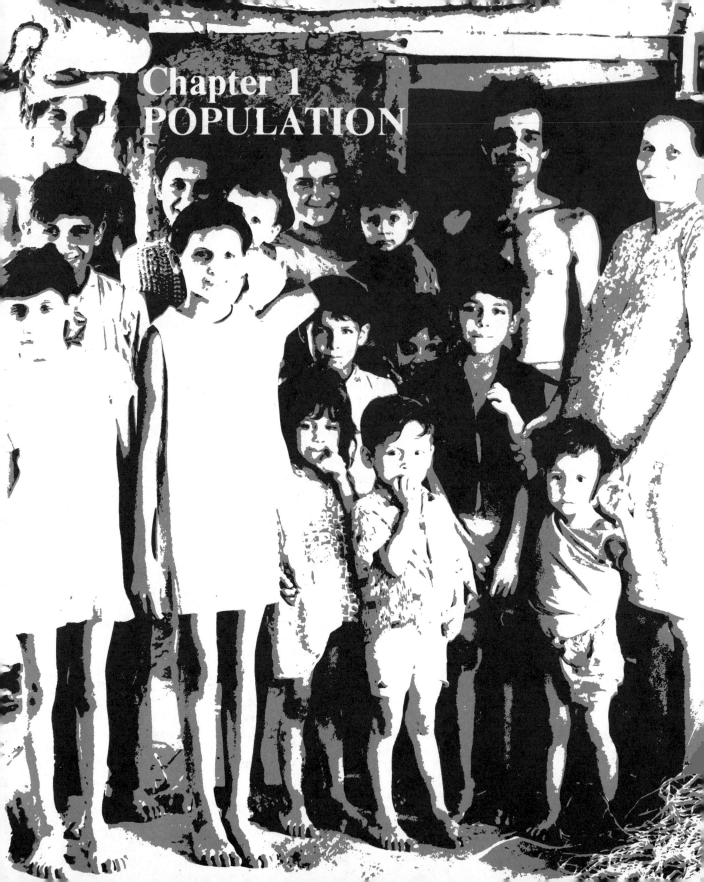

Chapter 1
POPULATION

Introduction

Rapid population growth is widely regarded as one of the world's most pressing problems. Almost daily we are asked to help starving children around the world. We read about natural resources that are being depleted quickly by the growing numbers of people. We hear the forecasts of "standing room only" in the world of the future.

The facts about population growth thus far make the predictions seem inevitable. The world's population, which took thousands of years to reach 1 billion, needed only 80 years to double that number, and only another 45 years to reach 4 billion. If this growth rate persists, there will be 8 billion early in the next century. Before the year 2100 there could be 40 billion people on earth, struggling for a share of the earth's life-supporting resources.

In 1978 the *UNESCO Courier* reported that world population increased by 2% during 1977, while world food production rose by only 1.5%.

Such large populations would aggravate every economic and social problem facing the world today. The main issues of the future would become the feeding, clothing, housing, educating, and employing of growing legions of people.

The following extracts give you an idea of the size and complexity of the population issue.

Today, 20 per cent of the entire male labour force in the developing world is unemployed. This fast growing unemployment trend is due to the rate of population growth and the economic growth policies followed by the poor countries in the fifties and sixties. Increased child survival and longevity have increased labour supply.

UNESCO Courier 1970 10

...While other countries take steps to limit the growth of their populations, the Soviet Union...is heading full speed in the opposite direction.

"Our policy is to struggle against the one child family," Boris Urlanis, Soviet demographer, wrote last year. He cited full employment, sparsely inhabited areas and unexploited natural resources.

The Toronto Star 1973 5 19

ANIMAL CRACKERS

Reprinted by permission of *Toronto Star* Syndicate. Copyright (1973), CTNYNS.

Saudi Arabia has banned contraceptives following a ruling by the World Moslem League that "birth control was invented by the enemies of Islam."

...

With four million citizens, this desert kingdom needs more manpower for development. Already more than a million foreigners work in Saudi Arabia.

The Saudis observe the injunction of the Koran that women are to "stay home, bear and rear children, only."

"The kingdom needs more and more males for work, and more and more females to bear and rear babies," an official said.

The Globe and Mail 1975 5 7

With so many people coming into the world if there are no jobs, there is going to be more and more social chaos, political instability. As a matter of fact, I think there are some very densely populated areas of the world that are rapidly approaching the point where they are ungovernable.

The Globe and Mail 1972 6 28

Orthodox Rabbi Norman Lamm, who raised the question in a recent speech in Milwaukee, admits that world population control is a "moral imperative," but maintains that it must be balanced by a concern for survival of all human groups. "Jews are a disappearing species," he says, "and should be treated no worse than the kangaroo and the bald eagle." Lamm's recommendation: each Jewish couple should have four or five children.

The Toronto Star 1975 3 25

...A number of Latin-American nations actively oppose birth-control efforts. Brazil's military government sees family planning as an effort of the more industrialized nations to keep Brazil in a semideveloped state of bondage to the more developed nations.

"Birth control is the work of American imperialists," insists a colonel attached to the staff of Gen. Emilio Garrastazu Medici, Brazil's military President. "We have plenty of unused land and we need more people to populate it."

Christian Science Monitor

In its 29 years of independence, India has increased its population more than the United States has in all the 200 years of its history. To its 628 million people it is currently adding some 13 million annually, which is equivalent to absorbing an Australia a year.

One has only to walk the feverishly teeming streets of India's cities and see the tiny paddies and plots of its crowding countryside to be appalled at the prospect—just 25 years from now—of an *additional* Indian population in itself nearly twice that of the entire United States. Looking down this abyss, Indian officialdom—state and national—is more than dreaming of a way out never before attempted by government. Compulsory sterilization to limit the number of children a couple can bring into this world is an imminent reality of Indian life.

Prime Minister Indira Gandhi, who on less compelling issues has shown a readiness to subordinate private rights to those of the state, talks bluntly of "strong steps which may not be liked by all" to be taken in the interest of family planning. "Some personal rights have to be kept in abeyance for the human rights of the nation—the right to live and the right to progress."

New York Times Service 1976 3 11

There Are No Simple Solutions. Only Intelligent Choices.

In the body of this chapter we will examine in detail the extent and nature of world population growth, some of its associated problems, and some of the different developments that are taking place around the world. Our study will conclude with a look at the population problem in one specific country, India.

Section A
The Apparent Problem

1. Attitudes to World Population

We have little reason to assume that early people were concerned with the population question. Few persons worried about the existence of others, except when the need to defend themselves arose, or when they wanted to trade with their neighbours. Gradually, as the number of people grew, some individuals began to concern themselves with population. The reading "From Confucius to Malthus" gives an excellent summary of some of these early views on population growth.

From Confucius to Malthus . . .

Since antiquity men have asked:
'Is there an optimum population?'

Man has been concerned with population problems since ancient times. From antiquity, statesmen and thinkers have held opinions, based on political, military, social and economic considerations, about such issues as the most desirable number of people or the need to stimulate or retard population growth.

Ideas and theories on population have nearly always revolved round the real or supposed problems of individual societies and have stimulated the most response when directed specifically towards those problems. Thus the ideas of the philosophers of ancient Greece dealt mainly with the population questions faced by the city-state with a relatively small population. In the Roman Empire the views on population reflected the populationist outlook of a society in which population was considered a source of power.

The thesis that excessive population growth may reduce output per worker, depress levels of living for the masses and engender strife is of great antiquity. It appears in the works of Confucius and his school, as well as in the works of other ancient Chinese philosophers.

Some of these writings suggest that the authors had some concept of optimum population, as far as the population engaged in agriculture was concerned. Postulating an ideal proportion between land and population, they held the government primarily responsible for maintaining such a proportion by moving people from over-populated to under-popu-

A *city-state* is a self-governing and fully independent political unit, much as Singapore is now. However, they were most common in the ancient world of Babylon, Greece, Assyria, and in Renaissance Italy.

The *populationist* view holds that an increasing population is an advantage to a state.

Optimum population can be defined as the ideal population size for a specific area. If this number is exceeded, each person will receive a reduced share of the wealth produced. If the population falls short of this number, there will not be enough people to create the area's maximum wealth; thus the total wealth and the amount given to each person will be reduced.

lated areas, although noting also that government action was reinforced at times by spontaneous migration.

These ancient Chinese writers also paid some attention to another aspect which has occupied an important place in subsequent literature on population theory, that is, the checks to population growth. They observed that mortality increases when food supply is insufficient, that premature marriage makes for high infant mortality rates, that war checks popultion growth and that costly marriage ceremonies reduce the marriage rates, although they paid little attention to the manner in which numbers adjusted to resources. Despite these views on population and resources, the doctrines of Confucius regarding family, marriage and procreation were essentially favourable to population increase.

The writers of early Greece were more concerned with the formulation of policies and rules for population than with theories about it. Plato and Aristotle discussed the question of the "optimum" population with respect to the Greek city-state in their writings on the ideal conditions for the full development of man's potential.

They considered the problem of population size not so much in economic terms, but more from the point of view of defence, security and government. The thought was that population should be self-sufficient, and thus possess enough territory to supply its needs but not be so large as to render constitutional government impossible.

. . .

The Romans viewed population questions in the perspective of a great empire rather than a small city-state. They were less conscious than the Greeks of possible limits to population growth and more alert to its

advantages for military and related purposes. Perhaps because of this difference in outlook, Roman writers paid less attention to population than the Greeks. Cicero rejected Plato's communism in wives and children and held that the State's population must be kept up by monogamous marriage.

The preoccupation with population growth, the disapproval of celibacy and the view of marriage as primarily and fundamentally for procreation was mainly reflected in the Roman legislation of that time. Particularly the laws of Augustus, creating privileges for those married and having children and discriminating financially against those not married, aimed at raising the marriage and birth rates.

The Hebrew sacred books placed much emphasis on procreation and multiplication and, for this reason, unfruitfulness was regarded as a serious misfortune. In general, Oriental philosophers appear to have favoured fertility and multiplication. An exponent of some of the views on population for the period dating back to some three to four centuries B.C. is *Arthasàstra*, a book written as a guide for rulers and attributed to Kautalya. The work discusses such aspects as the desirability of a large population as a source of military and economic power (although recognizing that the population may become too large); the effects of war, famine and pestilence, and the colonization and settlement of new areas.

Early and medieval Christian writers considered questions of population almost entirely from a moral and ethical standpoint. Their doctrines were mainly populationist but less so than those of Hebrew writers. On the one hand, they condemned polygamy, divorce, abortion, infanticide and child exposure; on the other, they glorified virginity and continence and frowned upon second marriage.

The main arguments in favour of celibate practices are found in the teachings of St. Paul. Some early Christian defenders of ecclesiastical celibacy resorted to economic arguments not unlike some of those later used by Malthus. Referring to the growth of the known world's population, they attributed want and poverty to this cause and cited pestilence, famine, war, etc. as nature's means of reducing excess population.

The prevailing tendency, however, was to favour, as in earlier times, population growth. The high mortality which was found everywhere and the constant threat of sudden depopulation through famine, epidemics and wars predisposed most writers towards the maintenance of a high birth-rate. The opposition to birth control, for instance, was based not only on church doctrine but also on a fear of depopulation.

The views of Muslim authors on population resemble those of the Hebrew and Christian authors. Special mention should be made, however, of the interesting but long unrecognized work by Ibn Khaldoun, an Arab author of the fourteenth century. His opinions are noteworthy in two respects.

In the first place, he held that a densely settled population was conducive to higher levels of living since it permitted a greater division of labour, a better use of resources and military and political security.

Secondly, he maintained that a State's periods of prosperity alternate with periods of decline and that cyclical variations in the population occur in rhythm with these economic fluctuations. Favourable economic conditions and political order stimulate population growth by increasing natality and checking mortality. In the wake of these periods of economic progress come luxury, rising taxes and other changes which in several generations produce political decline, economic depression and depopulation.

At the dawn of the modern era, the emergence of the nation-states and the related issue of power led mercantilist writers to emphasize once again the advantages, both political and economic, of a large population. Malthus's contrary theory had its roots in political, economic and social issues which existed during his time. The same can be said of Marxist views on population.

More recent developments in population theories have been influenced predominantly by two factors. The first of these was the upsurge of population growth, especially in the developing countries. This fact has created a need for a better understanding of the factors in population growth. Secondly, the nearly universal preoccupation with the problems of development has called for a considerably more penetrating theoretical framework for assessing the interrelations between population and economic and social development.

The search for an acceptable population theory has thus gained importance. If such a theory could be elaborated, it would provide a better insight into the development process, and could constitute a basic element in policy-making and planning for development.

UNESCO Courier 1974 7-8

This text is abridged from the chapter on population theory in "The Determinants and Consequences of Population Trends", a 2-volume study published by the U.N. Department of Economic and Social Affairs, New York, December 1973.

Mercantilism is the doctrine that a country's economy is important and should be strengthened by protecting industries through tariffs, increasing foreign trade, and emphasizing manufactured exports. The possession of colonies as a source of raw materials is seen as an advantage, and the operation of armies to maintain these colonies a necessity. According to this doctrine, large populations are an asset, for they provide a labour supply, markets, and troops as demanded.

Malthus believed that populations tended to grow too fast to be supported adequately by available resources. He forecast eventual disaster if populations kept on increasing.

Marxist population beliefs are guided by the principle that wealth is the product of the efforts of the workers, and that if more wealth is required then more workers are also required. These beliefs are broadly *populationist* in nature.

Discussion and Research

1. Which philosophers and writers argue in favour of population growth? What are their reasons?

2. Which philosophers and writers argue against population growth? What are their reasons?

3. What factors appear to influence a society's attitudes toward population growth? Give examples with your answer.

About the year 1800, some European countries began to count their citizens. Many of the census-takers could not count accurately, and sometimes they could not be bothered going to remote places. Accordingly the first census figures were only approximately correct. Even today no one knows exactly how many people there are in the world; some countries still do not count their people properly, while others do not count their people very frequently. For example, China has had only one full census. It took place in 1953, when the population was recorded at 574 205 940. Since that time there have been several estimates and various official proclamations, but we just do not know the exact number of people living in China today; 850 000 000 was a widely accepted figure in 1977. Most countries at least try to do a proper job, but we are still in the position of having to use *best estimates* instead of facts in many instances. Fig. 1-1 gives the accepted UN and other estimates of world and continent populations since 1800.

Fig. 1-1
Population totals and estimates, in millions, 1800-1980

	1800	1850	1900	1920	1940	1960	1970	1975	1980 (est.)
Africa	107	111	133	143	191	273	320	395	457
Asia	630	801	925	1 023	1 244	1 659	2 100	2 353	2 630
Europe	208	284	430	482	575	639	660	689	719
North America	7	26	82	116	144	199	225	243	260
Oceania	2	2	6	8	11	16	20	22	24
South and Central America	24	38	74	90	130	212	300	327	378
World Total	978	1 262	1 650	1 862	2 295	2 998	3 625	4 029	4 468

Compiled from data in Carr-Saunders, *World Population*; Willcox, *Studies in American Demography*; and *UN Statistical Yearbook*, 1972 and 1975.

Statistical Interpretation

1-1 Obtain some *4 cycle semi-log graph paper* (see Appendix 3), and plot on it seven time-series graph lines, one for each of the six continents and one for the world total, as shown in Fig. 1-1. For clarity use seven different colours, and label each line with its correct name. Write the name directly against the end of each line; do not use a legend. What are the chief points that emerge from the graph?

1-2 Using 1900 as the base year, so that we get figures for the twentieth century only, calculate index numbers (see Appendix 3) for 1975 for each of the six continents and for the world total, from the data in Fig. 1-1. For example, the index number for the growth of Africa's population from 1900 to 1975 is $\frac{395}{133} \times 100$, or 297. Index numbers tell you more precisely than a line graph just how quickly the populations of the different continents have been increasing this century. Why do you think North America has grown at a faster rate than Asia? Why do you think Europe has grown so slowly?

2. The Reasons for Present-day Concern

A look at world population figures shows that the population of the world is quickly increasing. Rapid population growth is a major concern today; this concern exists for several reasons. Perhaps the most basic reason is that the world seems unable to feed its present population satisfactorily, and so a growing population will increase the problem. Some people foresee massive food shortages and disastrous famines on a global scale.

There are several other causes of concern. It is feared that more people will mean more industry, leading to the exhaustion of the world's resources, especially minerals and fossil energy. Some people are worried that there will be too few jobs and too many unemployed people if population growth continues. Others foresee mass migrations as people move from areas that seem to offer little to areas that appear to be wealthy. There may even be conflict as different parts of the world attempt to protect their wealth, and as they develop politico-economic organizations to try to increase their output.

Taken together, all these worries constitute one basic concern; the potential deterioration of the existing quality of life. Many people argue that if larger numbers of people bring about the changes we have discussed, then the quality of life as it now exists will decline.

In later chapters we will discuss quality of life and the other concerns in detail; for the moment, however, it is enough to realize that these problems may result to some extent from rapid population growth. In the next section we will examine some factors leading to this growth.

Is this the future?

FAO/Canadian Hunger Foundation

3. The Causes of Population Growth: Birth and Death Rates

The basic cause of population growth is a high birth rate. Column D in Appendix 2 shows you the most recently available data regarding birth rates for the world's countries. You can see that the figures vary considerably, from a high of 52.3/1 000 (52.3 births per thousand people) for Swaziland to a low of 10.1/1 000 for West Germany. The map in Fig. 1-2 also shows these data. It is an example of a "graded shading" map, whose purpose is to depict by the graded intensity of the shading the pattern of variations in the data being mapped.

UNICEF / David Mangurian

Statistical Interpretation

1-3 **a)** Write an account of what you notice about the distribution plotted in Fig. 1-2.

b) Why do you think birth rates are so high in so many countries?

1-4 The *Rule of 72* is useful for calculating the time it takes a quantity to double. The formula is

$$d = \frac{72}{i}$$

where *d* is the number of years for doubling to occur, *72* is the formula constant, and *i* is the annual percentage rate of increase. For example, if a country has an annual population increase rate of 1.6%, then its doubling time is

$$d = \frac{72}{1.6} \text{ or 45 years.}$$

By using this formula and the population increase data in column H of Appendix 2, decide which countries will double their populations before the year 2000. When you have listed the countries, shade them in on a world map similar to that in Appendix 1. What do you notice about the plotted distribution? Does it bear any relationship to the map in Fig. 1-2?

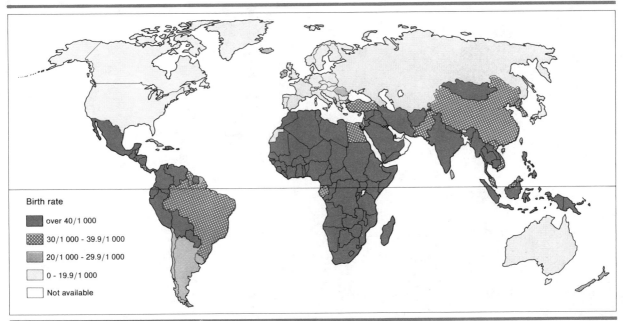

**Fig. 1-2
Variations in birth rates
throughout the world**

So far, the Women's Liberation Movement has affected economically advanced nations only, and has little meaning elsewhere.

There are many reasons for high birth rates throughout much of the world. A basic reason is security; people feel they will have their children around to care for them in their old age. Another is the desire to have extra help in the fields. Still another is the traditional domestic regard in which women are held in many societies. Also, in some countries there are religious reasons for large families, while in others there may be military or strategic considerations which cause the governments to favour large families.

While high birth rates (over 40/1 000) seem to be the main cause of population growth, they are not the only factors involved in the population explosion. Birth rates, indeed, were high in all societies around the world for centuries, and yet there was never a population explosion. Population growth has been a serious matter only in the last two hundred years; and oddly enough it is during this period that many countries have managed for the first time to *reduce* their birth rates. Obviously, then, there is more to population growth than just high birth rates.

For many thousands of years the birth rate was high, but the death rate was high too, and the world's total population therefore grew slowly. If a couple had ten children, perhaps three would die at birth or soon after, another two would probably die of childhood diseases, two more would likely be killed in riots or battles, and one might enter a religious order, thereby leaving two to look after their parents and to carry on the generations. Large families were therefore the norm. If the community produced a few additional babies who managed to survive, the population would grow slightly (and slowly).

" . . . Leaving two. . . . "

CIDA

There was a slight increase in the birth rates of most *incipiently advanced* countries about two hundred years ago, caused perhaps by better food. However, the basic reason for the start of the population explosion was not that people began to have larger families but that more children survived to have families in their turn. Death control, brought about by modern medicine, better hygiene, less disease, and better food all helped younger people to survive to a child-producing age. In the example given in the previous paragraph, therefore, out of an original ten children born perhaps only one would die of childhood disease, leaving nine to become teenagers. Of those, perhaps one would die in an accident or be killed in a war, thereby leaving as many as eight to reproduce.

Incipiently advanced countries are those that two hundred years or so ago began to develop a modern industrial structure. The first was England, followed closely by Germany and the United States.

▶ **Better medical care helps to keep more children alive.**

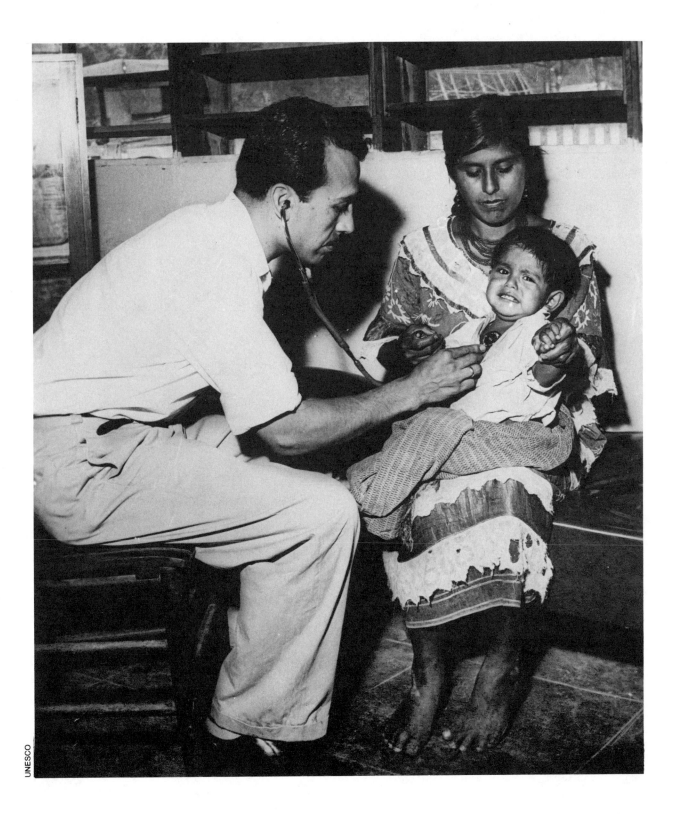

It is at this point that the population begins to grow rapidly. It continues to grow just as long as birth rates remain significantly higher than death rates. In every country of the world, death rates have always declined before birth rates, thus creating a widening gap called the *population explosion*. In some countries birth rates have subsequently declined, thereby closing the gap; but in many other countries birth rates have not yet started to come down, despite the lower death rates, thereby prolonging the period of population explosion. The gap between birth and death rates is called the *natural increase rate*, expressed as so many additional people per thousand in the existing population. The larger it is, the faster the population is growing.

Statistical Interpretation

1-5 Examine the death rate data in column E of Appendix 2. In nearly all cases it is lower than the birth rate. The difference, the natural increase rate, is given in column F. Draw a graded shading map to illustrate the natural increase (NI) data, in five classes:

30.0/1 000 and over	very bright red
20.0/1 000—29.9/1 000	bright red
10.0/1 000—19.9/1 000	pale red
0.0/1 000— 9.9/1 000	very pale red
under 0.0/1 000	pale blue

Can you explain any differences between this map and the one drawn in Fig. 1-2?

1-6 The map that you drew in assignment 1-5, showing *where* population is exploding the fastest, does not of course give you a full picture. It omits any reference to the size of the population. This is clearly a serious omission, for an extra 22.9/1 000 in Burma, which has a population of 31 240 000, will produce more people in a year than the same rate of 22.9/1 000 will produce in Burundi, with a population of only 3 760 000. Indeed, Burma will produce an additional 715 396 people (31 240 × 22.9), which is more than eight times as many as Burundi's 86 104 (3 760 × 22.9). What we need therefore is a map showing absolute quantities, so that we can see where population growth will be largest. This will complement the map in assignment 1-5 and help to give a fuller picture. First, then, calculate the *population impact factor* (i.e., the approximate numbers of additional people who will be created annually in each country), using the data in columns A and F of Appendix 2. To do this, multiply the number of thousands in the population by the natural increase rate, as shown above for Burma and Burundi. Don't worry about the fact that as the base enlarges over the years so will the number of additional people; you would need a computer to do those calculations. When you have finished, group the results into four classes and draw a graded shading map.

a) What should the title of this map be?

b) What are your conclusions regarding the distribution of impact?

1-7 A country with a very high rate of natural increase will tend to have a high percentage of young children in its population. The exact percentage can be well illustrated by a *population pyramid*, as shown in Fig. 1-3(ii). In such a pyramid, the bottom bar shows the percentage of the population that is under five years old, the next bar the percentage of the population between five and ten years old, and so on, with the percentage of the very oldest people in the top bar. Using the data for country F in Fig. 1-3(i), construct a pyramid.

a) What relationship does the shape of your pyramid have to those already drawn in Fig. 1-3(ii)?

b) Which named country is it most similar to?

Fig. 1-3(i)
Age and sex percentages for seven selected countries
(M = male, F = female)

	A		B		C		D		E		F		G		
	Mali		Brazil		Chile		Japan		East Germany		?		?		
Age	M	F	M	F	M	F	M	F	M	F	M	F	M	F	Age
80	0.1	0.1	0.2	0.2	0.3	0.5	0.4	0.6	1.0	1.6	0.3	0.1	0.9	0.9	80
75	0.1	0.1	0.2	0.3	0.3	0.4	0.6	0.8	1.0	2.0	0.3	0.1	1.0	0.9	75
70	0.1	0.1	0.4	0.5	0.6	0.7	1.0	1.2	1.8	2.9	0.5	0.4	1.4	1.3	70
65	0.5	0.5	0.7	0.7	0.8	1.0	1.3	1.6	2.4	3.5	0.8	0.6	1.5	1.6	65
60	0.8	0.7	1.0	1.0	1.2	1.3	1.7	2.1	2.3	3.7	0.9	0.8	2.0	2.0	60
55	1.1	1.1	1.3	1.3	1.4	1.6	1.9	2.3	1.5	2.5	1.0	1.0	2.3	2.4	55
50	1.6	1.3	1.6	1.5	1.6	1.8	2.1	2.7	1.9	3.2	1.3	1.4	2.5	2.7	50
45	1.9	2.0	2.0	2.0	1.9	2.0	3.1	3.2	2.2	3.1	2.0	1.6	2.9	2.9	45
40	2.3	2.6	2.3	2.4	2.5	2.6	3.7	3.6	3.0	3.0	2.4	2.0	3.2	3.3	40
35	2.6	3.1	2.6	2.6	2.8	3.0	3.9	3.9	3.6	3.5	2.6	2.4	2.9	3.1	35
30	2.6	3.4	2.9	3.0	3.0	3.0	4.1	4.1	3.9	3.9	3.0	3.0	2.7	2.7	30
25	2.6	3.1	3.6	3.8	3.3	3.6	4.4	4.4	2.7	2.6	3.4	3.4	3.0	2.9	25
20	3.4	3.3	4.5	4.8	4.0	4.4	4.7	4.7	3.7	3.5	4.4	4.0	3.8	3.6	20
15	5.1	4.6	5.4	5.5	5.0	5.2	3.8	3.7	4.0	3.7	5.4	5.0	4.7	4.4	15
10	7.6	7.3	6.3	5.5	6.3	6.3	3.8	3.6	4.2	4.0	6.4	6.0	5.1	4.6	10
5	7.6	7.2	6.7	6.5	7.0	7.0	4.0	3.9	4.0	3.8	8.0	7.1	5.6	5.0	5
0	9.8	9.6	8.1	7.9	6.4	6.2	4.7	4.4	3.3	3.2	9.4	9.0	5.3	4.9	0

Source: *UN Demographic Yearbook*, 1975.

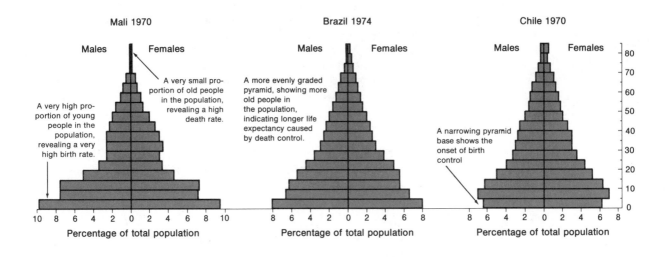

Mali 1970

Males   Females

A very small pro-
portion of old people
in the population,
revealing a high
death rate.

A very high pro-
portion of young
people in the
population,
revealing a very
high birth rate.

10 8 6 4 2 0 2 4 6 8 10
Percentage of total population

Brazil 1974

Males   Females

A more evenly graded
pyramid, showing more
old people in
the population,
indicating longer life
expectancy caused
by death control.

8 6 4 2 0 2 4 6 8
Percentage of total population

Chile 1970

Males   Females   80
                               70
                               60
A narrowing pyramid   50
base shows the
onset of birth   40
control   30
                               20
                               10
                                0
8 6 4 2 0 2 4 6 8
Percentage of total population

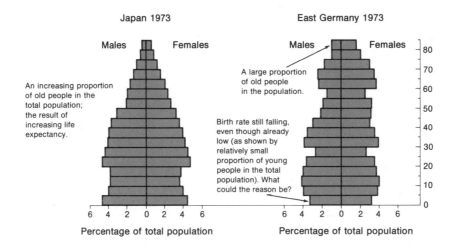

Japan 1973

Males   Females

An increasing proportion
of old people in the
total population;
the result of
increasing life
expectancy.

6 4 2 0 2 4 6
Percentage of total population

East Germany 1973

Males   Females   80
                               70
A large proportion
of old people   60
in the population.
                               50
Birth rate still falling,
even though already   40
low (as shown by
relatively small   30
proportion of young
people in the total   20
population). What
could the reason be?   10
                                0
6 4 2 0 2 4 6
Percentage of total population

Source: *UN Demographic Yearbook*, 1975.

About 1800, industrialization was taking hold in Europe; people were starting to leave their farms and villages to work in factories in the towns. This migration to towns, a movement still going on in many parts of the world, produced for the first time a highly visible number of people. The worriers began to worry about population growth, and partly as a result of this, census-taking became popular.

Fig. 1-3(ii)
Population pyramids for five countries, illustrating an evolutionary sequence

4. Malthusianism

One of the most famous worriers around the year 1800 was an Englishman, Thomas Robert Malthus, who wrote a "doom" book forecasting the possibility of widespread starvation. Malthus had a theory that the birth rate would grow faster than food supplies could be increased, and that for one reason or another the surplus people would die. Malthus held that people would tend to increase at a *geometric rate*, which means that they would *multiply* by a constant factor (in this case, 2) each successive generation. For example, if you start with 1 (or with 1 000 or 1 000 000 or whatever) you then go to 2, then 4, then 8, and so on. Meanwhile, food supplies, according to Malthus, would increase only at an *arithmetic rate*, thereby merely *adding* the same quantity over each comparable time period: 1, 2, 3, 4. The result would be as follows:

	units of time (*generations, for example*)				
	A	**B**	**C**	**D**	**E**
population (*geometric*)	1	2	4	8	16
food (*arithmetic*)	1	2	3	4	5

Obviously this could not continue for long. During periods *A* and *B* the food supply would keep pace with the growth of the population, but by period *C* some people would be going hungry, since there would be enough food for only three quarters of the population. By period *D*, even more people would be hungry, and some would die of starvation.

Discussion and Research

4. In a period *C* situation, which sectors of the population do you think will go hungry? Or do you think everyone will be just a little hungry?
5. When people are starving and death is in the air, what else is likely to happen?

The disasters that you suggested in answer to question 5 may be the same as those that Malthus thought of when he first wrote his theory: famine, disease or plague, riots, warfare, looting, and the overthrow of governments. They are commonly called the *Malthusian checks on population growth*. These factors effectively prevent a period *E* situation from developing; as soon as a period *C* or *D* situation is reached the Malthusian checks kill off enough people to return the

Famines can occur in large or small countries, wherever the population outgrows its food supply base. The Sahel region across the northern savannas of Africa provides a good example of a small population experiencing devastating famine.

population to a period *A* or *B* situation, and the whole process starts again. This is what happened in India after the great famine of 1770, when 10 000 000 died; and in 1877 when 4 000 000 died of hunger; and after the famine of 1943, when dead bodies were described as an eyesore over the landscape. Also, the 1971-72 failure of the monsoon across the Indian subcontinent saw death rates rise by as much as 25%.

When developing his theory, Malthus took into account the problems of famine and plague common at the time; he failed, however, to foresee the eventual elimination of these problems in Europe and North America. Nevertheless, famine and plague are still common in many parts of the world, and Malthus's early warnings are widely believed by many Neo-Malthusians today. You can read "Let's suppose...," an article published in the *UNESCO Courier* of 1974 7-8, and compare it with the extracts from "Population problem" by Donald Warwick.

Young men suffering severe starvation brought about by drought. This is in Ethiopia in 1974.

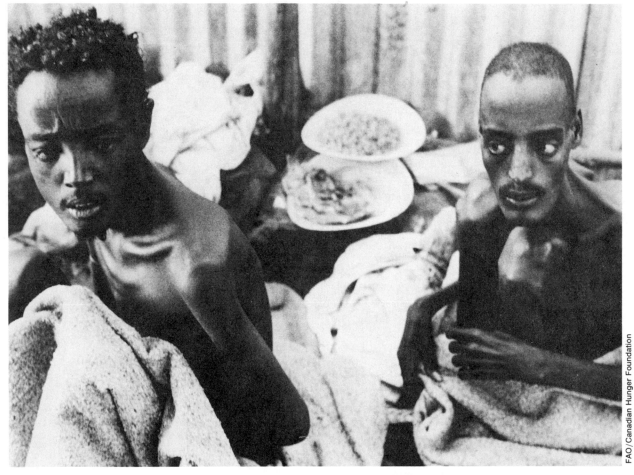

FAO/Canadian Hunger Foundation

Let's suppose...

A tale for the year 3550 A.D.
by ISAAC ASIMOV

Suppose the whole world became industrialized and that industry and science worked very carefully and very well. How many people could such a world support? Different limits have been suggested, but the highest figure I have seen is 20 billion. How long will it be before the world contains so many people?

For the sake of argument, and to keep things simple, let's suppose the demographic growth rate will stay as it is now at two per cent per annum. At this rate, it will take 35 years for the population to double, so it will take the present world population of 3.8 billion 70 years to reach the 15.2 billion mark. Then, fifteen more years will bring the world population to our 20 billion. In other words, at the present growth rate our planet will contain all the people that an industrialized world may be able to support by about 2060 A.D. That is not a pleasant outlook for only 85 years from now.

Suppose we decide to hope for the best. Let us suppose that a change *will* take place in the next 70 years and that there will be a new age in which population can continue rising to a far higher level than we think it can now. This means that there will be a new and higher limit, but before that is reached, still another change will take place, and so on. Let's suppose that this sort of thing can just keep on going forever.

Is there any way of setting a limit past which nothing can raise the human population no matter how many changes take place?

Suppose we try to invent a real limit; something so huge that no one can imagine a population rising past it. Suppose we imagine that there are so many men and women and children in the world, that altogether they weigh as much as the whole planet does. Surely you can't expect there can be more people than that.

Let us suppose that the average human being weighs 60 kilogrammes. If that's the case then 100 000 000 000 000 000 000 people would weigh as much as the whole Earth does. That number of people is 30 000 000 000 000 times as many people as there are living now.

It may seem to you that the population can go up a long, long time before it reaches the point where there are 30 000 000 000 000 times as many people in the world as there are today. Let's think about that, though. Let us suppose that the population growth rate stays at 2.0 per cent so that the number of people in the world continues to double every 35 years. How long, then, will it take for the world's population to weigh as much as the entire planet?

The answer is—not quite 1 600 years. This means that by 3550 A.D., the human population would weigh as much as the entire Earth. Nor is 1 600 years a long time. It is considerably less time than has passed since the days of Julius Caesar.

Do you suppose that perhaps in the course of the next 1 600 years, it will be possible to colonize the Moon and Mars, and the other planets of the Solar system? Do you think that we might get many millions of people into the other world in the next 1 600 years and thus lower the population of the Earth itself?

Even if that were possible, it wouldn't give us much time. If the growth-rate stays at 2.0 per cent, then in a little over 2 200 years—say, by 4220 A.D.—the human population would weigh as much as the entire Solar system, including the Sun.

We couldn't escape to the stars, either. Even if we could reach them; even if we could reach *all* of them; population would reach a limit. If the growth-rate stays at 2.0 per cent, then in 4 700 years—by about 6700 A.D.—the human population would weigh as much as the entire Universe.

So you see we can't go on forever at the rate we are going. The population rise is going to have to stop somewhere. We just can't keep that 2.0 per cent growth-rate for thousands of years. We just can't, no matter what we do.

Let's try again, and let's be more reasonable. Suppose we go back to considering the density of population on Earth.

Right now, the average density of population on Earth is 25 per km². If the population of the world doubles then the average density of population also doubles, since the area of the world's surface stays the same. This means that at a population growth-rate of 2.0 per cent per year, the average density of population in the world will double every 35 years.

In that case, if the growth-rate stays where it is, how long will it take for the average density of population to become 18 600/km²? Such a density is almost 750 times as high as the present density, but it will be reached, at the present growth-rate, in just about 340 years.

Of course, this density is reached only if human beings are confined to the land surface of the world. Perhaps human beings will learn to live on the bottom of the ocean, or on great platforms floating on the sea. There is more than twice as much ocean surface as there is land surface that would give more room for people.

That wouldn't do much good, however. At the present growth rate, it would take only 45 additional years to fill the ocean surface, too. In 385 years, the average density of population would be 18 600/km² over land and sea both. That would be by about 2320 A.D.

But a density of 18 600/km² is the average density of population of the island of Manhattan.

Imagine a world in which the average density everywhere, over land and sea alike—*everywhere*—in Antarctica and Greenland, over the oceans and along the mountains, over the entire face of the globe—was equal to that of Manhattan. There would have to be skyscrapers everywhere. There would be hardly any open space. There would be no room for wilderness or for any plants and animals except those needed by human beings.

Very few people would imagine a world like that could be comfortable, yet at the present growth-rate we will reach such a world in only 385 years.

But let's not pick Manhattan. Let's try the Netherlands. It is a pleasant, comfortable nation, with open land and gardens and farms. It has a standard of living that is very high and yet its average population density is 400/km² How long would it take for our population to increase to the point where the average density of the surface of the world, sea and land, would be 400/km²?

The answer is 200 years, by about 2175 A.D.

You see, then, that if we don't want to go past the average population density of the Netherlands, we can't keep our present growth-rate going even for hundreds of years, let alone thousands.

In fact, we might be still arguing in an unreasonable way. Can we really expect to have a world-wide Netherlands in the next 200 years?

No one really believes that mankind can spread out over the ocean bottom or the ocean top in the next 200 years. It is much more likely that man will stay on land. To be sure, there may be some people who would be living off shore in special structures, on the sea or under it. They would make up only a small fraction of all mankind. Almost everybody will be living on land.

Then, too, not every place on land is desirable. It isn't at all likely that there will be very many people living in Antarctica or in Greenland or in the Sahara Desert or along the Himalaya Mountain range over the next 200 years. There may be some people living there, more people than are living there now, but they will represent only a small fraction of the total population of the Earth.

In fact, most of the Earth's land surface isn't very suitable for large populations. At the present moment, most of the Earth's population is squeezed into that small portion of Earth's land surface that is not too mountainous, too dry, too hot, too cold, or too uncomfortable, generally. In fact, two-thirds of the world's population is to be found on a little over 1/13 of the land surface of the planet. About 2 500 000 000 people are living on 11 000 000 km² of land that can best support a high population.

The average density on the 11 000 000 square kilometres of the best land is 230/km², while the average density on the rest of the land surface is just under 10/km².

Suppose the population continues to increase at the present growth-rate and the distribution remains the same. In that case, after 30 years, the average population density of the less pleasant parts of the Earth will reach the 19/km² figure, but the density of the 11 000 000 square kilometres of best land will be 400/km².

In other words, we will reach a kind of world-wide Netherlands density-figure, for as far as we can go, in only about 30 years.

But will all the world be as well-organized and as prosperous as the Netherlands is now? Some of the reasons why the Netherlands is as well off as it is now, are that it has a stable government, a highly-educated population, and a well-organized industrial system.

This is not true of all nations and they need not expect to be as well off as the Netherlands when they are as crowded as the Netherlands. Indeed, if they have an agricultural way of life and a poorly-educated people, who don't have long traditions of stable government, then a population as dense as that of the Netherlands now is, would only bring misery.

In other words, the world can't keep going at the present growth-rate, even for tens of years, let alone for hundreds or thousands.

The matter of a population limit is not a problem for the future, then. We might just as well realize that the world is just about reaching its population limit *now*.

Of course, this entire argument is based on the supposition that the population growth-rate will stay the same as it is now. If the growth-rate drops, that obviously will give us more time before the limit is reached. If it drops to zero, the limit will never be reached. Even a 1 per cent per year population increase, however, is enough to bring disaster. So we can't just sit back and do nothing. We will have to do something.

This article is taken from *Earth: Our Crowded Spaceship*, New York: John Day Co., 1974. Reprinted by permission of the author.

Population problem

by DONALD P. WARWICK

Population doomsayers commonly present statistical descriptions about the current population situation, project them into the future and argue that the likely pattern in the year 2000 constitutes a "population problem." Such discussions often duck the question of just what makes something a problem, and why the projected demographic growth qualifies under that rubric. Any statement about a "problem" involves at least three elements: *facts*, such as statistical data on the present and past size of the world's population; *values*, or desired states which may be threatened or which may fail to materialize as a result of a given set of developments; and *assumptions* about the relationships between a given set of facts or projections and one or more values.

To make a convincing case that demographic growth is a problem, the analyst must present solid facts or reasonable projections about present and future numbers of people, indicate the values, such as survival, freedom, or economic growth, that will be jeopardized by such growth, and show just how population growth will affect the values at stake. It is not enough simply to pronounce that a doubling of the world's population will automatically imperil human freedom, cause revolutions, or produce mass famines. If one wishes to pass from scare-mongering to responsible social predictions, it is imperative to document the specific connections between population size or distribution and a given value, such as survival. We know from other efforts at social forecasting, including earlier predictions about the dire consequences of stabilized population growth, that these exercises easily lend themselves to the projection of

one's fears or fantasies onto a far-removed landscape. Further, the task of those who would argue for a "population problem" is not complete until they show why, from a moral standpoint, it is undesirable for a given value to be threatened. There is not much debate on the desirability of avoiding famines, but when it comes to the preservation of the political stability of authoritarian regimes, the value is very much open to question. In short, it is a form of intellectual sloth to proclaim the existence of a population problem without stating concretely the facts, values, and assumptions that underlie this assertion.

The greatest drawback to most discussions of "the population problem" is a failure to set forth the values threatened by demographic growth, and to show why such threats are problematic. Most of us would agree that the carrying capacity of the earth is finite, and that there would be an ultimate threat to the survival of the species if population should continue to double every thirty years. But since we are nowhere near that limit, and since it is very unlikely that the present rates of growth will continue for the next several hundred years, a breakdown in carrying capacity is usually not the issue. The values more commonly cited to demonstrate the existence of a problem include economic growth, nutrition, the ability of governments to provide such services as schools and housing, maternal and child health, and political stability.

But careful research into the relationships between population growth and almost any one of these values raises doubts about the existence of a straightforward problem even at the factual level. For example, despite dozens of treatises to the contrary, it is by no means evident that rapid population growth has a negative effect on economic growth. The debate continues among economists working in the field, but at this time it would be fallacious to argue that the bulk of the evidence clearly supports one or another position. The most we can say with any surety is that the relationships between population and economic growth are complex, and may well vary according to region, the type of political system, and similar noneconomic factors. The same is true for the relations between population growth and political stability. Rapid growth may indeed increase the pressures on a political system, for example, by raising the demands for public services in urban areas, but whether this turns out to be a healthy challenge or a crippling crisis depends on many other factors, including the legitimacy of the government, its economic resources, and the capacity of the rulers to govern. Similar ambiguities arise with almost every area of value used to define a problem.

A related fallacy is seen in the tendency to approach population questions in global rather than national terms, or to choose those national examples which best fit one's preconceptions about a problem. Again, when the question is the ultimate carrying capacity of the earth, a global focus is essential, but this has not been the predominant emphasis. To the extent that population problems are experienced, they are experienced mainly at the level of the nation-state. And it was clear at the World Population Conference at Bucharest that the countries of the world present a great diversity in population structure. Partly because this country neatly fits the preconceptions of those who would have us believe in a "population crisis," India has been by far the most common example in the population literature. Recently it has been joined by Bangladesh. If Bucharest did nothing else, it helped to show these two countries do not, in fact, represent the wide range of conditions found in Asia, Africa, and Latin America. Argentina, for example, is, like India, a large country, but most observers, including its own government, would consider it underpopulated in certain respects. To speak of impending demographic catastrophes for this country, which has experienced extensive rural depopulation in recent years and which is now actively seeking immigrants, is almost laughable. Similarly, within the African continent there are several countries or parts of countries whose "problem," especially as defined by the families involved, is sterility rather than excessive fertility. To lump all of these variegated situations together in all-encompassing statements about a "world population problem" is to show symptoms of demographic simple-mindedness.

Reprinted by permission by the author. *The Chelsea Journal* 1975 12

A *nation-state* is a state whose people are of fairly uniform ethnic or national origins. Canada is not a nation-state; nor is Switzerland. Japan, however, is, and so is Portugal.

Discussion and Research

6. Is the author of "Let's suppose . . . " a modern Malthus? Why?
7. "We will have to do something," says Isaac Asimov. What can you suggest?
8. While Asimov believes we have to do something about the growing numbers of people in the world, Donald Warwick says that talking about world population is "simple-mindedness", and that each coun-

try must be considered separately. Is either one of these authors right? Or are they both right? Give reasons for your answers.

9. Donald Warwick notes some values, such as political stability, that may be threatened by continued population growth. He thereby defines the problem primarily as an attack on existing values rather than as a matter of survival. Of the values he mentions, which do you think would be the first to be abandoned as population pressure mounts? Which do you think would be the last?

10. Why can't people simply be moved from overpopulated to underpopulated countries? Give examples of the problems that would arise.

Section B
Possible Solutions

1. Reduced Birth Rates

Malthusian checks are certainly one answer to the problem of population growth, and in some parts of the world today they are clearly at work. However, while famine and disease do kill millions of people, they do not affect the population growth of every country. A glance at

Fig. 1-4
Selected examples of birth rates, 1750-1970

Year	Canada	France	Italy	Japan	Sweden	UK	USA
1750	——	——	——	——	36.4	——	——
1760	——	——	——	——	35.7	——	——
1770	——	——	——	——	33.0	——	——
1780	——	——	——	——	35.7	——	——
1790	——	——	——	——	30.5	——	——
1800	——	32.9	——	——	28.7	——	——
1810	——	31.8	——	——	33.0	——	——
1820	——	31.7	——	——	33.0	——	55.2
1830	——	29.9	——	——	32.9	——	——
1840	——	27.9	——	——	31.4	32.0	51.8
1850	45.0	26.8	——	31.0	31.9	33.4	——
1860	40.0	26.2	38.0	31.0	34.8	34.3	44.3
1870	37.0	25.9	36.8	32.0	28.8	35.2	——
1880	34.0	24.6	33.9	34.0	29.4	34.2	39.8
1890	30.0	21.8	35.8	34.0	28.0	30.2	——
1900	30.0	21.3	33.0	35.0	27.0	28.7	32.3
1910	29.0	19.6	33.3	35.0	24.7	25.1	30.1
1920	25.0	21.4	32.2	35.0	23.6	25.5	27.7
1930	21.0	18.0	26.7	35.0	15.4	16.3	21.3
1940	25.0	13.6	23.5	37.0	15.1	14.1	19.4
1950	28.0	20.5	19.6	19.5	16.5	15.8	24.1
1960	20.0	17.9	18.1	17.0	13.7	17.1	23.7
1970	17.4	16.7	17.6	13.0	13.5	16.3	18.4

Source: B. R. Mitchell, *European Historical Statistics 1750-1970*; *Japan Statistical Yearbook*, 1977; *Historical Statistics of the US*, Bicentennial edition; and Urquhart and Buckley, *Historical Statistics of Canada*.

Note: 1) Reliable data are not available for the early years of certain countries shown.
2) There are no data for the less developed countries, so none of them can be included in the table.

column F in Appendix 2 reveals that many countries that we know are not unduly affected by famine and disease nevertheless have very low rates of natural increase. For these countries, examine the birth rate figures in column D; lower birth rates are the answer.

The histories of the birth rates of several countries indicate that when they have changed they have usually declined. For example, Canada's birth rate in 1850 was 45/1 000, while in 1975 it was down to 15/1 000. In the UK in 1850 the rate was 33/1 000; in 1975 it was 13/1 000. More details are shown in Fig. 1-4.

Statistical Interpretation

1-8 Plot the data in Fig. 1-4 as a multiple line graph (See Appendix 3). What do you notice?

The reasons for these declining birth rates are very complex, and not yet fully understood. Some of the possible causes include better birth control methods, better education, more job opportunities for women, more machinery to replace human labour, better pensions, more liberal abortion laws, later marriages, easier divorce, and preferred childless life styles.

The following articles illustrate some of the reasons that people give for a falling birth rate.

In the USA a particular case

NEW YORK (AP) — Midnight feedings, the patter of little feet, Scout meetings and orthodontist bills — these joys of parenthood Ken and Sandra Voit can do without.

They prefer another life style: living in a $71 000 condominium apartment in Hartford Conn., dining out up to five times a week, long, leisurely hours of reading at night unbroken by children's squeals, exotic vacations such as alligator hunting on the Amazon River or camping in Iceland.

. . .

"The best thing about not having children is the personal freedom. You can do anything you want any time you want . . . ," says Ken, age 34, a senior vice-president of an insurance company.

The number of couples choosing to remain childless is increasing in Canada and the US. Of wives ages 18-24, the percentage of those with no children and desiring no children has almost tripled in the US during the past five years — from 1.3 of the group in 1967 to 3.6 in 1972. Of wives ages 25-29, it has almost doubled — from 2.2 to 4.0. . . .

The Toronto Star 1972 10 19

in Russia too . . . more cases

"Couples would happily have children if more attention were paid to the public services. A woman spends much too much time in the kitchen and the store. The services must be improved, the queues ended, and there must be more cheap and comfortable restaurants to which one could go on days off and in the evening."

Thus, a woman named Savina writes to the editor of Moscow's lively Literaturnaya Gazeta. The newspaper has just set off an avalanche of mail with an article wondering if families should follow the fashion and have only one child, or have more.

The letters give one a startling glimpse of the private anxieties in a nation in which the size of the family is shrinking, life has become more complex, and the family's only child may find himself in a hostile world at school. The anxieties are broad—and sometimes they are not too different from our own.

Here is an engineer named Burilov: "I have only one child, a daughter. And though we have all the requisites—a good apartment, adequate income, a nursery in our building—my wife will have no more children. Our women are drifting away from their mothers on this question, and for no serious reason."

Or a woman named Alexandrova: "My husband wants three children, and I told him I won't have them, even if he threatens to kill me. We have a girl already, and one—or perhaps two—is enough. Our child is now 16 months old, and I am happy that soon it can be sent to a nursery and I shall cease being a domestic servant. I shall meet people again, hold a paying job, begin to wear good clothes. Don't judge me too harshly. I am still young. Must I give up personal life?"

The Toronto Star 72 11 25

and China...

SAN FRANCISCO (AP)—"Before liberation, it used to be the family wanted lots of children," Dr. Lin said. By liberation, she made clear she meant the formation of the People's Republic, but in her remarks in other cities the physician also has indicated she has meant a different role for women.

Infant mortality formerly used to be very high but "now has gone down tremendously. Mothers and grandmothers once wanted to have 10 children so that two would survive," but changes in prenatal and allied health care are keeping more infants alive, Dr. Lin said.

Still another factor is the present trend for later marriage, with rural girls delaying marriage to the age of 19 to 22, and city girls "not marrying until 23 to 25, or among the highly educated many do not marry until age 30," Dr. Lin said.

The Globe and Mail 72 11 1

Tomorrow the world...

Liberation lowers the birth rate, could save world, woman claims

NAIROBI (Reuter)—The Women's Liberation Movement could turn out to be the salvation of the world because it leads to a lowering of the birthrate, the World Council of Churches was told yesterday.

Six women from Africa, Asia, Australia, Europe and the Middle East addressed the WCC assembly on the theme Women in a Changing World.

In the most forceful of the speeches, Annie Jiagge, a judge of the Ghana appeals court, said statistics show that wherever women have a life outside the home, the population growth rate drops with or without incentives.

"But wherever women are illiterate, ignorant, house-bound and dependent on men, the growth rate increases even with the best possible incentives for a decrease," she said.

"Many third world women are of the view that the only effective way of achieving the zero rate of growth without doing violence to the dignity and worth of the human person is an accelerated plan for the advancement of women, especially in the poorest sector of society and in the poorest parts of the world."

The Globe and Mail 1975 11 29

Reprinted by permission of *Toronto Star* Syndicate. Copyright (1975) CTNYNS.

Discussion and Research

11. The birth rate in some countries has been falling. From your reading of the different articles, can you determine the values that people have put above child-rearing?
12. It is also clear from the clippings that birth rates have not fallen in isolation; other aspects of life have changed too. Can you decide what "other aspects" *must* change if birth rates are to fall?

2. The Birth Control Controversy

The easiest of all the solutions to the problem of population growth appears to be a widespread acceptance of birth control. However the solution is by no means simple. Birth control as an effective method of population control involves numerous factors, such as education of the public; for many reasons, it is a highly controversial issue.

Some people support birth control because countries are often unable to provide food and jobs for the growing numbers of people; as a result, there can be serious social, economic, and political problems. These problems can be a real threat to nations that are struggling to become self-sufficient, or that have gained a small measure of prosperity and are unwilling to lose it. The following articles illustrate just a few of the arguments and techniques used by those who favour birth control.

Children sing of birth control in Thailand

BANGKOK, THAILAND (UPI)—"I wish you subdued fertility in 1976," says Meechai Viravaidya as he hands out his calling card, a blue and white package containing brightly colored male contraceptives.

Meechai, formerly a government economist, now heads Family Planning Service, a private Bangkok-based organization devoted to battling Thailand's exploding population through introduction of birth control in the country's small villages.

. . .

"We have a serious population problem in Thailand. Three babies are born every minute, 1.5 million a year. If we can't curb the growth, the country's 42-million population will double in 20 years."

Meechai's 150-member staff visits small villages throughout Thailand to set up oral contraceptive distribution centres. They also try to educate schoolteachers about contraception.

The teachers in turn have their students sing a theme song which begins, "Too many children, too many children, too many children."

"Eighty per cent of the Thai population lives far away from cities," Meechai says. "And there is only one doctor for every 110 000 people. So we try to train a social leader in each village—a schoolteacher or shopkeeper—to prescribe and distribute contraceptives.

"So far we have covered about 8 000 villages, 10 per cent of the total. We have enough funds to cover another 5 per cent in the coming year."

The Toronto Star 1976 4 13

Singapore birth-control program penalizes 'irresponsible parents'

by LIM JIT MENG

SINGAPORE (Reuter) — Health authorities here are stepping up their family planning program in an attempt to arrest a rising birth rate which could seriously jeopardize the economic prosperity of this city state.

With two million people in a region with hardly any natural resources, the Government is anxious not to dissipate its hard-earned prosperity by having too many mouths to feed and jobs to provide.

Even now, more than 55 per cent of the population is under the age of 21 and this level is expected to rise.

The official view is that bigger families would greatly hamper the Government's attempts to improve the quality of life in Singapore.

Two ministers—Chua Sian Chin (Health) and Ong Pang Boon (Labor)—recently opened a new family planning campaign, drawing attention to the priority the Government gives to its population control program.

To give teeth to its population control program, the Government is ready to get tough with "irresponsible parents" who produce more children than they can afford to feed and bring up. From now on, large families will not be given priority when applying for low-cost Government flats.

Delivery charges at Government hospitals will increase proportionately with each additional child.

After the fourth child, working women will not be paid for leave taken to have a baby.

On the other hand, delivery charges will be waived for women who undergo sterilization, and generous medical leave will be granted to those sterilized after a delivery or an abortion, according to a Health Ministry pamphlet.

For couples who have as many children as they want, the authorities recommend sterilization as a safe, effective and permanent method of birth control.

The family planning and population board has set up a male counselling and vasectomy clinic and has also warned that the incidence of women dying at childbirth rises sharply after the fourth pregnancy.

"Family planning should be a national objective and should receive the active support of all in Singapore who want a higher quality of life for themselves and their progeny," Mr. Ong asserted.

The Globe and Mail 1972 8 11

Birth control pills being packaged in the United States.

US Information Service

Poster title: Plan for good birth control for revolution.

Birth Control in Dominican Republic

SANTO DOMINGO, DOMINICAN REPUBLIC (Reuter) The government of the Dominican Republic is conducting a birth-control program aimed at slowing down one of the severest population explosions in the Americas.

The republic, which shares the Caribbean island of Hispaniola with Haiti, has one of the fastest rates of demographic growth in the Western hemisphere, at 3.4 percent a year.

The government's program was launched in February 1968, and as a result of it, there are at least 60 family-planning clinics in the Dominican Republic now, six of them in this capital.

The program is administered by the National Council of Population and Family, and since its work began, more than 80 000 women aged between 14 and 44 have registered for help in planning their families.

The council, and the Dominican Association for Family Welfare, produce a radio program which is broadcast by 13 stations around the country for one hour every day, with the object of informing people in rural areas of family-planning possibilities.

A team of sociologists and social workers is carrying out an education campaign on a national scale using lectures, teach-ins, short courses, and group meetings.

Directors of the program are collaborating with the agriculture secretariat and community development office in order to penetrate rural zones.

About 200 000 women between 14 and 44 are expected to come into the plan by next year, representing 20 percent of their age group.

The council aims at reducing the birth rate to 28 per thousand in the next eight years.

The current rate is 48 per thousand, which means that between 160 000 and 170 000 children are born each year.

Christian Science Monitor 1973 9 6

The Chinese also pursue birth control with great fervour, as the following poster, reproduced in *Scientific American* in 1974 4, shows.

Courtesy of Victor W. Sidel, M.D., Montefiore Hospital, Bronx, New York

Although many people wish to extend the practice of birth control there are others who do not. There is, indeed, widespread opposition to the idea for religious, economic, and political reasons. There are also social difficulties; one of the greatest barriers to a wider use of birth control is the high rate of infant mortality in many parts of the world. Until parents are convinced that their first two or three children will survive, they will likely continue to produce large families. The following articles present a number of objections to birth control, and the problems involved in forming family planning programs.

Africa and Latin America

Progress in family planning is much more limited in Africa and Latin America than it is in Asia. Some African countries feel that population size and political status are directly related so that more people are wanted rather than fewer. Furthermore, in view of social customs and structures it is difficult for a family planning programme to get under way. The only real progress in mainland Africa has been made in Tunisia in conjunction with a number of social measures to abolish polygamy, modify the divorce laws, delay marriage and raise the status of women; but even there the birth rate still exceeds forty per 1 000.

The influence of the Catholic church has impeded the spread of family planning programmes in the whole of Latin America. Their raison d'être is improvement of maternal and child health and reduction in the number of abortions rather than restriction of population growth. But Catholicism is far from being the only factor; prestige of male virility is certainly another. Family planning is sometimes denounced as an alien ideal or an American trick to limit the numerical superiority of the Third World, 'the only superiority they have.' Many also regard Latin American LDCs [less developed countries]

as underpopulated with large open spaces available for development, and only capable of being developed by larger numbers of people. Whether this is true or not, the important point often not realized in the West is that many people in LDCs do not accept alarmist attitudes. Some people regard the family planning movement, and conservation for that matter, with undiluted suspicion as being aimed at maintaining existing economic structures and hierarchies. The emphasis on the population problem of the Third World is supposed merely to conceal the massive economic inequalities between the rich nations and the poor, although of course most of the world's 70 000 000 extra people each year will live among the poor.

J. I. Clarke, "Fertile people in infertile lands," *Geographical Magazine* 1973 5.

Africa

In 1973 the desired number of children, for most Kenyan couples, was six or seven. This desire, according to one observer, was based upon an awareness of the formerly very high infant mortality. The more children you had, the more you were likely to finish up with.

The infant mortality has dropped, but most people in the countryside are still not aware of it. It is the old

story brought over from Asia: the more children, the more hands to work, the more social security in age, the more status in the community.

There is a further complication, reminiscent to me of the situation as regards the Indian states. The tribes have proportional representation in the Kenyan Parliament. The larger the tribe, the more elected members it has to speak for it. In a situation where most tribes suspect and distrust each other, this is obviously no incentive for a tribal chief to tell his people to limit their families.

In 1967 the Government of Kenya rather warily said that it supported family planning, so long as it was accepted voluntarily—which meant that no incentives should be offered—and so long as it was done for reasons of health.

Samir Amin is Egyptian and persuasive. He has a quick rivery voice. He said that in the history of mankind the rise of population had been inducive to development. In certain areas of the world, he said, like India, this was not so. It was the opposite. But in tropical Africa it was so. "People actively don't want family planning in Africa," he said. "And growth in terms of population has to equal economic growth. The Senegalese Government has not the courage to face the opposed interest within the country. If the growth, economically, was quick, then perhaps family planning could come in to reinforce it."

As long as the problem of poverty was unsolved, Amin said, the question of family planning didn't arise. "There's a difference," he said, and I agreed with him, "between a national attitude and the attitude of a family. There's also a difference between the attitude of a nation and the attitude of an international body like the United Nations. When the Portuguese came to the Congo for the slave trade, they estimated there were a million people there. Three hundred years later, they estimated that there was a population of about 300 000. Black nations think of oppression on many levels, both past and present. If the whites ask black nations to reduce their population now, what are the black to think?"

Both from *A Matter of People*, by Dom Moraes, New York: Praeger, 1974. © UN Fund for Population Activities.

India

Some success has been achieved in the voluntary sterilization programme for men, with 5 500 000 operations reported, but when one considers that 90 000 000 married couples in the reproductive age group must be covered an idea of the scale of activities is indicated.

The production and distribution of contraceptives is an immense task and the problems of overcoming cultural opposition in the great mass of rural population is a gigantic exercise in communication. In the long term social change may provide the checks, and encourage the creation of smaller families, but in view of the lengthy period required to raise the economic expectations of traditional village communities and promote social mobility, the short-term picture is dark indeed.

William Kirk, "Frustration of the Indian Family Plan," *Geographical Magazine* 1975 2.

Indonesia

Family-planning programs here, as everywhere, involve a number of socially complex questions.

Since 20 percent of all children pass on before age nineteen, parents face their own advanced age more securely if they produce a large family. "A son's house is where one dies," a local saying goes.

The marriage age in Indonesia is almost universally low; consecutive marriages are very common.

And children are much loved here. "Every child brings his own blessing with him," a professor's wife with eight children once remarked. As a family planning official noted wryly, "There is never a question here of too many children—just too little income."

Christian Science Monitor 1973 10 3

Discussion and Research

13. Make a list of the practical problems involved in the implementation of birth control that are mentioned in the previous articles. How would you solve these problems?

14. What are some of the cultural objections to the practice of birth control noted in the clippings? Do you agree with them?

---

3. Population Policies

It is obvious that there is little agreement about controlled population growth. Indeed it may not even prove to be possible; there are so many different opinions, backed by strongly held values, that birth control may never become a universal policy. For a glimpse of the variety of opinions and the strength of the feelings involved, look at the next reading entitled "Population policy in Latin America."

Population policy in Latin America

Like other regions of the world, and perhaps even more than others, Latin America is a mosaic of widely varying attitudes, criteria and standards vis-à-vis the world-wide phenomenon which is known as the "population explosion".

Countries in this region have adopted very different and even completely opposed positions in their approach to this immense problem. There are countries, such as Argentina, which are categorically in favour of a policy of openly encouraging high population growth, while others, such as El Salvador and the Dominican Republic, are pursuing a no less categorical policy of birth control.

Whatever their positions, however, there is unanimous agreement among Latin American governments that the formulation of population policy is the sovereign right of each country.

. . .

A study prepared by the United Nations Economic Commission for Latin America (CEPAL), which was used as a basis for debate at the Costa Rica meeting, divides Latin American countries into five categories according to their attitudes on matters of population policy. These are as follows:

1 Countries whose governments have declared themselves in favour of accelerated population growth. This is the case of Argentina and Uruguay.

According to the Argentinian representative at the Costa Rica meeting, "Latin America should defend population growth as a positive factor in development." Argentina's new population policy has two main objectives: to increase the population at a more rapid rate and to ensure a more balanced distribution of the population throughout the country.

. . .

2 Countries whose governments consider that the present population statistics and their estimated future trends are satisfactory and that in consequence the State should avoid setting population standards and objectives. This is the position of Brazil and Peru.

The government of the latter country considers that understanding of the world population problem would gain in amplitude and depth if there were to be an objective analysis of existing relationships between demographic, social, economic and political factors. The Peruvian delegate to the Costa Rica meeting stressed the vital importance of "pointing out and rejecting the fallacy of those who consider that the problems of Peru (in other words, the problems characteristic of a developing country) are caused by high population growth and that the solution to these problems lies in curbing it."

The fact is, he declared, there is no harm in a demographic growth rate of 2.9 per cent "in a country with plenty of space and an adequate quantity and variety of natural resources, as is the case in Peru. The Revolutionary Government and the Peruvian people must therefore concentrate their attention and all their efforts on finding a radical solution to all those problems of a structural order which constitute the real source of difficulty for the people of Peru."

The Brazilian Delegate, Miguel A. Ozorio de Almeyda, emphasized the fact that in a number of Latin American countries a considerable population increase is essential for acceleration of their economic development.

3 The third group consists of countries whose governments have stated their intention of taking action through nation-wide programmes designed to have long-term effects on their birth-rates, but which have refrained from setting definite population objectives. This group includes Colombia, Mexico, Cuba, Costa Rica, Chile, Guatemala, Nicaragua, Panama and perhaps to some extent Ecuador.

Mexico is applying a qualitative rather than a quantitative population policy, whose essential aim is "to raise the standard of living of all Mexicans" and to make every effort "to provide greater opportunities for all with a view to bringing about continued change, and not as a limitation to protect privileges."

Cuba considers that under-development problems are not caused by population growth at all, and its efforts have therefore been directed not at controlling demographic processes, but at bringing about structural change aimed at stimulating development. The Cuban representative at the meeting expressed the view that a rigid population policy can only be defined in the context of overall development policy, which it should reinforce and complement; the history of world population growth shows that the adoption of population control is a corollary to development, not a prerequisite.

Within the same group, Guatemala also maintains that birth control is not the universal panacea, the unique formula for the solution of problems of population and their consequences. There is no national family planning policy in Guatemala, but there exist family guidance programmes adapted to the attitudes and motivations specific to the Guatemalan people.

4 The fourth group identified by CEPAL comprises those countries whose governments support special family planning programmes at the local level or on a limited scale.

5 The fifth and final group consists of countries which have formulated and applied overall policies designed to reduce population: El Salvador, the Dominican Republic and Honduras.

El Salvador, a country with high population density and intense demographic growth, advocates the formulation of an integrated population policy which its delegate defined as "a series of actions planned and coordinated by the public authorities", aimed at bringing about the greatest possible individual, family and social well-being by means of the "rationalization of population dynamics."

Finally, in the Dominican Republic, another of the decidedly antinatalist Latin American countries, the government gives its unqualified support to every type of action aimed at curbing the birth-rate, and actively promotes family planning programmes.

. . .

With so many variables, it is not surprising that Latin America does not speak with one voice in the great population debate.

UNESCO Courier 1974 8

---

4. Demographic Transition

Birth control may become a standard part of life, whatever official government policy says. As societies provide greater benefits such as old age security and more paid jobs for women, they will eliminate many of the reasons people give for having large families. We can therefore probably foresee a general reduction in birth rates based on individual choice, if not on government policy.

By observing past birth and death rates, researchers have been able to construct a theoretical "model", called the *demographic transition model*, which projects birth and death rates for a certain period of time. The construction of the model (see Fig. 1-5) involves some *inductive analysis*, and requires testing against the most recent birth and death rate figures.

Inductive analysis means taking a series of individual observations and trying to build a general theory out of them. The opposite is *deductive analysis*, which means that a theory is formulated, or a proposal put forward, and then evidence is sought to prove the validity of the theory.

Fig. 1-5
The demographic transition model

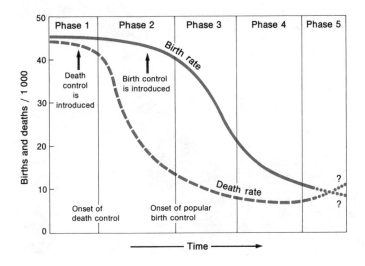

As current birth and death figures become available, they may suggest changes in the model, but for the moment we will accept it as providing a framework for analysis and use it for making cautious predictions.

In the demographic model, phase 1 occurs when both birth and death rates are high and uncontrolled. Very few parts of the world are still in this phase, since medical aid has succeeded in most places in bringing death rates under some degree of control.

Phase 2 is marked by a reduction of the death rate as people live longer. However, birth rates usually remain high according to custom, and the result is an ever-widening gap between the two rates. The

Novosti Press Agency

A 107-year-old man in the USSR. There are many old people in a demographically advanced society.

Throughout phases 2 and 3 the existence of death control means that many people live longer; in other words, they do not die as children or teenagers at the onset of a severe disease. Thus, *life expectancy* is increased. Countries going through these phases have populations of old people larger than those in phase 1 countries.

Intensive child care in the USA.

population explosion has begun, and increases in intensity as the gap widens. Its intensity is heightened by the fact that death control does more than just permit children to reach childbearing age; it also permits them to survive right through their fertile years. Phase 2 is therefore characterized by rapid population growth; the longer the phase lasts, the larger the population becomes.

Phase 3 starts as soon as birth control becomes common enough to cause a significant decline in the birth rate. At this time the death rate will usually remain at a fairly low level. Obviously the death rate cannot keep on declining forever; death can be postponed, but not avoided. During phase 3 the population explosion still continues, but at a slower rate, and so the gap between the birth rate and the death rate diminishes. Note, however, that a slower rate of natural increase does not necessarily reduce population pressure; the population base, which exploded through phase 2, is now much larger.

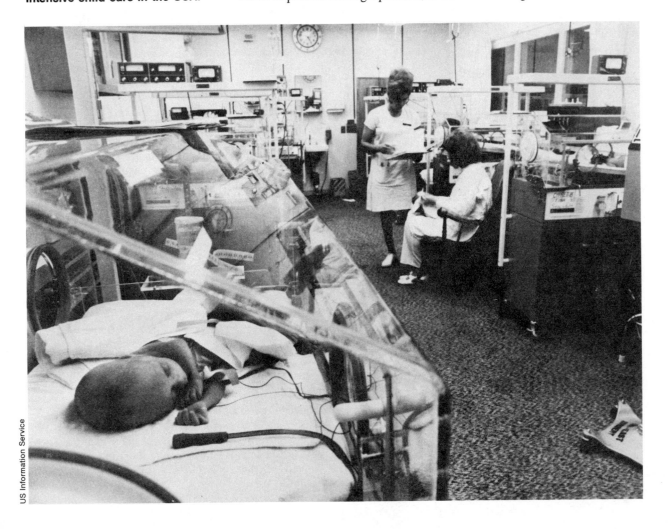

In phase 4 both birth and death rates tend to be fairly low and steady. The death rate may actually rise slightly, as older people form a larger part of the population. But it is not necessarily so; there may even be "baby booms". Although the details of the situation vary from country to country, the general trend is low birth and death rates and slow total population increases.

In the future it is possible that phase 5 will develop, wherein death rates will climb above birth rates because of the continued aging of the population. West and East Germany, with declining populations, are perhaps already beginning to move into phase 5. Many other countries are approaching this phase. Population growth slows, approaches zero, and then becomes negative. A declining population, however, does not mean the end of problems, as the following two articles show.

Declining birthrates worry Eastern Europe

by ERIC BOURNE
Special correspondent of The Christian Science Monitor

BUDAPEST While much of the world is concerned these days to curb population growth, Eastern Europe is anxiously looking for more people.

One by one, Communist regimes are refocusing increasingly serious attention on stagnant birthrates and aging population, on the escalating divorce rates and alcoholism and evidence of other frustrations among the young.

Paradoxically, the problems are in many cases worse in those countries which in recent years have achieved solid advance in living standards.

• Czechoslovakia, for example, with one of the world's best medicare services, also has both one of its lowest birthrates and highest figures on abortion. And it is, too, a nation of heavy liquor drinkers.

. . .

• Here in welfare-minded Hungary, where there has been a measure of political-cultural "liberalization" as well, abortions last year were greatly in excess of live births. There now are more Hungarians over 60 than between 1 and 15 years. In a population of only 10 million, a million Hungarian couples are childless. The country stands fourth in the world's divorce chart.

Christian Science Monitor 1973 11 21

Zero population growth —we must prepare now

by JOHN HERITAGE

WASHINGTON In a dramatic exception to America's growth-oriented philosophy, the country's population trends have gone into a strong downward spin. Between 1970 and 1973, the pace of population growth fell by a stunning 33 percent.

If the slowdown continues—and it began almost two decades ago—the U.S. could reach zero population growth more quickly than anyone had imagined. The bureau of the census says the momentous event could come in less than 60 years.

Some other observers say it is theoretically possible by the end of this decade.

Slower population growth could prove to be a blessing—if the country adequately prepares for the tough new problems that will come with it. Major adjustments will be required in the economy, in education, and in life-styles. And ultimately, there could be an era of much slower overall growth.

The birth-rate decline is already making itself felt in the nation's school systems. Total enrollment is dropping. Some schools are actually being closed due to a lack of pupils, a remarkable change from the bulging classrooms of last decade.

A spreading wave

And as the smaller baby crop reaches adulthood, the waves of change will spread. In the 1980s, there will be fewer young customers to buy automobiles; there will be fewer couples to buy houses; and there will be fewer new workers joining the labor force.

With a smaller stream of young people, the average age of the population will increase, a trend whose merits are sure to be debated. Innovation and productivity could be reduced—but so might status-seeking and restless mobility. Toward the end of the century, a higher ratio of aged persons to contributing workers will significantly increase the costs to the Social Security program.

Pluses are many

But after extensive research, the 1972 Commission on Population Growth and the American Future concluded that the U.S. economy can meet the problems posed by a levelling population. "Neither the health of our economy nor the welfare of individual businesses depends on continued population growth."

And the potential plusses would more than outweigh the drawbacks, the commission contends. Lower population growth could conserve energy and help control pollution. And it could bring improved public services by easing the demand for pell-mell expansion.

But others caution that the nation should not expect such benefits to come automatically. Pollution won't be curbed if couples have fewer children but spend more on luxuries, said sociologist George Grier of the Washington Center for Metropolitan Studies. Education won't be boosted if schools close facilities when classes decline, he added.

The worst thing that could happen, according to Mr. Grier, is an over-reaction to the problems posed by the declining population growth. To avoid such a reversal, he urges the nation to wake up to the implications of this historic change, so it can begin to maximize the good side and minimize the disadvantages.

Christian Science Monitor 1974 2 9

Discussion and Research

15. What problems are associated with a declining population? You should consider social, political, and economic aspects.

Fig. 1-6
Canada's birth and death rates, 1850-1975

Year	Births/1 000	Deaths/1 000
1850	45	22
1860	40	21
1870	37	19
1880	34	18
1890	30	16
1900	30	13
1910	29	12
1920	25	11
1930	21	10
1940	25	9
1950	28	8
1960	20	7.5
1970	17.4	7
1975	15.5	7.5
1980	15.0	7.0
1985	14.5	6.5

Source: Urquhart and Buckley, *Historical Statistics of Canada;* also *Canada Year Book,* 1968 and 1976-77.

Statistical Interpretation

1-9 Using the data in Fig. 1-6, construct a graph according to the demographic transition model, and mark in the phases which you think Canada has passed through since 1850.

1-10 Using the data for country G in Fig. 1-3(i), construct a population pyramid. What does it tell you about the rate of population growth in the country? How does it compare with the pyramid you drew for assignment 1-7? After examining the two pyramids alone, decide which country you would rather live in. Why?

If the transition model holds true then we should regard the present population explosion as a unique phenomenon, caused by the fact that death control has taken effect more quickly than birth control has. If this is so, then any country in phase 4 may be safely through the worst of the explosion. For countries in phase 3, the end of the explosion is at least in sight, because rates are to some degree under control; it will just be a matter of time before these countries reach the safety of phase 4. From the standpoint of population *problems* (housing, jobs, education, taxes, social security, food), the least fortunate countries are those in phase 2, where death control is well established but where birth control is not.

Statistical Interpretation

1-11 Assess the demographic phase of each country according to the following criteria:

	Birth rate	Death rate
phase 1	uncontrolled, 40/1 000 plus	uncontrolled, 40/1 000 plus
phase 2	uncontrolled, 40/1 000 plus	becoming controlled, below 40/1 000
phase 3	becoming controlled, 20-40/1 000	controlled, 0-20/1 000
phase 4	controlled, 0-20/1 000	controlled, 0-20/1 000

The figures are guides only; a few countries may not fit neatly into the categories, so use your discretion. When you have decided which phase each country is in, isolate the countries with exploding populations and plot them on a world map. Use a more prominent shading for phase 2 countries than for the phase 3 countries. You will now be able to see not only where the population explosion is concentrated in the world, but also which parts have passed the worst of the explosion already (phase 3) and which parts are still experiencing the worst effects (phase 2). What do you notice?

Case Study 1
India: Population Growth

India, a phase 2 country in the demographic transition model, is experiencing a population explosion. Of course other nations in the world are having similar explosions; the demographic characteristics shown in Fig. 1C-1 are typical of all phase 2 countries, many of which have populations growing even faster than India's.

Fig. 1C-1
Demographic transition in India

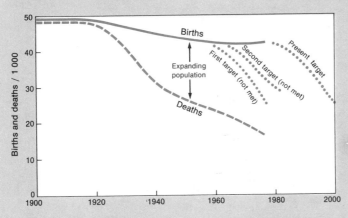

Compiled from data in the *Christian Science Monitor* 1973 1 12, *Globe and Mail* 1973 4 21, *Geographical Magazine* 1975 2, and American Geographical Society *Focus* 1974 5.

For example, while India's annual rate of population increase is 2.6%, the rate is 3.2% in Algeria, 3.4% in Kuwait, 3.4% in Mexico, 3.3% in the Philippines, and 3.3% in Venezuela.

However, India's demographic uniqueness rests in the *size* of the population explosion. Each year the population grows by more than 15 000 000; this figure is larger than the individual populations of two thirds of the world's countries. The only nation more populous than India is China, and as Fig. 1C-2 shows, India is expected to equal or surpass China around the year 2000 with a population of over 1 000 000 000.

Indeed, each day 60 000 Indians are born, while only 20 000 die, so that India's population increases by 40 000 daily.

Fig. 1C-2
Growth of population in India and China

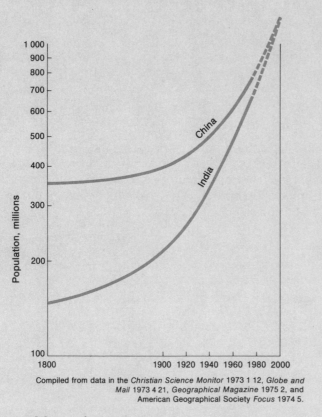

Compiled from data in the *Christian Science Monitor* 1973 1 12, *Globe and Mail* 1973 4 21, *Geographical Magazine* 1975 2, and American Geographical Society *Focus* 1974 5.

Many observers regard the combination of great population size and fast growth as a problem; obviously, most of the existing inhabitants can do little more than survive. Obtaining sufficient food has become the major concern of most Indians, and a matter of urgent priority for all levels of government. But there are other needs: housing, fresh water, jobs, education, and so on. Per capita GNP is below $150 a year, less than half that of China. All these deficiencies together with the size of the population make India the world's largest example of mass poverty. People elsewhere may survive in conditions no better than in India, but they do so in their millions; in India they survive in their hundreds of millions.

Governments have tried to do much. Early efforts after independence in 1947 were devoted to building industry, and a great deal was accomplished; India now has sophisticated industries capable of producing jet aircraft and space satellites. However, industries of this kind use large amounts of money but employ relatively few people. Therefore the government may have produced wealth for a few but it did not produce jobs for large numbers of people. In any event, the planners of the early Five Year Plans (1951-56; 1956-61) did not expect birth rates to remain high for as long as they have. The idea of family planning was officially adopted in 1952, but not really stressed until the third Five Year Plan (1961-66). During the third plan, family planning methods were introduced to the people mostly through advertising, but with little effect. And the situation was made worse by a series of poor harvests, culminating at the end of the Plan period in the great drought of 1965-66. The total food grain harvest in 1966 was only 72 300 000 t compared with a 1961 harvest of 82 000 000 t and a targeted 1966 harvest of 100 000 000 t. During this same period the population grew from 439 000 000 to about 490 000 000, thus reducing per capita foodgrain availability by almost 25% (from 0.187 t in 1961 to 0.147 t in 1966). The situation became critical, and remained so throughout the disastrous 1966-67 harvest, when the monsoons failed again and the harvest was only 75 900 000 t. Five year planning broke down, and was replaced by single year planning.

The doctor (at left) tries to persuade village men to practise contraception.

US Information Service

Massive birth control programs were mounted, but success has been minimal. By 1971 there were 547 000 000 Indians. Current estimates show that only about 6 000 000 people of reproductive age regularly use contraceptives, in contrast with about 350 000 000 who do not. The government is now moving more in the direction of comprehensive planning; medical care and social welfare in particular are being improved. If parents thought that their first two or three children would survive, and that their old age security was not in doubt, then perhaps they would have fewer children. As it is, however, the rejection of birth control by most people has been a thorn in the side of government planners; they see that any real gains in output are being lost to an increasing population.

Along with family planning programs, which were greatly expanded after 1966, India also put much effort into improving the farming situation. New high yielding varieties (HYVs) of rice and wheat were introduced on a large scale, and as a result, India's total foodgrain output rose greatly. By 1971 output was up to 107 000 000 t and per capita availability to 0.196 t. Officials claimed that India was becoming self-sufficient in foodgrains, but warned citizens that family planning efforts would have to be maintained, since increases in foodgrain output could not continue indefinitely.

After 1971, the country suffered several setbacks; the monsoon failed in 1972, and in 1973 the price increases of OPEC oil made fertilizers and pesticides very expensive. In addition, post-1968 Green Revolution technology left many farm workers jobless; many moved to the cities, where their arrival caused serious tensions. In 1974 the government was forced to take severe measures, and so normal democratic rule was suspended. Indira Ghandi tried to relieve some of the problems in 1977 by proposing compulsory sterilization, but she was defeated at the polls.

India's population explosion has been creating a variety of problems for many years. Clearly, though, the population/food problem is the most serious. It requires continuing attention if India is ever to be a self-sufficient nation.

POPULATION: Further Reading

The Crowding Syndrome, BIRD
The Population Bomb, EHRLICH
My Petition for More Space, HERSEY
Pronatalism, PECK & SENDEROWITZ
Be Fruitful and Multiply, FREMLIN
Compulsory Parenthood, WATTERS
Crowding and Behavior, FRIEDMAN
Ark II, PIRAGES & EHRLICH
The Biological Time Bomb, TAYLOR
Origins, LEAKEY

Conclusion

Population growth is indeed one of the most difficult issues facing the world. We know that the world population is increasing by some 70 000 000 people each year. Does this rate of growth present us with a crisis? At the very simplest level, will there be enough food for us all? If millions of people are malnourished or starving today, what will be happening in ten years? In one hundred years?

We have seen the haunting spectacle of India, a country where the population explosion threatens to outstrip food production. In spite of strong efforts at birth control, remarkable advances in food production, and serious attempts at land reform, India remains the obvious example of the population-food problem. It typifies the situation of many smaller countries in Asia, Africa, and South America.

There are grounds for hope, however. West Germany has a population that is actually declining, and yet it produces a large surplus of food. Russia and China appear to have a decreasing rate of population growth, and food production appears to be adequate. The population explosion is not expected to last. The UN predicts that the world's population will stabilize around the year 2100 at 12 or 13 billion people.

This is, of course, a huge number. Can the world be expected to feed an additional 8 billion people? The next chapter will help us to find answers to our questions, and provide a clear picture of the present and future food situation.

Chapter 2
FOOD

Introduction

The United Nations held two major related conferences in 1974, one on Population, which took place in Bucharest in August, and the other on Food, held in Rome in November. Two more allied conferences took place in 1977, one on Water, held in Buenos Aires in March and the other on Aridity, which took place in Nairobi in September.

According to the Secretary-General of the United Nations World Food Conference held in Rome in November 1974, "the food problem facing mankind today is probably the most serious one in the world's history . . . and carries with it the gravest implications for the peace and security of the world."

Famine has, indeed, stalked human societies since the dawn of time. The vast majority of people have always suffered the pains of hunger and the threat of starvation. What makes the lack of food so serious today is its widespread occurrence, and its potential for social and political turmoil. The United Nations Food and Agriculture Organization (FAO) estimates that 500 000 000 people around the world are suffering from hunger, and about 1 500 of them die every day from starvation.

The FAO says that the main reason for the growing food problem is the high rate of population growth in much of the world. It says that in the developing countries, where hunger is most common, the rate of population growth is at least twice that of the developed countries. The population is simply outstripping the food supply, as Malthus forecast.

Developing countries generally feel that the developed countries are largely responsible for the population explosion, because they introduced death control in developing countries through medical aid, without any of the accompanying social and economic factors that act toward a reduction in birth rates.

Another view of the problem is put forward by Roger Revelle, Professor of Population Studies at Harvard University and President of the American Association for the Advancement of Science. Writing in the *UNESCO Courier* of 1974 7-8, he claims that:

> The principal cause, however, is the low level of agricultural technology in most parts of the world. Instead of the 6.4 metric tons grown on a hectare in Iowa, the average Indian or Pakistani farmer produces only a little more than one ton of wheat or rice.

Output is relatively low in India not only on a per hectare basis, but also on a per person basis. For instance, India produces about 100 000 000 t of foodgrains a year from the labour of about 200 000 000 people directly engaged in farming, while the United States produces about 220 000 000 t from the work of about 5 000 000 people.

Other scientists say that there may be enough food grown, but that because of the losses to pests not enough reaches the people who need it. This point is made below.

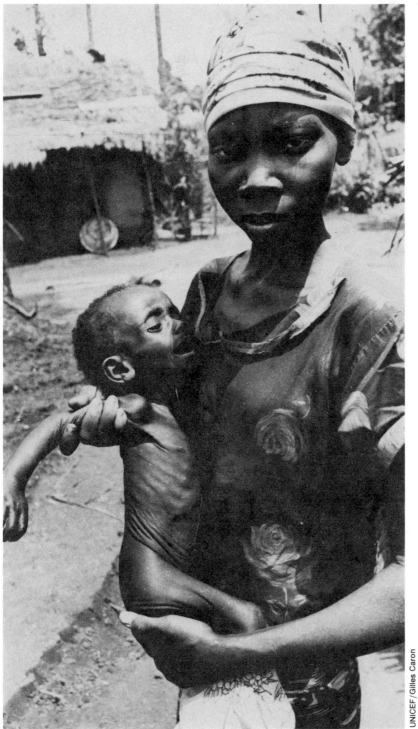

UNICEF / Gilles Caron

The FAO estimates that there are 500 000 000 people around the world suffering from hunger.

World losing half its food

LONDON (Reuter)—Insects, animal pests, diseases and weeds destroy no less than a half of all the food grown in the world, a British scientist said yesterday.

In Britain, nearly a third of the crops are wiped out by vermin and disease, according to Leonard Broadbent of Bath University's School of Biological Sciences.

But in tropical countries, where the climate favors man's competitors and agriculture is less well developed, food losses total more than two thirds.

"In the world as a whole, crop losses from pests and diseases alone are equal to the value of the world grain harvest plus the world potato harvest," he said.

"This would not matter much, apart from the wasted effort, if the population were stable and well-fed. But some 500 million people are seriously underfed, and 1.5 billion inadequately fed—and the world's population is expected to double during the next 25 years."

It is estimated, for example, that there are six billion rats in India, approximately ten per person. According to a newspaper article of 1977 2 10:

> ...they eat up between 10 and 25 per cent of the entire food grain output..., ruin even vaster quantities of rice and wheat with their droppings, carry between 35 and 40 kinds of infectious diseases, and breed prolifically.
>
> It is now generally admitted that the losses of grain in fields and warehouses would make up the difference in India between shortage and plenty.

The USSR Vice-Minister of Foreign Affairs, writing in the *UNESCO Courier* of 1975 5, suggests yet another reason for the food problem:

> Some explain food problems in terms of the population explosion but this is incorrect. Science in theory and in practice has proved that given certain social and economic conditions, there is great potential for food production. Talking about a population explosion appears to be an intentional attempt to veil real causes, which are in the social, economic and political fields.
>
> The solution to the problem of food supplies is first of all dependent upon peace in the world. Vast sums are spent on armaments and this undermines the confidence of countries in each other. We endorse the UN General Assembly resolution that permanent members of the UN Security Council reduce their arms spending by 10 per cent. The saving could be

applied to agricultural development in the Third World countries.

Colombia's Ambassador to Italy, writing in the *UNESCO Courier* of 1975 5, also feels that the causes of the problem are political and economic:

> The world is approaching the point where as many people die daily of hunger or malnutrition as were killed every 24 hours during World War II. The wielding of the world's economic power by a handful of nations has made it impossible to guarantee the majority of our fellow men even the most elementary human rights.

Whether or not these people are justified in placing the responsibility for the food problem on the developed nations, it is a fact that there are food surpluses in the richer parts of the world. The European community often stockpiles vast surpluses of meat, butter, tomatoes, wine, and milk; these abundances exist largely because of price supports which are given to keep the least efficient farms in production, but which cause efficient farms to overproduce.

Also, throughout the wealthier parts of the world, many people overeat and give large amounts of food to pets. There are other moral issues involved as well, as a newspaper article of 1976 2 25 notes:

> ... Is it right that we use approximately half a million acres of land in Ontario to maintain 120 000 horses for our pleasure— or that we use tons of fertilizer to keep our lawns and flower beds looking better than our neighbors'?
>
> Only you can answer such questions.

It is not only in the developed world that animals are allowed a large share of available food. In India, for example, cows are permitted to eat what they want, even off a street vendor's display, while ceremonial rats and monkeys are almost always fed by visitors to temples and other holy places.

Does it indeed matter to you if millions of people starve?

In this chapter we will examine the world food situation in more detail. We will look at the importance of food and its general availability; we will also investigate standards of nutrition, and explore ways of improving the situation. A case study of the Sudan illustrates the points made in the discussion.

Discussion and Research

1. What causes of the world food problem are suggested in the Introduction? What other causes can you suggest?
2. Is Malthus being proved correct?
3. What arguments can you suggest in favour of having the richer nations share their surpluses with the poorer nations? And what are the arguments against the idea?

Section A
The Present Situation

1. The Importance of Food

Why do we eat? The obvious answer "to remain alive" is inadequate. Food serves a variety of purposes; for example, it provides material for cell growth so that decaying cells can be replaced by new ones. Food serves many cultural and psychological needs, too. Stop for a moment and think of some examples.

✓ Food is also required for energy. The human body "burns" kilojoules of energy which are produced from food (a kilojoule is the amount of energy required to move a mass of one kilogram a distance of one metre at an acceleration of one metre per second each second). This energy is consumed in a number of ways, and for many different purposes. The greatest quantities of energy are generally needed for the maintenance of basic body functions called *basal metabolism*; such functions include breathing, muscle action, and blood circulation. The temperature of the body must also be kept at 36.9° C. The amount of energy required for this process will vary according to the climate; more energy is needed in the colder parts of the world, and less in the tropics. Therefore, the amount of energy used in basal metabolism, including body temperature maintenance, varies from 6 000 to 8 000 kJ/d. It is estimated that the average adult needs 7 000 kJ/d just to keep the body in working order.

Energy is also essential to physical growth. The requirements vary during a person's lifetime, rising during childhood to a peak at about 15-17 years, and then tapering off. Regular activities such as walking and talking have a fairly low energy requirement of about 1 000 kJ/d. This amount, which makes up 10% of our needs, does not vary much from person to person. Energy is also required for other activities, such as work. Obviously, the amount needed will vary with the type of work done; a job in construction, which requires much physical labour, will demand more kilojoules than a desk job.

Kilojoules come from three main sources: carbohydrates, fats, and proteins. Carbohydrates and proteins both yield 16.8 kJ/g, but a gram of fats can yield up to 37.8 kJ. Fats are therefore the most concentrated form of food energy. Rich supplies of fats are obtained from

Food energy has traditionally been measured in Calories. It is now measured in kilojoules. The conversion factors are:
1 Calorie (kilocalorie) = 4.2 kJ
1 kJ = 0.238 Cal.

butter, lard, liver, egg yolk, and vegetable oils. If all the energy contained in food eaten (carbohydrates, fats, and proteins) is not burned up, the body stores the unused kilojoules in the most concentrated form possible—fat. Sometimes fat can build up inside the body, resulting not only in obesity, but in susceptibility to heart disease.

Carbohydrates are widely available from sugar found in candy, and starch foods such as rice, wheat, corn, and potatoes. Starch foods are easy to produce, and so are literally the staff of life for billions all over the world.

Proteins come chiefly from meat, milk products, eggs, and fish. Some plants, notably cereals and soybeans, are also good sources. In

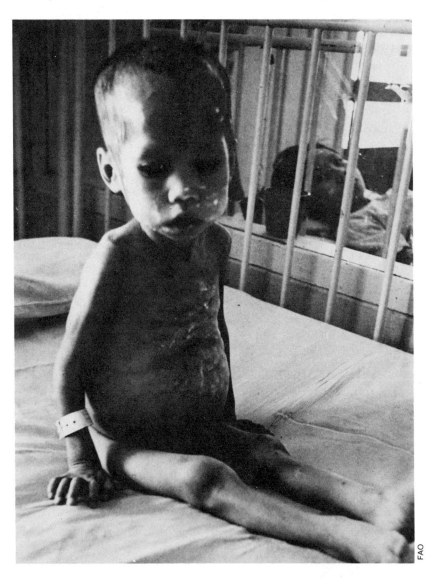

A child suffering from severe protein deficiency in a hospital in North Thailand.

FAO

our study of food, we are interested in both the quantity and quality of the energy-producing capacity of food. The total number of kilojoules available will measure *quantity*. And since the major sources of proteins are generally expensive and scarce throughout the world, and usually contain other important nutrients, it is possible to use proteins as a measure of the *quality* of a nation's diet.

Besides being a source of energy, proteins are part of every cell, and thus are the basic building material for the body. Chemically, proteins are made up of about 28 different amino acids. All these acids are found in meat, eggs, fish, and milk products, whereas only some are found in sufficient quantities in cereals, beans, and peanuts. An average person requires about 56 g/d of protein; one third of this should be animal protein. The amount of animal protein consumed can be used as another measure of the quality of food taken in by a country. Unfortunately, protein deficiency is a serious problem among many of the world's peoples.

A group of women in Sierra Leone being instructed in good nutrition.

UNICEF photo by Larsen

In addition to proteins, fats, and carbohydrates, the human body needs supplies for the following: minerals, such as calcium for bones and iron for *haemoglobin*; vitamins, such as A for good vision and B_1 (thiamin) for effective use of carbohydrates; fibre, which is the indigestible portion of many fruits, vegetables, and whole grain cereals, and which is necessary to promote good digestive action and prevent intestinal cancer; and water, which is more important even than food.

These needs are contained in different foodstuffs. For example, meat is a good source of fats, proteins, minerals, and vitamins, while bread provides carbohydrates, proteins, and vitamins. The aim of good nutrition is to eat the correct quantities of a variety of different foods so that the needs are met in total. Since no single foodstuff will supply everything (milk is the most versatile), a balance of different foods must be obtained. A proper balance means good nutrition.

Malnutrition is a lack of nutrients caused by an imbalance in the varieties of food eaten. It does not necessarily indicate starvation, which is a lack of food. People can eat all the food they want and still be malnourished. Thus malnutrition may be as much of a problem in North America as it is in tropical Africa. The following article describes the results of malnutrition in various parts of the world.

Haemoglobin is the substance in the blood that permits it to absorb oxygen from the air.

Nutrition in the developing world

Two-thirds of the world's children live in the developing countries and for most of them malnutrition is a fact of existence. The consequences may be death, blindness, irreversible mental retardation due to protein deficiency, or physical impairment, so that they are incapable of employment and of contributing to their countries' progress.

Nutrition as a reliable science is relatively young. The first vitamin to be identified was vitamin A, in 1913; the last, vitamin B_{12}, was not discovered until 1945. Nutritionists now know that about fifty substances must be present in the diet to sustain life and promote health. They can prescribe fairly accurately the necessary minimum allowances of these substances, but they still do not know the full consequences of excessive consumption of certain food elements.

Nevertheless, we know that while about a quarter of the world's people eat too much for their own good, the other three-quarters eat too little. Whereas North America produces 116% of the kilojoules needed by its population, Asia produces only about 90%, so that in that densely populated area of the world there is an overall "energy gap". Moreover, in every part of the world some people have plenty to eat while others have barely enough to sustain life.

The protein gap
The discrepancy in quantity between the diet of the "haves" and that of the "have-nots" is great, but the discrepancy in quality is even greater. In affluent countries, meat, milk, eggs, and other high-protein foods—valuable as elements of a balanced diet but having potentially dangerous concentrations of animal fats unless used in moderation—are consumed in amounts far in excess of recommended allowances. Indeed, they have practically become dietary staples, and in certain income groups a "meatless meal" is considered a genuine deprivation. In poorer countries, animal protein foods are often in such short supply that, except in the homes of the rich, they may be served only on special holiday or ceremonial occasions. The diet typically available to children in those countries is grossly deficient not only in high quality protein but in certain minerals and vitamins that animal protein foods provide.

There is good reason to suppose that malnutrition, in one form or another, is the most serious problem now facing the human race. On the one hand, an affluent few are inviting arteriosclerosis (an accumulation of hardened fatty deposits in the arteries) by consuming too much food rich in animal fats—a steady diet of fat-meat hamburgers, ham-and-mayonnaise sandwiches, ice cream, and the like. On the other hand, perhaps as many as two billion people are prey to infection and deficiency diseases because their diet does not give them the needed minimum of proteins, minerals, and vitamins. Among the latter, it is the children from one to five years old who suffer most.

Deficiency diseases

Where hunger and malnutrition exist, an unusually high percentage of babies born alive have a low birth weight and incidence of prematurity is higher. It is also considered that in any country a high mortality rate in the one-to-four-years age group indicates widespread malnutrition. While the immediate cause of death may not be a nutritional (deficiency) disease, malnutrition lowers the resistance to infectious diseases and the ability to recover. Even without infection, deficiency diseases can stunt, cripple, and kill. They claim many victims every day.

✓ Kwashiorkor

Kwashiorkor is the African name for a major deficiency disease of childhood in many less developed coun-

tries. It attacks infants who are weaned to a rigorous diet of starch foods which are often too coarse for the child's digestive system, with the result that he suffers from moderate kilojoule deficiency as well as grossly deficient protein intake. A child with kwashiorkor becomes puny, his hair and skin grow pale, his arms and legs become thin, and he develops a potbelly. In the acute disease, the child's face, hands, and legs may swell, his skin may break down as if burned, and he becomes apathetic; when this stage is reached, the disease is usually fatal. In earlier stages, the addition to the baby's diet of food rich in protein will clear up the condition.

Marasmus

The condition known as marasmus is a form of starvation not specifically related to protein. It may develop in a child after an attack of diarrhoea when the digestive system is unable to handle the food available. This disease takes the form of wasting; the skin becomes thin and wrinkled but does not break down and the child does not refuse food or become apathetic. As in the case of kwashiorkor, marasmus victims can be returned to

health if they are treated soon enough.

. . .

Some of the other diseases of malnutrition are *Beri-beri*✓ which is caused by lack of vitamin B$_1$ (thiamine); *Xerophthalmia*, a disease of the eyes brought on by lack of vitamin A, causing blindness, and curable by the inclusion of green leaves in the diet; *Pellagra*, caused by a deficiency of niacin found in meat, fish and whole grains and pulses; *Scurvy*✓ resulting from a lack of vitamin C; *Rickets*,✓ a bone disease caused by a lack of vitamin D; *Anaemia*,✓ an iron-deficiency disease.

In addition to the diseases caused by specific deficiencies in the diet, lack of food—hunger—is an all-too-common condition among the poor of the world. In many areas, population is increasing at a rate that is greater than the available food supply can support. Lack of transportation facilities in the developing countries hampers transfer of food from areas of plenty to areas of need. People are leaving the traditional rural economy and crowding into the cities where they can afford only the cheapest and least nourishing food.

Canadian UNICEF Committee 1971 10

✱ Anorexia Nervosa

BROOM HILDA

Reprinted by permission of *Toronto Star* Syndicate. Copyright (1977) CTNYNS.

Hunger
Starvation
Malnutrition

Discussion and Research

4. What are the cultural values that lead to malnutrition in North America?
5. Many of the effects of food deficiency are described in the previous reading. Most of these are physical effects. Suggest some of the social, economic, or political effects of food deficiencies.

2. Food Availability

Variations in the *quantity* of food available may be measured by means of kilojoules. However, the *quality* of food available is less easy to measure. In North America and Europe an imbalance generally results from an excess of fats and carbohydrates, but in most of the rest of the world unbalanced diets are usually caused by protein deficiencies. We will use proteins as a measure of nutritional quality, bearing in mind that protein is only the most obvious of the requirements for a good diet.

Statistical Interpretation

2-1 Using the data in column I of Appendix 2 draw a graded shading map of the per capita daily availability of kilojoules throughout the world. You might consider using a grading scheme such as:

12 000 and over kJ/person/d	very bright green
10 000 – 11 999 kJ/person/d	bright green
8 000 – 9 999 kJ/person/d	pale green
under 8 000 kJ/person/d	very pale green

What do you notice about the distribution of the countries that have a food availability below 10 000 kJ/person/d? How does it compare with the population growth maps in assignments 1-4 and 1-5?

2-2 To find the energy-producing capacity of the food consumed by different nations, calculate the kilojoules per gram (kJ/g) for each country from the data in columns I and J of Appendix 2. For example, Afghanistan's data are 8 274 kJ and 842 g, and the resulting kJ/g figure is 9.8 (8 274/842 = 9.8). Group your answers into four classes and draw a graded shading map to show the world picture. How do you explain the result when you compare it with the kilojoule map in assignment 2-1?

2-3 The graded shading map in Fig. 2-1 shows per capita daily protein availability in the world's countries. How does the pattern compare with the ones you have just drawn in assignments 2-1 and 2-2?

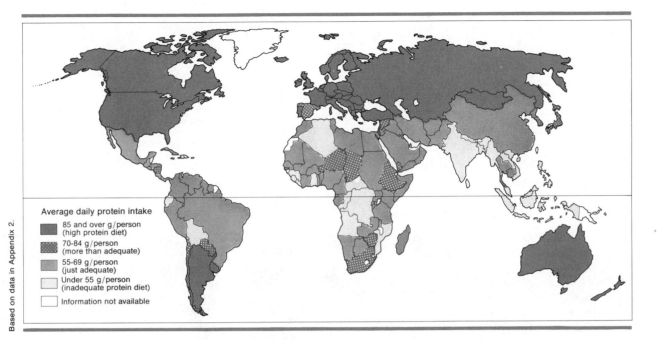

Based on data in Appendix 2.

Average daily protein intake

- 85 and over g/person (high protein diet)
- 70-84 g/person (more than adequate)
- 55-69 g/person (just adequate)
- Under 55 g/person (inadequate protein diet)
- Information not available

Fig. 2-1
National per capita daily protein availability in the world

North Americans and Europeans generally have more kilojoules and proteins than they need, but according to the maps drawn in assignments 2-1 and 2-3, there are large populations that have far fewer kilojoules and proteins than required. These are areas where starvation and malnutrition are widespread. There are two basic reasons for a lack of food: not enough food production compared with the demand, and a lack of commodities to trade for food produced in other countries.

Among the reasons for insufficient food production we should note the following:

a) The use of simple methods and implements such as water wheels, animal and human muscle power, shallow wooden ploughs, inadequate fertilization, hand seeding, and low quality seeds. For example, Denmark, with a population only 12% as large as Egypt's, uses just as much nitrogenous fertilizer, while Czechoslovakia, with about the same population as Kenya, uses almost one hundred times as much potash fertilizer.

b) Small and scattered landholdings. When plots of land are scattered farmers must waste time travelling from one plot to another; the small size of each plot also renders the use of machinery unlikely. Many countries face this problem, brought about by *gavelkind* laws of inheritance whereby all children share equally in the division of their deceased parents' holding. In time, this system produces a multitude of tiny plots which may be held in a scattered fashion by a few descendants. France began to consolidate its many small plots in the 1950s,

When crops are seeded by hand, the seeds are scattered haphazardly over the ground. The plants therefore are unevenly distributed and difficult to harvest.

The consolidation process in France is called the *remembrement* movement.

when it planned to join the European Common Market. India also began at about the same time with plans for inheritance law reform, but there is still much to do in the country. Other countries have scarcely begun on land reform.

c) The system of landholding, whereby most peasants do not own the land they work, and thus have little or no reason to improve farming conditions. This is a very explosive issue. One of the first aims of revolutionaries in agricultural societies is always the confiscation of large landholdings and the distribution of land to former tenant farmers. We should note that this in itself will not ensure greater food production.

Such confiscations took place in Italy under Mussolini, in China under Mao, in Russia under Lenin, in Cuba under Castro, and in Japan under MacArthur. In other countries such as Brazil and India the changes have been less revolutionary.

d) The loss of food to insects and other pests, caused by poor pest control and poor storage facilities.

Animal and human muscle power.

UNESCO

Small plots do not usually make for efficient food production.

United Nations

Photo/Péchiney-Progril, Paris

Wheat grains destroyed by weevils.

Simple implements.

A shallow wooden plough.

Julian Juez and Andrew Pearce

UNESCO/Gerda Bohm

Countries that cannot feed themselves can always buy food from nations with a surplus—if they have the money to buy it, as several European countries do. But most countries with a food deficit have little money, and few ways of earning it.

Some of the reasons for this are:

a) They cannot produce and sell manufactured goods in competition with big industrialized nations. There are important exceptions to this: Hong Kong, Taiwan, Korea, and Brazil.

b) They cannot produce and export enough raw materials. There are important exceptions here as well; Indonesian oil, Malaysian tin, Jamaican alumina, and Bangladesh jute are all widely exported. Often, wealthy countries which control the world market are thus accused of exploiting the less developed countries.

c) They do not earn money from "invisible exports" as some countries do. Exceptions to this are the profits from the banking, insurance, and shipping services provided by Singapore; the money that tourists spend in Hong Kong; and the money sent back to India, Pakistan, and Hong Kong by emigrants working in high-wage countries.

They may receive money in aid. The money is available in the form of *credits*, which permit the aid-receiving countries to purchase food from the surplus-producing countries by going into debt to them. Most developing countries are very heavily in debt.

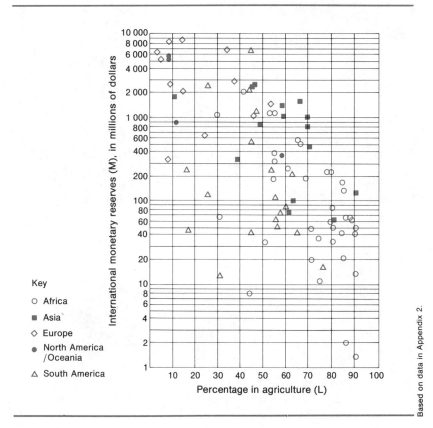

Fig. 2-2
Relationship between international monetary reserves and percentage of population in agriculture

Based on data in Appendix 2.

Generally, the lower the percentage of the population employed in agriculture, the greater the efficiency.

You can change US dollars for Canadian or Australian dollars at a bank. In effect you sell the US dollars to the *government* in exchange for Canadian or Australian dollars. In this way and others, the government comes to hold a large quantity of foreign money.

Fig. 2-2 shows a *scattergraph* (see Appendix 3) of the data in columns L and M of Appendix 2. Column L contains the percentages of each country's population employed in agriculture; these data are widely used as a test of agricultural efficiency. Column M gives information about the size of each country's *international monetary reserve*, which is a test of its trading ability. An *international monetary reserve* is the money held by a country's central bank in the currencies of other nations. In Canada, for example, the US dollars, Swiss francs, Japanese yen, and so on which are held by the Bank of Canada form the country's international monetary reserve. Normally this money is largely at the disposal of the government, which may use it for foreign purchases. In early 1977, for example, China is reported to have "dipped into its international monetary reserves" in order to purchase wheat from Canada.

Statistical Interpretation

2-4 What do you notice about the relationships shown in Fig. 2-2? What do you think are the chief causes of these relationships?

2-5 Select one of the data sets, L or M, and relate it to the quantity of food available in each country as expressed in kJ in Appendix 2, column I. Use the *phi (∅) coefficient* technique as outlined in Appendix 3.

a) What sort of relationship do you get for your data sets (I and L or I and M)?

b) Describe in words the sort of relationship that you would expect to obtain between I and the data set you did not choose (either L or M).

2-6 The FAO suggests that a large part of the food problem is attributable to the high rate of population growth in the developing countries. This view is shared by others, as the following item from the *UNESCO Courier* of 1975 5 demonstrates:

The major problem facing the developing countries, in spite of the remarkable expansion of their agricultural output in the 1950s and 1960s lies in the increased rate of demand—3.5 per cent—due to faster population growth. Although the degree of imbalance varies from country to country and from region to region, in the majority of developing countries the agricultural shortfall has become a grave impediment to the achievement of overall development.

A vicious circle of malnutrition leading to high death rates, which, in turn, motivates large families, is also set up.

The suggestion is that a high rate of population growth (column F in Appendix 2) not only correlates well with food deficits (column I), but also *helps to cause them*. We can test this idea mathematically by calculating the *coefficient of determination*, as shown in Appendix 3. It would be laborious to do this for all the countries listed without the help of a computer, so use only the *sample* of countries that are shown starred (*) in Appendix 2, namely Algeria, Brazil, Canada, etc. The number of countries in the sample = *n*. Your answer will vary between 0.0 and 1.0. A number close to 0.0 indicates that only a small degree of *i* (food availability) can be explained in terms of *f* (rate of population increase), while a number close to 1.0 indicates that a large degree of *i* is attributable to variations in *f*. The figure you have calculated also tells you the exact percentage of *i* that has been caused by *f*. For instance, if your answer is 0.62, then 62% of the variations in *i* can be accounted for by variations in *f*.

a) What is your answer?

b) What does it tell you about the *causal relationship* that exists between rate of population growth and food deficits?

c) Can you explain it?

d) What percentage of food deficits remains to be explained by factors *other than* rate of population growth?

e) What could these other factors be?

f) How would you test whether or not the factors that you suggest are really part of the cause?

Undoubtedly there are many things wrong with the world food situation. There are great inequalities in kilojoule and protein availability; starvation and malnutrition exist in spite of the excess amounts of food produced in some areas; there are conflicting views about the causes of hunger; and there are many different explanations for the inadequate availability of food. We should therefore try to establish some standards.

Section B
Standards of Nutrition

It is hard to say how much we should eat. Most of us know when we are hungry, even though we may not be able to say whether the reason is physiological or psychological. We also know when we have eaten too much, but not many of us know when we have eaten just the right amount. It is much more difficult for us to set standards for others, particularly when billions of people are involved.

There are no officially recognized standards of nutrition. One early proposal was the *standard nutrition unit*, formulated by the geographer L. D. Stamp. He took the basic requirement to support an average person for one year as 4 200 000 kJ, deducted about 10% for wastage, and divided the remainder by 365 to arrive at a daily figure of about 10 350 kJ/person. We can round this figure to 10 000 kJ/person/d, and call it the *modified standard nutrition unit*. This figure is an average for the population as a whole; babies and old people generally need less than the average number of kilojoules while adolescents and very active adults need more. A glance back at your map in assignment 2-1 will tell you how different countries relate to the modified standard nutrition unit. Some exceed the standard, but many fail to reach it, which suggests that in the latter countries a few may be well fed but most people are hungry.

All attempts to rank countries according to universal food standards meet with the criticism that tropical countries, which for climatic reasons do not need so much food as high latitude countries, will always appear as deficit areas if they are plotted against a universal standard. This is true. It is also true that medical research indicates much starvation and malnutrition in tropical countries. What do you deduce from this paradox?

In order to produce a fairly refined set of norms the Food and Agriculture Organization of the United Nations (the FAO) has calculated an individual norm for each country based on that country's climate, prevailing individual human body size, and age composition of its population. The norms, expressed in kJ, are given in column N of Appendix 2. The extent to which each country exceeds or fails to reach its FAO norm is given in column O.

Statistical Interpretation

2-7 Using the information in column O of Appendix 2, construct a map
to show those countries that meet or exceed their FAO norms.

OR

Construct a *linear dispersion diagram* as shown in Appendix 3 to
illustrate the data in column O, using a different colour for the
countries in each continent. Relate the graph to your map in assignment 2-1, and explain the results.

The nations of the world can now be seen to vary not only in their
ability to meet absolute food quantities (assignments 2-1 and 2-3) but
also in their capacity to meet individually tailored food norms (assignment 2-7). In either case many countries exist below the desired levels
of food availability. The situation must be improved.

Section C
Improving the Situation

Food is one of humanity's basic resources. It is also a renewable resource, and an increasable one. In this it is almost unique (how many other increasable resources can you suggest?). There are growing numbers of people in the world, and all will want sufficient amounts of food. However, until all areas of the world can feed themselves adequately, we should look for better ways of distributing existing food supplies.

1. The Distribution of Existing Food Supplies √

There are food surpluses in a few countries. These are supplies of food that no one will buy, and that are consequently stockpiled or destroyed by the producing countries. For example, Canadian milk has been poured down old mine shafts, English tomatoes bulldozed into the sea, German meat put into cold storage, and American cows killed and buried. Food may be destroyed to prevent prices from falling, since low prices make future crops unprofitable for the farmers. Of course, surpluses may be given away as foreign aid by the producing countries; some countries want this kind of aid, while others do not. Mexico and Senegal favour international reserve food stocks; these would be financed by the richer nations for use in countries that experience famines. The Minister of Rural Development in Senegal is quoted in the *UNESCO Courier* of 1975 5 as saying:

> There is still hope that a world seemingly dominated by egoism, with the "haves" wasting grains for feeding their animals...will be able to unite in the face of threatened famine.
> Immediate measures should be taken for the establishment of food stocks, particularly grains and proteins, in order to prevent crises such as those recently witnessed and still rampant, particularly in the Sahel. These stocks must be placed at strategic points near famine areas. The international community should urgently finance the necessary installations.

√ Food surpluses above the level of demand within a particular country (domestic demand) exist within several countries. In most cases these surpluses are produced in response to expected trade demands on world markets, and they are therefore only surpluses in a *domestic* sense. For example, Danish bacon is produced in quantities far greater than the Danes can consume, but it is sold, as expected, to buyers in Germany and Britain. It is an item produced for trade just like cars, for example, and is therefore surplus food domestically only.

Sometimes crops may not even be planted, in order to keep prices sufficiently high to maintain the farmers in business. Indeed, farmers may be paid by governments for not producing; they may even be fined if they produce more than the government says they should.

(Other developing countries want nothing to do with such a scheme; they say that the remedy should be sought within their own territories) as the following items from the *UNESCO Courier* of 1975 5 show.

Philippines

CARLOS P. ROMULO, *Secretary of Foreign Affairs*:

It is no use, it is indeed shameful and degrading to wait for the developed countries to come to the rescue every time we come to the brink of starvation. Of course, when millions are faced with misery, offers of assistance must be welcomed, as demonstrations of human solidarity. But we are not helpless—we must help ourselves.

Pakistan

MALIK KHUDA BUKHSH, *Special Assistant for Agriculture to the Prime Minister*:

The developing world will have to recognize that the solution of its food problems lies in its own hands and within its own countries. Agriculture will have to be accorded the highest priority.

Emergency famine relief in Upper Volta, June 1973. The sacks contain sorghum, donated by the USA and distributed locally by village chiefs.

FAO

Work being done under the World Food Program to enlarge a reservoir tank in Madhya Pradesh, India, for extra water storage.

Aid to needy countries takes a wide range of forms; different attitudes abound among those who give, and those who receive. At one end stand the countries whose people need aid—mostly food—in order to survive. Some of this aid is shipped in emergencies from individual surplus to individual deficit countries, but an increasing amount is being distributed through the UN *World Food Program.* Under this program, payments are made in food to local populations for their work on development projects. For example, workers on an irrigation ditch would be paid in food. The USA is the chief donor, providing 75% of all food aid. Canada gives 15%, followed by Australia, West Germany, and Japan (which has been delivering rice from surplus stocks since 1970). Individuals find it very difficult to send direct food aid, as reported in a newspaper article of 1975 4 2.

50 tons of food for starving, no way to send it

by PETER WHELAN

Terry Leonard never thought feeding hungry people could be controversial.

Nor did he expect to accuse Cabinet ministers to their faces of criminal negligence.

Mr. Leonard has 50 tons [45 t] of food in Toronto for the starving of Bangladesh.

His problem: to get it there quickly. He had the same problem a week and a month ago. Banglis have starved in the interim. They are starving today.

He is hoping for an answer today on an airlift plan. He is talking to charity groups and private corporations. "I am optimistic."

But the voice on the telephone reflects other words for his feelings, "confused, disenchanted."

Everyone says "somebody should do something". He admits saying it for most of his 32 years until he decided to be that somebody.

Consider it through his eyes. First the idea: ask Kingston residents to fast for a day, learn the pangs of hunger and donate the food-money saved to the Banglis. His wife Patricia and friends pitched in, the news media gave publicity and about 6 000 people donated $23 500.

The Leonards had a hectic but warm December. There was a direct feeling: from the dinner tables of Kingston to hungry hands in Dacca.

The question became how to use the money wisely. As district manager for Beaver Foods Ltd., Mr. Leonard has seen a lot of food wasted.

He consulted the federal Government with a faith he now questions. He did not like the answers.

"We have no right to let people starve," Mr. Leonard says. The statement is a keystone of his outrage. In his terms, some Canadians, men in power, are willing to let people starve. He is appalled.

CIDA, the Canadian International Development Agency, suggested he route the money to buy food on the spot from the Bangladesh Government. But it could not assure him this food would not be free aid being resold for personal profit by corrupt officials.

CIDA was not too interested in direct food aid. "They talked of diminished returns from simply sending food," Mr. Leonard said angrily.

It was his first experience with men and agencies influenced by the concept that hundreds of thousands in poor nations are inevitably to starve. The premise is that man's ingenuity cannot cope with population growth that exceeds even hoped-for food supplies. Only starvation and disease, in the end, will balance the scales.

Agriculture Minister Eugene Whelan said this, and called it a terrible thing to have to say.

"I do not believe in Malthusian population theories," Mr. Leonard insists.

The Canadian aid program for Bangladesh centres on efforts to pull together a staggering society, foster the stability needed to grow food, transport it and have homes in which to eat it. Projects are in effect for food tomorrow, not today.

In Mr. Leonard's opinion, CIDA is willing to let today's hungry become tomorrow's dead.

CIDA had no matching dollars for Kingston's $23 500. The Defence Department had no military plane to fly the food to Dacca. Those decisions came in January.

But who said what and when has

become important to Mr. Leonard. Belatedly—only this month—CIDA offered "with many conditions" to help ship the food by sea from Montreal. "They'll only pay $5 000 though. They can't tell me when it would arrive," he says.

CIDA moved only after publicity created bureaucratic discomfort, he says.

The food was settled on fairly early: 50 tons of a highly nutritious corn-soya-milk mixture. A milling company prepared it free, a paper company donated bagging and a drug company gave vitamins.

Cost figures of transporting it by air give Mr. Leonard the greatest difficulty in rejecting criticism of his approach to saving lives.

Commercial air freight would cost $179 000 by one estimate. He has a $60 000 estimate for an airline's costs alone, should one offer transportation at no profit.

In CIDA's books, food shipments from Canada—especially by air—are the least effective aid for Bangladesh. "If you have $1 000 to invest, it is better to put it into an agriculture development program than into food directly," Ian Thompson, CIDA coordinator for such private aid programs as Mr. Leonard's, said in an interview.

This approach admits to early starvation deaths, he conceded—"we don't usually put it that way—but fewer should die in the long run.

"It is a difficult situation you cannot put in simple terms. We start with a world spending $12-billion to $15-billion a year on aid, far from the needs, and $250-billion on the military."

Everyone, including CIDA, would have been happy had a Defence Department plane been available to carry Mr. Leonard's food to Dacca.

But the military training flights sometimes used for such shipments on the basis that the planes are going anyway, have been used up.

CIDA does favor quick, direct food aid in spot disasters, such as earthquakes and drought, Mr. Thompson said.

He called it unfortunate that Mr. Leonard had not chosen to work through a recognized aid agency. But he said CIDA felt it has helped all it could. "It's the taxpayer's dollars we spend, and we try to make best use of them."

In the end, Mr. Leonard does plan to use an international aid agency. He and his wife hope to fly to Bangladesh with the food. Once there, though, he wants experienced aid workers to supervise the distribution.

Is there an onus on governments to spend public funds to assist the foreign aid plans of private citizens? Mr. Leonard believes there should be.

It is not just getting $23 500 worth of food to a few thousand people. There are other benefits—the awareness of human needs and the sense of participation experienced by those who donate and organize.

His exuberance at the early sense of accomplishment was already fading when he went to the Ontario Government on Feb. 18.

He was invited to address eight Cabinet ministers whose fields brushed on his concern. Other subjects took the first hours of the ministers' meeting. Only four remained to hear him: Resource Development Secretary Allan Grossman, William Stewart of Agriculture, Leo Bernier of National Resources and William Newman of Environment.

He accused them of criminal negligence, for long-term government policies of farm quotas which reduce food production and inflate costs, and for apathy toward the world's hungry.

His plea for a matching grant was rejected.

Mr. Leonard says his 50 tons of food could keep 10 000 people alive for 40 days. The 41st day?

"We cannot just do nothing because we do not have complete answers. We must do our best."

The Globe and Mail 1975 4 2

Discussion and Research

6. If Terry Leonard had come to you for help how would you have responded?
7. What are the arguments for and against the destruction of food by governments in food surplus countries?
8. Should farmers in food surplus countries be discouraged from producing more than a certain amount of food, as Ontario's milk producers, American wheat growers, and others are at times?

It is important to remember that food is more than just nourishment; it is part of the tradition valued in every culture. The culinary tradition is arguably the strongest aspect of a culture. Immigrants gradually adjust to the culture of the area they have chosen as their new home, and lose some of their own traditions in the process of *acculturation*. These people may give up their clothing styles fairly quickly; they may retain their own language and religion for a longer period of time; but their old food habits often persist the longest. Indeed these traditional food habits may even be adopted by the new culture; Chinese food, for example, has become popular in North America.

Because of the cultural values attached to food, especially to certain foodstuffs, the problem of feeding the world's hungry is more difficult than it would otherwise be. Most food taboos have little to do with nutrition; for example, most North Americans do not eat snakes or dogs, even though these protein-rich foods are delicacies in some other parts of the world. But some food taboos affect nutrition, and may cause people to refuse healthy food that is readily available to them; an example is the avoidance of wild greens, rich in vitamins and iron, in southern India. Other examples are the avoidance of beef by Hindus and of pork by Moslems.

Rice, wheat, and corn are examples of foods acceptable to most cultures, but even these cannot always be substituted for one another. People who usually eat rice as a staple will not, for example, switch readily to corn or wheat, even in an emergency. Meats and dairy foods also have high acceptability, although there are some taboos attached to them.

Children in a Child Nutrition Centre in Thailand being served soymilk, a developed high protein food, to offset endemic protein deficiency.

FAO

The chief trouble with the most widely accepted staples is that they provide only a limited diet. Therefore to help solve the problem of malnutrition among the peoples of the aid-receiving countries, other acceptable and yet nutritious foods must be introduced. Donors often experiment to see just what is acceptable. Some of the successes include *incaparina*, containing 25% high quality vegetable protein that can be mixed with local flour and water; *milk biscuits*, developed by New Zealand to provide whole milk for children even in areas where there is no water; and *superamine*, consisting of a 20% protein mixture of wheat, lentils, peas, milk powder, and vitamins.

Meanwhile experiments continue with fish flour, which contains over 70% protein but is an unappetizing, tasteless grey powder. There are also food *analogues*, whereby substitutes for natural foods are made in a factory. Margarine is one of the oldest food analogues, substituting for butter. In the same way coffee creamers substitute for milk, and dessert toppings substitute for cream. There are even meat analogues made from soybeans—imitation steaks, hamburgers, and so on—which have excellent nutritional qualities but have met so far with low market acceptance. Researchers are even studying the use of bacteria for food; bacteria are rich in protein and they multiply at a fantastic rate. It is estimated that 1 000 kg of bacteria could produce as much as 100 000 000 000 000 kg of protein daily. Acceptance might present a problem, but think of the benefits!

2. Increasing the Quantities of Food Available

"Give a man a fish," runs an old proverb, "and you give him a meal. Teach him how to fish and you give him a living."

Many informed people agree that the best way to help the hungry populations of the world eat better is *not* to give them food. This belief is summed up well by Gene Gregory, writing in the *UNESCO Courier* of 1969 3:

> Food aid, while beneficial as a stop gap measure to relieve famine caused by drought or flood, tends to attack the symptoms rather than the causes. While necessary in times of distress, even when food aid is maintained for a few years only, it breeds an unwholesome attitude of dependence among the recipients and makes it very difficult for local agriculture ever to get properly organized in face of the competition from "free food".

Accordingly, aid should take the forms of education, technology, and capital, rather than food. In the 1975 5 edition of the *UNESCO Courier* the Minister of Agriculture of Mauritius describes the exact type of aid needed by hungry nations:

If you want to increase food production in the developing countries, the necessary facilities for which we have been asking for decades now must be provided. The constraints which lie in our way should be removed or mitigated. What are these constraints? Shortage and high cost of fertilizers, high cost of pesticides, high cost of farm machinery, lack of trained personnel, lack of finance and, most important of all, of a reasonable level of income for the farmers. This can only be achieved by guaranteed and stable markets and reasonable prices for farm products.

know-how?

BROOM HILDA

Reprinted by permission of *Toronto Star* Syndicate. Copyright (1975) CTNYNS.

When aid of any kind moves directly from country to country it is called *bilateral aid*; but increasingly the flows are being channelled through UN and other international organizations (*multilateral aid*). The chief aid channel is the Development Assistance Committee (DAC) of the Organization for Economic Cooperation and Development (OECD). The following countries are members of the committee: Austria, Belgium, Canada, Denmark, France, Italy, Japan, Netherlands, Norway, Portugal, Sweden, Switzerland, UK, USA, and West Germany. About 90% of all world financial aid comes from the DAC members, 40% from the USA alone.

The DAC has set a target of government aid from its members at a level of 0.7% of their own Gross National Products; at the present time the achieved level is about half that. However, there is a huge additional flow of aid from private citizens and commercial companies within the DAC countries, yielding a total aid flow (official and private) of about 0.8% of the GNP (compared with a target for all aid flows of 1%). Assistance also comes from a variety of countries that are not members of DAC, chiefly Finland, New Zealand, South

Africa, and Spain. The largest communist donor is the USSR, whose total aid is about 0.25% of its GNP.

As you go through the following articles, make a list of the things that need to be done with the aid that is received.

What are the prospects that poorer nations can in fact eliminate their food shortages?

On the production side, the opportunities are great despite the bleatings of those who paint pictures of doom. In that area of the world bordering on and between the tropics of Capricorn and Cancer, there is a vast potential for agriculture and food production almost untapped. Much of this area is farmed or grazed under technologies that differ little from those discovered thousands of years ago. Yet the basic ingredients of a productive agriculture—water, responsive soil, suitable year-round growing conditions, and abundant light—hold an immense promise for an abundance beyond anything yet attained by man.

The potential of those areas in the tropical and subtropical developing regions where there are large expanses of land still unexploited for agriculture is, however, probably surpassed by the potential of those other parts, now cultivated by traditional means, where modern farm technologies could greatly increase production. New crop varieties of the major grains and starchy roots offer significant advantages in yield and nutrient content over indigenous biological materials; modern methods of irrigation and rainwater harvesting have a potential water-use efficiency of close to 90 per cent, a sharp contrast with traditional irrigation efficiencies of between 10 and 20 per cent and multiple cropping and intercropping systems adapted to tropical climates and soils can increase land yields from 1 to 2 tons per hectare per crop to over 20 tons per hectare per year (in fact, yield per unit of land *per period of time* is now replacing yield per unit of land as the critical output measure for tropical circumstances). This is not all. New methods of using plant residues for integrated crop-livestock programs hold promise of higher returns to small farmers, of making efficient use of plant materials unfit for human consumption, and of yielding a major source of quality protein for human nutrition. New means of storing and processing food commodities will eliminate waste and open opportunities for rural industry and development. Improved implements for farming permit a better efficiency and timing of agricultural operations for higher production, while easing some of the drudgery of peasant work. New pasture grasses and legumes, new methods of controlling animal diseases, new techniques of animal and range husbandry, new breeds of livestock, open major avenues for increasing the yields of animal and grazing agricultures. These are only a few examples. Modern technology holds one of the keys to abundance, the geographic potential of the tropical world holds another ....

Canadian International Development Agency 1975 8

Rivers must be dammed for electrical power and water control; deep tubwells must be sunk to tap the underground rivers of the Ganges and Bharamaputra basins; land must be shaped for irrigation; canals and drainage channels must be dug; a whole new organizational pattern must be built among the cultivators; and new agricultural supply, credit and marketing structures must evolve.

Even for land not blessed with nature's largess, modern agricultural technologies offer great opportunities to enjoy the benefits of a prospering agriculture.

The irrigation technologies developed in Israel; the discoveries now being made in plant drought resistance and photosynthetic efficiency, in pest and pathogen resistance, and in maximizing the product of the symbiotic interactions of plant, soil water and sunlight are some.

Others are the improvements in the effectiveness of farm production inputs and in elimination of waste in processing and handling farm products; and the work under way to upgrade the nutrient quality of the food produced. All these open vast new frontiers through science to provide an assurance that all can eat.

The Globe and Mail 1974 4 12

Another area ready for further exploitation is the fish industry. Development of aquaculture needs to be given more priority in the future.

Most important of all are the human resources. Here is an immense potential waiting to be released, organized, and generously provided with the needed technological know-how and tools of production.

UNESCO Courier 1975 5

The small farmer equates agriculture with poverty and seeks desperately to find ways of leaving the land. Farmers must be given concrete evidence that farming is a profitable enterprise.

Jamaican Minister of Agriculture 1975

A grain with more nutrition than wheat, similar baking qualities, and hardy enough to grow where wheat cannot survive—that's what scientists are perfecting. It's called Triticale (a name coined from combining the generic names of its parents, rye and wheat) and it could have a major impact on world food supplies during the coming years of shortages.

Cooperation Canada 1974 9

World land resources are sufficient to feed all, even with a rising population. Developing countries have great reservoirs of natural resources and manpower. But one cannot expect full success in agricultural production without deep modifications in the social and economic structure.

Czechoslovakian Minister of Agriculture 1975

Land reform and consolidation of fragmented holdings will be needed in many developing countries not only to accelerate technological change and stimulate production in the long run, but also to generate rural employment.

UNESCO Courier 1975 5

But growing more food is a less effective answer than saving the food that is already grown. If attacks on waste were to save only 10% more of the wheat harvest, for instance, that would add nearly 30m tons to world supplies, making (in theory) nearly one-third more wheat available for international trade. The developing countries' food needs exceed actual supplies by more than 6% only in exceptional circumstances, and it would take only a small improvement in grain storage and processing to eliminate that gap.

But it is immediately after harvesting that the biggest savings can be made. Up to a third of a cereal crop can be lost in post-harvest handling, processing and distribution, and even higher proportions of perishable foods like fruit and vegetables.

At the Rotterdam conference, Dr H. A. B. Parpia, of the FAO, gave some measures of the damage done by rats, insects and various microorganisms. Six rats can eat the food of one man; and in a year a pair of rats can produce up to 70 offspring that survive to maturity. A state of emergency had to be declared in Mindanao, in the Philippines, in 1953, when rats destroyed nearly 70% of the crop. When the rat population reaches a density of 0.78 per square metre, as has happened in a food warehouse in Calcutta, the problem is worse than an emergency.

Less pests—more crops

	Pesticide (grams)	Crop yield (kilograms)
	per hectare	
Japan	10 790	5 480
Europe	1 870	3 430
USA	1 490	2 600
Africa	127	1 210
India	149	820

The threat from insects is less obvious, but just as damaging. The pulse beetle passes through eight overlapping generations in a year, and the progeny of 40 eggs can halve the weight of infested grain in six months, as well as contaminating what is left.

But waste of this sort is difficult to deal with in developing countries; about three-quarters of their basic food crops never enter western-style storage, processing and distribution channels, so there is little control over handling.

The Economist 1975 3 22

Discussion and Research

9. Can you group the recommended courses of action into those of a purely mechanical nature and those requiring cultural and value decisions? For example, bringing new land into cultivation may be a simple mechanical matter requiring only the will and resources to do it, whereas land reform may entail all sorts of cultural decisions about the sort of society that will emerge after reform. At another level, the decision to use pesticides or not raises other questions of values. Which group do you think it would be easier for a government to take action on? How would you suggest action be taken on the more difficult group?

Sprinkler irrigation involves the use of pipes and sprays rather than open ditches. Water losses by evaporation are thereby reduced, and the quantities of water applied and times of application can be more carefully regulated. In advanced systems of sprinkler irrigation there are humidity sensors in the soil next to the plants, connected to computers which switch sprinkler systems on and off according to the sensor readings. Fertilizers and/or pesticides can be mixed with the irrigation water for easy application, thus cutting costs. Drip irrigation, whereby dripping water is fed to individual plants by plastic tubing, is even more economical on water; and since only the plants receive water, weeds do not grow.

The methods of increasing available food quantities are varied, and often difficult to apply. However there are thousands of options open, despite cultural, social, political, and economic constraints. We can consider some of these options under the following six headings.

a) *New Techniques*

There is a need for mechanization, and improved techniques of fertilization and irrigation: canal irrigation can be replaced by the more efficient sprinkler or drip irrigation, old-fashioned tools can be redesigned, and seed drills can be used instead of hand seeding. There are also innovations in food production techniques. Hydroponics, for example, involves growing crops without soil; nutrients mixed in water are pumped into a gravel or sand base in which the plants grow. Other new techniques include weather control by cloud seeding; the breeding of quality animals through artificial insemination; the production of hybrid plants by means of genetic control; the raising of plants and animals in a controlled environment; the magnetizing of

Simple canal and ditch irrigation in Senegal. There is considerable loss of water by percolation and evaporation, and weeds abound.

Jean Gobeil

seeds so that they grow in alignment to the earth's magnetic field, thereby yielding greater tonnages per hectare; and the multicropping of the land so that two or more crops can be grown on the same ground during the year.

The latest development in multicropping is to plant the second crop before the first crop is even ready for harvesting. In this way the second crop takes root and is ready for growth by the time the first crop is harvested.

United Nations

An experimental farm being built in Laos under the United Nations Development Program.

There are hundreds of new techniques being applied around the world, many of them experimental. Much of the experimental work is done by United Nations agencies, particularly the FAO and UNESCO, as well as by independent multinational groups such as the Colombo Plan countries and the OECD. Frequently the research is carried out by university personnel (as at Guelph, Ontario) or by people working for major charitable foundations such as the Ford Foundation and the Rockefeller Foundation. One of the most spectacular events in the development of new techniques, involving the combined efforts of UN agencies, university personnel, and charitable foundations has been the so-called *Green Revolution*. Experiments with wheat and corn in the Centro Internacional de Mejoramiento de Maiz y Trigo (CIMMYT)—the International Maize and Wheat Improvement Centre—in Mexico and also at the University of Manitoba resulted in the development of high yielding varieties (HYVs) of these plants, together with a new environmentally resistant crossbreed of wheat and rye called *triticale*. Triticale offers the hardiness of rye with the heavier yield of wheat, thereby allowing more productive use of cooler lands. In addition, researchers at the International Rice Research Institute in the Philippines, sponsored by the Ford and Rockefeller Foundations, developed *IR5* and *IR8 rice plants* which yield 10-15 times more than do traditional varieties.

IR5 and *IR8 rice* is "Green Revolution" rice developed as the fifth and eighth experiments by the International Rice Research Institute in the Philippines.

The Indian government has made some effort to stop the buying-out of poorer farmers by instituting maximum sizes for farms. The economic trend toward larger farm units runs counter to the social desires of the government to give more peasants a share in land ownership; moreover, the government would rather the peasants have jobs in the farmland than be unemployed in the cities.

An Andean farmer happy with his improved wheat crop.

When these HYVs were first used in south and southeast Asia during the late 1960s there were dramatic increases in cereal output. For example, from 1965 to 1970 India's wheat production rose from 12 000 000 t to 20 000 000 t, a 67% increase, and its rice production from 46 000 000 t to 64 000 000 t, an increase of 39%. The increased output of the HYVs, however, requires a greater input of fertilizer, irrigation water, pesticides, and money for seed. Only the richer farmers, therefore, can easily participate in the Green Revolution, and accordingly they have grown richer, often buying out poorer farmers. Large numbers of landless peasants have thus been created, leading to social, economic, and political pressures.

FAO

An irrigation pumping plant on the Mekong River in Thailand.

The Green Revolution requires more knowledge and greater use of technology than traditional farming. Here, farmers learn about simple mechanization on a rice farm in Iran.

International Labour Office

b) New Organizations

Various organizations have been formed to increase food production. Some organizations, like farmers' unions, cooperatives, land banks, agricultural credit and loan societies, and competitive shows, are primarily economic in purpose; others, such as communes and kibbutzim, also serve social and political purposes. Communes, for example, have been the main instrument by which the Chinese communists (party members number about a quarter of a million) have sought to control the production and life styles of millions of Chinese peasants; kibbutzim have been the main means whereby the Israelis have colonized territory in the disputed areas in and around Israel.

One other new type of organization, found especially in developed countries, is the *agribusiness*. This is farming by a major commercial enterprise, such as Kraft Foods; the company buys or rents farms, and hires managers to run them as business operations.

c) Land Reform

The *Grandan* movement originated as the *Bhoodan* movement in 1951. Originally the government sought voluntary donations from landowners, equal to about one sixth of their holdings, for redistribution to the landless; but the Grandan movement seeks donations of entire villages from their landowners, so that the land belongs to the village as a whole.

Changes in landholding patterns are both useful and necessary. In many parts of the world, land has already been, or is in the process of being redistributed; in others it is still a matter for the future. There are different types of land reform, but basically they are concerned with *either* the bringing together of scattered holdings, as in the *remembrement* movement in France, *or* with the breaking up of large estates (often called *latifundia*) and their redistribution to landless peasants, as in the *Grandan* movement in India.

d) Development of Marginal Lands

For centuries, people simply cleared away the forest or plowed the grassland whenever they needed more land for crops. Today, most of the suitable land has already been put to use; indeed, the last great development of arable land occurred in the early years of this century with the opening up of the Canadian prairies. There is still much undeveloped land (about as much as is already cultivated), but it is less suitable for use. These areas are called *marginal lands*; "marginal" in this sense means "on the edge of being used". Marginal lands usually have some environmental economic disadvantages; they are extremely cold, wet, hilly, dry, or remote. However, these lands will be put to use if the potential crop will pay the costs of bringing the areas into cultivation. Heated underground pipes, artificial sunlight, greenhouses, and special fast-ripening seeds permit the extension of farming into colder areas; water-resistant crops and controlled drainage will make possible the farming of marsh areas. Meanwhile the Israelis have shown what can be done to utilize desert lands (see part 3 of this Section).

Wheat farming in Canada was extended northward because of the production of a faster ripening variety called *marquis*.

Greenhouse cultivation at Madagan in eastern Siberia.

Novosti Press Agency

Soviet Information Bureau

Construction of an irrigation pumping station in the drylands of Uzbekistan. The development of this region is part of the tenth five-year plan (1976-80).

Novosti Press Agency

Wheat production from the "virgin lands" of western Siberia. The legend on the first truck reads (at top) "Sosnovski bread for the homeland!", and (at front) "over and above the plan". The legend on the second truck shows it to be the ninth five-year plan. The photo was taken in October, 1973.

e) Cultivation of the Sea

Most fishing today is still a form of hunting, even with the aid of sonar to spot fish, and of migration-route tracking (as of Pacific tuna). To get the best yield from the oceans, however, we must turn to the techniques of farming, namely planting, tending, and harvesting. Fish hatcheries are already in common use, but mainly in inland waters, where tending and harvesting are much easier than in the sea. However, ocean bays and estuaries offer good locations for future hatcheries, especially if there are power stations nearby, because power stations offer a continuous supply of warm water, discharged as waste.

A Russian trawler of the Kamchatka fleet.

Novosti Press Agency

Fish-breeding in Malaysia. This is carp.

f) Synthetic Foods

Experiments to make food from other substances are in progress. Carbohydrates, fats, and proteins can all be synthesized artificially; petrochemical scientists have already produced edible material from rubber and oil bases. Flavour is a problem at the moment, but this will likely be overcome. Wood fibre is presently used in some bread in the United States, and has met with little or no consumer resistance. The following article presents a favourable view of synthetic food; the Blondie comic strip is a little more jaundiced.

Let us imagine the day when a country's economy is based on the manufacture of synthetic food instead of on traditional methods of food production. A few huge factories sited in different parts of the country where coal and petroleum are to be found, prepare all the food required by the population. Altogether, these factories occupy barely a few hundred square miles [kilometres]. Agriculture with its need for a vast labour force and its limited capacity for progress, has been abolished, with the exception perhaps of market gardens and horticulture.

There is no longer any need for the vast industry which formerly provided agriculture with its equipment —tractors, machines, tools. Nor for the metal used in making them, nor for the fuel used to power them. Nor for chemical fertilizers, pesticides etc. A large proportion of the population previously engaged in these industries and in agriculture itself is thus freed for other productive work. Only a minute part of this manpower is needed for the production of synthetic food.

The old food industry gives way to an entirely new industry, infinitely more compact. No more bad years, poor harvests, unproductive land. No more calamitous losses due to climate, natural catastrophes, parasites, plant diseases, all of which today still take their toll of a considerable part of every harvest.

All the conditions are on hand for the transformation of villages into towns and towns into garden cities. Food products, ready to eat, packaged or tinned like the products on sale today, but with the fundamental difference that they contain the normal amount of vitamins and have the highest nutritive value, have only to be heated.

The appearance of these dishes leaves nothing to be desired. With a standard composition (proteins, carbohydrates, fats, salts, vitamins) adapted to each age need, these foods are the best source of health and energy the human system can have, infinitely better, at all events, than the best natural products.

No more obesity, no more fatty degeneration of the heart, liver and other complaints of the kind. At the least sign of physical abnormality, special diets can be composed with more or less of one or other ingredient.

Vast tracts of land previously reserved for crop growing give way progressively to forests and parks. The silting and drying up of rivers is stopped and the abundance of food products leads to the solution of the world shortage of drinking water which at present is steadily worsening.

The society of the future gains on all fronts: economic, social and also moral, as the slaughter of animals, a cruel vestige of the past, is progressively done away with.

UNESCO Courier 1969 3

Reprinted by permission of *Toronto Star* Syndicate. Copyright (1973), King Features Syndicate.

Discussion and Research

10. The Green Revolution is indirectly producing "social, economic, and political pressures."
   a) What do you think these pressures are?
   b) In what ways can these pressures be minimized?
   c) What difficulties can you envisage in the application of your suggested solutions?

d) Which do you think is most important, more food or less socio-economic pressure? Or does it depend upon your viewpoint?

11. In recent years China has successfully fed its people largely from its own resources. One of the input costs of this greater output has allegedly been loss of individual freedom. Does increased agricultural output justify a loss of individual freedom? Give reasons for your answer.

12. Should a country such as Canada grow more food to give or sell abroad *or* should it admit some of the world's hungry people into its territory?

13. What sort of future can you envisage for synthetic foods?

Fig. 2-3
Arid environments

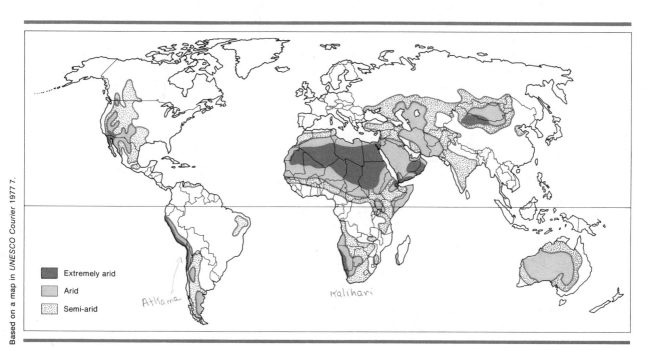

Based on a map in *UNESCO Courier* 1977 7.

Extremely arid
Arid
Semi-arid

Atkama

Kalihari

3. Coping with Dry Conditions

Heat and moisture are the basic requirements for crop growth. There are many areas in the world that are warm enough for good growth, but lack the necessary moisture. From the earliest times, however, people have farmed with some success in these desert or semi-desert lands. Some of their systems worked well for a stable population, but are unable to meet the demands of a population explosion. Among the old instruments and techniques used to bring water to dry areas are the *sakia water wheel*, the *foggara tubes*, the *shaduf*, and the flooded field. Other traditional methods used to cope with infrequent or sea-

Foggaras, or *quanats*, are tunnels driven into a hillside to trap and channel the water that percolates through the ground within the hill.

sonal drought include nomadic herding and farming, cistern storage, and emigration.

Modern technology, when available, provides a broader range of solutions to the problems of farming dry areas.

a) Bringing Water to Water-Deficient Areas

There are several potential sources of water for a water-deficient region. The closest source is often underground, although such water may be difficult to find or highly mineralized (thereby restricting its use to animals). Much farming in Australia and the United States depends on modern wells drilled into underground aquifers; in 1977 Egypt discovered a huge underground supply of sweet water sufficient to provide water for farming for several decades. The chief problem with such underground water is that it is replenished very slowly, and may be used faster than nature returns it. In the Santa Clara valley of California, for example, underground water was pumped out so fast that sea-water began to seep in to replace the fresh water, while in many other parts of California and Arizona the water table kept dropping while wells were driven deeper and deeper, until some actually dried up.

Rivers are another major source of water for water-deficient areas. While their sources lie outside the arid regions, rivers often flow through dry areas; they are called *exotic rivers*, because they are foreign to the arid regions. The Nile is the classic example. Other important examples are the Indus and the Colorado, both with huge dams and water distribution schemes.

No irrigation project is without problems. For example, exposed water surfaces in tropical areas provide breeding grounds for mosquitos, while bilharzia snails may spread within the water. The most common problems, however, are those downstream from the dam: the shrivelled river may not provide enough water for downstream users; sea-water may seep into the lower parts of the river valleys; and irrigated land may become waterlogged due to improper drainage. In parts of the Indus valley, especially downstream from the great Ghulam Mohammed Barrage, almost as much land is lost to farming by waterlogging as is gained by increased irrigation. Nevertheless, with adequate drainage, irrigation from exotic rivers offers good potential for increased food production.

Some of the larger "environment-moulding" projects are water-transfer plans based on the concept of exotic rivers. The Israeli National Water Plan is an example of this, and is summarized in Fig. 2-4. The more extensive California Water Plan is illustrated in Fig. 2-5.

Desalination, the removal of salt from sea-water, is another method of bringing water into arid regions. At present there are only

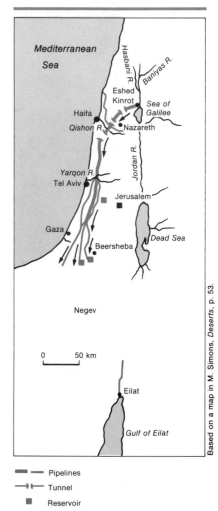

Fig. 2-4
Israel's National Water Carrier Plan

Based on a map in M. Simons, *Deserts*, p. 53.

▬ ▬ Pipelines

→├── Tunnel

■ Reservoir

Water is taken from the more humid north and piped southward toward the Negev Desert. The major irrigation works are between the Yarqon River and Beersheba, although farming continues to push south into the Negev.

Heavy precipitation, much of it as winter snow, throughout the mountains in the northern parts, especially the Shasta Mountains and the Sierra Nevada, is impounded at a series of dams and channelled southward toward the Mojave Desert. The main recipient of water is Los Angeles.

Irrigation is widespread in the Central Valley and the Los Angeles embayment. Farm productivity is very high under the computerized systems employed, and California ranks first among US states in farm income.

Based on information in *Journal of Geography* 1969 7.

Fig. 2-5
The California Water Plan

three practicable ways of desalinating sea-water: distillation, electrodialysis, and refrigeration. Distillation is the most common, with several large plants around the world, as in Hong Kong, Saudi Arabia, Kuwait, and Venezuela; there are also numerous distillation plants in the USA. Electrodialysis, the separation of salt and water by electricity, is not widely used since it is slow and requires a good deal of fuel. Refrigeration is used mostly in Israel, where the Zarchin method of separating ice crystals as they begin to form in the cooling process was developed. All desalination methods, however, are expensive, and the costs and problems of distribution still remain. California has frequently proposed towing icebergs from Antarctica to obtain a large supply of fresh water, while Saudi Arabia actually imports shiploads of water from New Zealand.

Rain-making is another method of obtaining water. It has never been proved that cloud seeding really works; the weather is unpredictable, and it is difficult to determine the amount of rain that might have fallen without the seeding. Rain-makers also face the risk of lawsuits from downwind farmers who feel that their rightful supply of rain has been taken from them by the upwind rain-makers.

UNESCO

A desalination plant in Kuwait.

US Information Service

A desalination plant at Key West, Florida.

Fig. 2-6
Desalination plants in Saudi Arabia
(circle sizes indicative only)

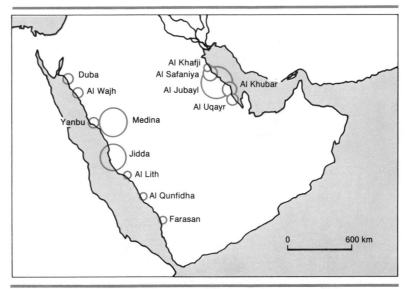

Based on a map in *Geographical Magazine* 1976 12, p. 172.

b) Adjusting to Water Shortages

Much skill and time has been, and continues to be invested in developing plants that will grow in very dry areas. These dry region plants may have long roots to tap underground water, waxy skins to restrict evaporation losses, short stems to minimize unnecessary plant growth, hairy leaves to trap overnight condensation, and juicy insides to permit water storage.

In addition, researchers are exploring the development of salt-resistant plants, for arid areas usually have a high level of salts in the soil. Some plants are naturally tolerant of salts; others are not. Cotton, barley, asparagus, and dates are tolerant, while beans, celery, lemons, and oranges are not. The aim of research is to extend the tolerances, so that new varieties with higher yields will grow in dry areas.

Research has also been done on methods of increasing the condensation of overnight dew. In Israel's dry south the farmers plant their crops in slight hollows lined with loose stones, in the hope that the stones, which cool rapidly at night, will chill the air around them and thus encourage condensation. The Israelis also cover plants with a polythene sheet pegged horizontally above the plants but weighted slightly in the centre by a pebble; moisture from the plants, normally lost by evaporation, is trapped when it condenses on the underside of the sheet, while the slight depression caused by the pebble in the centre of the sheet causes the moisture to trickle down to the underside of the sheet and drop back into the ground.

Summer fallowing is another useful technique for combating dry conditions. In this practice, the ground is left unused for a year, but is plowed and replowed to prevent rain from seeping away; as a result,

The salinity of the Nile delta has increased because the freshwater pressure provided by the Nile has been reduced now that much of its water is taken for irrigation in the Aswan project. The growing of cotton in the area is increasing as competition from crops less tolerant of salts diminishes.

some water is saved, and when a crop is planted the following year there is some moisture to help plant growth. Fields may thus be used every second year, so that at any one time only half the ground is being cultivated. Summer fallowing is common in the prairie wheatlands of Canada and the United States.

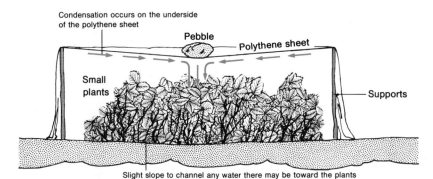

Fig. 2-7
A method of conserving plant water

These wheatlands are undoubtedly the major food surplus area in the world today, and their yields can be enormously expanded. Indeed, farmers in these areas are periodically asked *not* to grow more wheat, because if they were to do so then wheat prices would fall and many farmers would be driven out of business. Because of the bumper wheat crop in the United States in 1977, for example, farmers were told by the government to reduce the area of the 1978 wheatlands by 20%. To ensure an adequate supply of food, then, we must be sure that farmers make enough money to stay in business. Developed countries can generally afford this price, even though consumers grumble, but less developed countries can seldom afford it. In a developing country, people cannot afford higher food prices, and so farmers have little incentive to produce for a wide market. This means that farmers cannot afford to modernize. It is a vicious circle, and it is not helped by the importing of inexpensive food. A breakthrough is badly needed. In the case study that follows, we will examine the ways in which Sudan is coping with the problem.

Case Study 2
Sudan: Food Prospects

Sudan is one of the world's twenty poorest countries, but it has the potential of becoming the "bread-basket" of Africa. It could make a major contribution in the battle against world food shortages because it has large areas of unused arable land. At present only about 9% of the suitable land is actually farmed. Besides land, Sudan has a good water supply. What is needed, then, is careful planning, along with financial help and a united population willing to work toward improved agriculture.

Sudan is the largest country of Africa, with an area of approximately 2 500 000 km². This makes it larger than Western Europe. With a population of about 17 800 000 in 1975, the country has an average population density of only 7.1 persons/km². Thus, with a small population at home to feed, the opportunity to produce food for export is certainly feasible. The population, with a current yearly growth rate of 3.2%, will probably double before the year 2000, but this may mean a growing young work force, which will be needed to carry out major schemes involving the redistribution of water and the harvesting of huge new areas of cropland. However, an alarming increase in the exodus of skilled labour to neighbouring oil-rich nations is already becoming a serious problem.

Within Sudan there are other problems too. There are several different ethnic groups in the country, a situation that restricts the development of a cohesive society and a national identity. Although Sudan's people are of different racial origins, about 66% of the population is Muslim; most of these people live in the northern two thirds of the country. Christians account for 4% of the population, and the rest of the inhabitants follow a variety of local beliefs and practices. Almost all of the non-Muslim people live in the south. Differences are increased by the use of the Arabic language in the north, and English in the south. This language problem reflects the fact that, in the past, Egypt held Lower Sudan and Great Britain held Upper Sudan.

The Nile, which cuts through the country from south to north, has not been a unifying factor as you may expect. In the past, great swamps separated the Islamic Egyptian people of the north from the black Africans of the south. When Christian missionaries finally reached Southern Sudan, it was by way of East Africa, rather than the Nile.

The slave trade of the nineteenth century also created problems which have carried over into the twentieth century. The Sudanese Arabs of the north were the masters and traders, while the Sudanese Africans of the south were the slaves. The Arabs looked on the southerners as their inferiors, and the south developed a lasting fear of northern domination. After the creation of a Sudan independent of Britain and Egypt in 1956 this fear resulted in open warfare between the south and the north. Only since 1972 has there been any real peace. Part of the peace settlement involved the south being given more autonomy. English was also given more status as a language, after attempts to spread the Arab language and culture to the southern people failed. English is taught now throughout the schools of the south.

Fig. 2C-1
Place names and railways in Sudan

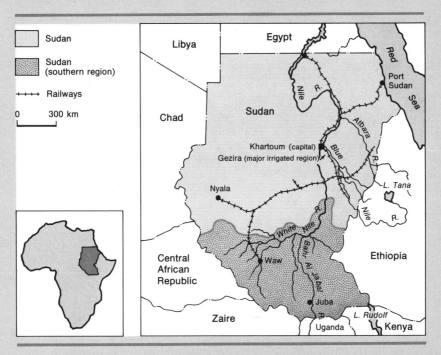

Source: Nelson, *Area Handbook for the Democratic Republic of Sudan*, 1973.

There is a government-sponsored free school system, but only about 20% of the school-age children attend school, and only 10% of the people are literate. Because there is a general lack of teachers and facilities, it is proving difficult to introduce the population to higher levels of technology. Moreover, the northern Arabs are better educated than the southern

Africans, and this does little to help the economic development of the south. Finally, not very much vigour or progress can be expected of a people with a life expectancy of forty years, few medical facilities, and a high rate of malnutrition.

On the other hand, the physical landscape offers few barriers to development. The country is primarily a broad plain, some 800-1000 km from west to east, and 1500 km from north to south. For thousands of kilometres only occasionl low rolling hills break the surface of the plain. There are only four rugged areas, namely the Red Sea Hills of the northeast, the volcanic Jabal Marrah in the west, the Nuba Mountains west of the White Nile, and the Immatong and Dongotona Mountains in the south. All these rugged areas are more of a benefit than a hindrance because they collect orographic (mountainous) rainfall and thus provide moisture, especially for the valleys between the mountains.

The northern third is desert, consisting of broad areas of sand, broken by occasional hills and outcroppings of bare rock. But the rest of the country is part of the great African savanna belt, with grasses, thorny shrubs, and small trees. It is in effect a transition zone extending from the southern edges of the Sahara Desert to the beginnings of the equatorial rainforest. With more water, development in this area is possible.

Fig. 2C-2
Vegetation in Sudan

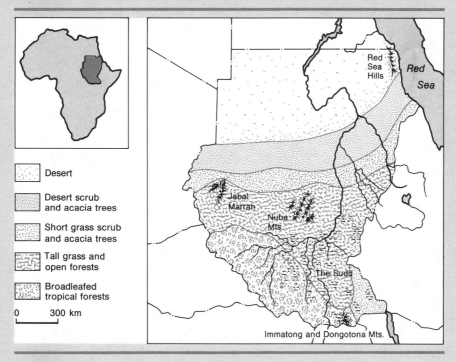

Source: Nelson, *Area Handbook for the Democratic Republic of Sudan*, 1973.

Southern Sudan contains a vast region of swamps and marshes called the *Sudd*. These are fed by the waters of the White Nile, or the Bahr al Jabal as it is known, whose headwaters lie in the Lake Victoria-Lake Albert region. The White Nile flows north from the Sudd, and is joined by the Blue Nile at Khartoum. The combined Niles then flow into Egypt. Because most of the White Nile waters are lost in the swamps, largely through evaporation, the amount of water the White Nile provides Sudan with is only 20% of the amount supplied by the Blue Nile; but the White Nile's supply is highest when the Blue Nile's is lowest.

The Blue Nile begins in Lake Tana in the Ethiopian Highlands. Most of its input to Sudan is due to torrential summer rains from the Ethiopian monsoon. The result is flooding in Sudan, and a high water flow about sixty times as large as its low water flow. Another important tributary of the Nile system is the Atbara River, which also brings summer floodwaters to Sudan. The large-scale water distribution schemes that have already been developed are all the result of harnessing the Nile and its tributary waters to irrigate the alluvial floodplains. Away from the floodplains, there are also numerous *wadis*, which carry intermittent streams. Some of these watercourses support local areas of agriculture, and many more could.

Although most of the surface water of Sudan is exotic there is also a great deal available locally. Most of the country has a tropical savanna climate, with rainfall developing from the humid air masses of equatorial regions which move northward as far as Khartoum in summer. Total yearly rainfall exceeds 1 250 mm in the south, falling to between 400 and 800 mm in the central areas, and down to between 120 and 250 mm at Khartoum. In the northern border regions, rain is almost unknown.

Temperatures are high throughout the year, and thus a year-round growing season exists. Frost is almost unknown, except in the upper mountainous areas. However, the high temperatures and dry air of most of the country create a very high evaporation rate. In the northern and central areas surface water generally disappears early in the dry season, which lasts from October through November. Various forms of water storage are needed, in the form of tanks, dams, and artificial basins. Some major dams and irrigation projects have been built on the Blue Nile, the Atbara, and the White Nile, the latest in 1969 at Roseires near the Ethiopian border.

Central Sudan is an area of clay soils and low ridges of sand deposited by the wind. In the rainy season the clay on the flatlands becomes waterlogged, while on the slopes its impermeability rapidly causes the precipitation to become run-off, thus increasing the risk of flooding in low-lying areas. In sandy areas, on the other hand, the water percolates quickly downward. It is therefore only where mixtures of sand and clay occur that a useful water-holding soil is obtained. There are some such areas across central Sudan, but any soil improvement policy here has to involve a major attempt to expand the areas containing a mixture of sand and clay.

A wind pump for obtaining subterranean water in northern Sudan. Note the carriers on the right.

UNESCO/Eric Schwab

Farther south, the swamps of the Sudd are underlain by impermeable clays. Along the southern edges of the swamp the clays rise to the surface where they support shrubs and grasses, and, in the extreme south, rain-forest. These southernmost soils are generally capable of supporting subsistence agriculture.

The best soils, however, are still the alluvial soils alongside the rivers. Other good soils may also be found in the volcanic area of the Jabal Marrah in the west.

Little mineral wealth has been discovered, so that it is to agriculture that the country must look for development. At present, agriculture, including herding, is the main source of livelihood for more than 85% of the population. The ratio of population to arable land is so low that on average the country is self-sufficient in all essential foods such as cereals, edible oils, and meat, although the average food intake per person is quite low.

Most food is grown without irrigation on land known as dryland. Such rain-fed cultivation usually involves thousands of small-scale subsistence farmers using old-fashioned methods. The country's chief crop is cotton, and the government hires about 15% of the population to grow and harvest this important export. The cotton is grown on large government owned and managed irrigation project areas along the Nile. The only exports from the traditional sector are sesame, peanuts, and gum arabic, which grows wild in central Sudan.

Dependent as it is upon seasonal rainfall or upon simple irrigative implements such as water wheels and shadufs, agricultural production varies greatly from year to year. Moreover, the country is too dependent on cotton as an export, especially in the face of competition from synthetic textiles. Efforts to diversify are being given top priority.

Modern agriculture is characterized by government ownership of much of the land, along with government supervision of the work done. The reason is the absence of a class of innovative farmers. Although some individuals or private companies have sponsored schemes, they usually do not wish to become directly involved. There are few incentives for improvement. Another disadvantage is that the cultivating tradition is not strong; few Sudanese study agricultural methods. There are frequent shortages of farm workers, and as a result, production declines.

In spite of all these problems, it is generally agreed that there is enough arable land for a tremendous increase in food production, using scientific and mechanized methods. Quick-growing *sorghums* (tropical cereal grasses) offer the best possibilities.

In most of the country a lack of water is the most serious problem. Particularly in the northern part the low annual rainfall makes irrigation essential for year-round cultivation. In the southern third, where rainfall is more plentiful, the farmer faces heavy forest growth, seasonal floods, and tsetse flies. The most valuable area for expansion and modernization, even without irrigation, is the vast clay plain of the centre, stretching across both the Blue and White Niles from west to east. Rainfall in this area ranges from 250 mm to 500 mm, diminishing northward. The growing season must be fitted into the seasonal rainfall pattern, but quick-growing sorghums would make possible great increases in food production. Expanding the use of the irrigated lands along the Nile is also possible; and plans to drain the Sudd by means of a canal could, if implemented, greatly increase the amount of naturally watered grazing land and cropland.

In 1976 the Arab oil-producing countries agreed to channel nearly $5 000 000 000 during the following 25 years into Sudan, mainly for agricultural projects. The main agency for this flow of aid is the Arab Authority for Development and Agricultural Investment (AADAI). Private Arab and Western entrepreneurs are also interested in Sudan in order to make money.

A nutrition clinic in the village of Hosh near the Blue Nile. The Sudan government is serious about improving the food situation in the country.

UNICEF/Almasy

In 1976 the government also passed the Agricultural Investment Act, which provides tax incentives, tariff protection, and land concessions to investors in Sudanese agriculture. The aim is a food surplus for export, together with crop diversification. It has recommended that $20 000 000 be allocated for the development of tea, coffee, and rice production in the south. More irrigation along the Nile is planned, especially in the Gezira, the triangular area between the Blue and White Niles. Here development is being concentrated on sugar production in a project which promises to create the largest sugar factory in the world.

Along with such agricultural schemes there are also plans to combat some of the insect pests. International efforts are being made to control the tsetse fly in the south, and the locust in the north. United Nations locust teams are already an accepted sight in the north, but much remains to be done.

The size of all these operations—agricultural development and insect control—will place enormous strains on the country's resources. Already the backers of the sugar project, including the Japanese as well as Arabs and the Sudanese, are considering buying their own trains. Better transportation is greatly needed, not only for the distribution of goods, access to market, and so on, but also in such vital areas as the shipment of seeds, fertilizers, pesticides, and machinery to farmers. Paved roads are not very numerous, and most roads are impassable at some time of the year. There is only one railway across the centre of the country and another running from the Roseires Dam on the upper Blue Nile to the Egyptian border, with a branch to Port Sudan on the Red Sea. Rail cars are so crowded that passengers ride on the roofs of the cars. A scheduled trip of two days often ends up as three. Port Sudan, the country's only ocean port, has some problems in handling the flow of goods efficiently; it is quicker for the south, for example, to export via Mombasa in Kenya. As for river navigation, only sections of the Nile are navigable from Khartoum northward to Egypt. Southward, the river steamer service to Juba, which is supposed to take 12 days, may well take up to 15 days.

Obviously there is a great need for aid to help make improvements. Sudan may still be to some extent a land full of potential, but it is also coming closer to fulfilling its promise.

FOOD: Further Reading

Food for People, RIEDMAN
Nutriscore, FREMES & SABRY
What Have You Been Eating?, HYDE & FORSYTH
Health Foods, MARGOLIUS
The Politics of Food, MITCHELL
Hard to Swallow, STEWART
The Food in your Future, BARRONS
This Hungry World, VICKER

Conclusion

It is clear that the global food picture is varied; some areas of the world have great surpluses, while others are suffering from a scarcity of food. These variations do not occur haphazardly. In examining food deficit and surplus regions, we can detect definite patterns. Comparisons of population growth and food production generally reveal that those countries with very slow population growth are also the ones with abundant food supplies, while the nations with rapid population growth usually appear to have food scarcities. These close correlations lead us to ask certain questions. For example, is slow population growth a reason for abundant food supplies, and rapid population growth a reason for food scarcities?

Questions like these are complex, and we would be oversimplifying the matter if we considered only food supply patterns and rates of population growth. We should consider other factors that may be responsible for the high negative correlation between population growth and food supplies. One factor that suggests itself is technology. If a country has a high level of food-producing technology, it is also likely to have the technology for effective birth control. The most visible sign of technology is industrial development. In the next chapter, therefore, we turn to an examination of the varying degrees of industrialization throughout the world.

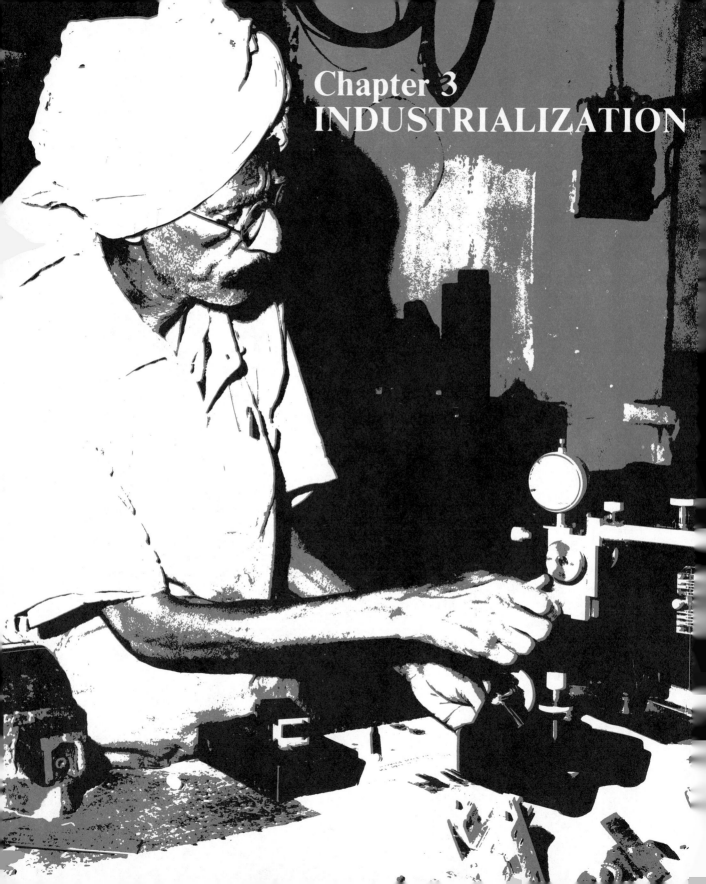

Chapter 3
INDUSTRIALIZATION

Introduction

For most people *industry* means factories, and *industrialization* means the process of acquiring factories. It is important to realize that industrialization is in fact much more complex than this. A society that becomes industrialized undergoes great changes in its social and economic order: mechanization and large-scale production are introduced; urbanization occurs as workers flock to the cities; and existing social systems and values come under great strain.

Many governments actively encourage the development of industry. This encouragement takes several forms, such as sponsorship of trade shows, low industrial taxes, tariff protection against competition from imports, and the building of technical colleges and other worker training schools. Governments even advertise their desire for more industry, as the two advertisements below indicate. They are taken from international business magazines, which are widely read by, among others, people who decide where new factories should be built.

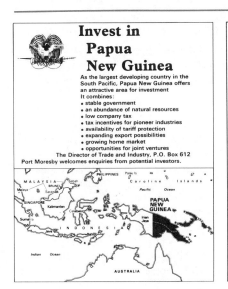

With acknowledgements to the Government of Papua New Guinea

Courtesy of Ontario's Ministry of Industry and Tourism

People and governments decide to start or expand industries for many reasons. Which ones can you identify in the following articles?

MEXICO CITY—Every day the streets of this bustling city are crowded with down-at-the-heels men and women cleaning cars, shining shoes, playing solitary trumpets, dancing in Indian costumes and selling everything from tropical fruit to contraband watches.

In a country where the Government cannot afford to sustain those without jobs, the unemployed have no choice but to make a living as best as they can. As a result the unemployment rate is · deceptively low, but the number who are without permanent jobs or whose long hours of street vending barely provide a subsistence income is growing dramatically.

According to official estimates, the underemployed exceed 40 per cent of the work force of 16 million.

Unemployment has been intensified over the past five years by inflationary and recessionary setbacks to economic growth and by the private sector's open distrust of the reformist social policies of the outgoing administration of President Luis Echeverria.

As a result new investment by Mexican and foreign businessmen has slumped, and despite vastly increased Government spending on major projects, new jobs have fallen far short even of the number of young people joining the work force.

Driven by hunger and despair, hundreds of thousands abandon the countryside every year and head for the overcrowded cities or even for the United States, which they frequently enter illegally, in search of jobs.

In Mexico City lucky migrants become maids or waiters, while the less fortunate become market porters, street vendors or prostitutes.

Because even a well-run agricultural sector could not sustain more than the present rural population of 25 million, the solution to the present and future unemployment problem must still be dealt with in the industrial and services areas of the economy.

The youthfulness of the population —more than half the 61 million Mexicans are under 18—will increase the burden carried by those with jobs during the coming decade. By the end of Mr. Lopez Portillo's term in 1982 a work force of 23 million, with perhaps 50 per cent underemployment, will have to support a population of 78 million.

The Globe and Mail 1976 7 5

Only the big landowner groups, with access to official credits, have succeeded in installing the necessary irrigation and drainage facilities and in procuring fertilizer, pesticides and so on. Some of them have made so much money that they have bought tens of thousands of tractors and thousands of combine harvesters....

UNESCO Courier 1975 5

While some people can provide good reasons for industrialization, others are aware of its problems and dangers. There are fears of resource exhaustion, pollution, inflation, excessive taxation, and even manual labour itself, as this newspaper article of 1975 10 1 indicates.

BOMBAY (CP)—"Many educated people in India regard manual work as undignified," lamented an editorial in the influential Bombay Times.

The Times went on to say that educated Indians would rather earn 300 rupees (about $85 a month) as a clerk than three times as much by becoming a mechanic.

. . .

Hem Bahuguna, chief minister of Uttar Pradesh, is deeply worried by the reluctance of educated young men to take up manual jobs. He thinks that this attitude cannot be changed through appeals but only by making a spell of manual labor compulsory for all high school and college students.

Henceforth, no student in Uttar Pradesh will get a high school or college degree unless he has worked on a development project like road building, planting trees or digging wells.

. . .

Many thoughtful Indians think their country's slower economic progress is partly because of the snobbish attitude of the educated classes towards jobs involving manual labor.

Toronto Star 1975 10 1

Discussion and Research

1. List some of the reasons for the desire to develop industry.
2. What are some of the problems that industry faces in a developing country?
3. What can governments do to help or hinder industrial development?

It is clear that opinion about industrialization is divided. In this chapter, we will take a close look at the arguments for and against it. We will start by examining the reasons for industrialization and then go on to assess the global extent of industrialization. Following that we will look at the prospects of industrialization, and then at some of the problems facing industrialized countries. A case study of Japan, a country which chose to industrialize, rounds out the chapter.

Section A
Why Industrialize?

Industrialization brings many changes to a society, changes that are generally welcomed. Among the effects of industrialization, the following are perhaps the most important: the production of material wealth, the creation of a money economy, the widening of personal choice, and the creation of jobs. For these four main reasons, societies will often choose to industrialize.

Industrialization is a process, not a single event. It may take many years for the process to occur, perhaps even several lifetimes.

1. The Production of Material Wealth

Before any society becomes industrialized the vast majority of its people live by farming. Life tends to be hard; harvests are variable, the storage of buffer stocks is difficult if not impossible, technology is limited, yields are low, output per worker is low, per capita returns are correspondingly small, and disease is endemic. Thomas Hobbes, a seventeenth century English philosopher, described life in preindustrial England as "nasty, brutish, and short." It is still like that in many parts of the world.

Industrialization changes a society. It stimulates technological progress, challenges old social structures, creates new opportunities, and generates higher per capita output. It raises the standard of living as it satisfies the varied needs and desires of the population. The wealth that industry creates is most noticeably *material* wealth: houses, hospitals, transportation systems, power grids, fertilizers, farm machinery, radios, cameras, newspapers, and so on. The list is endless and always growing. The key point is that industrialization creates all its material wealth *on a large scale*, gradually making goods accessible to everyone instead of just the privileged few.

Along with increasing material wealth come numerous other benefits. Better medical care enables people to live longer and healthier lives, better schooling reduces illiteracy; better transportation systems enable people to travel easily, and increase international contact and trade; and wider choices give consumers more satisfaction. Life becomes better in ways other than the material, and yet the improvements are made possible by material progress.

The large scale of industrial production is vital. It would cost an enormous amount of money to produce just one car, but if thousands are produced then the costs of the plant and machinery can be spread out over each one, and the cars cost less.

The start of industrialization stimulates technical progress.

UNESCO/M. Serraillier

2. The Creation of a Money Economy

The material wealth created is largely responsible for the growth of a money economy throughout society. In a non-industrial society it is possible for most people to do with little or no money; food is the basic product of almost all the population, and there is little need to trade. Subsistence is the norm. As industry develops, however, specialization begins on a large scale; most new industrial workers cannot eat or often even personally use their product, and trade becomes essential. Trade can take the form of direct barter, but money makes the process infinitely easier; thus a money economy is generated. Indeed, money is created to match the growing physical output of industry; people become richer in monetary as well as in material terms.

Even in a simple economy, barter is not easy. If you repair shoes and you want bread, you have to find a baker who wants his shoes repaired. Such a *coincidence of wants* is often difficult to find.

Industrialization creates large-scale material wealth. This is a television factory in Osaka, Japan.

3. The Widening of Personal Choice

In preindustrial economies most people live directly from agricultural work. There may be a few other jobs in trade, administration, religion, and craftwork, but they are very limited. Moreover, farming techniques cannot yield enough surpluses, even *exacted surpluses*, to feed more than a very small number of non-agricultural workers. Accordingly most people rely directly upon agricultural work. Industrialization changes this. It not only provides a battery of new techniques and materials with which to increase farming surpluses, but it also provides a choice of jobs not available before.

Exacted surpluses are those that are taken from the agricultural workers by force, by taxation, or by tithe.

Furthermore, although specialized workers must buy most of the products they need, they have more money to spend, and an increasingly greater variety of products to buy. Such freedom of choice as a consumer is a welcome quality for most people. This freedom is also increased by improved transportation and communication networks, which become available in all phases of early industrialization. Indeed, good transportation and successful industrialization are the two legs of progress.

A choice of jobs not previously available. These are Indians involved in an industrial expansion project in Durgapur.

PUNJAB FIGHTS
INDUSTRIAL RECESSION
By
DIVERSIFICATION OF
MACHINE-MAKING
CAPACITY
to Serve
FARMING AND
RURAL INDUSTRY
MERADO-1

UNESCO/M. Serraillier

4. The Creation of Jobs

Industry creates jobs that cannot be provided by farming alone. As technology is introduced into societies, farming becomes more productive, through the use of new methods, tools, and fertilizers. Farms require less labour; there often arises a state of "disguised unemployment" where there are more workers on a project than are needed. The unemployed seek jobs in the town, or in a different country. It is one of industry's major functions, and nowadays also one of its main purposes, to provide jobs. Farming alone cannot employ the numbers now on the earth. Indeed it probably will not be able to handle the present number of workers as it becomes more efficient.

Industry, therefore, faces a great task. Many less developed countries desperately want factories to employ their populations. Developed countries want to keep the factories they already have; they are in danger of losing them as companies expand into other parts of the world. During times of rising world prosperity, as through the 1950s and 1960s, it was not difficult for industry to accommodate both of these aims, because the total amount of industry in the world grew greatly. Even so, industry did not provide sufficient jobs; nor did it always provide the right sort of jobs. Throughout the 1960s, during what the UN called the First Development Decade, industry was encouraged to spread into the less developed countries. Both industry and the countries themselves, however, often saw this process in terms of steel mills, hydro dams, and airports, all of which ultimately provide regular employment for only a few people. Moreover the economic benefits of such projects did not usually spread far throughout society; most people remained unaffected by development.

A few of the unemployed people of West Africa.

International Labour Office

Throughout the 1970s, the so-called Second Development Decade, therefore, both the less industrialized countries and the industries of the industrially advanced world have been encouraged by the UN to take into account the overwhelming need for job creation, and the wider distribution of benefits throughout society. It may be better, for example, to have bicycle factories than car factories. To this extent, the world has followed the model of development set by China, where great stress was laid from the very beginning (after 1949) on local small-scale industrialization to foster independence, develop initiative, and provide employment. In order to oversee and channel these efforts at small-scale industrialization in the less developed world, the UN has established the World Employment Program. The following reading presents some of the background.

The global job crisis

As the Pearson Report (made by former Prime Minister Lester Pearson, who headed a World Bank Committee which reported on development assistance in late 1969) pointed out, "Development was too often only seen as a consequence of decision-making at the top. The vital need to bring about mass participation in development was at times sacrificed to the enrichment of special groups or individuals."

Thus there has been a shift in emphasis in planning for the Second Development Decade. Objectives have been included that reflect the specific results expected of economic development from the human angle: sufficient food, a lower mortality rate, education and employment. The supposition that economic progress is automatically followed by improved living conditions for the mass of the people is thus implicitly abandoned. But the time has now come to state it explicitly.

Employment-creation will have to be recognized as a major goal of development, a goal that will not be achieved automatically as a byproduct of economic growth.

. . .

In 1970 the world's population was about 3 600 million and the labor force some 1 510 million. Between 1970 and 1980 more than 280 million people will be added to the world's labor force, 226 million in the less-developed regions.

Although complete and reliable statistics on unemployment and underemployment are not available for the developing countries, evidence indicates that the situation has been steadily worsening. If no changes take place in the trends observed during the Fifties and the Sixties, the magnitude of the "employment gap" will become even more serious during the Seventies.

If unemployment and underemployment are allowed to spread, it will mean that growth has failed to achieve its essential purpose; very large numbers of the poor—precisely those whom economic growth was intended primarily to benefit—will be left on one side. At least in the short run (which may be for a whole generation) they will gain little, and might even lose, from the process of economic growth.

Venezuela, which enjoyed a growth rate of 8 per cent between 1950 and 1960, ended with more unemployment at the end of the decade than it had at the beginning. That is why a new orientation toward the attainment of social as well as economic goals has to be given to the whole concept of development assistance.

The major problem immediately ahead is likely to be unemployment and underemployment, which could easily reach half the labor force of developing countries by the end of the decade if the problem is not attacked. For employment is the foundation on which all other objectives of development rest.

Moreover, given the severe limits to capital accumulation and the nature of present-day technology, there is little hope for "structural change" in developing countries as a group, in the sense of a rising share of the labor force becoming fully employed in the industrial sector. Nor is there hope that the absolute numbers engaged in agriculture will fall.

Many countries will experience difficulties in reducing even the share of the labor force in the agricultural sector. Some that do will merely transfer unemployment, underemployment, and low-productivity employment ("disguised unemployment") from villages to cities.

In short, the grim prospect of the Second Development Decade is one of rising unemployment, increasing population pressure on the land, urban growth accompanied by increasing concentration of the worst aspects of poverty in the cities, and growing gaps in the level of welfare among social groups and regions in individual countries, as well as growing gaps among countries.

It has become apparent that problems of massive and growing poverty are not going to be solved by the mere injection of additional capital or by growth in GNP. Capital resources will, of course, be needed, and in greater amounts than in the past; but the use of these resources must be planned and production must be organized in such a way that they lead to far higher levels of employment. Employment-creation will have to be recognized as a major goal of development, a goal that will not be achieved automatically as a byproduct of economic growth.

Extracted from an article by Kalmen Kaplansky, Canadian director of the I.L.O., printed in The Globe and Mail 72 11 16

Discussion and Research

4. When examining employment, we find that the relationship between farming and industry is very close.
   a) Describe it.
   b) How does it relate to population growth?
   c) And to food production?
5. What sort of industries seem to be best for newly industrializing countries?
6. Can you think of any cultural or social qualities that might have prevented the wider diffusion of early industrial benefits during the First Development Decade? How do you think these qualities might have been (or still may be) changed to spread the benefits more widely?

Section B
Who is Industrialized?

There are two basic levels of industry: manufacturing industry and cottage industry. The term *industrialized* refers only to economies characterized by manufacturing industry. Economies characterized by cottage industry are called *preindustrial* economies.

In cottage industry, many single workers, or small groups of workers, are widely scattered throughout the locality. Most preindustrial countries, for example, have at least a local weaver or a local smith. These *artisans*, or skilled workers, supply a very personal level of input, with much muscle power and few mechanical aids. They earn little for their effort, because their physical output (product) is restricted by the scarcity of power and machinery.

Indian artisans in Ecuador prepare to take their woven mats to market.

Julian Juez and Andrew Pearce

A cottage industry tannery near Manila.

Manufacturing industry is very different from cottage industry. It takes place in factories, and it uses one or more of a wide variety of mass production techniques, with a great deal of mechanical assistance. When larger inputs of power and machinery are employed we find that industry tends to concentrate in a few places; this is called *point concentration*. Factories are set up at those points where power and machinery are accessible. The availability of power is initially an important factor in determining the locations of factories; areas around waterfalls are popular sites, since waterfalls are excellent energy sources. The use of machinery tends also to demand point concentration rather than scatter merely because machines are initially scarce, and usually bulky.

The start of industrialization. This is an artisan-owned workshop in Chandigarh, India. Note the precision machinery and the newspapers. The man is making scientific instruments.

UNESCO/M. Serraillier

The employment of power and machinery, and the ensuing agglomeration of industrial activity at certain places mark the beginning of factory industry. At first there is simply a collection of separate artisan-owned workshops. Soon the benefits of common action are recognized; a large forge, furnace, or press costs too much for one person, and requires several people to work it efficiently. Soon a number of people are working under one roof, making use of facilities that greatly increase their productivity. In time the organization of the operation into a single corporate entity is seen to be desirable; this corporation may be joined by other new enterprises. Agglomeration continues. Sophisticated power systems and machinery continue to be used in ever-increasing quantities. As the quantity and quality of the input increase, so does the output. Manufacturing industry has by now become established.

It is not easy to say just when a nation has become industrialized, and it is equally hard to know which countries have become industrialized, and which have not. To find out which stage of industrialization a nation is in, we must first select criteria. Any single factor can be misleading unless we check it out against another, so electricity generation will be taken and checked against the value of gross manufactured output; both factors are on a standardized per capita basis, of course.

Manufacturing is now established. This is the Lenin locomotive works at Tbilisi in the USSR.

Novosti Press Agency

Statistical Interpretation

3-1 We are going to try to obtain a *correlation coefficient* between per capita electricity generation (column P of Appendix 2) and per capita value of gross manufactured output (column Q). This will tell us the degree to which the two variables are related to each other, and thereby give us an approximate indication of the reliability of using either as a test of the extent of industrialization. Use the *grouped data technique* for obtaining a correlation coefficient, as illustrated in Appendix 3, and then:
a) Suggest why the relationship is less than perfect.
b) Comment upon the reliability of using either criterion as a meaningful test of the extent of industrialization throughout the world.

3-2 The scattergraph in Fig. 3-1 shows the relationship between per capita electricity generation and per capita value of gross manufactured output. The "line of best fit" shows the main trend.
a) Describe the main features of the graphed distribution.
b) Why are a few countries located so far from the line of best fit?
c) If a country wanted to achieve a per capita manufactured output level of $500 how much electricity should it plan on producing?

3-3 Examine Fig. 3-2 and suggest reasons for the uneven world distribution of manufacturing activity.

Fig. 3-1
Relationship between per capita electricity generation and per capita value of gross manufactured output

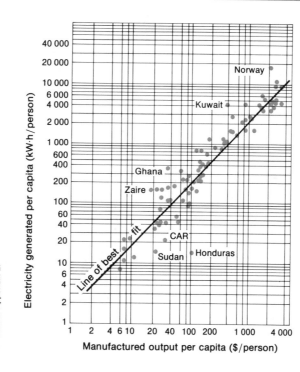

Based on data in Appendix 2.

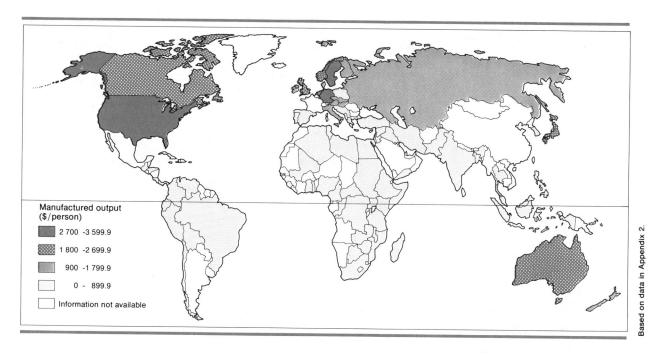

Manufactured output
($/person)

- 2 700 -3 599.9
- 1 800 -2 699.9
- 900 -1 799.9
- 0 - 899.9
- Information not available

Based on data in Appendix 2.

Fig. 3-2
Variations in per capita value of
gross manufactured output
throughout the world

Section C
What are the Chances of Becoming Industrialized?

The chances a preindustrial country has of becoming industrialized depend on the balance of the country's advantages and drawbacks. For example, one nation may be rich in mineral resources but lack good transportation systems, while another may have a large supply of labour but lack adequate energy sources. The chances of successful industrialization are clearly greater if a society's advantages greatly outweigh the disadvantages. We will look closely at advantages and drawbacks.

1. Advantages

a) Natural Resources

All industries rely to some extent on natural resources. The degree of reliance generally varies according to the bulk and consequent transportation costs of the raw material needed. For example, while pulp and paper industries are usually located close to timber areas, watch-making companies do not need to be situated near sources of iron ore.

The amount of energy available is often another factor that determines the location of industry. For instance, relatively cheap and plentiful supplies of hydro power in Quebec and British Columbia have favoured the development of aluminum industries in these provinces, although the raw material has to be imported from Jamaica.

The raw material is initially bauxite, a red soil-like material that is a product of the tropical weathering of rock. It is very bulky to transport, and is partly processed into *alumina* before shipment to Canada.

Natural resources do not necessarily consist only of raw materials and energy supplies. They also include landscape, climate, and position. Landscape can facilitate or hinder industrial growth; flat land makes transportation easy, deep-water channels make good harbours, and deep valleys allow for the construction of hydro reservoirs. A good climate offers obvious advantages; in some places the warmth means that factory heating costs may be eliminated, snow clearance minimized, and general operating costs thereby reduced. The southern half of the United States, the so-called "sunbelt", offers a good example of the attractions of warmth. In recent years there has been a noticeable trend for industries to move into the southern States. The following article of 1976 2 25 gives another example of the way climatic warmth can attract industrial growth.

VANCOUVER (CP)—Favorable climate and economic conditions are reasons given by officials of Canadian firms for their involvement in a major tree planting project in Brazil.

Work on a plantation that eventually will cover about 300 000 acres [121 458 ha] is being carried out by a Brazilian company 51 per cent owned by MacMillan Bloedel Ltd., B.C.'s biggest forest firm, and 49 per cent by Toronto-based Brascan Ltd.

More than 2 000 acres [810 ha] were planted last year.

Companhia Catarinense de Empreedimentos Glorestais, or Embrasca, is developing an area on the south Brazilian coast in the state of Santa Catarina, about 600 miles [960 km] from Rio.

John O. Hemmingsen, executive vice-president of natural resources for MacMillan Bloedel, said in an interview the project began about 18 months ago. It is expected to be completed in eight years.

"We are in the pulp and paper industry in a big way and there is not much opportunity to expand in B.C.," he said.

"If we want to expand where there is a lot of suitable forest, Brazil is attractive for a number of reasons. The government is stable, the economy a fast growing one and the trees grow very rapidly there."

For example, eucalyptus trees can be cut when they are six to seven years old and pine trees can be used for pulp in 12 years. In Canada it takes 70 years to grow a tree for pulp.

Hemmingsen said the yield from Brazilian trees is better than that of Canadian species.

He said 1 500 to 2 000 people, almost all Brazilians, are working for Embrasca.

The Toronto Star 1976 2 25

Can you suggest other industries that would be attracted by a warm climate?

As far as the other factor—location—is concerned, the best locations are those on or near major transportation routes. For example, Singapore, at the junction of South Asia and the Far East, has always had good industrial potential.

b) Labour Supply

Rapid industrialization in the past has usually been based on an equally rapid growth of population, thus enabling an expanding industry to draw successfully upon an adequate supply of labour. This was the case in England in the seventeenth and early eighteenth centuries when the increasing population not only supplied England's developing industries with labour, but also made up the empire-building armies, and helped colonize North America, Australia, and South Africa. The same was true in the United States during the late eighteenth and early nineteenth centuries, when the world's most powerful surge of industrialization was largely based on continuing massive immigration. In West Germany, successful industrialization after the devastation of World War II was helped to a great extent by the influx of 10 000 000 refugees from behind the Iron Curtain and by millions of *guest workers* from southern Europe. It was also the case in Japan after World War II, when the industrial labour supply was augmented by millions of people who left the increasingly efficient farms of the countryside and poured into the towns in a tide of new urbanization.

The present preindustrial world (see Fig. 3-2) seems to have plentiful labour, and industrialization is seen as the main source of jobs for these large populations. Not all countries, though, possess sufficient labour for extensive industrialization; a glance at the population data in column A of Appendix 2, for instance, shows that many of the preindustrial nations have very small populations. For example, Belize has a population of 140 000, Botswana 690 000, Cyprus 640 000, Equatorial Guinea 310 000, Gabon 530 000, and Gambia 520 000. Nevertheless there are some other countries with much "cheap labour". This term is used to describe labour that is usually less skilled than in industrialized nations, and that is often in surplus supply in its own country. Labourers in these countries accept low wages because if wages get too high, the owners or the industry will be tempted to use more machinery, thus reducing the number of jobs available. A large supply of cheap labour is therefore an advantage possessed by some of the less industrialized countries. The extent to which this is an attraction can be seen in the following article.

The global scramble for cheap labor

West Germany's Rollei-Werke for years has been losing sales to Japanese rivals, whose low wage costs enable them to sell cameras for less than half the price of a Rolleiflex. Fighting to overcome that handicap, Rollei executives recently decided to try to beat the Japanese at their own game. The German firm is investing $12.6 million in a new plant in Singapore. There workers will turn out cameras for sale in the U.S. and East Asia at wage rates only one-sixth as high as in Germany, and two-thirds below those prevailing even in Japanese camera plants.

How long Rollei's advantage will last is problematic. Low as they are by European standards, Japanese wages more than doubled between 1963 and 1969. Logically enough, Japanese industrialists are also discovering the advantages of shifting some production to lands where no wage explosion has yet begun. Within the past four years, at least 40 Japanese firms have set up plants in Taiwan alone. The factories turn out lingerie, computer parts, kitchenware and TV sets—though not yet cameras—at wages averaging only 30% of what their owners would have to pay in Japan.

Willing Workshops.
Both Rollei and the Japanese firms seem likely to have increasing company in their new locations. All over the industrialized world, accelerating wage inflation is pushing manufacturers into new efforts to tap the vast pool of willing and cheap labor in poorer countries. They are farming out production of component parts, subassemblies, and even finished products, sometimes for export to other areas but often for use back home. In the process they are not only cutting their own costs but speeding the industrialization of underdeveloped countries, some of which are coming to relish the role of workshops for distant, richer lands.

U.S. companies started the trend for an obvious reason: since they pay the world's highest wages, they have the most to save by manufacturing offshore. They began by subcontracting work to locally owned firms in Japan and Western Europe, and are still expanding that practice. Ford Motor, for example, has signed up Tokyo Shibaura Electric to make most of the generators that will go into its 1971 models, and is dickering to have another Japanese firm, Diesel

Kiki, supply many of the compressors needed in auto air-conditioning systems.

Lately a growing number of American firms have gone further to set up their own component-manufacturing operations in the lower-wage Asian nations. Signetics Corp., a Corning Glass Works subsidiary, for instance, flies components to Seoul, South Korea, where workers assemble them into integrated circuits that are flown back to the U.S. to be fitted into computers. The operation makes economic sense because Signetics pays the Korean workers only $45 a month *v.* the $350 or so it would have to pay an employee in Sunnyvale, Calif. Fairchild Camera and Instrument conducts a similar assembly operation for integrated circuits in Singapore.

Changing Roles.
As wage costs balloon, a growing list of companies in Western Europe and Japan are seeking similar savings—sometimes next door, sometimes at the other end of the world. Sweden's Saab has just completed a plant in Uusikaupunkt, an undeveloped area of Finland, to roll out 15 000 cars a year, about one-third of which will be sent back to Sweden; the Finnish workers get about half the pay that Saab's Swedish employees do. West Germany's Daimler-Benz has invested $6.6 million in a Yugoslav truck and bus plant and supplies technical help, in return for which it will get spare parts made for Daimler-Benz's German plants at low Yugoslav wage rates. Japanese manufacturers are dickering with India for component parts for sewing machines, autos, radios and bicycles.

Even countries that have themselves been traditional suppliers of cheap labor have now begun to look offshore for still lower-priced labor. Italian manufacturers make many of the refrigerators and other appliances sold in the European Common Market, often under German, French or Dutch brand names, because their wage rates were the lowest in the six-nation community; they also make aircraft parts for U.S. firms. Wage rates in many northern Italian plants, however, have now climbed to equality with other parts of the Common Market, and Italian unions are demanding that the same scales be extended to workers in the depressed south. One result: Società Generale Semiconduttori, the country's biggest maker of electronic components, is building a $1.3 million transistor plant in Singapore, where wage costs will be only one-tenth what they are in Italy.

Dividends of Discipline.
To the poor countries, such investments offer not only jobs but desperately needed foreign-currency earnings and a chance for local workers to acquire skills that home-owned industries cannot teach. Rollei, for example, is already bringing groups of workers from Singapore to its main plant in Braunschweig for training in camera making. Westerners have been impressed by how swiftly unskilled Asians respond to such training. George A. Needham, head of Motorola Korea Ltd., says that it takes only six weeks to teach girls in Seoul to assemble transistors—or two weeks less than the training period for girls hired by Motorola's other semiconductor plant in Phoenix. His explanation: "These girls need the work more and the discipline in Korea is harder. Life is tough here."

For all these reasons, the leaders of several underdeveloped countries, particularly in Asia, have switched from their traditional insistence on developing locally owned industry to welcoming, or even actively seeking foreign manufacturing operations. . . .

Time 1970 9 21

Discussion and Research

7. Do you approve of firms from industrialized nations setting up operations in a less developed country in order to take advantage of lower labour costs? Who benefits and who loses from such a transfer?

---

c) *Favourable Government Action*

Potential industrialists can readily see the natural resources and the supply of labour in a preindustrial country. Less obvious are the invisible advantages of political stability and favourable economic

Even while Ontario advertises its attractions for industrial growth, Ontario manufacturers occasionally expand outside Ontario. For example, Ontario firms manufacture hockey equipment in Barbados, and ship it back to Canada for sale. The reason is the lower wage costs in Barbados. Ontario firms also manufacture carpets and other goods in New York State; they then have access to the giant US market without having to go through customs.

policies. Governments of nonindustrialized countries often have to advertise their policies in order to compete with other areas. Advertising of this type is not confined to less developed countries, as the advertisement at the beginning of the chapter shows. All countries and regions with high unemployment want job-creating industries, and so Ontario is trying to attract industry just as much as is Papua New Guinea. Indeed, New York State even advertises in Ontario!

Some countries offer extraordinarily generous government help in order to attract industry. For example, Singapore offers tax advantages to new companies for five years, extended for a further fifteen years if they expand; a tax of 4%, instead of 40%, on earnings from exports; no limit on the employment of foreign nationals; tariff protection against imported competition; and free *repatriation* of profits (sending profits back to the homeland). In competition, the Republic of Korea offers five years at no taxes, followed by three years at half taxes; no commodity import duties for raw materials; permanent income tax exemption for foreign nationals; export promotion by the Korean Trade Corporation; and unrestricted repatriation of profits. If you were an industrialist seeking to expand, how would you choose?

As a result of this government help, much of the new, labour-intensive manufacturing in the world is shifting gradually to a small number of less developed but highly ambitious countries.

d) Favourable Attitude toward Multinational Companies

Multinationals are firms that have their home base in one country but their operations in many other nations. They are usually owned by stockholders, although they may be owned by governments. Many of the multinationals are among the largest companies in the world, and a number of them engage in more manufacturing than do some entire countries. Indeed, of the 100 largest economic units in the world,

Fig. 3-3
The ten companies with the largest sales in the world, according to the 1977 *Fortune* list

Company	Sales (in dollars)
Exxon	48 630 817 000
General Motors	47 181 000 000
Royal Dutch Shell	36 087 130 000
Ford Motor	28 839 600 000
Texaco	26 451 851 000
Mobil	26 062 570 000
National Iranian Oil	19 671 064 000
Standard Oil of California	19 434 133 000
British Petroleum	19 103 330 000
Gulf Oil	16 451 000 000

(units for which an annual balance sheet is published), 50 are nations and 50 are multinational companies. As an indication of the multinational shift in manufacturing, consider this: in 1901 there were 47 overseas manufacturing subsidiaries of US firms; by 1950 there were 988; by 1959 the number had increased to 1 891; and by 1967 there were as many as 3 646 subsidiaries. As Ford's vice-president for international operations said, "It is our goal to be in every single country there is. We at Ford Motor Company look at a world map without any boundaries." The present forces of industrial *dispersion*, or spreading out, thus in evidence are of course the opposite of the earlier trends to agglomeration.

Multinationals offer huge advantages to preindustrial countries, and so the governments of many of the less developed nations adopt an attitude favourable toward these companies. Multinationals are seen as one of the prime agents in the spread of technology into less developed countries; they bring ideas, methods of organization, and contacts; they provide training in management as well as in shop skills such as welding and fitting; they promote international trade; they draw less developed countries into the mainstream of the modern world community.

Multinationals have certain drawbacks, however. In the receiving country they may be regarded as exploiters of local resources, and as organizations that will act in their own interests rather than in the interests of the host country, if the interests clash. As multinational companies move their operations abroad, they can create unemployment in the home country. In the USA the AFL-CIO contended that during the years 1966-70 there was a net loss to the States of 700 000 jobs because of the transfer of work abroad. As an example, in 1969 the General Instrument Company shut down operations in Massachusetts and opened up 12 000 new jobs in Taiwan instead.

AFL – CIO = American Federation of Labor and Congress of Industrial Organizations

The major problem, though, concerns sovereignty; who has the authority, the company or the country? This is especially true in those countries that either feel exploited or want to control their own future. Therefore, countries wishing to become industrialized welcome multinationals, but set down certain conditions designed to limit the power of the companies. For instance, India now insists on a measure of local participation in any foreign enterprise that wishes to operate in the country; the Philippines requires 60% local ownership, and foreigners are restricted to 5% of the total labour in any job category; Peru has decreed 51% local ownership; Canada has its Foreign Investment Review Agency.

Canada also has its own multinationals, such as Brascan, Seagrams, Canadian Pacific, Moore Corporation, Abitibi, George Weston, Alcan, and Inco. The following article is a study of one of Canada's multinational companies.

Brascan is the Canadian-owned firm in Brazil that operates most of the power production and distribution in that country; Seagrams is the world's major distilling group; Canadian Pacific operates railroads, paper mills, hotels, mining companies, and airlines in many countries; Moore Corporation is the world's largest manufacturer of business forms; Abitibi is the world's largest manufacturer of newsprint; George Weston is one of the world's leading food processing and retailing companies; Alcan is a major producer of aluminum; and Inco is the world's largest producer of nickel.

Massey-Ferguson: A global corporation

Massey-Ferguson is among the world's largest manufacturers of farm machinery, industrial and construction machinery, and diesel engines. These products are made in 92 factories located in 30 different countries, half of which are nations of the less developed world. Combines are manufactured in Brantford, Ontario, general farm machinery in Brazil, and tractors and diesels in Britain; tractors are also made in Detroit in the US, as well as in West Germany, Italy, Iran, Pakistan, Turkey, Poland, and Libya. In addition there are factories in several of these areas for the manufacture of industrial and construction machinery.

The USA is Massey-Ferguson's largest single market, accounting for about 23% of all sales. Brazil accounts for 10%, Britain 9.8%, West Germany 7.8%, and Canada 6.9%. Sales are made to countries on all continents. The most important product is tractors (42% of all sales), followed by diesel engines (18.3%), industrial machinery (11.8%), and grain harvesting equipment.

Like many multinational corporations, Massey-Ferguson operates a variety of factories under its own name in many of the world's countries. For instance, in Brazil the company is called Massey-Ferguson do Brasil S.A., and it operates plants at Canoas (for the manufacture of combines and other agricultural machinery), Sao Paulo (for tractors), and Sorocaba (for industrial and construction machinery). In addition, Massey-Ferguson also owns or partly owns companies with other names. In Brazil, these companies are Motores Perkins S.A. (with diesel engine plants at Sao Bernardo and Sao Paulo), Progresso Metalfrit S.A. (with a foundry at Sao Paulo), Companhia Industrial de Pecas para Automoveis (with a forging plant at Sao Paulo), and Piratininga, Implementos Agricolas Ltda (with a farm implements factory at Butia).

Sales also take place within the multinational organization. It is quite normal, for instance, for the diesel engine division (called Perkins) to buy castings and parts from companies owned or partly owned by Massey and to sell its engines to tractor and machinery plants also owned by Massey.

While Massey-Ferguson emphasizes mechanical aids for farming, it does not ignore the demands of farmers in less developed countries. The Malavi subsidiary, Agrimal Ltd., specializes, for example, in the manufacture of hoes and animal draft equipment. Nevertheless, the corporation confidently expects that the world demand for its main machinery lines will continue to expand in the future. In its forecasts for 1978-82, Massey expects that the increased demands for food arising from a growing world population will necessitate the output of an additional 125 000 000 t of grain a year and the use of an additional 50 000 000 ha of land. "It is clear", Massey states in its annual report for 1977, "that the developing countries must provide much of the increase and to do so they will require large inputs of farm machinery, fertilizers, improved technical and management skills, and food processing and distribution functions."

The problems faced by the company are in many ways similar to the problems of all multinationals. Fluctuating exchange rates, for example, cause some branches to become more profitable and others less so. By 1978, Massey's German subsidiary had become so unprofitable because of declining sales caused by an appreciating mark that Massey considered closing it. Inflation also poses problems in some countries. Throughout 1977, for example, Massey's factories in Argentina were closed because they were unable to carry on business while the country suffered from an annual inflation rate of over 100%.

On the other hand, Massey enjoys benefits that are not shared by all multinational corporations. It has generally escaped hostile government action, partly because of its widespread employment of local labour and management, but also because government policies in most countries tend to favour businesses that encourage increased farm productivity.

Information from the *Massey Ferguson Annual Report*, 1978

2. Drawbacks

We have seen that natural resources, cheap labour, government assistance, and an acceptance of multinationals are advantages in industrial-

Fig. 3-4
Development criteria and data for some less developed countries

Country	MO	A	B	C	D	E	F	G	H	I	J
Guatemala	98	5.54	38	.007	.01	.04	38.27	—	—	1.25	0.04
Algeria	88	16.78	20 28	.01	.014	.07	68.12	.10	.036	—	1.02
Congo	84	1.35	20 28	—	.008	.03	5.93	—	.327	1.63	—
Mozambique	83	9.24	7	.002	.006	.04	—	—	—	1.00	—
Philippines	81	42.51	72-100	.006	.01	.06	24.42	.033	.0003	0.83	—
Egypt	77	37.23	26 36	.001	.013	.11	10.50	.006	.015	—	—
Ecuador	72	6.73	67	.008	.019	.05	35.81	—	—	0.52	—
Iraq	67	11.12	24	.004	.012	—	139.66	—	—	—	0.14
Yemen Democratic Rep.	66	1.69	10	.003	.006	.04	44.97	—	—	—	—
Libya	60	2.44	27	.04	.02	.13	371.72	—	—	—	—
Botswana	56	.69	—	.01	.009	—	—	—	—	—	0.47
Kenya	51	13.40	25	.002	.009	.02	17.39	—	—	0.86	0.87
Cameroon	47	6.23	15	.006	.004	.04	8.19	—	—	1.30	—
Pakistan	38	70.26	16	.001	.003	.03	6.82	—	—	0.13	0.16
Ghana	35	9.87	25	.003	.006	.11	19.15	—	—	1.02	2.15
Jordan	35	2.69	31	.02	.016	—	115.99	—	.402	—	—
Uganda	35	11.55	20	.001	.003	.02	—	—	.002	1.27	—
Togo	33	2.25	10	.003	.003	.01	16.89	—	1.01	—	1.82
Central African Republic	31	2.61	10	.002	.002	.01	0.77	—	—	0.92	0.25
India	27	598.10	34 47	.001	.003	.03	1.91	.037	.0002	0.20	0.36
Sri Lanka	27	13.99	76	.004	.005	.02	6.22	—	—	0.34	0.05
Thailand	27	42.48	68 94	.005	.006	.05	30.65	.005	—	0.43	0.35
Nigeria	26	62.93	25	.001	.002	.01	9.41	—	—	0.95	0.55
Malawi	25	5.04	22	.002	.004	.01	13.29	—	—	0.87	—
Bolivia	23	5.63	40	.006	.009	.06	12.79	—	—	0.76	0.13
Malagasy (Madagascar)	23	6.75	39	.57	.004	.01	10.07	—	—	0.83	1.30
Sudan	23	17.76	15	.001	.003	.01	3.43	—	—	1.19	—
Tanzania	21	14.76	20	.003	.004	.01	9.82	—	—	—	—
Zaire	19	24.90	20	.003	.002	—	9.44	—	—	0.59	—
Somalia	11	3.17	5	.003	.002	.002	11.04	—	—	—	—
Indonesia	9	127.59	43	.001	.002	.01	6.32	—	—	0.99	—
Bangladesh	7	76.82	22	.0003	.001	.01	—	—	—	0.14	—
Ethiopia	7	27.95	5	.0004	.002	.01	6.33	—	—	0.87	—
Mali	7	5.70	5	.001	.001	.006	7.37	—	—	0.51	—
Rwanda	6	4.20	10	.001	.001	.006	3.81	—	—	0.93	—

Source: *UN Statistical Yearbook*, 1975.

MO: Per capita value of gross manufactured output

Development criteria:
- **A** Population in millions
- **B** Literacy rate percentage
- **C** Commercial motor vehicles in use per person
- **D** Telephones installed per person
- **E** Electrical generating capacity in kW/person
- **F** International monetary reserves in US $/person
- **G** Iron ore production, iron ore content in t/person
- **H** Phosphate and potash production in t/person
- **I** Roundwood production in m³/person
- **J** Research and development funds in US $/person

ization. Now we will examine some of the drawbacks of preindustrial countries; some of these are powerful enough to reduce the chance of industrialization.

Among the most powerful disadvantages are illiteracy and lack of *infrastructure*. These problems seriously hinder industrialization since, to establish itself, new industry depends on literacy and the infrastructure. Development plans from the start, therefore, should include elements of literacy and technical training, as well as numerous improvements, such as road building, telephone installation, creation of banking facilities, institution of vocational training, and of course, factories. Everything must fit together.

Infrastructure is the technical name for all the facilities that help to support an efficient manufacturing economy. It includes transportation and communication media, banks and capital markets, education and health facilities, employment exchanges, and power utilities.

There are, therefore, certain problems involved in starting development programs, especially when a nation lacks infrastructure. For example, the Nigerians had problems in the mid-1970s when they tried to import large quantities of cement for new dock construction. They didn't realize until there were about five hundred ships anchored off the coast that the existing dock facilities were incapable of handling the ships. In consequence all other shipping to Nigeria was backed up as well, and piracy began to flourish. Pirates from the mainland would sneak out to an anchored cargo ship and steal its cargo while holding the crew back at gunpoint or knifepoint. Many shipping lines started to drop Nigerian ports from their calling lists.

Uganda, as a military dictatorship, offers another example of the need for a strong infrastructure. Because massive amounts of money were put into military equipment during the 1970s, ordinary commercial and industrial development gradually ground to a halt. In *Time* 1977 3 7, it was reported that "only one in twenty trucks registered in Uganda moves" and that "everything from breweries to cement factories has broken down."

While the lack of industry in a country certainly presents problems, industrialized societies are not problem-free either, as Section D shows.

Statistical Interpretation

3-4 We are now going to try to assess an *index of development potential*. The problem of criteria selection is, of course, ever-present, so we will use those given in Fig. 3-4. The countries listed are those that have the least manufacturing industry as shown in column Q of Appendix 2; that is, those with a per capita value of gross manufactured output *less than* $100. They are listed in order from Guatemala with $98 down to Rwanda with $6, and information relating to ten criteria is given.

Devise an index of development potential to help industrialists choose the future location of their factories. There isn't a single correct method of formulating an index; there are several. Try two or three different methods and see if you get comparable results. If you get different results from different methods, what do you say to the industrialists who are waiting for your report?

3-5 Design an industrial development brochure for the nation that you found to have the highest index of development potential.

3-6 Each of the criteria in Fig. 3-4 is important because it *represents* a sector of the country's economy. Can you explain why each criterion was chosen, and what it represents?

3-7 Before making a decision to invest, an industrialist may require information on other aspects of the country. What are some of these other aspects?

Section D

What Problems Face Already Industrialized Countries?

While some countries vigorously pursue a policy of industrialization, others hold back. They see some of the problems that the industrialized countries face. As the President of Zaire said in 1972:

> We have certain advantages in being underequipped. We have to be proud that we have never made errors such as those which are regretted by some countries considered as completely developed. Therefore, we refuse to follow blindly the trend of developed countries which want production at any price. We do not believe that peace and happiness are derived from the number of cars in the garage, the TV antennas on the roof, or the volume of noise in one's ears.... How does it help to have innumerable factories if their chimneys spread poisonous products over us all day and night? We do not want these destructive industries which kill the fish in our rivers, depriving honest people of the pleasure of fishing or drinking clean water.... We desire only that when scientists will have transformed the world into an artificial one, that in Zaire an authentic nature will remain.

The president has pinpointed several of the disadvantages of industrialization, which we will now examine in detail.

1. Pollution

Pollution is a term applied to the production of waste materials in quantities greater than the environment can handle. The environment has always had "cleaning cycles" of its own; thus dirty water becomes purified through the water cycle, and dirty air is cleansed in the oxygen cycle. As industry has grown, however, the traditional cleaning cycles have become overloaded and incapable of handling the amounts of waste produced.

In the past, there have been a number of pollution disasters. One of the worst incidents was probably the "killer smog" of London in 1952, when a mixture of fog and industrial pollutants caused the deaths of hundreds. After that tragedy, London banned the use of coal in domestic fireplaces and worked to control factory emissions. As a consequence, London's air became much cleaner, and by 1975 the sunshine was visible for twice as many hours per year as it had been in the early 1950s.

Another disaster occurred in Japan in the 1960s, when a factory near the fishing village of Minimata put unwanted mercury wastes directly into the sea. No one thought much about this until several fishermen became seriously ill; some became blind, while others lost control of their nervous systems. Gradually the disease was traced to the large numbers of fish eaten, and from there to the mercury in the water.

Environmental pollution has become a matter of public concern, and most industries now try to control the amount of waste they produce. Even so the risk of contamination remains, and different levels of government have passed laws giving themselves the right to order factories to shut down during times of excessive pollution.

The use of coal was not banned at a single stroke, because most homes had no alternative source of heat. Nevertheless, smokeless fuels were invented and smokeless zones gradually extended over the whole of Greater London.

Dangerous atmospheric pollution does not generally occur at times when factories are busiest but when the atmosphere itself is calmest. This usually happens during anticyclonic high pressure conditions, especially if accompanied by temperature inversions. Normally, the movements of the atmosphere disperse any pollutants until they are diluted and totally harmless, but if the air is calm this does not happen. Under high pressure, moreover, the downward drift of air pins pollutants close to ground level, thereby restricting dispersal even more.

2. Environmental Aesthetics

Quarrying, dumping, blasting, and the emission of *toxic* fumes generally make the environment unattractive. The landscape near Sudbury, Ontario, for example, became world famous in the late 1960s when the lunar astronauts practised there. The rocky surface, laid bare because smelter gases had destroyed the vegetation, was the closest thing to the moon's surface they could find on earth.

Much can be done to improve the appearance of industrial operations; factories can be landscaped, tree screens can be planted, and even the barren land resulting from strip mining can be resodded and planted over. The beautiful Butchart Gardens near Victoria, British Columbia, is an excellent example of what can be done to mask former quarrying operations.

3. Resource Depletion

Many people think that the world is exhausting its resources, and they want to stop industrial expansion. They ignore the fact, however, that at any time in history there is only a limited quantity of *known reserves* of any resource. By known reserves, we do not simply mean those resources that are known to exist, but those that can be developed at existing prices.

The reason for this limited quantity of known resources is partly that industries do not waste time or manpower looking for or develop-

Even if an inventory were to list just the known deposits of, say, iron ore, there would still be the problem of defining the level of iron content needed to qualify the rock as iron ore. The problem is enormous because the only criterion that would determine whether or not the rock qualified would be the price of iron in comparison with the cost of mining, and those future prices and costs are unknowable.

ing resources that are unlikely to be needed for thirty or forty years. Another reason is that resources are important to industry only if they can be developed at current prices. Usually it costs more to develop the deeper parts of a mine, or the remoter areas of a forest. Industries prefer to avoid these more expensive resources, and so they use the cheapest first. The more costly resources are counted among the known reserves only when the market price rises to cover the costs of developing them. Thus it is meaningless to try to make an inventory of resources; we cannot know the future, and we cannot judge now just when a resource will become worth developing. Still less can we know what substitutes might be developed, for that too depends on a balance of prices and input costs. An inventory would be of no real use to industry today.

4. Disease

Some kinds of industry can be dangerous to the worker, and can cause such new diseases as asbestosis and silicosis; these are serious lung disorders caused by breathing air contaminated with asbestos and silica particles. Indeed, most industrial health hazards are linked to contaminants in the air, although danger is also presented by work in radioactive surroundings, and by work involving contact with acids and other toxic substances.

Health risks are not necessarily restricted to plant workers; industry may also endanger the health of the surrounding community. One of the more interesting examples was the discovery of radioactivity in Port Hope's new school in 1975. Some of the landfill had been taken unknowingly from a dump created and used years thirty years previously by Eldorado Nuclear Ltd.; at that time this company had been helping to make the first atomic bomb which was detonated at White Sands in New Mexico prior to Hiroshima. As a result of the radioactivity, some people became sick, property values decreased, and houses and the school itself were closed down. The school was reopened in 1977. You can probably think of other instances in which people's health has been endangered by industry.

5. The Loss of Jobs to Less Developed Countries

Many undeveloped nations offer relatively cheap labour and government policies favouring industrialization, and many companies have taken advantage of this. However, these new operations can cause problems for the workers in the original home plants in three ways. In the first place, they may be laid off as the firm shuts down a high-cost plant in an industrialized country in order to open a replacement plant in a low-cost preindustrial country. Secondly, workers lose the chance of increased job opportunities themselves, and the unemployed in the industrial country fail to get an opportunity to become employed. And thirdly, workers face the risk of having their factory shut down in the future as the products of lower-cost factories in preindustrial countries compete at a lower price. The following newspaper report of 1976 4 19 illustrates the problem.

Again we're asked "Want to pay extra for a Canadian shirt?"

OTTAWA (CP)—The Canadian textile and clothing industry is again engaged in a public battle with the federal government about protective tariffs and import quotas, this time using the Senate banking committee as the forum.

At issue is one of the oldest and most basic questions facing the country in the last century. How much should Canadians, given their small market and relatively high labor costs, be willing to pay to protect domestic industries from foreign competition?

In the case of the textile and clothing industry, why should consumers pay $14 for a Canadian-made shirt when one from Taiwan can be bought for one-third the price? Or why pay $40 for a dress or $150 for a suit when imported products are available at less than half those prices?

The industry traditionally argues that it directly provides about 200 000 jobs and that a domestic textile capacity protects Canadians against the whims of international cartels.

Clothing and fabrics from countries with cheap labor, such as Taiwan, Hong Kong, Malaysia and the Philippines, are cutting into the domestic market. The Canadian companies told the committee the domestic share of the Canadian market had slipped to 46 per cent in 1975 from 64 per cent in 1964.

The issue has always been politically sensitive, given the concentration of the industry in the traditionally high-unemployment areas of Quebec and eastern Ontario.

The industry already enjoys a protective tariff wall of between 22 and 27 per cent, one of the highest accorded any domestic industry and one of the highest textile tariffs in the world.

But in recent years, although the industry pays among the lowest wages of any manufacturing sector in the country, labor costs relative to the cheap-labor countries have soared. Imports have had little difficulty getting over the tariff wall and selling at a fraction of the cost of Canadian-produced goods.

In recent years, the department has put quotas on certain categories of imports to counteract this trend. Industry spokesmen say it isn't enough and want the quotas extended to a wider variety of products.

"There is no way," J. I. Armstrong, president of the textiles institute, told the Senate committee, "that any industry, whether it is textiles or any other industry, in Canada, the United States or any other industrial nation with our standard of living can possibly compete with a country where a skilled tailor can take an hour and 10 minutes to finish a jacket and be paid 14 cents. There is just no way."

The Toronto Star 1976 4 19

---

6. Materialism

Materialism is the overwhelming interest that people have in bettering their own material situation. People with a materialistic attitude often meet with criticism. Consumers are accused of worshipping the "almighty dollar", of having lost their "traditional values", and of being part of the "rat race". Industrialists are accused of exploiting the workers, of cheating the consumers, and of being motivated solely by greed. Anti-materialism becomes a creed, and both consumers and businesses alike are scorned. As the ultimate expression of this scorn, many people today are trying to stop the growth of industry, or trying to remove themselves from the industrial society itself. A slow drift back to the "organic" land and a sympathy for the "natural" life have developed. Some young people set up rural communes; some city people shop at health food stores.

7. Anti-growth

In the industrialized world, especially North America and Western Europe, there has been considerable debate over the issue of continued growth. A computer study entitled *Limits to Growth*, published in 1972, calls for zero or restricted growth. It forecasts doom before the year 2100 if growth continues at the same rate and recommends certain policies of growth limitation to help avoid disaster. Restricted growth has become the watchword for many people, as the following extract from *Time* 1972 1 24 indicates.

The worst is yet to be?

The furnaces of Pittsburgh are cold; the assembly lines of Detroit are still. In Los Angeles, a few gaunt survivors of a plague desperately till freeway center strips, backyards and outlying fields, hoping to raise a subsistence crop. London's offices are dark, its docks deserted. In the farm lands of the Ukraine, abandoned tractors litter the fields: there is no fuel for them. The waters of the Rhine, Nile and Yellow rivers reek with pollutants.

Fantastic? No, only grim inevitability if society continues its present dedication to growth and "progress." At least that is the vision conjured by an elaborate study entitled *The Limits to Growth* [prepared by Dennis Meadows for the Club of Rome].

Meadows, 29, had studied the new field of "systems dynamics." His mentor was M.I.T. Professor Jay Forrester, the brilliant developer of a computer model that could simulate the major ecological forces at work in the world today. Forrester's model begins with the recognition that all these factors are interlocked. Human population cannot grow without food for sustenance. Since just about all

the globe's best land is already under cultivation, farm production can rise only through use of tractors, fertilizers, pesticides—all products of industry. But more industrial output not only demands a heavier drain on natural resources that are scarce even now; it also creates more pollution. And pollution ultimately interferes with the growth of both population and food.

. . .

The question Meadows had to answer was: How long can population and industrialization continue to grow on this finite planet? Unlike the doomsday ecologists who predict that man will drown in pollution or starve because of overpopulation, Meadows's system concludes that the depletion of nonrenewable resources will probably cause the end of the civilization enjoyed by today's contented consumer.

End in Collapse
The sequence goes this way: As industrialization grows, it voraciously consumes enormous amounts of resources. Resources become scarcer, forcing more and more capital to be spent on procuring raw materials,

which leaves less and less money for investment in new plants and facilities. At this stage, which might be about 2020, the computer's curves begin to converge and cross (*see chart*). Population outstrips food and industrial supplies. Investment in new equipment falls behind the rate of obsolescence, and the industrial base

Projection for disaster adapted from computer-output chart in "The Limits to Growth" report.

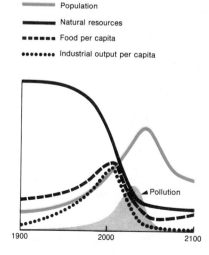

- ▬▬ Population
- ▬▬ Natural resources
- ▪▪▪▪▪ Food per capita
- •••••• Industrial output per capita

Pollution

1900   2000   2100

begins to collapse, carrying along with it the service and agricultural activities that have become dependent on industrial products (like medical equipment and fertilizers). Because of the lack of health services and food, the world's population dwindles rapidly.

In an attempt to find a way out of this basic dilemma, Meadows postulated other scenarios. He assumed that there are still huge, undiscovered reserves of natural resources, say, under the oceans. Testing that possibility, Meadows' computer shows that industrialization will accelerate—and the resulting runaway pollution will overwhelm the biosphere. Might not new technological devices control pollution? Sure, says the computer, but then population would soar and outstrip the ability of land to produce food. Every advance in technology consumes scarce natural resources, throws off more pollutants and often has unwanted social side effects, like creating huge and unmanageable unemployment. What if pollution was abated, the birthrate halved and food production doubled? The readouts are no less glum. There would still be some pollution from every farm and factory, and cumulatively it would still trigger catastrophe. After running thousands of such hypotheses through the computer, Meadows sums up his conclusion tersely: "All growth projections end in collapse."

The Meadows team offers a possible cure for man's dilemma—an all-out effort to end exponential growth, starting by 1975. Population should be stabilized by equalizing the birth and death rates. To halt industrial growth, investment in new, nonpolluting plants must not exceed the retirement of old facilities. A series of fundamental shifts in behavioral patterns must take place. Instead of yearning for material goods, people must learn to prefer services, like education or recreation. All possible resources must be recycled, including the composting of organic garbage. Products like automobiles and TV sets must be designed to last long and to be repaired easily.

Discussion and Research

8. Anti-materialists accuse people of having lost their traditional values. What values do you suppose they mean?
9. What does the term "rat race" mean?
10. Do you as a consumer feel exploited by industrialists? If so, how could the situation be remedied?
11. Would you pay extra for a Canadian shirt?

Other people regard those who would limit growth as shortsighted pessimists; they argue that continued growth is not only possible but also desirable. They say that resources exist in plenty, that new resources will in any event be made available by developing technology, and that the world's people clearly do not yet have enough material wealth. The following reading from *The Economist* of 1974 6 29 analyzes the progrowth view.

A little more time

Even if there are no improvements in existing technology, the world is not likely to be threatened with a physical shortage of raw materials until about AD 100 000 000

This may be the time to finish off the dying cult of extreme ecodoom. Professor Wilfred Beckerman has long made thoughtful people his debtors by writing into the Club of Rome's equations his admirable product called Beckermonium, named after his grandfather who failed to discover it in the nineteenth century. Ever since his grandfather failed to discover it in about 1856, the world has had no supplies of Beckermonium at all, which on the Club of Rome's equations should have made the world come to a halt some time soon after 1857: especially as, even in 1974, the things we have not yet discovered are far more important and numerous than the things we have so far discovered. Anyone can play the Beckermonium game by defining it as something unknown in their grandfather's day but found to exist since.

This is probably the best quick way of understanding the flaw in the extreme econonsense; but, as some people do not see it yet, it is good now to have a whole book from Mr. Beckerman on the subject [In Defence of Economic Growth. By Wilfred Beckermann. *Cape, £3.95.*], full of admirably numerate facts. This article will pinch some of the best of these facts without further attribution, and spice them with his and our own comments. A continuing demolition job on the cult is important, because its wrong—if well-meaning—views have been responsible for a number of deaths. These include malaria victims in Ceylon after the banning of DDT; burned children after the wrongly-based anti-phosphates campaign against detergents had destroyed fireproofing in some clothing; and pneumonic victims in brownouts caused by conservationist opposition to power stations.

A prolific mile

The prophets have assumed four limiting factors on the world's economic growth, in ascending order of respectability: they say the world will run out of raw materials, will suffer ever-increasing pollution, will have too large a population, and too little food.

On raw materials, the Club of Rome reached its equations by assuming that actual reserves of any material cannot be more than two to five times "known reserves", with nil elasticity of supply and substitution after that. It then asked the computer what would happen if demand for precisely these things went on expanding exponentially. The computer replied, naturally, that everything would then break down.

This mode of argument could always have proved that world production of most things stopped long ago, because "known reserves" of most materials all through history have been only a few decades' worth of demand. This is because, if reserves of any material represent more than that, it is not worth looking for more of that material for a while. At present, "known reserves" of most metals are historically rather high—about a hundred years' supply —but random samples suggest that the natural occurrence of most metals in the top mile of the earth's crust is about a million times as great as present known reserves, so we could probably extract one hundred million years' supply of metals from that top mile by existing technology. Towards the end, it would be a bit uncomfortable to mine to the depth of one mile at every point on the earth's crust, but by AD 100 000 000 we may be able to think up something.

Even without mining, sea water is now known to contain about a billion years' supply of sodium chloride and magnesium, 100m years' supply of sulphur, borax and potassium chloride, more than 1m years' supply of molybdenum, uranium, tin and cobalt. Most of these are materials with a rather high elasticity of substitution. Those who say we should be worried by AD 100 000 000 also seem to assume that, in the rather long period between now and then, there will be no advances in recycling, in producing substitute materials, or in production techniques. In practice, there are going to be huge technical advances in all of these over a very short period ahead. Scientists already nearly know how to mine manganese nodules from the seabed (according to a World Bank report, a mining rate of 400m tons a year should be possible for a literally unlimited period of time at production costs "a fraction of current costs"): technical improvements in the past few years will allow low-grade porphyry copper to last for 600 or 700 years at present rates of use; a large part of the earth's land mass has not been explored for any minerals in any detail; new mining techniques (such as softening rock through chemical or vibrational action, and the use of induction heating and hydraulic jets) are on the point of breakthrough.

. . .

In listing "pollution" as its second cause of coming breakdown, the Club of Rome supposed the most "optimistic" possible assumption was that the ratio of pollution to output might be reduced by one quarter over the next hundred years. Actually, smoke pollution per unit of industrial output in London had then already been reduced by 85 per cent in the fifteen years after 1953, and in the United States during the present decade all air pollution is expected to fall to about one-tenth of what it was. Some ecologists say that today's technologies are steadily more pollutant and dangerous than yesterday's. **But usually the opposite turns out to be true.** Recorded accidents in Britain's industry in 1900 were six times those in Britain's much larger industry in 1970; ecologists who complain that the carbon monoxide concentration around Oxford Street may reach about 20 ppm (parts per million) for about two minutes a day at peak travel times (compared with 50 ppm all day long in many factories) should note London's 1847 report on drainage and sewerage that "the space bounded by Oxford Street, Portland Place, New Road, Tottenham Court Road, is one vast cesspool", which makes it unsurprising that 20 000 people then still died from typhus in England every year. If a Club of Rome had rightly forecast Britain's present quantum of travel, industry and urban workforce exponentially forward from 1850, it would have proved that this plague-ridden, industrially maimed nation must long since have disappeared beneath several hundred feet of horse manure.

. . .

The third reason for supposed èco-doom is the growth of population. The breakthrough in reducing infant mortality rates all over the world after the late 1940s (itself, surely, a good thing) did by the early 1960s seem to threaten such a population explosion. It then brought its natural antidote of breakthroughs in both birth control technology (the pill, etc) and often in birth control attitudes (permission of abortion, etc). Now the World Bank reports that "of the 66 countries for which accurate [fertility] data are available, as many as 56 show a decline". This includes poorer countries. The real problem is that in the next twenty years doctors may break through into conquering some of the great debilitating diseases, allowing us to keep many more old people alive, just as we started to keep many more children alive in the twenty years after the 1940s: that is the real problem we should now be humanely debating.

The world's food problem has nothing to do with physical limits on food production. Even if there were no new discoveries in food-growing technology from now on, and we continued to cultivate only the very small proportion of the earth's surface now used as farmland, a raising of all other countries' efficiency of cultivation to that of the Netherlands would already suffice to feed 60 billion people (today's world population is 3.7 billion). Those who say that more intensive cultivation always ruins the soil should note that the land in Holland has been farmed with increasing intensity for 2 000 years. Some big improvements in food-growing technology are almost certain during our children's lifetime. . . .

If the rate of growth of rice yields in India and Pakistan in 1965-71 were continued for a century, all of mankind would indeed die, because the surface of the earth would be covered with rice to a depth of three feet. But this should not obscure the world's two real agricultural problems. First, about 60 per cent of the world's workers still labour on farms; with modern techniques, every country will soon be able to feed itself with under 10 per cent of its workers there; this rather imminent threat of technological unemployment for half the world's workers is a major turning point in history. Secondly, the flock away from agriculture to the towns will be handled least well in the poorest countries, from which the biggest flight from the land is still to come.

Crusades that are needed

Extreme environmentalism is now on the wane. Mr. Beckerman quotes reports that sales of the main ecological newspaper have already fallen by 80 per cent from their peak. He is sternly critical of those who drove or leaped on the bandwagon: the middle classes who interpreted environmentalism to mean that other people should not disturb their peace and solitude, radical youth eager to condemn materialism, the newspapers and clergymen and academics who told what some must eventually have known to be untruths because this inflated their importance, the alarmingly innumerate scientists. Yet there was a real passion for doing good among very many of those who interested themselves in these issues. Those who prefer to stick to facts rather than fancies should consider why they fail to attract this potential force for doing good to the crusades that are needed—such as the devising and financing of performance contracts for all who will bring re-employment opportunities, modern urban management systems, and nutrition programmes (of which transport, not cultivation, will be the key) to the world's growing urban poor. Such things, however, need action, not just nice spine-chilling calls for inaction.

Discussion and Research

12. What arguments could the leader of a poor country use to persuade an anti-growth adviser that growth is desirable?

13. If the anti-growth philosophy were to be adopted, what values would have to be given up by (a) the wealthy nations, and (b) the poor nations?

14. To what extent does economic development depend on people's knowledge of their environment?

15. How is the environment changed by industrial growth?

Case Study 3
Japan: Industrialization

Japan was the first non-western nation to become industrialized. It has been highly successful, developing from a traditional preindustrial society to the world's third major industrial power in little more than a century.

Preindustrial Japan was a closed feudal society run, under the nominal rule of the emperor, by the *shogun*, a military governor. In essence, he maintained Japanese society in a rigid pattern; people were bound by ties of obligation to group first (to Japan, and to the feudal lord, for example) and family second. Loyalty was a paramount value. Emigration was neither allowed nor desired; immigration was forbidden; trade was not sought. The whole world outside Japan was ignored and change was frowned upon.

Nevertheless the shogun kept a finger on the pulse of change in the west by means of a carefully controlled trading concession to the Dutch awarded at Nagasaki. In return the Dutch had to make annual reports to the shogun on recent developments in Europe and North America. Thus, in the early 1800s the shogun knew of the beginnings of European industrialization and of the growth of European overseas empires; he wanted no part in these developments. Thus, when the Dutch brought a German scientist to teach medicine at the school in Nagasaki in 1823, the Japanese found a way to prevent his teaching; they expelled him for having in his possession a map of Japan.

However, the seeds of western science had been planted. Japanese scholars worked hard at translating western books, and by 1853, when Commodore Perry's warships pried open the closed society with the threat of force and demands for trade, the Japanese were themselves ready to set up a research institute for such "foreign" sciences as mathematics and geology.

As a result of Perry's efforts, foreign ships and guns were seen by many Japanese to be as efficient as foreign knowledge in breaking the traditional isolation and closure of Japanese society. The lesson was repeated in the Namamugi incident of 1862 when the British destroyed some Japanese forts in retaliation for the samurai killing of a British subject who had not dismounted from his horse at the approach of the local warlord.

Under the pressures of both western knowledge and force of arms, therefore, the shogunate began to crumble, and full power was restored to the emperor in 1868. The Emperor Meiji and his advisers realized that Japan might well be next on the list of potential European acquisitions, so they immediately set out to make Japan a modern military power capable of defending itself against imperialist armies. This meant rapid industrialization, along with educational and technological improvements.

Japanese Ministry of Foreign Affairs

This is the Emperor Meiji, in whose reign Japan started to become an industrial nation. The streetcars at right are from woodcuts of the Meiji era.

In order to avoid any sort of colonial domination, the Japanese rulers decided that as far as possible Japan should industrialize itself without foreign help, and certainly without foreign multinationals. Selected Japanese were therefore sent to Britain and the USA to learn industrial technology, so that they could return and teach it to other Japanese. They imported the required books, bought the necessary machinery, and hired six hundred western engineers at high salaries to help organize the start of industrialization.

The process was costly. The building of a heavy industrial complex large enough to supply armies and navies capable of defending Japan was too heavy a drain on a feudal society. Other sources of money were required.

Export earnings were seen as the best source of additional money. The first exports were silk goods, but the list was soon expanded to include cotton textiles. As a newcomer to the industrial scene, Japan was able to start with the latest equipment, and use huge supplies of low-cost labour. Success was achieved, especially since the nation was competing with older countries which tended to have less modern equipment and costlier labour. The strategy of opting for export growth in order to pay for heavy industry at home worked well. Iron and steel furnaces were obtained in 1887, and the first steel ship was launched in 1890. Meanwhile, light manufactured goods such as toys and bicycles were added to the export list.

Japan also improved its educational facilities. The Bureau of Geography and a school of technology were instituted in 1871, and public elementary schools in 1872. Tokyo University was started in 1877 and education was made compulsory by 1886. In 1893, Japan stopped using foreign teachers and all instruction passed into the hands of Japanese teachers.

These were great changes for Japan, and they were forced very rapidly by the Meiji government. This transition was peaceful largely because of the unquestioning loyalty to superiors displayed by all Japanese. An order given by the emperor was passed down the line until it reached the appropriate level, where it was carried out by people who genuinely believed they were doing the task for Japan. Under these conditions it was possible to maintain for many years the competitive advantage of low wage rates. The government was careful to censor all mention of western standards of living, because this topic was considered to be dangerous.

By 1900, only thirty years after starting the process of industrialization, Japan had almost caught up to some of the European industrial powers: textiles, shipbuilding, machine tools, iron and steel, coal mining, and electrical power were all important. Basic research was also proving to be very successful, as shown in 1900 by the discovery of adrenalin.

It was World War I, however, that finally made Japan an industrial society. During the war the European allies ordered a multitude of armaments and ships from the Japanese, and Japanese industry prospered accordingly. By 1919 manufacturing had become Japan's largest source of employment, and heavy industries were firmly established. Japan's own war preparations helped growth through the 1920s and 1930s; in search of a new supply of resources, the nation even invaded Manchuria (1931-45).

World War II, on the other hand, was devastating to industrial development. Most factories were destroyed or dismantled, and all work in atomic energy (for which a Japanese scientist later received the Nobel Prize), aeronautics, and armaments was forbidden.

By 1950, Japanese industry had struggled back to its 1940 position. The Korean War (1950-53) then provided an opportunity for industrial growth similar to that of World War I. As the closest supplier of arms, Japan's industry got another boost, and after the war it kept on growing. Industry, at last on a firm base, was now permitted to supply the home market first, and workers were allowed to share increasingly in the wealth produced.

Since 1955 or so Japan's economy has grown by about 10% a year, so that the country has been doubling its wealth every seven or eight years. About 90% of Japan's products have been absorbed by the Japanese themselves, who have seen their wages rise higher than those of most European workers. Fig. 3C-1 presents some statistics illustrating the country's remarkable growth.

Fig. 3C-1
Japan: Selected statistics

1 Steel output (t)		2 Ships built (GRT)	
1950	8 000 000	1950	250 000
1955	13 000 000	1955	750 000
1960	22 000 000	1960	1 750 000
1965	41 000 000	1965	5 500 000
1970	93 000 000	1970	10 000 000
1975	102 000 000	1975	15 227 000

3 Annual car production		4 Electricity output (mkW·h)	
1950	5 000	1950	46 000
1955	20 000	1955	65 250
1960	165 000	1960	115 500
1965	700 000	1965	192 125
1970	3 000 000	1970	359 538
1975	4 570 000	1975	475 794

5 Number of TV receivers owned		6 Rice yields (t/ha)	
1950	—	1935	2.740
1955	166 000	1945	3.210
1960	6 860 000	1955	3.840
1965	18 224 000	1960	3.890
1970	22 818 000	1965	3.810
1975	26 545 000	1967	4.430
		1968	4.410
		1970	4.341
		1975	4.763

7 Persons employed in major activities		
	Farming	Manufacturing
1950	19 000 000	5 000 000
1955	16 000 000	7 500 000
1960	13 900 000	9 500 000
1965	11 500 000	1 1 600 000
1970	8 000 000	1 3 800 000
1975	6 200 000	1 3 500 000

There are many reasons for the huge success of Japanese industry, some not easily appreciated by westerners. One of the most important factors has undoubtedly been the loyalty trait, which makes workers put their factories or firms above all else except Japan itself. Thus people willingly work 6 days a week, 51 weeks a year, and feel deprived if they cannot. In return the firm is loyal to its workers, firing none, and providing care from cradle to grave even to the extent of establishing holiday hotels. Another factor has been the consensus, or general agreement, form of decision-making, which not only avoids confrontation but also secures cooperation in the carrying out of the decisions. Still another factor has been the huge pride the Japanese have in economic growth.

And what of the future? In the matter of gross output the Japanese look forward to overtaking the USSR sometime in the 1990s (as Fig. 3C-2 shows).

Fig. 3C-2
GNP data and projections

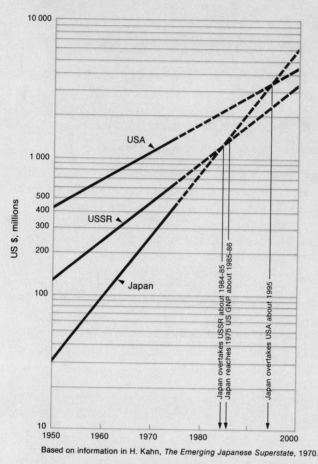

Based on information in H. Kahn, *The Emerging Japanese Superstate*, 1970.

Since the population has apparently stabilized in a slow growth phase 4 situation at about 110-120 million the Japanese confidently expect that on a per capita basis they will be the richest people on earth well before 2000. They see the first signs of a labour shortage, which develops in a growing economy whenever rural migration dries up or population growth slows down. This is being met in two ways: first, by expanding operations into new industrial areas with low labour costs; and second, by developing fully automated labourless production techniques.

The policy of overseas expansion is one which the Japanese refused to permit others to practise in Japan in 1868, and so they are a little wary of practising it themselves now. They will never intrude where they are not

Workers were permitted to share increasingly in the wealth produced.

wanted, but where possible, they use the "human flood" technique, dispatching mass missions to areas of potential investment. At present, most investment is being made in South America, chiefly Brazil (where the largest number of Japanese emigrants live), as well as throughout south and southeast Asia, Oceania, North America, and the Middle East. Africa and Europe see relatively little Japanese investment.

The policy of full automation offers more peaceful possibilities for Japanese trade. The Japanese have stressed the development of computers and robots, and already have a totally automated oil tanker, the *Seiko Maru*, which travels between Japan and the Middle East without the need of a crew (though it carries one in case anything goes wrong). They also have fully automated factories, where machines called "magic hands" do all the work. The Japanese are also working hard on a completely labourless shipyard.

Because of Japan's industrial development, the Japanese may well realize their expectations about being the world's richest people before the year 2000.

INDUSTRIALIZATION: Further Reading

The Franchiser, ELKIN
Takeover Bid, GAINHAM
The Eco-spasm Report, TOFFLER
The Master of the Mill, GROVE
In the Name of Profit, HEILBRONER
The Story of Unions in Canada, WILLIAMS
Silent Spring, CARSON
Limits to Growth, MEADOWS
No Safe Place, TROYER

Conclusion

Industrial growth is undoubtedly a controversial topic. Many countries are now experiencing the benefits of industrialization, and other nations want to share in these advantages. Comparisons of industrial expansion with population growth and food production show that a high level of industrialization correlates well with a low rate of population growth and high levels of food production. Does this mean that industry holds the key to the future of many overpopulated or hungry countries?

On the other hand, many people are worried about the problems caused by industrial growth. They point to the pollution of the environment and the depletion of resources. If we share this viewpoint, we may feel that a large part of the world's population is doomed to a future of starvation and material poverty.

Arguments rage over the consumption of resources; energy resources, in particular, which are essential to industrial prosperity, are a major concern. If energy can be produced in abundance, then we can fairly safely assume that the necessary technology will also facilitate the continued growth of industry. But if energy is really scarce, as some maintain, then the prospects for industrial expansion are indeed dim. In the next chapter we take a close look at the energy situation.

Chapter 4
ENERGY

Introduction

Much confusion surrounds the energy issue. Will the world run out of energy within a few decades, or is it virtually unlimited? Are oil spills inevitable? Are nuclear power stations safe? Will thermal waste gradually cause the polar ice caps to melt? Should we cut back now on the use of energy and start to change our life styles?

Confusion arises because there are several different answers to each of these questions; experts (and so-called experts) have conflicting views on the energy situation, and so the rest of the world is caught in the middle, not knowing what to believe.

It is generally agreed that energy is one of the major concerns of the present time. Its continued availability is of vital interest to farmers and industrialists alike, in all parts of the world. The average person relies on energy for transportation, communication, construction, climate-control, entertainment, and other needs and comforts. In order to act wisely, then, and discover our own answers to the many questions involved in the issue, we should learn as much about energy as we can.

In this chapter we will study the main sources of energy in the world, as well as the chief energy consumers. In addition, future sources will be discussed. Finally, we will look at OPEC, one of the major forces in the world's current energy situation.

Doug Sneyd

"It's called Energy Crisis."

Reprinted by permission of *Toronto Star* Syndicate.

Section A
Energy Production

Every country is capable of producing energy. The sun is the world's primary energy source, and thus the amounts of energy generated by a nation will depend to a large extent on its technological ability to convert solar energy to other useful forms. Throughout history, people have always depended on the sun for energy. They have gradually discovered and learned to extract solar energy from various sources.

The form of solar energy first used by human beings was *food energy*. Food energy is largely solar energy converted by *photosynthesis* into a form that animals and people can employ. Animal and human labour are therefore basic products of the sun. Even today, all nations depend on food for basic energy; some are more successful than others in obtaining it. An examination of column I in Appendix 2 indicates the national differences in getting energy from food. The average daily amount of energy taken in by an individual ranges from 7 182 kJ to 14 322 kJ, a ratio of 1:2. This is a very large variation for something as essential as food. There is a much narrower range in the amounts of food energy required each day by an individual. These figures are given in column N, and are calculated by the FAO on the basis of climatic demands, body size, and age composition of national populations; they range from 8 835 kJ to 11 377 kJ, a ratio of only 1:1.29. We should note that the range of energy achieved overlaps the required range at both ends. This indicates that some countries produce far more food energy than they need, while others produce far less. Thus, while people have always converted solar energy into food, some societies do it more efficiently than others.

Fire, or the burning of plant matter, is another simple form of solar energy conversion. The discovery of fire was one of the main steps leading to advanced technology. Today many societies still depend on wood as a fuel, and thus some areas with increasing populations face the danger of severe deforestation. India, for example, depends heavily on wood as a source of fuel. The country is trying to protect its few remaining forests, so Indians face a wood fuel crisis more serious than any oil crisis confronting the more developed countries.

Photosynthesis is the process by which the chlorophyll in plants uses the energy of sunlight to transform carbon dioxide and water into carbohydrates and oxygen. All life ultimately depends upon this process.

All plant matter, including timber, is the direct product of photosynthesis.

In the Sahel region of Africa, all the wood near the villages has been cut; the villagers have been forced to journey farther afield in search of it. Wood has become extremely scarce, and the arid land has become unprotected. A process called *desertification* has set in, whereby the formerly wooded land has gradually turned into desert.

Flowing or *falling water* is another example of converted solar energy, used by societies at all levels of technical achievement. Water-wheels and mills are primitive methods of tapping the energy of the solar-powered water cycle. At a higher technical level, hydroelectric generating stations serve the same purpose, but more efficiently.

Another important step leading to advanced technology occurred when some societies learned to extract the solar energy stored in *coal and oil*. Much of the world's coal is formed from the compacted remains of forests that existed millions of years ago. This coal is found in rocks that date back about 250 000 000 years to the Carboniferous period of geologic time. Thus the burning of coal *now* represents the

The Kariba dam on the Zambezi River. This is a technologically advanced way of tapping the energy of the water cycle.

S. T. Darke, Salisbury, S. Rhodesia

use of fossilized solar energy millions of years old. This is also true of oil and natural gas, except that the conversion of solar energy is more indirect (sun ➡→plants➡→marine life➡→oil and gas, rather than sun➡→plants➡→coal). Because coal, oil, and natural gas are forms of energy stored from the past they are usually called *fossil fuels*. These fuels take millions of years to form; once they are used up, it will be millions of years before new supplies are available.

The ability to extract stored solar energy from fossil fuels permitted some countries to develop as industrial powers. Societies that used fossil energy—initially coal—were greatly changed. In this period of change, which is called the *Industrial Revolution*, countries also learned to produce food energy with greater efficiency. In turn, they developed a new attitude; the industrialized countries began to feel that the physical environment was full of opportunities and challenges that could be met with new and better technology. These societies saw that people were free to choose from the many life styles offered by the environment. This attitude, or philosophy, is called *possibilism* and is the opposite of *determinism*, an attitude generally found in preindustrial societies. Determinists argue that the physical environment determines human responses and therefore people have little choice of life styles.

Developments in energy production have allowed people to make use of their environment in a number of ways. Today, in many parts of the world, people can choose from a wide range of foods, jobs, residential locations, and leisure activities. Solar energy conversion technology, then, has become one of the main aspects of human progress, freeing people from the bondage of insufficient food production and its accompanying poverty.

Statistical Interpretation

4-1 As a symbol of energy conversion technology we will use per capita electricity generation as shown in column P of Appendix 2. We want to know how well it correlates with the ability to grow food as indicated in column I of Appendix 2. Use the *rank correlation technique*, explained in Appendix 3, for the *sample* of countries marked with an asterisk (*) in Appendix 2.
    a) Calculate the value of ρ (rho).
    b) Suggest explanations for the degree of correlation between the two variables exhibited by the value of ρ.

√ 4-2 Construct a map of the world with *proportional circles* (see Appendix 3) to show the percentage regional distribution of energy production given in Fig. 4-1.

Fig. 4-1

Energy production by major region, all forms of energy in *tonnes of coal equivalent* (tce)

Major Region	Production	
	Total (tce)	Percentage
Africa	456 480 000	5.8
Asia (excl. USSR)	323 030 000	3.8
Central America (incl. Colombia/Venezuela)	323 690 000	3.8
Communist Countries	2 774 020 000	32.4
Europe	652 730 000	7.6
Middle East	1 508 050 000	17.6
North America	2 305 100 000	27.0
Oceania	115 790 000	1.4
South America	95 880 000	1.1
World total	8 554 770 000	100.0

Source: *UN Statistical Yearbook*, 1976.

Tonnes of coal equivalent is a measure used to make comparisons possible between different countries, some of which may use little coal. Values are obtained by converting the energy content of oil, gas, hydroelectricity, and other fuels to the amount of coal that would be needed to produce the same amount of energy.

The main sources of energy in the world differ from region to region. The Middle East, for instance, produces very little hydroelectricity or coal but a great deal of oil, whereas Europe produces large quantities of coal and hydroelectricity but relatively little oil. Production data for the major sources of energy are given in Figs. 4-2 through 4-5. Are there any surprises?

Fig. 4-2

The world's major coal-producing countries

Country	t
USA	568 158 000
USSR	484 668 000
China	470 000 000
Poland	171 625 000
UK	128 616 000
West Germany	96 755 000
India	95 890 000
South Africa	69 440 000
Australia	61 726 000
North Korea	35 000 000
Czechoslovakia	28 383 000
France	23 652 000
Canada	21 710 000
Japan	18 999 000
South Korea	17 585 000
World total	2 367 900 000

Source: *UN Statistical Yearbook*, 1976.

Fig. 4-3
The world's major oil-producing countries (* = OPEC member)

Country	t
USSR	491 000 000
USA	413 090 000
Saudi Arabia*	352 394 000
Iran*	267 623 000
Venezuela*	122 150 000
Iraq*	111 168 000
Kuwait*	105 232 000
Nigeria*	88 440 000
United Arab Emirates*	80 458 000
China	80 000 000
Libya*	71 533 000
Canada	67 778 000
Indonesia*	64 116 000
Algeria*	45 057 000
Mexico	36 456 000
Qatar*	21 102 000
Argentina	20 773 000
Australia	20 159 000
Oman	17 016 000
Romania	14 590 000
Gabon	11 375 000
Trinidad and Tobago	11 125 000
World total	2 646 290 000

Source: *UN Statistical Yearbook*, 1976.

Fig. 4-4
The world's major natural gas producing countries

Country	m^3 (thousands)
USA	546 578 340
USSR	298 000 000
Netherlands	90 140 106
Canada	75 800 000
UK	36 074 000
Romania	32 048 000
Iran	21 834 000
West Germany	18 921 000
Mexico	14 991 000
Italy	14 578 000
World total	1 245 000 000

Source: *UN Statistical Yearbook*, 1976.

Fig. 4-5
The world's major hydroelectricity - producing countries

Country	mkW·h
USA	303 195
Canada	202 404
USSR	125 987
Japan	85 906
Norway	77 496
Brazil	71 991
France	59 892
Sweden	57 669
Italy	42 116
India	33 247
Switzerland	33 069
Spain	28 750
Austria	23 745
Yugoslavia	19 317
West Germany	17 111
New Zealand	16 868
Australia	15 217
Mexico	15 140
World total	Not available

Source: *UN Statistical Yearbook*, 1976.

Statistical Interpretation

4-3 Looking at Figs. 4-2 through 4-5, would you say that the generation of power depends more on technological expertise or on geographical location? Give reasons for your answer.

4-4 The world uses coal, oil, natural gas, and hydroelectricity in very approximately equal quantities. Clearly the USA, which ranks first in possession of all four energy sources, is the top producer. Can you calculate which other countries are among the top ten energy producers?

4-5 Fig. 4-6 is a graded shading map illustrating the geographical distribution of the production of electricity. How does this map compare with others drawn for population increase (Chapter 1) and degree of industrialization (Chapter 3)? What explanations can you suggest for the variations in energy production around the world?

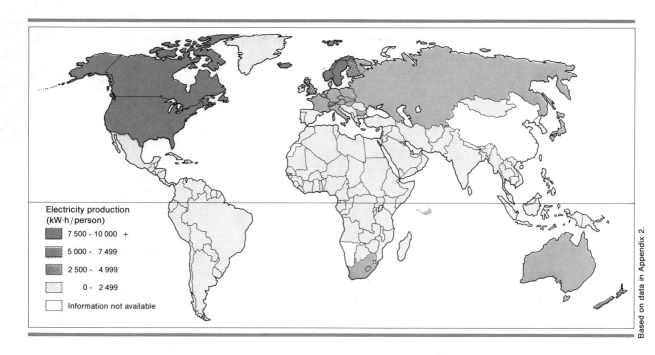

Based on data in Appendix 2.

Electricity production
(kW·h/person)

	7 500 - 10 000 +
	5 000 - 7 499
	2 500 - 4 999
	0 - 2 499
	Information not available

Fig. 4-6
Geographical distribution of
production of electricity

Section B
Energy Consumption

Every country uses energy, even if it is mainly in the food its people consume. This basic energy is used in the business of daily living: walking, playing, and most of all, working.

Most societies have now progressed beyond this basic level. They use energy for additional purposes: some to pump irrigation water and provide light and heat for their people; others to drive powerful machinery and transport people and goods from place to place. As the technical ability of a society develops, that society makes increasing demands on its own power-producing capacity. Increases in industry and trade cause a society to make the best use of its power sources, and also to seek new and more efficient methods of power generation.

Electricity is the product of some of the most efficient methods of power generation, and its large-scale production may therefore be taken as representing the energy achievements of any particular country. It has been used more and more often in the last few years, and its use will probably continue to increase for many years to come. It is clean at its point of use, immediate in action, and versatile. Accordingly, the demands for electricity have often outstripped the supplying abilities of hydroelectric generating stations. Therefore coal (mostly), oil and gas, and uranium (increasingly) have been brought in to help generate greater quantities of electricity. Indeed, about half the coal produced in the world is used for generating electricity. Electricity generated in this way is called *thermal electricity*, to distinguish it from hydroelectricity. Thermal electricity is now more important than hydroelectricity, and will probably become more so as the demand for electricity outstrips the capacity of even big new hydro projects.

Energy consumption is related therefore to technical ability and level of industrialization. Fig. 4-7 shows you some data on energy consumption.

Fig. 4-7

Energy consumption by major region, all forms of energy in *tonnes of coal equivalent* **(tce)**

Major region	Consumption		
	Total (tce)	Percentage of world total	kg/person
Africa	157 580 000	1.9	393
Asia (excl. USSR)	673 680 000	8.4	545
Central America (incl. Colombia and Venezuela)	166 260 000	2.1	1 174
Communist Countries	2 589 640 000	32.4	2 075
Europe	1 467 520 000	18.3	4 023
Middle East	126 580 000	1.6	1 055
North America	2 575 610 000	32.2	10 888
Oceania	100 740 000	1.3	4 782
South America	144 590 000	1.8	813
World total	8 002 200 000	100.0	

Source: *UN Statistical Yearbook*, 1976.

Statistical Interpretation

4-6 Using the data in Fig. 4-7 construct a located proportional circle map in the manner shown in assignment 4-2 and Appendix 3. What significant differences do you notice between the production and consumption maps? How would you explain these differences?

4-7 From the data in the totals columns of Figs. 4-1 and 4-7, calculate consumption: production ratios. For example, North America's ratio is 1:1.08, indicating that it is only just self-sufficient in energy. Which is the least self-sufficient region? The most self-sufficient? How do per capita consumption figures affect your observations about self-sufficiency?

4-8 Classify the world into regions of energy surplus, energy balance, and energy deficit. Suggest some possible solutions to a deficit situation.

4-9 List the world's major energy flows (e.g. from the Middle East to Europe) from the information given in Figs. 4-1 and 4-7. Construct a map to show these flows, and indicate which flows are major, and which are minor.

As a result of these energy movements and their importance to the deficit areas, it is little wonder that half of the world's trade is in oil and that half of the world's shipping tonnage consists of oil tankers. Indeed, it is no surprise that tankers are the largest ships afloat and that oil tankers are the products of the world's most advanced shipbuilding technology. Nor is it surprising that Japan and Europe, with their dependence on the world's major energy flows, are the world's largest shipbuilders.

The Organization of Petroleum Exporting Countries (OPEC) has demonstrated that the energy-deficit regions cannot rely on the cheapness—or the security—of trade with the surplus regions. Since 1973, OPEC has made the deficit areas aware of the extent of their dependence.

The price of crude oil in the Middle East in 1950 was about $15/m^3, while in 1970 it was about $11/m^3. Throughout the 1950s and 1960s the oil-deficit countries consumed oil at bargain prices. At the same time, the oil-surplus countries felt increasingly aggrieved at the one-sided nature of the bargain. Accordingly they were in a mood to organize a cartel, or selling arrangement, to raise the price of oil. Conflict between Arabs and Israelis in 1972 provided the key opportunity, and the Arab oil exporters used the political problem to provide added leverage in their effort to raise the price of oil. Oil embargoes were instituted against countries supporting Israel; quotas were introduced on sales to other nations, to make them switch their policies to a definite pro-Arab position. At the same time, prices were driven upward within a matter of months to about $70/m^3.

The deficit areas have responded in various ways. One way has been to attempt to cut back consumption; from 1973 to 1976 actual world consumption of oil fell by 2%, against a price increase for crude oil from OPEC of about 600%. OPEC does not supply the total world market, of course, but it nevertheless makes a significant contribution, and its price rises certainly trigger increases in other oil producers' prices. Consumers do not usually use less fuel when prices are increased; their inability to use less fuel despite rising prices is called *demand inelasticity*. The more developed countries, which are also largely the energy-deficit ones, have a very high demand inelasticity for energy. This means that their populations do not reduce their energy consumption, even when prices are extremely high. This is why OPEC can feel reasonably secure in raising oil prices.

There are, however, some constraints upon its ability to raise prices limitlessly. The chief constraint is the technological capacity of the deficit regions. If oil prices are *too* high these countries can turn to their own more expensive supplies, or to other energy sources altogether. Their own supplies may be locked away in remote areas such as the Arctic, or the sea bed; their oil may be found in deposits such as the Alberta tar sands and the Colorado oil shales, where it is difficult to extract. It is only when international oil prices rise to *more than* the equivalent cost of Arctic or tar sands production that it becomes worthwhile to open up these new areas or develop new methods of extraction. This new development may be valuable for other reasons as well, such as national security or the assurance of supplies.

An underground mine in the oil shales of Colorado.

The energy consumption picture is a fine balance of competing views: the deficit regions want energy at as *low* a cost as possible but they also want security of supply; the oil exporters want as *high* a price as possible but they also want security of markets. It is of no benefit to oil exporters to charge $500/m³ if most users then turn to another source. There is also disagreement among the countries that export oil: some want to sell their oil *now* so that they can buy economic development quickly; others want to *conserve* their oil because they think they will be able to sell it at a higher price in the future. Most users generally want to *increase* their own supplies to continue economic expansion, but some want to *reduce* consumption now to ensure a supply in the future.

Discussion and Research

1. A few of the advantages of electricity are mentioned in the text. Can you suggest more? Can you suggest any disadvantages?
2. It is claimed that North America contains only about 6% of the world's population and yet uses about 35% of the world's energy.
   a) What is the implied criticism in this statement?
   b) What would be the probable general value system of a person who makes such a criticism?
   c) How would you answer the criticism?
3. Why do you think energy flows are probably more important to deficit regions than to surplus regions? What advantages do both sides obtain, and who gains most?
4. What are all the likely effects of a rise in the price of energy? What if the price of oil alone goes up relative to the other energy sources? What if oil becomes cheaper again?
5. What values are appealed to by calls for greater national energy independence?
6. Can you justify calls for a reduced rate of growth of energy production?
7. If you were an OPEC minister, what arguments would you present to justify a further increase in the price of oil?
8. Within OPEC there are many different views regarding price policy and the rate of oil extraction. Suggest what these different views are, and why.

Section C
Future Sources of Energy

need depends on life style

There has been much talk of an energy crisis. Some people think that we have come to rely too much on energy for the maintenance of our ways of life. Others see no problem; indeed, there are those who want even greater energy production.

People's opinions about energy production and consumption will be determined by the life styles that they value. The matter of life style is important. A society's way of life affects its demands for industrialization and trade; these demands in turn bring about patterns of energy production and consumption. For example, in a wealthy society, where people insist on the latest comforts such as dishwashers or new cars, industrialization is great and much energy is consumed. The amount of energy produced and consumed by a society, then, depends on the life styles of its members.

However, would it not make equal sense to say that the amount of energy produced determines the types of life styles that develop in a society? In a less developed country, starving peasants almost certainly do not prefer their life style to others. The society's lack of technology and its inability to produce energy are largely responsible for the peasant's condition.

Energy-producing capabilities are the result of complex factors; *good education, a spirit of scientific enquiry, capital* for development programs, and *effective market demand* for worthwhile production. Once again we see the need in a less developed country for everything to be programmed together; *sectoral planning* brings no rewards. In a less developed country, market demand is not great and so little power is produced. The lack of generating capacity, then, determines basic life styles. In more developed countries, however, the situation tends to be the other way around; life styles generally determine energy-producing capacity.

In the more developed world we should therefore first determine our preferred life styles. There are two basic ways of life from which to choose: a highly powered life style full of comfort and convenience; and a low-powered life style centring on a stable environment and a

Sectoral planning is planning for the development of a sector or part of the economy only. For example, planning for the reduction of birth rates is sectoral when no plans are made at the same time for improved old age security and for all the other changes in economy and society that a reduction in birth rates brings.

UNESCO

belief in anti-growth philosophy. The likelihood and pace of future developments depend, therefore, upon our beliefs, and ultimately upon our values. Meanwhile, what do you think the less developed countries will be trying to do?

If future energy developments are desired, they could occur in the following areas.

1. Conventional Oil and Gas

Production can be maintained, even increased, by employing more efficient, but also more costly extraction techniques in existing fields. Also, new fields may be opened up. When an oil field is first opened up the trapped oil will usually be under pressure; drilling produces "gushers" and the pressure must be controlled. Eventually, as production continues, the natural pressure lessens and the rate of oil flow diminishes. Simple pumping (*primary extraction*) is then added to maintain the desired rate of flow, and in time more powerful pumps are needed. Costs inevitably rise. Under natural pressure, an oil field may yield about 10% of its contents; with pumping another 10% or so can be extracted.

Some of the remaining oil can be obtained by what are called *secondary extraction* methods. In secondary extraction, shafts are drilled to below the level of oil, and the rock is flooded with water pumped down under great pressure. Oil is then driven upward by the water into the areas near the well, where it is available for pumping. Another 30% of the field's contents may be obtained in this manner. About half of North America's oil production is currently obtained by secondary extraction techniques.

Even after secondary extraction has been used there is still a huge amount of oil left in the field. The recovery of some of this remaining oil requires the use of special chemicals instead of water in the underground flooding process. Carbon dioxide has been used in such *tertiary extraction*, but oil companies are looking increasingly to special

If a well "gushes" these days it is regarded as a problem, because it denotes poor drilling control techniques. In the early days, a "gusher" was a reason for joy; oil had been found. However, the danger of fires and explosions is now given greater attention.

Fig. 4-8
Secondary oil extraction

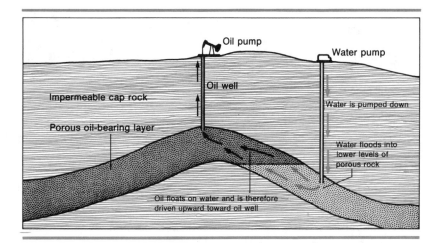

Oil pump

Water pump

Oil well

Impermeable cap rock

Water is pumped down

Porous oil-bearing layer

Water floods into
lower levels of
porous rock

Oil floats on water and is therefore
driven upward toward oil well

low-viscosity fluids. Costs naturally go up. Whether or not it is worth engaging in tertiary production depends upon the selling price of oil. If it is too low, the oil stays in the ground, and is not even counted as known reserves. But price rises make tertiary recovery worthwhile, and so known reserves increase and even double without the need for new drilling. It is not yet known what limits there are to oil recovery from existing fields, because production depends on a combination of technology and price. There can be oil in wells that have been closed down; it is simply too expensive to recover at prevailing prices.

Even within existing oil fields not all oil pools have yet been discovered. Continued drilling still reveals new pools which can be brought into production whenever the price is right. There is still more exploratory drilling in Alberta and Saskatchewan, for instance, than in the Arctic, partly because the prairie basin is not yet fully worked over, partly because drilling costs are cheaper in the prairies than in the north, and partly because the connection of a producing well to the existing pipeline system is cheaper in the prairie provinces than in the Arctic.

It is also possible to increase oil production by developing new areas. Generally the lowest cost areas, where extraction is easiest, are opened first; more difficult and higher cost areas thus remain unused until the price of oil rises sufficiently to make their development worthwhile. The cost of drilling an exploratory well on the Arctic mainland, for example, is about 20 times higher than in Alberta; if it is on an Arctic island the cost is 40 times higher; if it is in Arctic offshore waters the cost can be as much as 150 times as high as in Alberta. And remember that these are just exploratory wells, drilled before oil is even found.

In addition to the higher drilling costs in "frontier areas" there are also problems connected with securing access to markets. Pipelines are the most efficient means of transporting oil and gas, but their capital

Novosti Press Agency

Within the last decade the USSR has moved into the position of a major oil producer. This is a drilling rig in the newly discovered Tyumen oil field of western Siberia.

Even with the aid of advanced geological testing and accumulated knowledge of underground structures, oil companies never know whether or not oil actually exists in the ground until a well is sunk. About one well in ten strikes worthwhile oil.

Novosti Press Agency

Pipelines are very expensive but extremely efficient. They are ideal when large quantities need to be moved regularly. This is near Omsk.

cost is enormous. They are only worthwhile if huge quantities of oil and gas are available and if there is sufficient demand in the consuming area. The quantities of oil in a remote area have to be much larger than in a more accessible field before transporting oil in pipelines is even considered. In addition, the price of oil and gas has to be high enough to cover the costs not only of exploratory drilling and actual production but also of transportation under difficult conditions.

2. Non-conventional Oil and Gas

Oil and gas will continue to be available even when all existing and frontier fields are economically exhausted; the fuels will come from sources that are now tapped only experimentally. The non-conventional sources of oil are tar sands, oil shales, heavy oils, and coal. Vast quantities of oil are locked away in these non-conventional sources; for example, in the Athabasca Tar Sands alone there are about 130 000 000 000 m³ of oil. In 1975, Canada's oil consumption was about 120 000 000 m³, so given the development of appropriate technology, these tar sands would provide Canada with oil for quite a while. In the USA there are even larger deposits of oil shales throughout Colorado and Wyoming, equal to 255 000 000 000 m³. Heavy oils, as at Cold Lake in Alberta, offer other sources of energy once the technology necessary to extract the oil has been developed.

Synthetic oil and gas from coal represent yet another huge reserve. The technology is not new: *gas* has been made from coal for over 150 years, although it has been replaced in most areas by natural gas; *oil* was made from coal in Germany during World War II (and in South Africa today). However large-scale operational technology is needed if synthetic oil and gas are to be an important source of energy in the future.

Non-conventional crude oil does not flow like conventional crude. It is very thick and requires some sort of processing before it can be used. The oil in the tar sands, for instance, has to be separated from gritty sand particles. In its natural state it is virtually a solid rock, and it requires mining rather than drilling and pumping.

The technique of oil distillation from coal, used by the Germans in World War II, has been lost; scientists have died, and papers have been destroyed.

3. Coal

Production can be greatly expanded under existing technology. One of the reasons that coal has been neglected for so many years is that it was rejected in favour of cheaper and cleaner oil and gas. But OPEC has changed that, for oil is no longer a cheaper fuel, and since the early 1970s coal has been increasingly important. Reserves are vast in many countries: Canada alone has enough known reserves to last nearly 4 000 years at current rates of use. In addition there are huge supplies of lignite—or soft coal—which offer the possibility of direct thermal electricity generation at the mining site. However lignite has a low thermal efficiency in comparison with coal, and it poses transportation problems because it is prone to explode spontaneously.

4. Hydroelectricity

Most of the productive sites close to major markets have already been developed, and there is little prospect of making them more efficient. Therefore, developments are being forced into remoter locations, where the most productive sites are used first. Since it is not worth building expensive transmission lines unless quantities of electricity are large, projects in remote sites, such as Churchill Falls and James Bay in Canada, must be huge. Electricity is neither cheap, nor easy to

Even though it is inexhaustible, hydroelectricity is to some extent limited. Water will certainly never disappear from the earth, (although it may change form as in ice ages), but it will never be increased in quantity either. The only way to increase hydroelectric capacity is to use the same water many times over, either through a series of hydro dams along a river, or pumped storage facilities, wherein the used water is recycled during off-peak hours back to a reservoir upstream from the dam so that it may be used again.

Novosti Press Agency

Part of the engine room of a dam on the Yenisei River in southern Siberia. These dams are among the world's largest.

Work on the gigantic Krasnoyarsk hydro station in southern Siberia.

Novosti Press Agency

transport, despite popular assumptions to the contrary. The operations involved in developing hydroelectricity in remote areas are just as complex as those used in the mining of frontier oil and gas. However, once the necessary equipment is installed, hydroelectricity has one great advantage over oil and gas; it is an inexhaustible source of energy.

5. Nuclear Electricity

This can be produced close to large urban and industrial markets. However, its major disadvantage is that people are nervous about radiation which can be given off in a number of ways. One source of radiation is radioactive waste. Nuclear electricity is currently produced by a variety of fission reactors, which all produce radioactive wastes. Experimentation is going on in the development of fusion reactors, which yield no waste, but scientists say it may be around the year 2000 before anything worthwhile is developed.

The following letter and diagram present some reassurances in the matter of nuclear wastes.

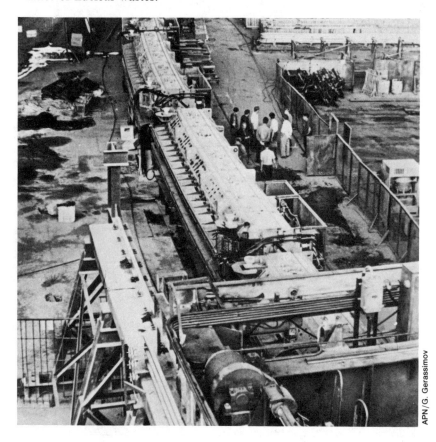

Experiments are taking place to develop power from nuclear fusion, which produces no radioactive waste. Scientists expect to succeed eventually.

APN/G. Gerassimov

Nuclear power

I have just read Dr. Gordon Edwards comments (May 24) on my address, Why Nuclear, to the Manitoba Electrical Association and felt I should reply on the question of nuclear waste disposal.

. . .

Dr. Edwards' main criticism of our program is that no geologist can give him an absolute guarantee that a geologic structure is going to remain undisturbed for several hundred thousand years. Of course they can't. No one should expect them to. However, you don't have to be a geologist to come to the conclusion that, if a structure has remained undisturbed for the past several hundred million years, through several ice ages and all the other natural phenomena that have occurred over that period, there is a high probability that it will remain undisturbed for the next few hundred thousand.

Furthermore, we plan to incorporate the wastes into an insoluble matrix so that, even in the remote chance they are disturbed, they will be released to the environment at such a slow rate that they should not cause any significant damage.

. . .

Dr. Edwards raises the question of retrievability. Yet he knows full well that we intend to maintain the wastes in the geologic repository in a retrievable manner for several decades to allow us further time to demonstrate the technology. He also knows that we have developed and are demonstrating surface repositories into which the wastes can be safely placed in the very unlikely event that they have to be retrieved.

We, in the industry, do not claim that there are no risks associated with nuclear energy. We do claim that the risks are low in comparison to those arising from other human activities and natural phenomena and the experience record bears us out. It was this relative risk and the relative benefits which I was trying to deal with in my address.

R. G. HART
Vice-President
Atomic Energy of Canada Limited
Whiteshell Nuclear Research Establishment
Pinawa, Man.

Letter to The Globe and Mail 1976 6 3

Accident risks estimated for the entire US population as the result of the operation of 100 nuclear power plants are compared here with the risks from several leading causes of accidents in terms of the average number of deaths per year attributable to each cause. (The averages for the latter categories are rounded to the nearest 1 000 fatalities). The figure for the risk of death from nuclear accidents is based on the conservative assumption that there is likely to be one major release of radioactivity in the US every 1 000 years, resulting in about 1 000 eventual deaths from cancer, and that once in 10 000 years there could be a more serious accident resulting in approximately 5 000 eventual deaths. The average risk from nuclear reactors is obviously extremely small compared with other risks that society accepts.

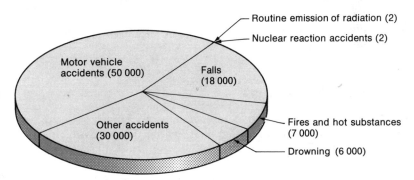

Scientific American 1976 1

Discussion and Research

9. In June of 1976 the State of California held a referendum, called Proposition 15, on the subject of the continued development of nuclear power in the state. The move to ban development was defeated two to one. How would you vote if a similar referendum were held in your area? How would you persuade others to support you?

10. In 1974 India exploded a "nuclear device", using nuclear technology it had acquired from Canada. Since then Canada has sold nuclear reactors to other countries, notably Korea and Argentina. "The less developed countries need power for development," say the proponents of the sales; "We cannot refuse to share our abilities; we would be supporting poverty and starvation if we did not help." The opponents claim that sales are unwise in view of India's explosion. Would you sell nuclear power stations to other countries?
11. India has the ability to generate nuclear power; it also has the ability to make nuclear bombs. Many of its people are starving. What are some of the arguments for and against India's manufacture of nuclear bombs?

6. Wood

Wood is a primitive fuel, but it is still important in many areas. Its use could easily be expanded; indeed new designs of wood-burning stoves show great improvements in efficiency. In New England the local electric utility is even thinking of building a wood-burning thermal electric generating plant. Also, a fuel called methanol can be made from wood and used to drive cars. But it is improbable that wood power could be made available in the quantities required for large-scale production. There are too many other demands upon the world's forests, and the thermal efficiency of wood is quite low.

The Science Council of Canada has estimated (1977 9) that if methanol were used to replace gasoline in cars then an area the size of Nova Scotia would be needed to grow trees to fuel 10 000 000 cars for a yearly average of 15 000 km.

7. Animal Excrement

Animal excrement is a source of methane gas, which is used for a variety of purposes including lighting, heating, and driving machines and motors. There are many methane gas extraction plants around the world, mostly on farms.

Animal excrement is in use on all continents of the world: for the Chinese it is a major local source of energy; in India, dried dung makes up half the country's fuel supply; in Britain, the methane gas extracted from the excrement is used to drive experimental cars, and in Canada, it is used as a heating source on some prairie farms. While increased use is possible, this source of energy is naturally limited.

8. Garbage

This is another publicized source of energy, especially in urban areas. Garbage is already widely used in Europe to generate steam heat, and its use is increasing in North America too. Two of the major advantages of burning garbage for energy are that first, it eases the pollution problem, and second, it eliminates the need for landfill sites which waste valuable space. The main problem with using garbage as an energy source appears to be the time and trouble it takes to sort the suitably combustible material from the rest of the garbage. We can look for further developments in this area.

9. The Wind

Energy supplies are available from the wind. The wind's power has traditionally been used for milling grain and pumping water, but the latest wind-powered machines are designed for generating electricity. In Canada, wind turbines already produce power for the Magdalen Islands in the Gulf of St. Lawrence, and they are proposed for local use throughout the northland. In the USA there is even a radio station run by wind power, although its broadcasts are a little erratic. The possibilities for local power production are considerable, especially in persistently windy locations.

10. Tidal Power

This was first developed in northwest France at the mouth of the Rance River. It works well, except for two disadvantages: there is a dead time of about an hour or so at high tide, and another five hours later, at low tide; also, the times of the tides become progressively later on succeeding days. There has been much talk in Nova Scotia of harnessing the Fundy tides; it is technically possible, but it has not yet been considered economically worthwhile.

11. Solar Power

This was also first developed in France, at Mont Louis in the Pyrenees. The solar oven is very effective; the sun's rays, reflected and concentrated by giant mirrors, are capable of melting steel. There is no doubt that solar power harnessed at ground level has great potential, probably more for space heating than for anything else.

One of the main disadvantages of a ground-level solar station is the amount of land that would be needed to make it economical. It has been estimated that a station in Southern California would have to cover as large an area of land as the town for which it was providing energy. Near Toronto, a solar plant would require a land area of at least 130 km² for each 1 000 MW of electricity produced, and would require an as yet nonexistent energy storage system to make it practical. In order to avoid these problems, engineers are increasingly thinking of locating the huge stations in space, and beaming the collected solar energy by microwave down to compact receiving stations on earth. The following newspaper article of 1978 2 9 gives details of one such project.

An experimental wind-powered electric generator in Russia.

**The solar oven at Mont Louis in
southern France.**

Gigantic satellite urged for U.S. energy

WASHINGTON (Reuter-Special)—A staggering scheme for gigantic solar power satellites measuring 29 kilometres (18 miles) long by 6½ kilometres (4 miles) wide to be built in space has been put to the United States.

The scheme calls for 500 workers to man an orbiting factory to build the satellites, which could beam down enough solar power to supply half the U.S. energy needs by the year 2000.

The proposal that the U.S. undertake the largest space project in history at an estimated cost of $40 billion to $80 billion came yesterday from the Boeing Aircraft Corporation.

"The technology is in this country now," Boeing scientist Ralph Nansen said before meeting with presidential science adviser Dr. Frank Press.

He suggested that the satellites could be built in low earth orbit from materials ferried up by large, unmanned space freighters similar to the U.S. space shuttle now undergoing tests in the U.S.

Nansen, a mechanical engineer who headed Boeing teams involved in several previous U.S. space projects, said the corporation has been

An experimental solar cooker at Dakar in Senegal.

studying the solar energy concept for about 10 years.

It proposes that after construction in low orbit, a solar power spacecraft weighing about 110 000 tons, would be moved out into orbit 35 000 kilometres (21,750 miles) above the equator.

The solar cells on its vast platform would transform the sun's light into microwave energy and beam it to antennas on earth measuring about eight kilometres by 11 kilometres (7 miles) which would convert the microwaves into electricity.

One platform could supply the energy needs of a million homes and Boeing officials said 100 of them would supply twice the current U.S. energy capacity. "With proper care they could literally last hundreds of years," said Nansen.

The Toronto Star 1978 2 9

12. Geothermal Power

This is now produced in only a few countries, chiefly Italy, USA, and New Zealand. Small amounts are also produced in Japan, Mexico, California and Iceland. Geothermal power is created when volcanic activity produces steam under enough pressure to drive turbines. The areas of volcanic activity are highly localized; therefore, future developments, though possible, are unlikely to be significant in the total energy picture.

13. Water

This may yet prove to be *the* major energy source of the future, since there are huge amounts of it on earth. For example, its energy could be tapped by a wave converter which would turn the energy of waves into usable electricity. The British are in fact experimenting with wave converters off the west coast of Scotland.

Water is most important, however, as a source of hydrogen. Water can be broken down into hydrogen and oxygen, the hydrogen piped away for burning as a fuel, and the oxygen "waste" used for purifying the environment. And when hydrogen is burned it combines with oxygen and turns back to water. The concept is excellent, but no one yet knows how to break water down into hydrogen and oxygen *cheaply enough*. It can be done, but it requires large amounts of electrical energy. The solution may come when electrical power generation becomes cheap.

Nuclear power may prove to be the answer to the problem of cheap electricity, and thereby the widespread use of hydrogen, *if* experimental breeder reactors prove successful and *if* fusion becomes viable. These two energy sources—nuclear power for stationary use and hydrogen for mobile use—could well provide an answer to the age-old search for "something better".

What do you think of Glenn Seaborg's vision of the future in the following article?

Nuclear energy and our future

by GLENN T. SEABORG
Nobel Prize, 1951

Man lives by energy. The more he can put to work, the better he lives. By harnessing energy, he can flick a switch to pump water, start a train, heat a home or light a city.

In the 21st century, most of this energy will come from the nucleus of the atom, and by using it wisely man can improve the way he produces food, uses water and raw materials, handles waste and builds cities.

The need for improvement is evident. By the year 2000, experts predict the earth's population will double. Some expect an eventual population of 15 thousand million people, five times today's total.

But the earth itself will not grow, and to support these extra thousands of millions we must learn to use and reuse our resources with an efficiency we rarely even approach today.

Energy is a resource, and by far the most important contribution the atom will make to the world of tomorrow will result from the combination of very cheap electricity and heat for use in manufacturing processes which it can make possible, particularly with the full development of breeder reactors which create more nuclear fuel than they burn.

One must emphasize that having a large amount of cheap energy is not a panacea in itself. We must develop the technology to take advantage of this energy; it must be applied skillfully, productively and wisely by people who have the tools and training to use it.

Some scientists have considered the concept of using these huge amounts of energy in giant nuclear powered industrial complexes, which we have called "Nuplexes", the energy heart of which would be breeder reactors, with a generating capacity in the multi-million kilowatt range.

A variety of industrial plants coupled to the energy centre would interchange goods and services through a maze of underground arteries, conveyor belts and pipelines.

. . .

If we can develop the sophisticated chemical techniques to capitalize on the cheap power, we might some day be able to completely recycle all our materials and water so that we would have an endless supply of raw materials and a virtually junkless civilization.

It should be emphasized, however, that planning, setting up and successfully operating facilities like this will be a mammoth undertaking requiring great advance study, a massive infusion of capital and, above all, the devotion and hard work of a great many talented people.

Yet the prospects are so great that they have excited the imagination of many of us.

A study conducted last year at the U.S. Atomic Energy Commission's Oak Ridge National Laboratory looked into the possibility of placing nuclear agro-industrial complexes in arid areas such as desert coastal plains.

We know already, for instance, that the economic use of nuclear energy to desalt water is not far off. A large dual purpose nuclear powered electric generating and water desalination plant has been planned for construction in the United States near the city of Los Angeles.

A report on energy centres by the Oak Ridge National Laboratory, which will be available later this year, indicates some exciting prospects for coupling large dual-purpose plants located in coastal desert areas with highly scientific farms or "food factories."

One study in this report considers the energy heart as a huge breeder reactor which could generate 1 000 000 kilowatts of electricity and desalt 400 million gallons [1 800 000 000 *l*] of water a day. At the same time, power from the plant could be used to make ammonia fertilizer and phosphorus-bearing fertilizer. It could be that many other by-products from the seawater brine could be produced and used locally or exported.

Electricity from the plant would be used for highly mechanized farming and food processing, as well as to supply light, air-conditioning and power for transport and communications for the personnel operating the complex.

On 200 000 acres [80 000 ha], irrigated with the desalted water and fertilized with locally manufactured products, crops would be grown which were specifically bred for the area. Hardly anything would be left to chance or the whims of nature.

Such a food factory could produce a thousand million pounds of grain each year, enough to feed almost 2 500 000 people at a level of 2 400 calories a day. In addition, it could export enough fertilizer to other agricultural areas to cultivate another 10 000 000 acres [4 000 000 ha] of land.

In our concern over the world's food supply we tend to concentrate our thoughts on the production of more food, often forgetting that one-fifth of the world's entire annual food crop is lost or destroyed by pests and spoilage.

By the year 2000, we expect to have largely perfected the techniques of food irradiation so as to greatly reduce such losses. Carefully controlled doses of radiation from certain radioactive isotopes can destroy pests, extend the shelf and storage life of fresh foods and help create new and hardier crop strains.

Whenever and wherever man can benefit from heat and electricity, nuclear energy in its many forms can help bring about a better world. Several other nuclear uses of the future deserve at least a brief mention.

Nuclear power could be coupled with tube-well pumps to tap the vast water resources which lie deep underground in many arid areas and which are being identified by the United Nations Hydrological Decade studies.

Radioisotopes will power batteries in weather, navigation and communications satellites. And they may even serve as power supplies for surgically implanted artificial hearts.

Before the end of the century, nuclear reactors no larger than a small car will be used to propel space craft for manned missions to Mars. Life support systems for space travel will be nuclear powered and some day nuclear reactors may help man create a habitable environment for a future moon colony.

In the future, it may be primarily nuclear energy and its associated technologies that allow man to explore and exploit the oceans.

Nuclear-powered deep sea research vessels are already being developed.

By the 21st century, man may be harvesting food from the sea, mining its mineral resources, perhaps even living for extended periods deep beneath the surface.

If present development programmes are successful, engineering with nuclear explosives could help to release deeply contained gas and ore reserves and create underground reservoirs to hold rainfall in regions where rapid surface evaporation takes place.

Peaceful nuclear explosives might also be used to build a canal, a new harbour or cut through a mountain barrier.

Because nuclear fuel is compact and long-lived, the atom's benefits are less tied to any accident of geography which gives one country fuel while denying it to another.

. . .

Since real economies in nuclear reactors are most often in large size plants, the future may see several nations joining together, in cooperation with the advanced nations and the International Atomic Energy Agency, to share large nuclear generating plants as they now share research machinery in centres such as the European Organization for Nuclear Research (CERN) in Geneva, which Unesco helped create.

This drawing together of men from many nations to work together and to share scientific knowledge and technological benefits can be a very important spin-off of nuclear energy.

It would be naive of me to ignore how nuclear energy was introduced to the world. I have not forgotten nor should my optimism on the power of the peaceful atom be taken to indicate that I am not realistic about the ever present question of nuclear annihilation. I have lived very close to this question for more than 20 years.

But I have also seen the birth of nuclear power to light homes and run factories, to drive ships across the ocean, to power satellites in orbit. I have seen the atom used to study life, to help create knowledge, to improve agriculture, to save lives and to make living more understandable and more enjoyable.

There is a cosmic 'glue' that binds the nucleus of the atom. It is a force stronger than any other force found in nature. As that cosmic force is released to the probing of man, and as we put it to work for man, perhaps another force will come into existence —one that will bind men together in a universal way, matching our human will with the physical powers we have learned to wield.

If this comes to pass, we may expect quite a future, and I think it might well be one far beyond that which you or I could dare to imagine today.

UNESCO Courier 1968 7 8

Discussion and Research

12. Glenn Seaborg describes a view of what some people would call Utopia, or the perfect world.
    a) Is it realistic, or just a dream?
    b) What aspects of life, human nature, culture, values, etc. would have to change if Seaborg's view were to become a reality?
    c) What aspects of life are likely to lead in the direction of Seaborg's Utopia?
    d) What would your Utopia be like?

Case Study 4

OPEC: The Geopolitics of Energy

The Organization of Petroleum Exporting Countries (OPEC) began in 1960 when a group of oil-exporting countries, namely Iran, Iraq, Kuwait, Saudi Arabia, and Venezuela, decided that together they could stand up to the price squeeze being put on them by the big international oil companies.

Prior to 1960 the so-called "Seven Sisters" of the oil world (Exxon, Shell, Texaco, Mobil, BP, Socal, Gulf) had run things fairly well to their own satisfaction. They cooperated in managing supply to match demand; they did not try to flood the market with cut-price products; they shared the market by agreement. They feared a glut that could be caused by someone trying to undercut their long-term price structure, someone who might be trying to make a "fast buck" at the expense of long-term security of supply. For example, during the hectic East Texas oil boom of the 1930s the oil majors fought to stop unregulated output; indeed the National Guard was eventually called out to close the independent, *maverick* (non-conforming) oil fields.

The oil companies also sought to eliminate competition in the search for oil in the Middle East. At one time a red line was drawn on a map of all the potential Middle Eastern oil countries, except Iran and Kuwait, where oil exploration was already a British monopoly, and within this Red Line Agreement area the "Seven Sisters" agreed not to compete for concessions. Naturally, this limiting of competition had a depressing effect on the prices the Middle East rulers could secure for oil concessions. The rulers felt mistreated as the years passed. Their aggravation was heightened as they saw foreign governments using money from oil taxes for all sorts of expenditures. The major oil companies themselves, the "Seven Sisters", faced with the growing burden of taxes on their products, tried to keep actual production costs as low as possible—hence the price squeeze on the oil-producing countries in 1960. At that time the producing countries got an oil royalty of about $0.50/bbl, which rose to about $1.00/bbl in the early 1960s.

During the 1960s there was tremendous economic growth in the developed countries of the world, which promoted new searches for oil.

Successful exploration was carried out in many parts of the world, though most newly discovered fields proved to be more expensive for production than the Middle Eastern fields. Some of the newer producing countries decided to join OPEC, even though the oil majors disapproved. Thus Qatar joined in 1961, Libya and Indonesia in 1962, Algeria in 1969, and Nigeria and the United Arab Emirates in 1971. Gabon and Ecuador joined subsequently. Fig. 4C-1 summarizes some of the facts about OPEC members.

The most significant new member turned out to be Libya, which sold concessions to a maverick oil company, Occidental Petroleum, in 1966. Libya was Occidental's only source of supply so when the new militant rulers of Libya put pressure on Occidental for higher royalties in 1970, Occidental had no choice but to agree. In 1971 Iran quickly followed Libya's lead by forcing higher royalties out of another maverick, Getty Oil. By the middle of 1973 the members of OPEC had managed to raise their average royalty rate to nearly double the 1966 price.

Fig. 4C-1
Important facts about OPEC members

	Population 1975	Oil production 1975 bbl (billions)	Oil revenue 1975 $ (billions)	Known oil reserves in 1975[3] bbl (billions)	Known oil reserves bbl/person in 1975	Life index in 1975[4] years
Algeria	16 780 000	.345	3.5	7.37	439.2	21.4
Ecuador	6 730 000	.073	0.7	5.70	847.0	78.1
Gabon	530 000	.073	0.7	1.50	2 830.2	20.5
Indonesia	127 590 000	.547	5.0	10.50	82.3	19.2
Iran[1]	33 020 000	1.953	20.0	64.50	1 953.4	33.0
Iraq[1]	11 120 000	.818	8.0	34.30	3 084.5	41.9
Kuwait[1]	1 000 000	.752	7.5	68.00	68 000.0	90.4
Libya	2 440 000	.544	5.5	26.10	10 696.7	48.0
Nigeria	62 930 000	.839	8.0	15.00	238.4	17.9
Qatar	90 000	.161	1.5	5.85	65 000.0	36.3
Saudi Arabia[1]	8 700 000	2.584	26.0	175.00	20 115.0	67.7
United Arab Emirates[2]	220 000	.620	6.0	32.00	145 455.0	51.6
Venezuela[1]	11 990 000	1.058	10.0	14.00	1 167.6	13.2
Canada (for comparison)	22 830 000	.730	7.5	9.00	394.2	12.3
				800.00*	35 041.6*	1 100.0*

Compiled from data in *The Economist* and *Business Week*, 1976.

[1] Founding members of OPEC in 1960
[2] Abu Dhabi, Dubai, Sharjah, Ajman, Umm al Qaiwain, Ras al Khaimah, Fujairah
[3] Note that oil reserves are not true reserves; they are only what it is worth extracting at current prices.
[4] Life index is an approximate measure of useful quantity; it is derived by dividing known reserves by current annual production. Note that oil producers rarely explore for more than 20-40 years ahead. The 1975 OPEC average was 41.5 years.
* With tar sands

This royalty increase came about because of several factors. The chief one was the economic growth of the developed countries: demand pressed hard on the capacity to supply; alternate production sources of oil proved to be vastly more expensive to operate than the Middle East sources; and the existence of mavericks created weaknesses in the oil majors' control. Meanwhile the oil-exporting countries continued to be annoyed at the oil taxation revenues being generated by governments in other countries. The Arab members also knew that if Israel was to be forced from the Middle East, money would be needed for training and equipping efficient armies. Additionally, the members of OPEC considered themselves to be part of the less developed world, and they all wanted to get out of it.

The conditions were all set therefore for a major move on the part of OPEC. The Arab-Israeli war of late 1973 provided the opportunity. By December 1973 the royalty rate was 75% higher than the rate of July of the same year; OPEC put an embargo on exports to the Netherlands and the USA because of their support of Israel. The developed world complained, talked of a new "balance of power", and even mentioned invading the Middle East; however, it took little action. Anti-growth people of the developed world started preaching conservation, advocating smaller cars, and proclaiming the need for a new society with "conserver" values. Thus realizing their power, the OPEC members raised royalty rates over and over again. By December 1974 their royalties were five times higher per barrel than in July 1973—and twenty times higher than in 1960!

At that level they realized that if they pressed harder they would not only bring about the economic development of competing oil sources, such as Alberta's tar sands or Colorado's oil shales, but also create economic hardship for the developed world, neither of which they wanted to do. Their aim in fact was to raise the royalty rate to as high a level as possible *without* creating competition or causing economic collapse. In this sense the price they managed to obtain was a real *economic* price, though it was achieved neither by purely economic means nor for purely economic motives.

The motives, as we noted, were political as well as economic. While the Arab-Israeli war made sharp price increases possible, anti-Jewish sentiments accounted only partially for the rise in oil prices. A large part of the Middle Eastern countries' vast income was and continues to be spent on armies and weapons. However, most of this expenditure is due not to hatred of Israel, but to fear of other countries. Saudi Arabia, which is the closest OPEC member to Israel, keeps the best parts of its army along the northern border to guard against Iraq; Iran, which isn't even an Arab state, keeps its huge army as a bulwark on its northern border against the USSR. Indeed, almost half the OPEC members are not Arab, and do not therefore share the Arabs' political feelings. Five members are not even located in the Middle East.

The desire for development is a much more basic reason for the royalty increases. One of the driving forces for development is the realization that a better life is possible and desirable. The possibility has been seen by the OPEC states ever since they first knew they had oil (e.g. 1933 Saudi Arabia, 1938 Kuwait, 1970 United Arab Emirates), but the desire to change their way of life has come more slowly.

Some member countries, chiefly Iran, Nigeria, Venezuela, Indonesia, and Algeria have started massive growth programs. Better food, better health, and more education are needed by their large, poor populations. These countries spend their oil revenues on infrastructural developments and industries; they want to improve the quality of life of their many people, who live now in obvious poverty. Oil gives them that chance, but even so, it will take a long time. Indonesia's per capita GNP was $150 in 1974, Nigeria's was $240, Algeria's $650, Iran's $1 060, and Venezuela's $1 710; this hardly indicates wealth when compared with Canada's $6 080.

The idea of change has been accepted more slowly in Libya and the thinly populated Arab countries around the Gulf, which all have mammoth oil reserves. In these countries the traditional ways of life have been protected by the rulers. For example, in accordance with the teachings of the Koran, thieves still have their right hands chopped off. Women are still veiled; they are not allowed to have jobs nor are they permitted to drive cars. Alcohol and movie theatres are forbidden to all citizens; public prayers are compulsory five times a day; religious police patrol the cities. Absolute monarchies prevail in most states and top jobs go to relatives. In Saudi Arabia, for example, the founder of the modern state, Ibn Saud, married 300 different women, 4 at a time, and thereby laid the foundations for the present ruling elite of 4 000 princes.

Nevertheless, the Arab oil states now realize that economic development is essential if the future is to be secured. They expect that their oil will not last forever, and that oil will be replaced as a major fuel source by new sources of power, such as hydrogen engines. The oil states do not want to have to go back to a life of poverty. Thus, they invest in desalination plants, roads, schools, hospitals, chemical factories, iron and steel works, cement plants, and so on. They are now building for the future.

They are also saving for the future. Most of their unspent cash, running into billions of dollars each year, is invested in North America and Europe. Generally the Arabs do not want to buy up the productive capacity of the developed world; they want a share of it, though, because that will guarantee an income when their oil is no longer in use. This investment money will work like long-term pension funds.

In addition, the Arab oil states give aid to poorer countries. Perhaps they feel guilty being rich while others are poor; in any case, they have a duty under Islam to share their wealth. Aid is therefore given liberally, to several percentage points of GNP as compared to the 1% given by the Western world and about 0.1% from the Communist world. Kuwait is the most generous and best organized donor; it gives aid chiefly to non-oil Arab countries, through the Kuwait Fund for Arab Development and the

Arab Fund for Economic and Social Development. Saudi Arabia concentrates its aid through the Islamic Development Bank on non-Arab Moslem countries such as Pakistan. African countries are taken care of through the Special Arab Fund for Africa, while Latin America gets aid from Venezuela. Whatever OPEC has done for our oil prices, it has been of great benefit to many of the less developed countries of the world.

ENERGY: Further Reading

The Terror of the Tar Sands, COSGROVE
The Tar Sands, PRATT
James Bay, RICHARDSON
Fuelling Canada's Future, ROWLANDS
The Prometheus Crisis, SCORTIA & ROBINSON
Exxoneration, ROHMER
Ultimatum, ROHMER

Conclusion

The pattern of world energy production is not identical with that of world consumption. Some regions, such as Europe and Japan, experience energy deficits and need to draw upon the surpluses of other areas such as the Middle East. A growing trend in the world is greater self-sufficiency on the part of the deficit regions, leading them to lessen waste while seeking to develop new energy sources. Meanwhile, the major surplus region, the Middle East, is attempting to use more energy itself by opting for programs of economic development. Must the developed world become a "conserver" society or will its technological skills permit it to tap new sources of energy? Must the surplus regions continue to support economic growth elsewhere by exporting fuel, or will they seize prosperity for themselves?

While such questions are difficult to answer, one thing at least is certain; changes in energy production patterns will affect the life styles of people in countries around the world. Of course, energy production is just one of the many factors that influence the level of life in a nation. Other factors include those that we have discussed in previous chapters—population growth, food supplies, and industrialization. In examining the effect of various factors on a country's level of living, we are in fact dealing with its quality of life. Because each country has its own advantages and problems, the quality of life will vary around the world. Moreover, since countries are constantly subject to change, their quality of life will evolve. In the next chapter we will discuss this complex topic, quality of life.

Chapter 5
QUALITY OF LIFE

Introduction

Quality of life is a difficult concept to define. Basically, it includes such diverse considerations as food and good health, political and religious freedom, opportunities for intellectual and spiritual growth, and wide choices of material consumption. The multitude of factors that blend together to yield a particular quality of life are unique to each society. Even within a single society, different features and opportunities are not evenly distributed, so that the quality of life can vary from area to area.

It is also difficult to specify the features that are essential to an acceptable or desirable quality of life. All human beings give priority to different sets of factors. To some people, the quantity and quality of food determines, to a large extent, quality of life. To other people, a desirable quality of life means space for living, good job opportunities, access to green spaces, uncrowded expressways, cheap air fares, or women's rights.

PEI Ministry of Tourism, Parks, and Conservation

UNICEF/Bernard Wolff

The Klong Toey district of Bangkok, Thailand.

A family in Prince Edward Island, Canada.

Discussion and Research

1. The two photographs illustrate different levels of material existence. Does this affect the quality of life? How do different levels of material existence affect the quality of life?

2. The quality of living available to people varies substantially in the world. To what extent are the variations caused by technology? Or the lack of it?

3. Can you make a list of the things that affect the quality of *your* life? Rank ten items in order from the most to the least important. Can you persuade your fellow students to agree with you? Does it matter if you can't? Why is that?

In this chapter we will examine some of the factors that people find desirable for a satisfactory quality of life. It is impossible to rank these factors objectively, since people have different preferences. There are undoubtedly some factors, such as good health, that all people would place near the top of their priority list; other factors, such as the opportunity to eat ice cream every day, are of pressing concern to relatively few people. We will discuss factors of various importance, and propose a list of universal concerns in the first section, Desirables. We will then examine three different levels of concern and attempt to measure quality of life. The chapter ends with a case study of California's quality of life.

Section A
Desirables

Any discussion of the factors that make up a desirable quality of life centres to a great extent on the topic of **choice**. Choice is made necessary by the fact that the things we have—on a material, spiritual, and intellectual level—are limited. We cannot get everything we want, nor fulfil all our dreams; choice, therefore, is an inescapable fact of life.

Like individuals, all societies must make choices. Generally, the amount of choice available to a society varies with its spiritual, intellectual, and material wealth; rich societies have more resources, and thus have to make more decisions regarding their use. Since various courses of action are open to all societies, priorities must be established. Each society must determine what it wants to accomplish, and settle on certain desirables; it then must act according to these priorities. Should the society clear the rats from its granaries, for instance, or should it use its resources to raise the level of literacy? What should be done about a factory that would go out of business if it had to pay for pollution control? Should it be closed down to prevent pollution, or should it be allowed to stay open for the sake of the jobs it provides?

The choices facing less developed countries are generally few and basic. For example, food is more important than housing or clothing, so it gets priority in any decisions that are made. In more developed countries, neither food nor clothing present problems, so housing may get priority. As a society's wealth increases, so do the number of desirables; rich societies for instance may be concerned about pollution or public parks or funding for the arts.

We know that each society has its own sets of concerns; the various features seen as desirable will depend on a society's character and degree of wealth. Yet, some factors are essential for survival, and thus should be desired by *all* people. We can attempt to rank features and distinguish these essential or *universal desirables* by examining the way people are affected by the absence of certain factors. The choice presented by universal desirables is always basic: with them we can survive; without them we die. People who are starving and disease-ridden do not survive. Therefore food and good health can be regarded as universal desirables. People do not die without freedom, but as history attests, millions have been prepared to die to obtain it. Thus, while freedom may not be a universal desirable, it nevertheless is important. We can examine these significant desirables in more detail.

1. Adequate Food

Since we have examined the world food situation in Chapter 2, there is no need to discuss the problem at any length here. We should only remind ourselves that in the world there are millions of starving people who are concerned only with obtaining food.

Statistical Interpretation

5-1 Using the data in columns R and S of Appendix 2, construct a scattergraph in the manner shown in Appendix 3. Scale the vertical axis to show food production indices (column R) and the horizontal axis to show population growth indices (column S). Draw in an *equal change line* (a line that joins all points that represent the same degree of change on one axis as they do on the other; i.e., 0 and 0, 1 and 1, 2 and 2 etc.), and mark in the world indices of 132 and 124 respectively by means of a distinctive symbol. Use contrasting symbols to indicate the continents to which the different countries belong.

a) What does the space below the equal change line mean? What does that say about the quality of life of any country currently in this space? Which continents have most of their countries in this space? Can you identify the country that has made the least progress in improving its quality of life as measured by food availability?

b) What does the space above the line mean? Which continents are best represented here? Which individual country has made the best progress?

5-2 Using the data in Column T of Appendix 2 (per capita food production) draw a graded shading map to show four classes as follows:

126 and over	bright orange
101 - 125	pale orange
76 - 100	pale black
75 and under	dark black

a) What do you think the class divisions signify?
b) Why are two colours used?
c) In which parts of the world are the countries that have an index of one hundred or lower located?
d) Suggest some solutions to their problems.

2. Good Health

Good health is partly a matter of adequate food and proper nutrition and partly a question of a disease-free environment. Much has been done to provide sufficient food supplies and to eliminate sickness. One of the most important products created to serve both purposes was DDT (dichloro-diphenyl-trichloroethane).

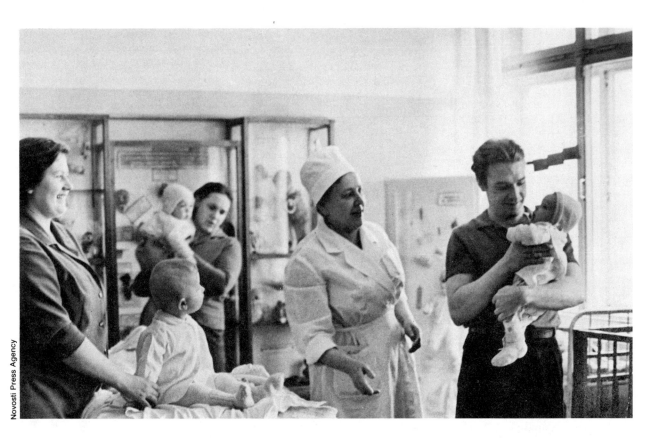

A children's clinic in the USSR, where health care is a top priority.

DDT has improved the quality of life for millions of people by reducing disease-carrying pests and improving food production. Nevertheless the product is banned in North America, and is being used less in other parts of the world because it is a poison that persists within the environment. It does not break down readily, and gathers at the top of the food chain where it kills organisms that experience the accumulations. However, because it destroys pests so effectively, DDT has many proponents; one is Norman Borlaug, who was awarded a Nobel Prize for developing hydrid corn and wheat, and thus promoting the Green Revolution. His views are summarized in the following article, taken from the *UNESCO Courier* of 1972 2.

In defence of DDT

by NORMAN E. BORLAUG
Nobel Peace Prize 1970

Civilization as it is known today could not have evolved, nor can it survive, without an adequate food supply. Yet, food is something that is taken for granted by most world leaders, despite the fact that more than half of the population of the world is hungry and an even larger proportion malnourished.

If the high-yielding dwarf wheat and rice varieties were the catalysts that ignited the Green Revolution, then chemical fertilizer was the fuel that powered its forward thrust. The responsiveness of the high-yielding varieties has greatly increased fertilizer consumption. The new varieties not only respond to much heavier dosages of fertilizer than the old ones but are also much more efficient in its use.

The continued success of the Green Revolution will hinge, however, upon whether agriculture will be permitted to use the inputs — agricultural chemicals — including chemical fertilizers and pesticides, both absolutely necessary to cope with hunger. If agriculture is denied their use because of unwise legislation that is now being promoted by a powerful lobby group of hysterical environmentalists — who are provoking fear by predicting doom for the world through chemical poisoning — then the world will be doomed but not by chemical poisoning, but from starvation.

The current vicious, hysterical propaganda campaign against the use of agricultural chemicals, being promoted today by fear-provoking, irresponsible environmentalists, had its genesis in the best-selling "half-science, half-fiction novel" *Silent Spring*, published in 1962.

...

Silent Spring convinced the general public that the use of pesticides — and especially DDT — was upsetting the "balance of nature" and was doing great damage to wildlife, especially birds and fishes. It implied that a number of species were facing extinction because of its use.

I am in complete agreement that we should try to preserve all forms of wildlife as part of our heritage, as far as it is possible to do so. On the other hand, let us not become egotistical to the point of assuming supernatural powers. A glance at the book of rocks tells us of the impotency of many species, including man, against the forces of nature. Yet it is incredible that only a few, if any, of the leaders of the current environmentalist movement have studied palaeontology and the "parade of the species," in the geologic past.

Spencer estimates that 99 per cent of all the species that have lived, since the candle of life was first lit on the planet earth about 3.2 billion years ago, have flunked the adaptation imperative: "evolve or perish," and consequently have now become extinct.

Rhodes, Zim and Shaffer estimate that there are at present approximately 1 100 000 species of animals, many of them very simple forms, and 350 000 species of plants that currently inhabit the planet earth. Of these, the United States Fish and Wildlife Service in 1966 listed 33 species of mammals, 49 species of birds and 9 species of reptiles and amphibians, and 38 species of fish in the U.S.A., which were either rare or endangered.

In discussing the causes for reduction in numbers and possible disappearance of these 129 species, the destruction of the habitat and disturbances resulting from man's activities were paramount. Pesticides were mentioned as possible contributing

factors in only two cases. In the past three or four years there has been much propaganda, but little convincing scientific evidence, put forward by environmentalists indicating that DDT has contributed to the decline of the Bald Eagle, Peregrine Falcon, American Osprey and Californian Condor.

One does not need a thin egg shell hypothesis due to DDT to explain the reduction in the population of these species. The truth of the matter is that many ornithologists had reported on the reduction in populations of these large birds of prey as far back as the 1880s and 1890s, long before the time of DDT. It is almost a foregone conclusion, for anyone who uses some common sense, that one or more of these species is about to flunk the imperative "evolve or perish." Their habitats are being destroyed by the encroachment of man.

The cliché "in balance with nature," which is in common usage today by modern environmentalists is very misleading. It implies we would have a favourable "in balance with nature" to assure the protection of our crop species if the "balance of nature" were not upset by man. This, of course, is not true. Nor is there in existence a single "in balance with nature" ecosystem. Rather there is, within a given area, an infinite number of local and many more extensive merging ecosystems.

None of them are in static equilibrium. They are in a constant state of dynamic change, responding to the changes in the environment. At different times, the selection pressure provoking change is drought, floods, frosts, heat, insect or disease attacks, or invasion of the habitat by other species.

Early in my career as a forester working in a large primitive or wilderness area completely isolated from the

This is part of a DDT spraying program in Paraguay, designed to keep malaria-spreading mosquitoes down.

influence of man, I learned of the fickleness of nature. I have seen 20 forest fires ignited by a single "dry thunder (electric) storm". Some of these fires started by lightning destroyed or damaged vast areas of several forest types (ecosystems).

In the same area I have seen tens of thousands of acres of lodgepole pine killed by Dendroctonus spp., infestation. The havoc done by the Dendroctonus beetle should not have happened according to some pseudoecologists, for it was, after all, a native insect pest with its entire army of natural predators, parasites and pathogens, and consequently should have been "in balance with nature."

The World Health Organization (WHO), with the assistance of the Pan American Health Organization and the United Nations Children's Fund (UNICEF), in 1955 launched a worldwide campaign against malaria, based on spraying the interior of all houses with DDT, so as to kill the Anopheline vector and break the cycle.

Of the 124 countries and territories in the tropics where malaria has existed, the disease has been eradicated from 19. There are 48 other countries in which eradication programmes are in progress and an additional 37 where extensive control programmes are under way. There remain only 20 nations in malarial areas where no programmes have yet been initiated.

There is also dramatic evidence from Ceylon of what can happen if a programme is stopped before eradication is accomplished. When the campaign was initiated in the mid 1950s there were more than two million cases of malaria in Ceylon. By 1962 it had dropped to 31 cases and by 1963 to 17, at which point the spray programme was discontinued for budgetary reasons. By 1967 the number of cases had jumped to 3 000 and by 1968 to more than 16 000. Before the

programme could be re-established, in late 1969, two million cases had reappeared.

In summarizing the progress in this world wide malaria campaign on February 2, 1971, officials of WHO made the following statement:

"More than 1 000 million people have been freed from the risk of malaria in the past 25 years, mostly thanks to DDT. This is an achievement unparalleled in the annals of public health. But even today 329 million people are being protected from malaria through DDT spraying operations for malaria control or total eradication.

"The improvement in health resulting from malaria campaigns has broken the vicious circle of poverty and disease resulting in ample economic benefits: increased production of rice (and wheat), because the labour force is able to work, and the opening up of vast areas for agricultural production.

"The safety record of DDT to man is truly remarkable. At the height of its production 400 000 tons [362 880 t] a year were used for agriculture, forestry, public health, etc. Yet in spite of prolonged exposure by hundreds of millions of people, and the heavy occupational exposure of considerable numbers, the only confirmed cases of injury have been the result of massive accidental or suicidal swallowing of DDT. There is no evidence in man that DDT is causing cancer or genetic change."

I repeat what I have said many times before: without thinking, conservationists and environmentalists and only partially-informed people in the communications media have embarked on a crusade designed to end the use of agricultural chemicals, such as pesticides and fertilizers. They give no thought to the end result of such action: the eventual starvation and political chaos that will plague the world.

Clean water is another important requirement for good health. In many parts of the world insanitary water creates many problems, while high temperatures may foster the breeding of pests and parasites on or near bodies of water. It is thus that millions contract cholera, malaria, or bilharzia.

Fig. 5-1
Incidence of river blindness in part of West Africa

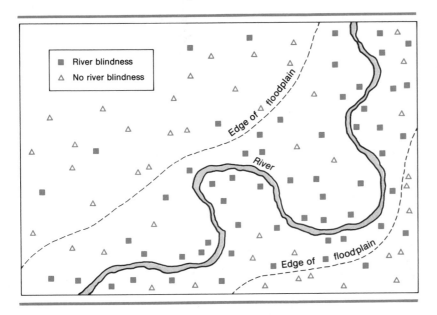

Statistical Interpretation

5-3 Fig. 5-1 is a map showing the locations of settlements in West Africa in which "river blindness" used to be common. Ascertain the ϕ (*phi*) *coefficient of relationship* between the incidence of river blindness and the location of settlements on the floodplain of the river; use the technique explained in Appendix 3. It was the use of just such techniques that led to control of the *simoleum fly*, which breeds along the water's edges and is responsible for transmitting river blindness.

People depend on large supplies of clean water to survive. However it is not always in a state that can be readily used by human beings. Most of the world's water is found in oceans and it is too salty for use without expensive *desalination* plants. In the Middle East, for instance, where most of the world's desalination plants are located, water is almost more precious than oil. Most of the remaining water in the world is found in polar icecaps; some Californians have considered

Saudi Arabia also has plans to tow Antarctic icebergs across the ocean. The plans call for the icebergs to be covered with giant polythene sheets so that losses by evaporation are minimized.

Water pollution is a serious problem in many parts of the world. This is a stream in Brazil.

satisfying their water needs by towing giant icebergs from Antarctica. The world's population is therefore almost entirely dependent for water on the 1% or so of the earth's fresh water found in aquifers, rivers, and lakes. Fortunately, it is this 1% that is constantly being recycled through the water cycle.

UNESCO/Patrice Fury

River water has long been used as a means of getting rid of undesired wastes. This was an acceptable course of action until the advent and growth of large-scale industry; so many wastes were disposed of that the rivers became overloaded. Rivers have a natural cleaning capacity, but too much waste produces pollution. Indeed, pollution can be defined as an excess of waste products, an amount that surpasses the natural cleaning capacity of the environment. In the more developed world the factories that produce too much waste are now taking steps to limit the amounts they dispose of. This means extra costs for the factories, and these expenses are reflected in higher product prices. But the choice has been made; clean water is seen as more important than the lower price of industrial products. Some of the problems related to water pollution are discussed in detail in the following reading.

Wastes from industrial processing can often be reduced by such means as filtering and settling.

Controlling water pollution: what is needed?

by RICHARD HARTLAND-ROWE

"Animal wastes must not be dumped in rivers, ditches or other waters near towns or cities; prosecution under this statute may result in a heavy fine." This sounds like a fairly modern anti-pollution law since we all know there was no pollution in the good old days. Or was there? This quotation is a summary of a law passed by the British Parliament in 1388, during the reign of Richard II. Clearly water pollution is not a recent phenomenon; it has existed ever since man began living in large stationary communities.

Natural waters have the capacity to purify themselves. Up to a point, biodegradable materials are processed and broken down by the organisms naturally present in the water (bacteria, fungi and other microorganisms), without resulting in adverse changes in the waterbody. The thoroughness of this process of biodegradability depends upon various characteristics of the waterbody and climate. But, if this limit is exceeded, changes may

occur with more or less obvious deterioration.

Water which is polluted for one use may still be unpolluted for another. You can still wash the car in undrinkable water. Water is used for many things, from drinking and washing to transportation and waste disposal, as well as for recreational and aesthetic purposes; therefore, possible degrees of water pollution vary enormously.

With such a range of possible kinds of pollution, the number of potential pollutants is immense, but they can be classified into a small number of categories.

Biodegradable pollutants include not only sewage but almost all other materials derived from plant or animal tissues and wastes, such as pulp-mill effluents, abattoir wastes, run-off from feedlots, and so on. Such pollutants create two types of problems. *First*, although they are not necessarily poisonous, they can create conditions which kill organisms; they provide food for organisms such as bacteria and fungi. These, like most other organisms, require oxygen. If there is an abundance of biodegradable material available, the organisms may multiply enormously, producing

a huge population of these very quickly. Such a population can create so high a demand for oxygen that the oxygen dissolved in the water is diminished, or even depleted. The resulting lack of oxygen will then result in mass mortality of many kinds of organisms, especially those like most fish which require high concentrations of oxygen in the water.

Since the detrimental effects of biodegradable material result largely from the oxygen depletion they cause, the amounts of such materials are often described in terms of the "Biochemical Oxygen Demand" or BOD, a measure of the oxygen demand created by micro-organisms which feed upon biodegradable material. All natural waters have some BOD, since there are always natural biodegradable materials present, such as dead leaves, excreta and corpses of animals. Usually natural BOD levels are too low to result in serious oxygen depletion. Even in polluted waters, BOD gradually diminishes with time as biodegradable material is used up. As oxygen enters the water again, either by diffusion from the atmosphere or from the photosynthesis of plant life in the water, conditions may once again become favourable for fish and other animals.

Biodegradable materials are also responsible, however, for *a second type of problem*. When they are broken down and the bodies of the micro-organisms, too, are broken down by other micro-organisms, many substances are released. Among these are various plant nutrients, especially phosphorus and nitrogen compounds. These plant foods, and particularly the phosphorus compounds, are of extreme importance because they are usually present in natural waters in such low concentrations that they limit the amount of plant growth possible.

. . .

The addition of biodegradable material to a waterbody may thus promote excessive plant growth. When the plants die, as they usually do in the fall in temperate climates, their biodegradable remains may create a high BOD, and oxygen depletion may occur. At worst the oxygen depletion may be total and cause obvious damage such as massive fish kills. Even if this does not happen, the increase in plant life may itself create undesirable conditions.

Lakes which contain low concentrations of nutrients are called oligotrophic (meaning unproductive). Little plant life can grow, and the waters are thus usually clear and attractive. If excess nutrients are added, the minute algae that live suspended in lake waters may multiply to an extent which makes the water green and turbid. The lake has become productive, or eutrophic. Of course, many natural lakes are eutrophic, having natural supplies of nutrients which permit substantial plant life. But many formerly oligotrophic lakes have begun the enriching process of eutrophication as a result of the inadvertent or deliberate release of nutrients into the lake by man. Apart from the well-known changes in the Great Lakes, the process of eutrophication can be seen in progress everywhere in Canada. The Okanagan lakes in British Columbia, for example, are undergoing eutrophication to varying degrees, almost certainly as a result of human settlement in the area.

Another type of water pollution should be mentioned. This is thermal pollution, resulting from the addition of heat to water. Water is used in many industries for cooling purposes, cold water being removed from the river or lake, and warmed water being returned. Since many organisms have rather specific temperature requirements, such a change may be harmful or even fatal. Trout, for example, are cold water fish, and if warm water is added to their river, they will either depart or be killed.

Although these various categories of pollutants have been listed separately, waters usually receive mixtures of pollutants of different types, simply because people live where industries exist. A biodegradable effluent from a sewage works will probably enter the same river as toxic or thermal effluents from industrial plants. It is not surprising that pollution detection is a complex business and pollution control an expensive one.

Two things are necessary before embarking on a program of pollution abatement. The first is the ability to detect pollution, particularly in its incipient stages when corrective action may be taken at comparatively low cost. The second is the means of assessing the costs of pollution control, to be able to establish realistic economic targets for action.

There are two main ways of detecting the presence of water pollution. The most obvious is by making chemical analyses of water samples to check for pollutants. This would seem to be a simple matter, but there are two problems. Since only a small number of potential pollutants can be monitored or frequently analysed, it is not usually possible to assess early stages of pollution unless the pollutant happens to be one of those being monitored. Nor does intermittent analysis of water samples give us much chance of detecting short-lived events.

Fortunately another technique is available which permits detection of such situations. This is the use of organisms that live in the water as built-in monitors. Usually some change in the organisms gives the first hint of trouble, like fish kills, or the growth of unusual organisms like sewage fungus, a whitish mould which grows in highly polluted waters.

Observations of the fauna and flora of lakes and rivers can be used as a biological monitoring system since the plants and animals do not change as rapidly as the chemical changes which affect them. For example, after a spill of toxic wastes into a river, the chemical effects may be undetectable after the spill, since the substance will have been washed downstream. But if plants or animals have been killed, they do not reappear instantaneously, and their absence indicates that something has happened in the recent past.

Probably the most complex aspect of water pollution control is the evaluation of its costs, because the costs may be in financial terms (how much will better sewage treatment cost?), ecological terms (should this waste be put in the river, or on the land, or incinerated into the air?), or aesthetic terms (is it worth spoiling this view of the river by damming it?).

Although cost assessment is difficult, it is essential that such an assessment be made as a basis for making decisions about pollution control. Ideally, pollution should be reduced to the point where the cost of its control is balanced by the benefit of having reduced it. This point is difficult to determine in cases where the benefits are often impossible to evaluate. How do you put a price on the aesthetic value of a river?

In the past many waters have become polluted because damage to the environment has not been taken into account by water users. Much recent legislation has the effect of internalizing the costs of minimizing damage; that is, water users are required to maintain certain quality standards in their effluents, and the price for achieving these standards within the plant is a direct or internal cost of running the plant, inevitably to be recovered by higher prices for products sold to customers, rather than an external charge to be borne by society generally, either in the form of public expenditure on pollution abatement, or in the form of a degraded environment.

It is impossible to decide arbitrarily what should be spent on pollution control since it is largely a matter of judgment by society, which eventually has to determine what is acceptable or tolerable and what is not. Most city dwellers take it as a matter of course that the water which comes out of the tap is safe to drink, and the cost of producing drinkable water is paid without question. Likewise there is public indignation when gross pollution episodes occur, such as the 1970 oil tanker spill in Chedabucto Bay, N.S. Yet even in the 1960s one of our largest cities, Montreal, gave no treatment at all to 90% of its sewage.

One thing is certain, and that is that the price of water pollution has to be paid sooner or later. It may be paid as an internal cost, reflected in increased prices of articles or services that involve use of water. It may be paid by society at large as an external cost, through the use of public funds on pollution control. Or it may be paid, now or in the future, in the form of a degraded environment requiring reclamation sooner or later. It is essential to determine what level of pollution is acceptable and then to ensure that the price can and will be paid to maintain that level.

Extracts of an article published in the *Canadian Geographical Journal* 1975 11

3. Freedom

While political freedom is not essential for survival as are food and good health, it is still a much desired factor in life. History is full of examples of people who value it highly. Millions have gone, voluntarily or by draft, to fight for political freedom. Millions have been willing to suffer ill health and other physical privations to obtain it. Time and time again throughout the centuries, people have lost their homes, possessions, and even their homelands in pursuit of it. Freedom would appear to be one of the most desired features of life. Yet not all people are politically free today. Even though empires have largely disintegrated during the twentieth century, there are still many subject peoples. The 1970s have witnessed struggles for freedom in Angola, Mozambique, Rhodesia, and South Africa, among other countries. Some have succeeded; others continue to fight.

Discussion and Research

4. With reference to the arguments in *In Defence of DDT*, what would you recommend about the use of DDT?
5. Many people value certain desirables so highly that they talk of them as "rights".
   a) What do they mean by this?
   b) Can "rights" exist?
   c) What happens when different "rights" clash, as for example, work and clean water?
6. Is democracy a "right" or one of the privileges of achievement?

Opinions about what is most wanted will differ even within a society close to the survival level; some people may want freedom above all, others may prefer food and stability. Revolutions and wars of independence succeed only when the forces for freedom gain supremacy over the forces for stability.

A hierarchy is a group of people or things that are arranged in a graduated series. A good example is the army, in which people are put into levels from private to general. Hierarchies also exist in business and in most social organizations. Generally, the group at the top receives more than its share of the wealth. For instance, the upper 5% of a society usually receives more than 5% of that society's income.

4. Other Desirables

Within any given society it is unlikely that there will be a general coincidence of individual priorities. There will be differences. The differences, however, will be least among the members of a society operating close to a survival level; people will generally give top priority to the universal desirables. As societies secure sufficient food and a healthy environment, they raise their levels of achievement. People are offered more opportunities and thus must make more choices. Attention is given to the *other desirables* in life.

Wealth tends to be distributed throughout any society in a more or less hierarchical manner; the wealthy groups will naturally have concerns different from those of the poor. For example, the wealthy may be concerned about wildlife, and want to protect it by banning insecticides; the poor, however, may fear that the banning of insecticides will cause food prices to rise. There are many conflicting drives in a wealthy society.

Since all people are different, they will rank their concerns differently. It is therefore very difficult, if not impossible, for us to rank these other desirables. Priorities are established according to the tastes of the individual. People generally rank various courses of action by assessing the degree of personal satisfaction they will gain from the course of action *in relation to* the amount of effort that must be put into it. People try to discover whether a course of action gives long-term or short-term satisfaction; they take into account the amount of satisfaction the action has given in the past. If the enjoyment is worth the amount of effort required, then the activity will be placed high on the list of priorities. For example, people decide what freedom means to them, and if they value it enough, they will fight and die for it. An evening at the theatre gives much satisfaction too, but people will not risk their lives for a theatre ticket. However, the satisfaction may be great enough so that some persons will wait in line all night to obtain tickets; others of course will not.

Quality of life thus means different things to different people. While it may be relatively easy to identify the concerns of a society operating at a fairly low level of material achievement, it becomes exceedingly difficult to categorize the concerns of a society with a high level of material achievement.

Section B
Levels of Development

Societies that are at different levels of development have different concerns about their quality of life. The following examples illustrate these differences.

1. Basic Survival: Bangladesh

Bangladesh is concerned with survival. It has an area of 144 000 km², a population of at least 77 000 000, and a density of at least 534 people/km². It is the most crowded large country in the world. Its people get only 80% of the food they need; 71% are engaged in agriculture; the per capita GNP is $100/yr; the *total* GNP is only about the same as Puerto Rico's, where the population is one twenty-fifth the size of Bangladesh's. From 1965 to 1974 the population grew by 46%, yet food production increased by only 17%; only 22% of the people are literate; annual energy consumption per capita is a low 29 kg coal equivalent.

World Bank Group Staff

Cyclones, or South Asian hurricanes, are blown toward Bangladesh by the prevailing southwesterly winds of the summer monsoon. The extraordinarily low atmospheric pressure within the cyclones causes the sea-water in the Bay of Bengal to rise well above its normal level. This, coupled with the onshore direction of the cyclones, brings flooding on a vast scale all across the very flat delta lands of Bangladesh. Not only does the sea-water pour in over the land, but the river water is backed up, thus causing it also to flood over large regions.

Typical cyclone damage in Bangladesh. This is part of the village of Patharghata after the cyclone of November 1970.

In addition, Bangladesh is the only place in the world where cholera is endemic. It is the country where cyclones drown thousands, where Bay of Bengal salt water is driven in over the flat delta lands, killing cattle, ruining crops, and spoiling the soil. The country has lost much of the valuable Ganges flood water to India, which, in order to feed its own hungry millions, has erected barrages to divert the water into the thirsty Deccan area.

Bangladesh *suffers*; its people are struggling to survive. The following item illustrates some of its basic concerns.

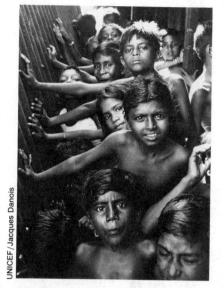

Children in Bangladesh. How do they see the future? What are their prospects?

Famine likely in Bangladesh, Waldheim says

© *New York Times Service*

UNITED NATIONS—Secretary-General Kurt Waldheim reported yesterday that despite an enormous and successful effort to avoid a famine in Bangladesh in 1972, the prospect of one was now "more serious and more threatening" than it was at the beginning of last year.

Mr. Waldheim's report attributed the bleak outlook to the poor December grain harvest, which was regarded as critically important in filling the food needs of Bangladesh.

The harvest was small because the monsoon rains were 40 per cent below normal during the critical growing months.

In addition, attacks by pests were greater than usual and supplies of fertilizer were insufficient at the crucial time of transplanting.

Because of the poor harvest, Mr. Waldheim said he wanted to make it clear that "only member states interested in the lives of the people of Bangladesh can provide the supplies and funds essential to deal with the situation."

In his report to the Security Council and the General Assembly, Mr. Waldheim noted that last year's effort to save the people of a single country by the international community had been on a scale never matched before.

During the year, just over $1-billion in aid was contributed and as a result, Mr. Waldheim said, the lives of 75 000 000 people were sustained and no deaths attributed to famine were reported.

The Globe and Mail 1973 1 2

2. Mid-development: The USSR

The USSR is an example of a country in the midst of development. It is a vast land with just over 250 000 000 people and a density of only 11.4 people/km². It is rich in natural resources of all types; it ranks highly in world production listings. But its people individually are not as well off as these figures imply. When the wealth produced by the USSR is averaged on a per capita basis, the position of the country in world rankings is low in some cases (e.g., cars) and high in others (e.g., health care). The differences in rankings permit us to say that the USSR is in the stage of mid-development. Its people, satisfied in many ways, still have other concerns about the quality of their lives.

Many people are still worried about basic desirables, such as food. The USSR would like to produce more; its people would like to eat better. In efforts to provide greater food variety and better nutrition, the government has encouraged farmers to increase their meat production. This means that they must feed part of the grain harvest to livestock; but the grain harvest has been erratic, and on several occasions the Russians have been forced to buy the grain on world markets. These purchases, made from Canada and the USA, have had two results: they have forced up the price of grain on world markets, and they have reduced the amounts available for purchase by other countries.

Another matter of great concern to many people in the USSR is good housing. As in most other countries, people have migrated to the towns for work, and a serious housing shortage has accordingly developed in the major cities. Moscow, for example, has constructed hundreds of apartment blocks, but people still have to wait years to get an apartment.

Inside a tractor driver's home.

Part of Magnitogorsk.

The home of a department head on a collective farm.

Political freedom is also a matter of great concern. This freedom does not exist *de facto* for many: there is only one official political party; advancement—social, political, and economic—often depends upon party membership; travel into other political jurisdictions is severely restricted; nationalistic minorities such as the Latvians, Ukrainians, and Kazakhs are forced to conform to national policies.

Nevertheless, these concerns do not affect the entire population. The USSR provides other important desirables such as good education. Over 99% of the people can read and write, giving the USSR one of the world's highest literacy rates. Medical care is also excellent; there is 1 physician for every 421 people in the country. In many respects, the USSR is well beyond the survival level.

In sum, the USSR has many advantages, but its people still lack sufficient housing, material possessions, and freedom of choice. The following items illustrate some of the concerns that Russians currently have about the quality of their lives.

A small-town Russian department store.

The report they wrote was as scorching as any I have seen. Each store, they noted, had crowds come to look at the displays, but there were no buyers. The warehouses were jammed with local and out-of-town shoes that no one wanted.

Why? The answers provided by the trio offered a glimpse of the problems that beset not only the shoemakers but all consumer industry as well.

The main reason the shoppers come in—and then quickly walk out—is the poor quality of the shoes. One distribution trust alone returned to the manufacturers a million pairs, or 20 per cent of all the shoes received from them, as unusable. Some factories have had a quarter of their output sent back.

Oddly, the system favors the maker of defective footwear. The workers and directors are given bonuses for turning out the most shoes, and not the best. Last year, Kazakhstan's stores lost $2.4 million on unsellable shoes—but the men who made them still received their bonuses.

Each factory, of course, has quality inspectors. But their own income depends on the quantity of shoes shipped out, and so they each check their 800-1200 pairs of shoes only cursorily.

Mark Gayn, *The Toronto Star* 1972 11 4

Beyond the inefficiency of centralized planning, the deadening impact of a system that places everything from housing to travel to the press under rigid state supervision kills individual initiative and breeds apathy. The Soviet man in the street is indifferent not just to the country's leaders, who appear on television or in the newspapers as depersonalized titans, but also to his job. The most obvious symptom of this malaise is the extraordinarily low productivity of labor in the U.S.S.R. as compared with that in every other developed country. Many people are unwilling to put in a day's work for the state if they can help it. Says a Western businessman who is a longtime resident of Moscow: "The real problem with this place is that the average worker doesn't give a damn." A recent study, based on Soviet statistics, showed that each day about 1 million people out of an industrial work force of 84 million do not turn up for work in the U.S.S.R.

Goofing off on the job is a way of life for an incalculable number of people, who are not impressed with being called the owners of the means of production. That is notably true of peasants, who still resent the imposed system of collectivized agriculture. The peasants concentrate their energies on their acre-size [0.4 ha] private plots, which constitute only 3% of the total farm acreage but produce 25% of the total agricultural output. Their productivity per acre is as much as eight times that of the government land. Farmers and industrial workers are notoriously careless of their machinery. Their indifference, combined with a chronic shortage of spare parts, has created what Kosygin has euphemistically called an "immobilization of equipment." Thus, despite the billions of rubles that have been poured into new agricultural machinery, the majority of Soviet peasants still work the land by hand.

The working man and particularly the working woman (85% of all working-age women have jobs) spend an inordinate amount of time tracking down scarce consumer goods. The ubiquitous mesh shopping bag is familiarly called an *avoska*, (perhaps) bag, meaning "Perhaps I'll find something to buy today, perhaps not." Although Moscow is by far the best-supplied city in the Soviet Union, TIME Correspondent Marsh Clark last week reported that "soap, toothpaste, perfumes, detergents, toilet paper, hairpins and matches were either of inferior quality or not available at all. The soaps don't clean, the mint-flavored toothpaste is harsh and repugnant, and the perfumes smell like overripe raspberries." The shortages are so commonplace that people will join any queue they see, then ask what it is for.

City dwellers constitute about 60% of the population, and housing construction scarcely keeps pace with continuing migration from the countryside. The shoddy quality of the new buildings is the butt of considerable ridicule. As one *Krokodil* car-

toon says: "It's good luck to let your cat go into a new apartment first." The drawing captures the startled expression of a family on the threshold of their new home as the weight of their cat walking into the living room causes the floor to give way.

In Odessa, a street vendor has been doing a brisk business in used light bulbs at 20 kopeks (26.5¢) each. When asked what purpose these might serve, he replied, "Take them to your office, screw them into the light sockets and take home the better ones." Moscow taxi drivers, instead of cruising for passengers, sometimes stash their vehicles in courtyards and let the motor run, while the back wheels, held up by a jack, spin away for hours. Keeping the wheels off the ground burns up gasoline very efficiently, while the odometer goes up. The drivers, who are state employees, are thus able to claim miles of fareless cruising and get reimbursement for gasoline on the basis of phony mileage.

Despite the corruption, the frustrations and the shortages, the average Soviet citizen is, in most respects, bet-

ter off than he was two decades ago. At the end of the Stalin era, collective farmers, when they were paid at all, earned 24 kopeks (about 6¢ at the time) for a day's work—enough to buy one pair of trousers in the course of a year. Now the average peasant makes about 98 rubles ($129) a month. Salaries for workers and professionals have also risen, while prices of basic commodities, even though they are not always available when wanted, have remained relatively stable. Ivan Ivanovich may not have everything he wants, but at least he can now dream of trading in his old black-and-white TV for a color set, of riding to work in a four-passenger Zhiguli instead of on the bus, of having enough rubles to buy nice toys for his son's birthday.

Life in the Soviet Union also has some agreeable surprises for outsiders. "There is little violent crime compared with the U.S.," reports TIME Moscow Bureau Chief Marsh Clark. "It is safe to walk the streets at night in Moscow." Heavy steel locks are not needed on apartment doors. Kidnapings, which have become epidemic in Europe, are not known. There is almost no jaywalking. The cities are immaculate. People do not throw cigarette butts on the ground; receptacles are provided for such things and are expected to be used. When it snows, it seems as if every citizen comes out to clean off his little patch of sidewalk. Graffiti, that Western abomination, are unknown here. For one thing, anyone defacing a statue of Lenin or a public building would be running a very serious risk indeed.

Perhaps the most significant improvement in the quality of Soviet life is scarcely ever mentioned, least of all by top party officials. Exactly 20 years ago this month, at the 20th Party Congress, Nikita Khrushchev delivered his celebrated de-Stalinization speech that heralded the end of the vast "Gulag Archipelago" of concentration camps in which Stalin imprisoned at least 12 million people every year. Today, perhaps 10 000 people are still being held in Soviet prisons, camps or police-run psychiatric hospitals because their political or religious views are regarded as dangerous to the state. But notable dissidents are now more likely to be exiled than jailed. Some, like Sakharov, survive within the Soviet Union, openly challenging and embarrassing the Kremlin inquisitors.

Ivan Ivanovich may be indifferent to Sakharov's insistent calls for greater freedom in the Soviet Union. He does care, however, that his material wellbeing is improving, however erratically, and that he has far less to fear from the arbitrary midnight knock on the door. And that is no small blessing.

Time 1976 3 1

A beach on the Black Sea.

Novosti Press Agency

A district in Baku.

3. Mature Development: North America

The countries in North America (and some European countries as well) are at high levels of achievement. They have solved the problems related to survival. The essential desirables have ceased to be a cause of worry; in addition, most of the other important desirables have been provided. In general, questions about quality of life centre on aesthetics, convenience, and humanity. The range of areas in which North Americans are trying to improve their already high level of life is wide; this is true of all developed countries which offer vast choice to their populations. We cannot examine all possible concerns, but the following selection of items should give you a reasonable idea about the factors that, according to many North Americans, influence the quality of their lives.

Aid to the needy
by N. BRUCE MCLEOD

Christmas in Canada this year could be the great obscenity of 1974. For we are getting ready to celebrate "peace on earth" by practices which unconsciously work to break the earth apart.

The same magazine that advertises "Three wisemen in gleaming sterling at $20 for the Christmas tree that has everything." describes over the page how 460 million people are chronically hungry and most are under 5 years of age.

Why are they hungry? Not because there are too many of them; not because they are dumb or lazy; not because there is not enough food to go around. They are hungry because we have and keep what they need to live. Worse, we wrap it up and give it to each other, and make sure our children write thank-you notes for what our economy programmed them to need and requires them to have for it to carry on.

The world is like four apples and four people. One person has three of the apples, and is biting into the fourth.

We are near the peak of the gigantic annual rip-off that, to keep our Gross National Product growing, hustles money out of our pockets for plastic gewgaws and gimcracks and machine-tied ribbon bows. My bank has had a Christmas tree in the corner since Oct. 1. Tomorrow morning in Dacca, Bangladesh street sweepers will decide whether bodies are alive and should be left, or are dead and should be carted away.

The Toronto Star 1974 12 19

Urban living
A Meadowvale childhood comes free with each new home.

"What if we have to live here for ten or fifteen years?" "What if my children were to live out their childhoods in this neighbourhood?"

It's a train of thought that can derail a decision to buy an otherwise very nice house.

Because a lot of okay homes are being built in neighbourhoods that will be downright deadly places for children to grow up.

This year in Meadowvale New Town, almost twenty different builders are creating some of the most exciting new housing in North America.

You could spend two weekends househunting in Meadowvale and not see the same model twice.

But it's when you look a few years into your family's future that Meadowvale will spoil you for anywhere else.

Because Meadowvale is parkland trails at your front door when the baby's ready for his stroller.

And daycare centres full of happy toddlers when mother has other things to occupy her day.

For trikes and bikes, miles of parkland bicycle paths take kids to the store, the school, and back again in traffic-free safety.

When it's time for hiking, camping, cowboys-and-Indians and all sorts of Huck Finn adventures, the whole Credit River Valley lies alongside our eastern verge.

It brings fishing and horseback riding, cross-country skiing and conservation areas into every Meadowvale child's life.

When it comes to recreation, Meadowvale's million dollar sports budget is going into swimming pools, a hockey arena—all kinds of playing fields, tennis courts and even a toboggan hill. (We're practically surrounded by golf courses, too.)

And for the more city-style pursuits and interests of the Meadowvale teenager, such as part-time jobs and movies, our towncentre, with its shopping, cinema, cafes and offices, clustered around a 12 acre [4.8 ha] man-made lake, will lend a bustle of city-style excitement.

You can come see the Meadowvale that is today, and will be ten years away, at the expo-style Meadowvale Information Pavilion 200 yards [183 m] south of Highway 401 on Mississauga Road. (We're open 9 a.m. – 8 p.m. weekdays, 11 a.m. – 6 p.m. weekends.)

Then, our hostesses will send you to see some fabulous homes that fit your needs and your homebuying budget.

Meadowvale.

It's where you'll buy if you're buying for the next 10 years.

Courtesy of Markborough Properties Ltd.

Physical fitness

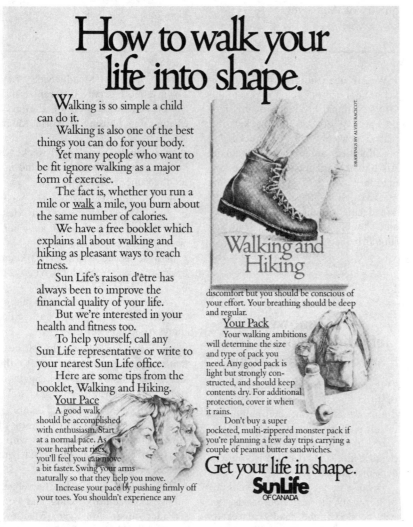

Courtesy of the Sun Life Assurance Company of Canada

Noise pollution

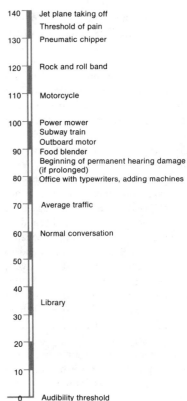

Level	
140	Jet plane taking off
	Threshold of pain
130	Pneumatic chipper
120	Rock and roll band
110	Motorcycle
100	Power mower
	Subway train
	Outboard motor
90	Food blender
	Beginning of permanent hearing damage (if prolonged)
80	Office with typewriters, adding machines
70	Average traffic
60	Normal conversation
50	
40	Library
30	
20	
10	
0	Audibility threshold

The Canadian Rockies are rapidly becoming a major tourist area.

A beach in Florida.

Pet Control

Should we limit Toronto's pet population?

YES!
Says Maurice Cowper-Smith, Toronto Humane Society

City aldermen tell me that they get more complaints about dogs than about any other issue. Municipal representatives in other cities confirm that experience.

. . .

Experience at the Toronto Humane Society has shown that, although there are people who have several dogs and look after them responsibly, owners with many dogs are more likely to be careless about where they permit their dogs to go and how much noise they permit their dogs to make.

The simple answer then is that there should be a limit on our pet population. But the real question is how many dogs can the average person look after responsibly?

One could say arbitrarily that the limit should be, say, three. Many municipalities have established such limits—Scarborough, York, Burlington and Cambridge being examples. But this discriminates against owners who may be able to care responsibly for, say, five dogs—or more.

. . .

Owners who refuse to confine their dogs, who let them breed indiscriminately or who neglect to get licences which identify them in the event of loss, are irresponsible and perhaps their dogs should be confiscated.

. . .

Prospective pet owners should be required to prove competence and adequate resources. The Toronto Humane Society already recognizes this philosophy in its "adoption" program.

This envisions a permit the application for which would reveal the size of a person's home, including the area of the fenced-in back-yard; whether or not an animal has been owned previously and, if so, what happened to it; whether or not there are infants in the family; whether the applicant is committed to the desirability of pet sterilization; and whether he or she can afford $200 a year in costs to keep a dog properly.

Another option is to charge prohibitive licence fees for second, third or more dogs. This has been done in some areas—but only the good citizens buy the second licence!

So yes—we should limit Toronto's pet population, not numerically but by requiring that pets have responsible owners. And that requirement may be best achieved through education, on which the Toronto Humane Society spends a lot of time and effort.

NO!
Says D. B. Macdonald, People's Animal Welfare Society

A bylaw to limit the number of pets a family may keep is unnecessary. Moreover, even when they've wanted such a bylaw public officials have never been able to devise a fair and effective way to limit the pet population.

Statistics show that the pet population can be effectively controlled by pet owners themselves. All they really need is the support of a local animal control department which will provide low-cost spay-neuter clinics rather than the existing, ineffective policy of impounding and killing strays.

If a limit of, say, three dogs per family were introduced, it would not make much difference to the public because the majority of families now own less than three anyway. If the limit were lowered, it wouldn't reduce the dog population so much as discourage owners from registering their pets.

Besides, when one considers that dogs can vary from five pounds to 150 pounds, the numbers aren't so important.

Our pet overpopulation today is the result of inept animal control policies and will continue until such policies change. The wasteful slaughter of pet animals and the tax burden this imposes is unnecessary.

. . .

No function of municipal government has distressed so many concerned people over such a long period as has the "impound and kill" system of animal control, and no function of municipal government has experienced such a long and costly history of failure.

Rather than impose limits on the number of pets or impose tough fines, Toronto could eliminate surplus and unwanted animals by establishing low-cost municipal spay-neuter clinics as has Los Angeles.

Another step would be to ban the importing of pets from puppy and kitten mills in the United States. Backyard breeding could also be discouraged through zoning and taxation.

Promiscuous breeding could be further discouraged by increasing license fees for pets that are not spayed or neutered at the low-cost clinics.

All these would be more sensible steps than passing a bylaw that says any one pet owner can only have a certain number of pets.

The Sunday Star 1978 4 2

4. A Development Game

In trying to forecast the future, experts often use the theory of games to see how a situation can be resolved. We can study Bangladesh and Russia by reducing their problems to symbols in a model, and examining the main elements involved (Fig. 5-2).

Fig. 5-2
The survival model

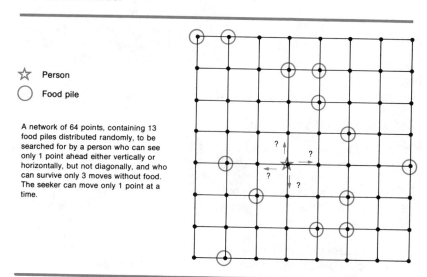

☆ Person

◯ Food pile

A network of 64 points, containing 13 food piles distributed randomly, to be searched for by a person who can see only 1 point ahead either vertically or horizontally, but not diagonally, and who can survive only 3 moves without food. The seeker can move only 1 point at a time.

In the survival model the network represents a society's environment and the food piles represent the survival chances. There are three main components; first, the number of food piles, or survival chances, available to the society; second, the length of time the seeker is able to survive without finding a food pile, namely three moves; and third, the distance the seeker can see ahead, namely one point at a time. As you examine the network it is fairly obvious which points the seeker should follow, but to the seeker, who can see only one point ahead, the path is not obvious.

At the simplest level the seeker, representing society, stumbles along, finding food piles at random. Perhaps the seeker follows the same pattern over and over as the annual harvests renew the food piles. The seeker who fails to achieve a successful pattern does not survive.

As the seeker becomes more aware of the environment's patterns, three new ways of improving the situation are seen to exist. First, the number of food piles, or in other words, the material wealth of the society can be increased. Translated into real-life situations, this means that the seeker does not need to spend so much time searching for food or other products; supplies are readily available. Second, the seeker can be allowed to survive more than three moves. In reality this means that the seeker gains improved storage capacities, so that failures to obtain certain commodities can be more easily survived. Third, the seeker can develop the ability to see more than one point ahead. In other words, education and other service levels of the society are improved so that the seeker becomes more aware of the environment and of what can be done.

Bangladesh represents a society still stumbling along, often needing the help of other societies. The USSR represents a society that has successfully built up its educational and general service levels but that is still lacking in material wealth. North America, on the other hand, has successfully solved all three problems, at least for most of the population.

Statistical Interpretation

5-4 Set up the survival model as a game between two sides. One side distributes the food piles (fewer than thirteen to make the game harder; more to make it easier) in a random fashion, *unknown to the other side*. The seeker can start anywhere, and is permitted to know what, if anything lies at the adjacent vertical and horizontal points only. After a one point move in a vertical or horizontal direction the seeker is again permitted to know what lies at the adjacent vertical and horizontal points. The seeker is allowed three unsuccessful moves before failing to survive. Variations of the game should be tried:

a) an increased or reduced number of food piles (material wealth);

b) longer or shorter survival periods (storage); and

c) the ability to see farther ahead than one point (education).

Which of these three variables is in practice the one most likely to influence the outcome of the game? *In order to guarantee survival in real life*, would it be better for a society to put its development effort into more current material production, greater capital accumulation and storage, or improved education?

Discussion and Research

7. To what extent should the quality of our lives depend upon the amount of help we give to less developed countries?

8. How would you respond to Bruce McLeod's argument that the world is like "four apples and four people"?

9. Is there a "geography of happiness"?

Section C
Assessing the Quality of Life

The problems of assessing the varying quality of life around the world are enormous; so many of the desirables are intangible and immeasurable. How do you compare the aesthetic values of a forest and a seascape? Or the ability to hear a live performance of Beethoven's Ninth Symphony with the ability to hear the cry of the loon? Choice is the inevitable problem.

Nevertheless we will try an assessment. There are two ways in which it can be approached: first, we can select many criteria and apply them to a few sample countries; or second, we can use a single representative criterion and apply it to all countries. Neither method will give us a total picture, but the alternative of applying many criteria to all countries is difficult without the aid of a computer.

We will use both of these methods, because the map that we develop will be made more meaningful by an analysis of a few sample countries. The criteria we will use are listed in Fig. 5-3. We can use

How do you assess the value of certain qualities of life? This is a tea-room in the Tajik Republic of the USSR.

Novosti Press Agency

only items for which measurable data are available; this means that we must omit the extent of religious freedom or minority rights, the general efficiency with which things get done, the moral climate, and so on. These factors can influence the quality of life from place to place, but we cannot assess them numerically.

Fig. 5-3
Criteria for assessing the quality of life
Note: Data for criteria are listed in Fig. 5-4.

Criterion	Unit
A Population density	people/km²
B Life expectancy	years
C Food adequacy	kJ/person/d
D Food production efficiency	percentage of population in farming
E Trading wealth	international reserves/person
F Electricity generation	kW·h/person
G Material wealth	gross manufactured output/person
H Education	literacy rate (percentage)
I Health	people/physician
J Communication ability	telephones/100 people
K News availability	radio receivers/1 000 people
L Ease of travel	cars/1 000 people
M Total goods and services	GNP/person
N Crime	murders/100 000 people
O Dissatisfaction levels	suicides/100 000 people

Fig 5-4
Criterion data (note that communist countries do not provide sufficient data, so they are not included in this chart)

Country	A	B	C	D	E	F	G	H	I	J	K	L	M	N	O
Canada	2.3	72.9	13 356	8	260	11 854	2 685	97	633	52.8	865	326	6 080	2.3	12.2
USA	22.8	71.3	13 986	4	70	9 254	3 265	98	621	65.7	1 752	493	6 640	9.1	11.7
Sweden	18.2	75.0	11 802	9	311	9596	2756	99	681	59.4	32	308	6 720	1.1	20.3
France	96.7	71.5	13 482	14	164	3 339	2 191	98	721	21.7	329	269	5 190	.9	16.1
W. Germany	248.7	70.5	13 524	9	535	4 825	2 722	98	543	28.7	332	267	5 890	1.4	21.2
UK	229.3	70.8	13 398	3	116	5 044	2 687	98	787	34.0	672	244	3 360	.8	7.7
Italy	185.3	72.0	13 356	21	117	2 651	1 040	98	544	22.9	227	245	2 770	1.1	5.8
Portugal	95.1	68.0	12 180	37	332	1 147	370	65	957	10.9	176	90	1 540	.7	8.2
Greece	68.6	72.4	13 398	47	117	1 651	426	80	579	18.7	111	39	1 970	.5	2.7
Israel	162.8	71.5	12 432	11	570	2 740	1 061	84	364	20.8	221	75	3 380	10.4	6.7
Thailand	82.3	56.3	10 752	77	33	171	27	68	7 971	.6	76	7	300	12.7	4.5
Japan	298.0	73.2	10 542	21	113	4 339	2 242	98	867	35.5	658	134	3 880	1.3	16.8
Australia	1.8	70.9	13 776	8	434	4 935	2 336	98	792	35.5	213	343	4 760	3.1	12.5
Kenya	23.0	49.1	9 912	80	19	58	51	25	16 292	.9	41	9	200	11.4	.2
Jamaica	185.2	64.6	9 912	27	65	1 080	329	82	3 918	4.3	376	45	1140	1.0	1.5
Bolivia	5.1	49.7	7 980	58	14	169	23	40	2 422	.9	288	4	250	11.2	1.4
Ecuador	23.7	52.4	8 442	54	36	166	72	67	2 928	1.9	279	5	460	9.1	2.3
Venezuela	13.1	66.4	10 206	26	214	1 452	550	77	978	4.6	182	56	1 710	9.7	6.4

Source: *UN Statistical Yearbook*, 1971-75, and *UNESCO Statistical Yearbook*, 1974.

Statistical Interpretation

5-5 Use the technique of *percentage deviation from the mean*, as explained in Appendix 3.

a) For each set of data for the different criteria given in Fig. 5-4, calculate the group mean.

b) Calculate the percentage deviation of each datum from its appropriate group mean.

c) Decide whether deviations over or under the group mean add (+) to the quality of life or subtract (−) from it. Insert appropriate + or − signs to *all* your calculated percentage deviations. Thus, if X represented road deaths per million people, then the fewer the better, so the deviation of 41 below the mean would be a plus (+41). If, however, X represented average weekly dollar wages, then the more the better, and a deviation below the mean would be a negative quality (− 41). Use your discretion here.

d) Add the deviations *across* the columns, so that all the deviations for one country are accumulated into an empty column on the right. Do not forget that the negative values must be subtracted.

e) Rank the countries in order from highest to lowest.

f) Evaluate the results.

g) In which areas could the quality of life in Canada be improved in relation to the other sample countries?

5-6 Using the GNP/person data in column U of Appendix 2 as representative of the *choices available* to a country, and therefore indirectly as a measure of the level of concerns about the quality of life, draw a graded shading world map showing four classes, as follows:

$3 000 and over	bright gold
$2 000 - 2 999	gold
$1 000 - 1 999	pale gold
$ 0 - 999	very pale yellow

a) How does this map compare with any population maps you may have drawn in Chapter 1? Do you draw any conclusions from this?

b) How good is the GNP/person data as a means of measuring quality of life? Could you pick a country to live in solely on the basis of GNP/person?

Case Study 5
California: Quality of Life

California is one of the richest areas in the world, with an average annual personal income in mid-1977 of about $7 500. It has already achieved a standard of living that many other areas in the world are still seeking.

It produces food in abundance, it has varied industries, and it has a highly literate population. It has been described as "the cutting edge of the future", and even as "paradise".

The concerns of California's people, as you may expect from an economically developed society, generally exclude such problems as food availability and daily survival. They also exclude questions of political freedom, good health, and sound education. Indeed, it is arguable that Californians are among the freest people on earth, and there is little doubt that their health care and educational facilities greatly exceed most world standards. In a survey of the quality of life in all US states in 1973, the Midwest Research Institute rated California top in the quality of both its state and local governments, and very highly in its provision of health and educational facilities. In other words, Californians are well past the stage of basic needs, and are already enjoying a very high level of living.

Despite its high quality of life, California does have certain problems. There are at least seven concerns—one minor and six major. The minor concern, unrelated to the others, is earthquakes. The six interrelated problems are: water availability, ethnic minorities, population, future energy supplies, environmental pollution, and continued economic growth.

The danger of earthquakes is considered to be unrelated to the other problems because it is as yet outside our control. The other concerns, however, arise to a great extent from our ability to improve the quality of life. These six basic problems sum up the difficulties faced by all economically advanced countries.

1. Earthquakes

The most notorious of California's earthquakes was the one that took place in San Francisco in 1906. Early on the morning of April 18, when most people were still asleep, an earthquake of 8.3R (8.3 on the Richter scale) totally destroyed 500 city blocks, caused 700 deaths, and was responsible for damage worth about $5 billion at 1977 prices.

But there have been other earthquakes, notably in Owens Valley, 1872 (8.3R); Long Beach, 1933 (6.3R); Imperial Valley, 1940 (7.1R); Kern County, 1952 (7.7R); and San Fernando, 1971 (6.6R). Seismologists in California, based at the US National Center for Earthquake Research at Menlo Park, just south of San Francisco, confidently predict that another major earthquake of at least 8.0R will occur on or before the year 2000. This prediction is based on the observed behaviour of the rocks along the edges of the two major *tectonic plates* (great segments of the earth's crust) that meet in California (see Fig. 5C-1). These rocks "creep" against each

Fig. 5C-1
The meeting of two major tectonic plates along the San Andreas Fault in California

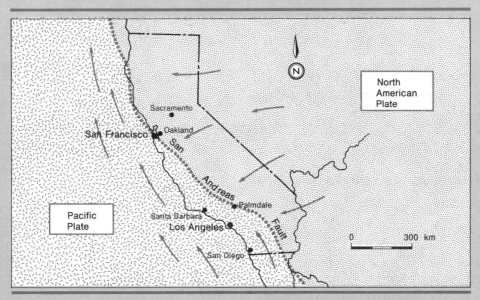

Based on a map in *Scientific American* 1975 11, p. 91.

other, producing tensions and distortions that build up where movement is inhibited until there is a major slippage to release the built-up pressure; this slippage causes an earthquake. Another observation which supports the possibility of a major earthquake within the next thirty years is the *dilation* (expansion) of the rocks along the line of the San Andreas Fault. This occurs because the rocks crack open slightly under tension, thus causing their volume to increase. Under tension, therefore, the ground bulges upward, exactly as it does at the Palmdale Bulge 60 km north of Los Angeles (see Fig. 5C-2).

These phenomena are sufficient to have caused California to set up a Seismic Safety Commission, in order to minimize human disaster resulting from earthquakes. Most of the group's work is concentrated in the San Francisco Bay area, which is regarded as the most hazardous zone because of the number of faults in the region (see Fig. 5C-3). Forecasts of

Fig. 5C-2
The Palmdale Bulge

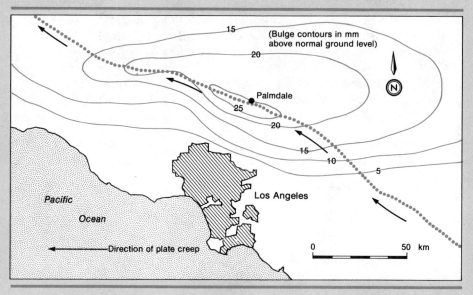

Source: *Time* 1976 4 19, p. 43.

Fig. 5C-3
Major faults in the San Francisco Bay area

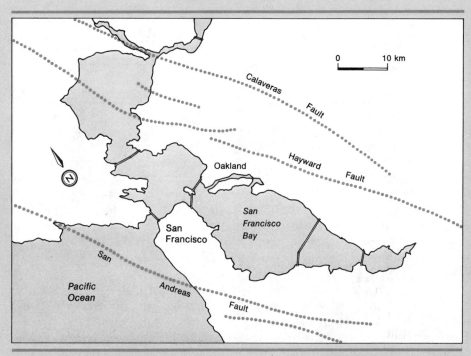

Source: White, *Natural Hazards*, 1974.

damage to San Francisco from another 8.3R earthquake run as high as $40 billion; 350 000 people may die, depending upon the time of day and the possibility of advance warning. To minimize losses, the Seismic Safety Commission is trying to have old buildings replaced as swiftly as possible, because these present the major threat to life. However, there is opposition from conservationists. To further reduce losses, construction on lands liable to be submerged if dams break is being avoided; balconies and parapets have been removed from existing buildings; and earthquake emergency services have been established.

2. Water Availability

Eighty percent of the population of California lives in the southern part of the state, but 80% of the precipitation falls in the north. There is a critical water shortage in the south, aggravated by the continued and explosive growth in that area in the last 100 years, particularly in the last 35-40 years. Most of the water is needed for farm irrigation, but much is also needed for industry; green lawns and swimming pools also make demands on the supply. As population grew in the south, water from local wells (although still used) gradually became inadequate. Water was then sought from the Owens River district of the Sierra Nevada and, later, from the Colorado River by way of the Parker Dam, Lake Havasu, and the Colorado River Aqueduct. Continued population growth has placed even these sources under great pressure; plans are currently being carried out in the California State Water Project to transfer water from northern California by a series of canals, pumping stations, and pipelines through the Central Valley and across the Tehachapi Mountains to southern California.

It is expected that if population growth continues, and that if people continue to use more water, even these sources will be inadequate. Plans have accordingly been made to bring water from Oregon and Washington, which, in turn, will draw water from British Columbia and even the Yukon. Meanwhile, desalination plants have been opened, notably at San Diego, and there has been talk of towing icebergs from the Antarctic.

Water availability has in fact become a matter of real concern to most Californians, especially in the south. Adequate water is important to the state's quality of life.

3. Ethnic Minorities

The enormous growth of California's economy, particularly in the period 1940-65, increased the inward migration of people from all areas of the world. For many years, persons from all parts of the world have moved hopefully to California, and as a result there is a great mixture of people in the state. Many have fitted easily into the society, just as the half-million or so Canadians in Los Angeles have done; but others have formed visible communities of their own. One of the oldest, largest, and most colourful of these ethnic communities is that of the Chinese in San Francisco. More recently established large groups include Koreans in San Francisco and Los Angeles, and blacks and Mexicans in Los Angeles. While the oriental areas generally serve as a highly valued tourist attraction, the Mexican and black areas often provide examples of urban poverty.

One of the most significant attempts to map the quality of life was made in 1965 in Los Angeles. At that time, the state of California hired the Space-General Corporation to study quality of life, and to predict areas of unrest resulting from a low quality level. The corporation used five criteria (median income less than $5 000; blacks 75% or more of the population; maximum drop-out rate from school; maximum crime rate; maximum population density) and produced the map for the Los Angeles area shown in Fig. 5C-4. Later in 1965 some of the most violent urban poverty riots were staged in Watts, giving credence to this new type of predictive mapping.

Many of the migrants to California, especially to Los Angeles, have been Mexican. Indeed, Los Angeles now houses more people of Mexican origin than any other city in the world except Mexico City. Most of them

Fig. 5C-4
Quality of life mapping in the Los Angeles area

Source: Space General Corporation.

are in California legally, and the Mexican quota of 20 000 immigrants is filled early every year. However, a large number have entered the state illegally. This illegal entry creates many problems, including the following: the depressing effect of illegally low wages; unemployment for more highly paid native US citizens; low health standards in some Spanish-speaking communities; the burdens imposed on school and welfare services; and embarrassment to legally admitted Mexican-Americans.

Nevertheless, as Fig. 5C-5 shows, illegal immigrants pour in, despite all attempts to stop or deport them. There are Mexicans and Americans who earn their living by smuggling illegal migrants into California, especially along the border east of Tijuana. About 80% of the "illegals" are caught and returned, but many still get through.

Fig. 5C-5
Illegal immigrants to the United States. (Immigration and Naturalization Service)

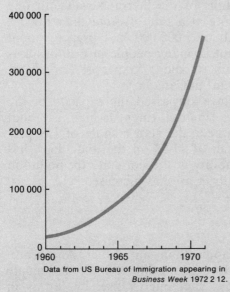

Data from US Bureau of Immigration appearing in
Business Week 1972 2 12.

Mexicans migrate to California, both legally and illegally, for numerous reasons. Among them the following motives are important:

a) Historical association. Mexicans inhabited the region well before it became part of the United States, and many of them strongly believe that it is the Americans who are the immigrants. Mexicans therefore feel they should be free to move in as they desire.

b) Historical employment. For many years Mexicans were brought in under the federal *bracero* program as cheap migrant labour to work in the fruit and vegetable fields. The US stopped the program in 1964, but by then many Mexicans had decided to settle permanently in California.

c) Higher wages in California than in Mexico. Wages in Los Angeles, even the illegal wages paid below the state minimum wage, are from five to ten times higher than in Mexico, and are a powerful attraction to potential immigrants, who have been conditioned by the defunct *bracero* program to look north for employment. Along with higher wages, migrants see the chance to better themselves as individuals.

d) Population pressure in Mexico. Mexico has one of the world's fastest rates of population increase; thus despite large economic gains, there is a great shortage of many things, including jobs. Outward migration to areas of better economic opportunity has always relieved this sort of population pressure. Mexico is no exception. This is one reason why the Mexican government is much less concerned than the US government about illegal migration; for Mexico, migration is a safety valve.

4. Numbers

People have flocked to California ever since the January day in 1848 when gold was discovered in the foothills of the Sierra Nevada. In one period, 1940-65, immigrants were arriving at a rate of more than 1 000 a day, so that the 1940 population of about 7 000 000 had risen to about 18 000 000 by 1965. There are now about as many people in California as there are in all of Canada, at a density of about 55 people/km², compared with a density of only 2.5 people/km² in Canada.

Population growth now seems to have surpassed the capacity of the state to support its people comfortably. Unemployment is high, at about 1 000 000; freeways are frequently jammed; the state's share of US personal income, which had risen to a peak of 11.5% in the mid-1960s, has fallen to about 11%; future water availability is a major concern; pollution has become a problem; and crime and drug use has increased.

5. Energy

Californians use more energy per capita than any other Americans. Indeed, high energy use is a characteristic of the life style of the people and of the economy of the state. The chief energy use, by far, is in transportation; there are about 18 000 000 cars in the state, and numerous trucks, buses, and planes. About 45% of California's energy is used for transportation, and the total amount of energy consumed is almost 20 times the amount used in India. Industry accounts for another 25% of the energy consumption, followed by commercial operations (15%), domestic use (10%), and farming (5%).

For many years, California has relied largely on local oil and gas for its energy supplies. Local production is now declining, while offshore drilling is being strongly resisted by conservationists, especially after the major oil leak at Santa Barbara in 1969. Alaskan oil and gas will provide a temporary solution, but long-term alternatives in other fields are being sought and developed. Geothermal power is available, as at the world's largest geothermal plant at Geyserville, north of San Francisco, but its potential is quite limited. Solar power is also in use, especially in the sunny south, but this form of energy production involved large areas of land. Meanwhile, as Fig. 5C-6 shows, the major supplies of energy in the future are expected to come from nuclear fuels. This is a problem, because many people object to nuclear power stations situated in a region so prone to earthquakes. They fear disaster at worst, from meltdown to clouds of plutonium dust; but they also fear inadequate safety standards. These low standards could lead to radioactive leakage, incomplete security in transportation of radioactive material, and unsafe disposal of radioactive wastes. Those who favour nuclear power point to a proven high safety record, and say that jobs and life styles for millions are threatened unless energy is provided. In 1976 a state vote was held on the matter of continued nuclear construction, and those in favour won by two to one. This still leaves millions of people concerned about the risks of nuclear energy production.

Fig. 5C-6
Expected sources of energy in California, 1975-2000 (Rand Corporation)

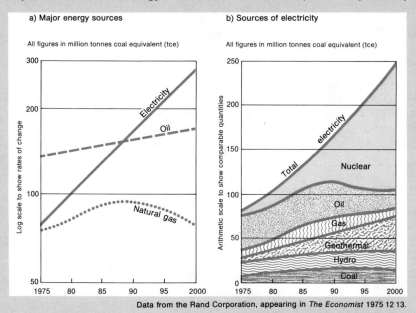

Data from the Rand Corporation, appearing in *The Economist* 1975 12 13.

6. Pollution

Massive inward migrations, rapid development of the economy, and high standards of living have put great pressure on the natural environment in California. This has aroused strong reactions; many Californians settled there because of the beauty of the natural environment, and they are still immensely proud of it. It is no coincidence that environmentalist societies such as the *Friends of the Earth* and the *Sierra Club* originated in California, nor that the state has the world's strictest car pollution controls.

The number of cars in California is astounding, especially in Los Angeles, where per capita car ownership is now the highest in the world. Before the 1970s, the quantities of untreated exhaust gas resulted in huge masses of smog, due to a chemical reaction between the exhaust gases and the bright sunshine. Sometimes when the smog was bad, people were advised to stay indoors and avoid energetic activity. Eyes watered and reddened, people complained and rebelled. Environmental care came of age; by the early 1970s the environmentalists were receiving broad support, and legislation followed. The situation began to improve.

7. Growth

Many Californians are alarmed about continued growth. Already there are concerns about pollution, water and energy supplies, and illegal immigration. Increased numbers of people can only serve to aggravate the situation, since they will seek housing, employment, and services.

There is nevertheless a strong and perhaps overwhelming drive for continued growth in California. Many, perhaps most, of the people who settled in California did so because it represented the future to them. Thus in 1960 *The Economist* described California as "The State of the Future"; in 1962 *Look* wrote of "Tomorrow's hopes and headaches... here today"; and in 1974 *Newsweek* noted that "California is where everything good or bad...seems to happen first."

However, the economy slowed down in the 1970s, and there were reductions in space research in California. These factors, together with the other concerns that we have discussed, may have slowed down the rush of people heading for California.

QUALITY OF LIFE: Further Reading

The Book of Eve, BERESFORD-HOWE
The Terminal Man, CRICHTON
The Man Who Fell to Earth, TEVIS
Fever, FULLER
The Poverty Wall, ADAMS
Making It, FINNIGAN & SONICK
Cabbagetown, GARNER
Reservations are for Indians, ROBERTSON
But not in Canada, STEWART
The Tin Flute, ROY
Playground, BUELL

Conclusion

Quality of life is, as we have seen, an elusive concept, open to many interpretations. An individual's life style is made up of a number of features, and this life is said to be "rich" if it consists of a variety of interesting experiences. In this chapter we have found that some societies offer a wider range of experiences than do others. The reasons for this may be rooted in some of the matters discussed in the first four chapters, or they may exist elsewhere. For example, the degree of crowding or the amount of open space available can affect a person's quality of life quite significantly; so also can the quantity and quality of food available. Industrialization may benefit some people and harm others. At the same time, quality of life may be influenced by political considerations, or by religious, moral, or intellectual factors.

Since quality of life involves so many different elements, it is only partially a geographical concern. Yet undoubtedly its variations have one of the most profound and persistent geographical effects of all—migration. The mass movement of human beings over the face of the earth is largely a result of people's desire to find a better life. In the next chapter, we accordingly examine migrations.

Chapter 6
MIGRATIONS

Introduction

Migration is the act of moving from one place to another, or the changing of locations. Migrations have been a common aspect of the human race from the earliest times. From their origins, probably in East Africa, people have spread over the globe in increasing numbers, earlier groups of migrants being pushed into remoter areas by later and more powerful groups. Earlier migrants usually tried to hold on to the best areas of land they had settled, and there was often bitter and bloody conflict as later migrants tried to push them out. History is full of examples of conflicts resulting from migration: "barbarians" (bearded ones) overran the Roman Empire and finally, in the fifth century, sacked Rome itself; the Spanish and Portuguese conquered Central and South America in the sixteenth and seventeenth centuries; and the Europeans fought the North American Indians for land, a conflict that has continued even to the present day (though now it takes place in the law courts rather than on the land itself).

Why do people migrate? Where do they come from? Where do they go? We will attempt to answer these basic questions in the first three sections of the chapter. In the last sections, we will examine the benefits and problems of migrations, and the different ways that migration is related to urbanization. To finish off the discussion, the case study deals with migration in a particular country, Turkey.

The following items provide a general idea of the main issues in migration today.

Report urges 100 000 immigrants a year to offset decline in births

OTTAWA (CP)—Canada needs at least 100 000 immigrants a year to offset a declining birth rate, but a special parliamentary committee said yesterday there must be a reasonable limit to admissions.

Mr. O'Connell told reporters that a revised immigration policy should consider four main factors: family reunification, lack of discrimination, the state of the economy and accommodation of refugees.

Refugees as well as immigrants sponsored by their immediate families would not be part of the annual target recommended by the committee, which did not propose any ceiling.

"We haven't attempted to consider a maximum." Mr. O'Connell said, adding that it would be "far too complex a matter."

Nevertheless, he suggested there had to be a limit.

He said Canada had more than 600 000 immigration applications in 1974, but "I don't think anybody really feels that Canada can handle 600 000."

The minimum of at least 100 000 was relatively easy to arrive at, however, because readily available figures show that the population will start declining in 25 years at the current birth rate.

"Canada must continue to welcome a minimum of 100 000 immigrants a year as long as present fertility rates prevail," the committee said. It said it was divided on whether to recommend a ceiling, but did not go into detail.

In the draft report, the committee said some of its members "would like to see Canada receiving up to 1 per cent of its population," about 220 000 persons a year at present.

Whatever the solution, the committee rejected the view expressed in some of the 1 200 submissions it received that Canada should close its doors to immigrants. It also concluded that an open-door policy was not the answer either.

"The committee's preference is for a policy of moderation between these two extremes."

The Globe and Mail 1975 11 7

Slums of hope... slums of despair

by APRODICIO A. LAQUIAN

In almost all large cities in developing countries, slum and squatter communities mar the otherwise beautiful and exotic landscapes. Known as *favelas, tugurios, bustees, ranchos* or *gecekondus*, they crowd inner city alleys, cling precariously to hillsides, clog smelly canals and drains, line railroad tracks and occupy road rights-of-way. They cluster like malignant cysts in the city or encircle it like dirty bath tub rings.

A study of slum and squatter conditions in eight million-size cities in as many countries recently finished with support from the International Development Research Centre (IDRC) revealed the critical lack of services and amenities in these settlements. In Bandung, Indonesia, the fastest growing city in the world, more than a fourth of the inhabitants are squatters. In the communities studied, only 33.2 per cent had access to clean drinkable water, 44.2 per cent had toilets, and 51.6 per cent had electricity. The city of Caracas, the wealthiest urban area of Latin America's oil-rich country of Venezuela, has been plagued with *ranchos*, illegal makeshift dwellings. Despite massive housing projects (called *super-bloques* appropriately enough), a fourth of Caracas still lives in hillside hovels or shanties at the bottom of ravines. The ancient city of Istanbul has its *gecekondus*, instant communities built by those that literally "fly in the night" and build their shanties faster than the government can tear them down.

In the cities of Kuala Lumpur, Lagos, Lima, Manila and Seoul which were also surveyed for the study, similar stories of the sad plight of squatters and slum dwellers were found. Kuala Lumpur, the beautifully planned capital city of Malaysia, has been trying to relocate its squatters to better areas for decades but they still make up more than a third of the population. Lagos, another well-planned capital city, has received the brunt of Nigeria's massive rural-urban migration, resulting in almost half of its people living in slums and squatter areas. The Peruvian capital city of Lima has, perhaps, done more than most cities to cure its problem of squatting. Through some admirably practical schemes, such as self-help housing, community organization and use of local resources for housing materials, Peru has been able to keep its squatters under control. The *pueblos jovenes* program (typically, squatter communities are called "young settlements") has been remarkably successful. Still, about a million people of Lima still live in poor communities, and conditions are worse in other cities such as Chimbote, where more than half of the people are squatters or slum dwellers....

Cooperation Canada (CIDA) 1974 9

Discussion and Research

1. What different reasons for migrating can you suggest?
2. What are some of the problems connected with migration?
3. If you were to migrate, what would motivate you most, idealism or reality?
4. What would you expect to be the likeliest problems when people of different culture groups come into contact through migration? In what ways could you reduce or even solve such problems?

Section A
Why Do People Migrate?

Most people have some sort of affection for their place of birth. The feeling may be expressed at different levels as local allegiance, regional loyalty, or national pride. It may also be expressed with different degrees of intensity: some people will close their minds to other people and places; others will seek to travel and meet other peoples, to "broaden their minds". *Xenophobia*—a hatred of anything foreign—is the opposite of an acceptance of the exotic, and immobility is the opposite of mobility.

Migration is therefore most likely to appeal to the more mobile and open-minded people in a society. Nevertheless there are ties that must be broken, and problems that must be solved. Friends and relatives must often be left behind, pensions and social benefits abandoned, and seniority and established positions given up; a new start must be made. The reasons for migrating must be powerful enough to overcome such factors.

Prospective migrants must think of the pros and cons of migration. They must compare their life at home with what they know of a new country. For example, job opportunities, wages, standards of living, and social services may appear to be better in one area than in another. Such perceived advantages then have to be weighed against any expected disadvantages, such as the possible need to learn a new language and to adjust to a different culture.

Some migrants are able to make a choice of destination; others are forced to migrate, and may not be able to choose. In some cases people migrate almost regardless of destination, in order to escape political, military, religious, social, or even economic persecution. Examples of such forced migrations include those of Chileans from Chile (1975, political), non-Lebanese from Lebanon (1976, military), Jews from Germany (1930s, racial), US blacks to Canada (nineteenth century, social), and US southern blacks to the northern US (nineteenth and twentieth centuries, economic).

There are other reasons for migration. First, governments often sponsor colonization projects, which either encourage or force people

One of the strongest barriers to migration is inertia. Many people feel that migration is too much trouble, and they accordingly remain where they are, even though they may be discontented.

Migrants are people who move. They include *emigrants*, who move out, and *immigrants*, who move in.

to move. Such projects account for the migration of Russians to Siberia, Brazilians to Amazonia, and Chinese to Manchuria and Sinkiang. Second, there is often a demand for cheap labour; for this reason West Indians are brought in to Ontario's fruit and tobacco fields. Third, people move to escape overcrowded conditions and find "room to breathe". Thus Britons move to Australia. Fourth, there is often an urge for a warm and sunny climate, and so retired North Americans, for example, go to Florida. Finally, people often yearn for a homeland; this accounts for the migration of Jews to Israel.

Statistical Interpretation

6-1 In 1966 the Canadian federal government started a program to bring Caribbean workers to Ontario to harvest the fruit, vegetable, and tobacco crops. Seasonal workers from Europe and the USA were also brought in. Fig. 6-1 shows the main details, as well as the area of land under tobacco in each year and the annual weight of the crop. Do you think Canada is justified in importing cheap labour for its fruit, vegetable, and tobacco harvests? Who gains from such an arrangement? Who loses?

6-2 Fig. 6-2 gives information on the number of immigrants arriving each year since 1901 in both Canada and the USA. Answer the following questions for either Canada or the USA (or both).
a) Calculate the ratio, lowest year: highest year.
b) Can you find or suggest reasons for this great variation in the level of immigration?
c) Plot the actual data from 1901 as a normal line graph.
d) Calculate a ten-year moving average as shown in Appendix 3, and then plot the moving average data as a regular line graph, starting in 1910.
e) What do you notice about the long-term trends in immigration? Can you explain them in terms of your answer to (b) alone?

Fig. 6-1
Immigrant seasonal labour and the tobacco crop in Canada

Year	Seasonal labour			Tobacco crop	
	European	US	Caribbean	Area planted (ha)	Production (kg)
1966	576	2 544	264	53 225	106 225 100
1967	—	—	1 077	57 013	96 745 584
1968	—	—	1 258	54 623	99 338 378
1969	—	962	1 449	53 765	112 349 110
1970	—	377	1 279	43 826	100 725 800
1971	675	377	1 271	39 503	101 883 040
1972	675	223	1 531	41 830	84 823 544
1973	1 193	—	3 048	48 951	116 820 100

Source: Food Prices Review Board, *Hired Farm Labour in Canada*, 1975 3, p. 13.

Fig. 6-2
Immigration to Canada and the USA since 1901

Year	Canada	USA	Year	Canada	USA
1901	55 747	487 918	1939	16 994	82 998
1902	89 102	648 743	1940	11 324	70 756
1903	138 660	857 046	1941	9 329	51 776
1904	131 252	812 870	1942	7 576	28 781
1905	141 465	1 026 499	1943	8 504	23 725
1906	211 653	1 100 735	1944	12 801	28 551
1907	272 409	1 285 349	1945	22 722	38 119
1908	143 326	782 870	1946	71 719	108 721
1909	173 694	751 786	1947	64 127	147 292
1910	286 839	1 041 570	1948	125 414	170 570
1911	331 288	878 587	1949	95 217	188 317
1912	375 756	838 172	1950	73 912	249 187
1913	400 870	1 197 892	1951	194 391	205 717
1914	150 484	1 218 480	1952	164 498	265 520
1915	36 665	326 700	1953	168 868	170 434
1916	55 914	298 826	1954	154 227	208 177
1917	72 910	295 403	1955	109 946	237 790
1918	41 845	110 618	1956	164 857	321 625
1919	107 698	141 132	1957	282 164	326 867
1920	138 824	430 001	1958	124 851	253 265
1921	91 728	805 228	1959	106 928	260 686
1922	64 224	309 556	1960	104 111	265 398
1923	133 729	522 919	1961	71 689	271 344
1924	124 164	706 896	1962	74 586	283 763
1925	84 907	294 314	1963	93 151	306 260
1926	135 982	304 488	1964	112 606	292 248
1927	158 886	335 175	1965	146 758	296 697
1928	166 783	307 255	1966	194 743	323 040
1929	164 993	279 678	1967	222 876	361 972
1930	104 806	241 700	1968	183 974	454 448
1931	27 530	97 139	1969	161 531	358 579
1932	20 591	35 576	1970	147 713	373 326
1933	14 382	23 068	1971	121 900	370 478
1934	12 476	29 470	1972	122 006	384 685
1935	11 277	34 956	1973	184 200	400 063
1936	11 643	36 329	1974	218 465	394 861
1937	15 101	50 244	1975	187 881	386 194
1938	17 244	67 895	1976	149 429	305 071

Compiled from Urquhart and Buckley, *Historical Statistics of Canada; Canada Year Book,* 1972 and 1976-77; *Historical Statistics of the US,* Bicentennial edition; and *Canadian Statistical Review* 1978 3.

Discussion and Research

5. Why have people migrated to Canada in particular?

6. What sorts of persons migrate?

7. Fewer people migrate than may wish to. What stops them?

Section B
Where Do Migrants Come From?

1. Origins

Early members of the human race are believed to have originated in the plains of East Africa and pulsed out in waves as periodic phases of overpopulation and starvation occurred. Several hundreds of thousands of years later in eastern Asia, the Han Chinese had become the predominant oriental strain and gradually pushed out from their home in the Wei valley to the limits of the East Asian mainland. On the other side of Eurasia the peninsulas and islands of Europe were peopled by various groups pushing westward: the nordic group in the north, the alpine people through the centre, and the mediterranean races in the south.

The origins and behaviour of early humans are subject to much speculation. While the earliest people seem to have originated in East Africa, there is evidence that other early humans originated elsewhere, as in China and Indonesia.

2. European Empires

The creation of the European overseas empires, beginning in the fifteenth century and continuing until the early twentieth century, provided another strong movement of migrants. Colonists and settlers were actively sought to populate the new lands. As early as 1634 for instance, William Penn opened a migration office in London, England; even earlier, in 1608, Samuel de Champlain founded Quebec City, and established the seigneurial system in New France, to get landowners or "seigneurs" to bring over colonists from France itself.

European empires, especially those of Britain, France, Portugal, Spain, and Holland, were also responsible for the mass movements of non-European peoples. In many parts of the tropics death control methods were slow to penetrate, populations were often small, and labour was frequently scarce. Accordingly, Europeans took people from areas where the population was more than large enough to fill European needs (e.g., West Africa and India) and transferred them to areas where a labour force was needed to work in mines or on plantations. Throughout South America, the Caribbean, and the southern part of the United States, imported black African slaves were used for work in sugar, coffee, and cotton plantations. Throughout the Indian and Pacific basins, Indians were frequently transplanted by the British; as a result, large numbers of Indians can now be found in places as different as East Africa, South Africa, Malaysia, and Fiji. Chinese too were sometimes seized to work on ocean clippers and on railway gangs, resulting in the dispersal of Chinese groups to many of the world's major seaports.

But the enforced movement of non-Europeans was little compared with the voluntary emigration of millions of Europeans. The empires founded by European countries were especially useful during the phase of industrialization, as the population of Europe increased because of better medical care. The new lands provided a valuable safety valve for the developing population pressures in Europe; settlers were also needed to establish firm claims to the colonies. Millions of

Chinatown in San Francisco.

US Information Service

Fig. 6-3
Approximate extent of European influence in 1900

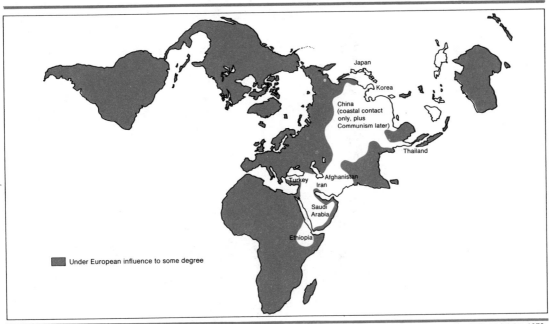

Japan
Korea
China
(coastal contact
only, plus
Communism later)
Thailand
Turkey
Afghanistan
Iran
Saudi
Arabia
Ethiopia

■ Under European influence to some degree

Source: J. P. Cole, *Geography of World Affairs*, 1972.

Fig. 6-4
Approximate present state of European influence (1970s)

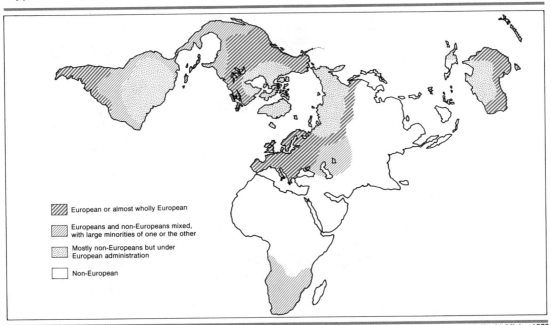

European or almost wholly European

Europeans and non-Europeans mixed,
with large minorities of one or the other

Mostly non-Europeans but under
European administration

Non-European

Source: J. P. Cole, *Geography of World Affairs*, 1972.

Europeans therefore migrated during the nineteenth and twentieth centuries, so that there are now about as many people of European origin outside Europe as there are in Europe itself. (There are probably over one billion people of European ancestry in the world.) Very few areas of the world were left untouched by European influence (see Fig. 6-3); even today, European influence is widespread, despite the fact that European countries have dissolved their empires and reduced colonization (see Fig. 6-4).

In many instances, people of European origin are now drifting back to Europe. They are moving chiefly from areas where they form a cultural minority, and especially from those where they have also become politically weak. Examples include the mass return of the Dutch from Indonesia and the Portuguese from Angola. In much the same way, the English in Rhodesia found their position weakening as compared with the black majority in the 1970s, and so they began to return to England. In order to prevent these people from leaving, the government forbade emigrants to leave with more than $1 500.

One of the legacies of former Dutch rule in Indonesia is the large number of Indonesians in the Netherlands. Among these are the South Moluccans, who use occasional terrorist tactics to pressure the Dutch government into trying to persuade the Indonesian government to grant independence to the Moluccan Islands.

3. The Non-European World

Now that industrialization and death control have begun to affect the non-European areas of the world, the same population pressures are building there as developed in nineteenth-century Europe. One of the results of this has been the gradual elimination of European control; another has been a heightened pressure for urban-industrial jobs, and for emigration. An additional factor encouraging migration today is the greater awareness of other areas held by people in the source regions. In the past, information about prospective destinations was usually sketchy and often coloured by travellers' tales. Nowadays, this is less likely to be the case; information is more detailed and its sources are more varied and authoritative. Moreover, radio, television, and newspapers have done much to open people's minds. It is thus that the international attractions of North America and Europe have become known.

The attractions of large towns within any particular country have become known in a similar fashion. However, rural-urban migration has become an increasing problem, since most cities in the less developed countries cannot cope with their growing numbers of citizens. The alternate solution of emigration to new lands is not so easy as it was to Europeans of the nineteenth century. The less developed countries have no empires to colonize, and there are few relatively open lands (i.e., lands with no strongly centralized government) left in the world to go to. Moreover, different cultural and educational backgrounds often make it difficult for migrants to adapt to those countries that still take immigrants.

Despite the problems involved in migration, the numbers of non-European migrants are growing around the world. Today the major sources of migrants are Hong Kong, Korea, the Caribbean, and the Indian subcontinent.

Statistical Interpretation

6-3 The city of Toronto is a major recipient of international migrants. The ethnic composition of its school system reflects the sources of migration. Fig. 6-5 presents data on this ethnic composition.

a) On a world map, simply shade each country that is listed as a source of migrants to Toronto.

b) Select the 20 chief countries or country groups that are sources of student-migrants, and obtain the square roots of their student-migrant totals. For instance, Portugal ranks first with a total of 5 379 students, and the square root of 5 379 is 73.3. Divide all the calculated square roots by 4, and use the answers as the radii in mm to plot located proportional circles on a world map such as the one in Appendix 1.

c) For all the countries listed as supplying migrants to Toronto, calculate the number of students each has in Toronto per million of domestic population (see column A of Appendix 2 for domestic populations). For example, Italy had a 1975 domestic population of 55 810 000, and the students of Italian origin (born in Italy) in Toronto numbered 3 146. This means that for every million people living in Italy there were 56.4 Italian students in Toronto (3 146 ÷ 55.81 = 56.4). Similarly, the West Indies, with a total domestic population of 26 560 000, were represented by 151.4 students per million of domestic population. It is obvious that large countries will tend to supply more immigrants than smaller countries will, other things being equal. What are we therefore attempting to find out by performing these calculations?

d) Rank the 20 highest answers from (c) in order from the highest to the lowest. Does this list correspond with the 20 chief countries listed in (b)? If it does not, what explanations can you suggest?

e) Toronto had 27 654 immigrant students in its school system in 1975. This represents about 7 students per million of total world population. Your answers to (c) ranged both above and below this world average. Such deviations from an average which may be used as a predictor are called *positive residuals* (above the average) and *negative residuals* (below the average). Thus, Greece, with a domestic population in 1975 of 9 050 000, could be expected, in conformity with the world average, to be represented in the Toronto school system by about 63 students. In fact it was represented by 2 053 students, about 33 times more than are predicted by using the world average. This is a very large positive residual for Greece. India and Sri Lanka, on the other hand, with a combined domestic population in 1975 of 612 090 000, were under-represented, with only 823 students (1.3/million) as compared with a predicted 4 285 students (7/million). This is therefore a large negative residual for India and Sri Lanka. On a world map, shade all the countries with positive residuals red and those with negative residuals blue. What does this map suggest about the areas of origin of Toronto's immigrant students?

Fig. 6-5
Countries or country groups in which at least four students in the 1975 City of Toronto school system were born

Country	Number of students	Country	Number of students
Portugal	5 379	Burma	48
West Indies	4 022	Uruguay	48
Italy	3 146	Switzerland	46
China and Hong Kong	2 528	Austria	45
Greece	2 053	Kenya	44
UK	1 737	Malaysia	42
USA	1 010	Turkey	39
Guyana	839	Israel	36
India and Sri Lanka	823	Egypt	35
Yugoslavia	729	Fiji	34
Poland	465	Indonesia	33
Ecuador and Peru	415	Romania	28
Philippines	357	Morocco	26
Korea	324	Mexico	24
Germany	289	New Zealand	19
France	191	Persian Gulf countries	14
Venezuela and Colombia	187	Bulgaria	11
Brazil	177	Lebanon	11
Taiwan	162	Angola	10
Tanzania	162	Mauritius	10
Australia	148	Nigeria	10
Argentina	144	Singapore	9
Cyprus	138	Syria	9
Pakistan and Bangladesh	137	Ethiopia	6
Czechoslovakia	116	Ghana	6
Malta	111	Jordan	6
Ireland	103	Albania	5
Scandinavia	94	Mozambique	5
Spain	82	Paraguay	5
Japan	82	Thailand	5
Netherlands and Belgium	80	Congo	4
Chile	73	Guinea	4
South Africa	71	Rhodesia	4
Hungary	68	Vietnam	4
Central America	63	Zaire	4
Uganda	62	Zambia	4
USSR	53		

Source: *The 1975 Every Student Survey*, by the City of Toronto Board of Education.

Section C
Where Do Migrants Go?

Migrants go wherever they believe the quality of life will be better, *provided they can do so*. Over the last two centuries or so this has generally meant a movement to the new lands: Australia and New Zealand, South and East Africa, and South and North America. Most of the emigrants have been European, but of late there have been growing numbers of Chinese and Indians. The qualification *provided they can do so* has become more restrictive over the years. In the early phases of European migration, it was customary for the migrants to crush the resistance of the natives by force of arms. Thus the Aborigines of Australia, the Maoris of New Zealand, the Bantu of East Africa, and the Indians of South and North America all met with the overwhelming power of the Europeans. There was a clash of cultures, and the technologically superior Europeans nearly always won. The Europeans expanded not only because they wanted to, but also because they *could*.

By settling in large numbers in the new lands, the Europeans have taken control of the world's current migration opportunities. Australia, for example, excluded Chinese and Indian migrants until 1972 by means of its "White Australia" policy; North America sets quotas and qualifications. There are no open new lands available now to international migrants, and the potential migrants of today lack the superior technology that took the Europeans successfully into so many parts of the world. Migration today is therefore more controlled than it was in the past. Governments have a larger part to play, and migrants cannot go where they want to; they go where governments will let them.

In these new lands, the ex-Europeans have changed their attitudes as they have developed. This change is perhaps due to their own conscience and humanitarianism. Europeans in new lands now feel they have to crush different racial groups militarily, guilty longer feel the need to transport slaves around the globe for guilty benefit. Instead, they talk of native rights, and occasionally power to about the violent deeds of their ancestors; they give poli

One of the invisible allies of the Europeans was disease. Many native people had no resistance to European diseases introduced by the migrants, and countless thousands fell to influenza and tuberculosis. However, thousands of Europeans also died of diseases that were foreign to them, such as sleeping sickness and malaria.

native majorities; they hold values different from those of past settlers. There are exceptions; Rhodesia and South Africa have old-style European colonists who believe that they are as South African or Rhodesian as the Bantu: these whites are technologically superior to the native blacks, and retain their position of power by force.

This change in attitude of most ex-Europeans has meant that migration has become somewhat easier for non-Europeans in the past few years. Canada, for example, had a quota system loaded in favour of Europeans until 1962; by 1968 it had been changed to a quality-loaded points system. In this system, people are awarded points on the basis of their personal qualities, such as age, education, and job skills, and not on the basis of race or nationality. The result was a change in the ethnic mixture of people admitted into the country; 79% of the migrants were European in 1960 but only 42% in 1972. During the same time span, Asian immigration rose from 4% to 19%, and Caribbean from 1% to 8%. The USA, still the world's chief destination for migrants, allows entry to 170 000 people from the eastern hemisphere compared with only 130 000 from the western hemisphere, with a maximum of 20 000 from any single country (plus as many relatives as desired). It too has seen the ethnic composition of its immigrant population change markedly over the last few years; whereas Canada, the UK, and Germany used to be the chief sources of migrants in the early 1960s, the main sources now are Mexico, the Philippines, and Korea.

Despite this loosening of barriers, there are still many obstacles to immigration. New Zealand will not admit anyone over 45 years old, nor anyone with more than 4 children; Switzerland will allow only 20 500 new residents a year; Britain will allow entry only to Commonwealth citizens who have at least one parent born in Britain, except for foreign doctors, dentists, and nurses; the Bahamas will not issue work ╌mits to anyone wanting a job that a Bahamian might be able to do ╌d. Some countries even have barriers to stop people from leaving ╌untry. The Berlin Wall is a classic example of a physical barrier, ╌ssian red tape and exit taxes are legal barriers that help ╌ge emigration. It is also quite difficult to migrate from China ╌Thailand, and blacks find it almost impossible to migrate ╌th Africa. In nations like these that restrict emigration, there ╌igration to different areas of the same country. In fact, ╌gration is often officially sponsored: Russians go to Siberia, ╌ the stimulus of wages three or four times higher than in ╌ussia; Chinese migrate to Sinkiang, Tibet, and Manchuria ╌nd availability; and black South Africans move into the ╌tu nations such as the Transkei, usually to escape from ╌sion.

╌s Europeans that pushed into so many other culture ╌f their population growth during the industrial revolu-

The Mexican quota, for example, is filled rapidly every year, while the German quota is never filled. Some people believe that the United States should let other countries use these unfilled quotas, but there is much opposition to this idea.

For example, an exit tax in the USSR requires emigrants to pay a sum equivalent to the cost of their public education from kindergarten through university.

There are many new Russian cities in Siberia. This is Irkutsk.

Novosti Press Agency

tion, it is ironic that Europe is now experiencing the characteristics of the most recent phase of the demographic transition model. Populations are static or merely edging upward; labour is scarce rather than abundant, and so there is a need to import rather than export workers. The following article forms a small case study of this aspect of migration in Europe.

Migrant Europeans

by JOHN GOSHKO
Special to The Star

BONN—Just as North America once relied for its development on the muscle and sinew of immigrants, the countries of northern Europe, with their low birth rates and chronic labor shortages, have become dependent on an army of newcomers to keep their factories and public services functioning. To a very large

extent, western Europe owes its phenomenal economic expansion during the 1960s and 1970s to this steady inflow of cheap and abundant foreign labor.

However, this new immigration is also fast turning into what Dr. Patrick Hillery, vice-president of the European Economic Community Commission, calls "the burning problem in Europe today." Through the importation of unskilled labor in such massive numbers, northern Europe has created a new *lumpenproletariat*—

an enormous, culturally different and unassimilated minority at the bottom of the economic ladder.

Now, many officials like Hillery are becoming increasingly worried that the tensions, frustrations and resentments generated by this group could explode and confront Europe with its own version of the social and racial unrest that hit the United States during the 1960s.

In polite circles the newcomers are generally referred to as "gastarbeiter" or "guest workers"—a euphemism originated in Germany and now used universally throughout the continent.

•••

Like most immigrants, they have been turned into wanderers, because they come from poor countries where work is scarce. To them, the Eldorado that North America represented to an earlier generation of migrants is the northern half of their own continent.

So they trek north to take on the hard, dirty tasks that the prosperous Germans, Scandinavians, Swiss, French and others are no longer willing to do. They man the assembly lines of automobile plants in Stuttgart, sweep the streets in Paris, collect the garbage in Zurich, wash dishes and wait on tables in the restaurants of Brussels and dig subways in Munich and Rotterdam.

In staggering numbers the new migrants have dispersed over the continent from Scandinavia down through the southern reaches of the Alps and the Pyrenees. Collectively, they total more than 11 million people. Some experts, making allowance for the large traffic in illegal and unrecorded immigration, contend that the number is actually closer to 15 million.

What's more, despite recessions, layoffs and the fresh uncertainties of the energy crisis, the number continues to grow. In just one southern country, Turkey, the list of applicants for jobs in northwestern Europe contains more than 1 million names.

Should the migration continue at its past pace, the United Nations estimates that it will climb to 22 million people by 1980. That would be a figure equivalent to half the number that emigrated from Europe to the New World in the great waves of the 19th and early 20th centuries.

But the current migration differs markedly from that experienced by the earlier generation in North America. The people who went to the U.S. and Canada went to stay—usually to become citizens and to see their children turned into Americans and Canadians.

By contrast, the countries of Europe have never regarded themselves as melting pots. For centuries they have existed as homogeneous societies, too cramped, too crowded and too nationalistic to welcome the idea of assimilating millions of strangers. To them, the foreign workers are a necessary evil to be suffered for the sake of a healthy national economy.

The first impetus came in the mid-1950s with the formation of the Common Market and its rules permitting the free movement of labor across the borders of member states. At the time one of the original community members, Italy, was struggling with severe unemployment problems in its parched southern regions, and before long Italian migrants were streaming north toward the factories of Italy's more prosperous community partners.

Then in the early 1960s the stream turned into a torrent as West Germany entered the boom period that made it the industrial powerhouse of Europe. Previously West German employers had filled their needs by absorbing scores of refugees disenchanted with the Communist system across the border in East Germany. But that ended in 1961, when East Germany forcibly dammed the tide by throwing up the Berlin Wall.

West Germany had to reach out even farther for helping hands, and soon German recruiters were scouring Italy, Spain, Portugal and Yugoslavia in their quest for workers. In the process West Germany became the single biggest employer of migrant labor. Today it has a gastarbeiter population of 2.6 million that amounts to slightly more than 10 per cent of the total West German work force.

So competitive has been the hunt for workers that the recruiters have had to cast their nets in ever widening circles. As countries like Italy, Spain and Yugoslavia began to dry up as "suppliers of flesh," the employers in recent years have gone farther afield to Greece, Turkey and, especially in the case of France, to Algeria and Morocco.

For a long time the zeal of the recruiters was matched by the governments of the countries from which the workers came. By sending their people abroad to work, these governments came to rely on the migrant system as a safety valve with which to relieve the pressure of a large domestic unemployment problem.

At the same time the so-called "exporting countries" have profited handsomely by the money—an estimated $2.5 billion last year—sent home by their expatriate workers.

Typical is Yugoslavia, which is able to keep slightly more than 4 million of its working-age citizens employed at home. But Yugoslavia also has between 300 000 and 400 000 unemployed. The only thing preventing this dangerously high unemployment rate from becoming intolerable is Yugoslavia's ability to keep approximately 1 million workers—almost 20 per cent of its labor force—employed abroad.

Elsewhere, the story is the same. In both Spain (almost 2 million people abroad) and Portugal (1.6 million emigrants), the remittances sent home by migrant workers are the second biggest source of foreign-exchange earnings. The backward economies of Greece and Turkey would probably collapse completely if they had to take on the twin burdens of reabsorbing millions of workers and losing their remittances.

Clearly, at the top levels of government and industry, there has been a vested interest in propagating the system. For a long time even the migrants themselves did not question their status.

In the north they earn what frequently are fantastic salaries by the standards of their homelands. By living frugally, often in miserable self-deprivation, many send as much as 70 per cent of their wages to relatives or put aside a modest nest egg with which to realize their dream of acquiring a house, a farm or a small business.

For many others, though, loneliness breeds the desperation that causes them to squander their earnings on prostitutes and drink, or expensive luxuries like cars and radios. Then, because they do not want to return home as penniless as when they left, they decide to stay in the north longer than the one or two years that was originally the custom.

This has radically altered the whole focus of the system. Many who came with the intention of remaining only a year or so have now been in the north for a decade or longer. As the stays grow longer, it becomes harder to resist bringing their families with them.

That has put enormous strain on the housing, schools and health facilities of the cities where the migrants cluster. It has produced ghettos— Kreuzberg in West Berlin, Oude Westen in Rotterdam, Goutte d'Or in Paris, Schaerbeck in Brussels—that would make a Harlem or a Watts seem lavish by comparison.

Inevitably, it also has brought the first ominous rumblings of a "backlash" from natives of the host countries. Now, after ignoring the social implications of migration for too long, officials all over the continent are worrying anxiously about a European replay of the violence that a few years ago rocked such U.S. cities as Los Angeles, Newark and Detroit.

So far that hasn't happened. But small-scale ghetto incidents between natives and foreigners already are quite common in Europe's big industrial centres. In France, with its large numbers of North Africans, the knifing of a Marseilles bus driver by a demented Algerian last summer touched off an orgy of "Arab bashing" in which 11 persons lost their lives.

The Toronto Star 1974 10 19

Discussion and Research

8. What do you think may be some of the values held by the different parties involved in the current migration pattern in Europe?
9. Would it be better if the countries of northern Europe were to offer citizenship to their guest workers? What would be the advantages and disadvantages?
10. If demographic evolution and rate of industrialization are out of phase, as they are in both northern and southern Europe, should migration be used to solve the problem, or should adjustments be made in demography and industrialization?

Section D
The Benefits and Problems of Migration

1. Benefits

Benefits obviously exist, otherwise migrations would not continue. Migration may start up because of promised benefits, but if the benefits are not real the movement rapidly disappears. Indeed, if the benefits are not long-lasting the migration trend may even be reversed; an example is the movement of West Indians from England back to the Caribbean, which started in the early 1970s. In the 1950s England had recruiting offices in the Caribbean; now there are offices in the UK for West Indians who want to return home.

The benefits of immigration to the receiving country are varied. It is claimed that one of the most important is a larger labour force, which is necessary to a country if its domestic economy grows at a faster rate than the domestic population. The growth of the domestic labour force helps the growth of the domestic market. As the labour force grows, so does the size of the total wage packet, and therefore the purchasing power of the total community (i.e., the *market*). This, in turn, helps industry to gain greater *economies of scale*. What this means is that the average cost of production per unit tends to fall as more and more goods are made. A larger firm, for example, can buy more cheaply in bulk. The main reason for the drop in production costs, however, is that *fixed costs* can be spread out over more units of production. For example, it may cost $5 000 000 for dies to stamp out car bodies. If 100 cars are produced, then each will cost $50 000 for the dies alone; however if 100 000 are produced, this cost drops to $50 per car. Many industrial products must be produced in hundreds of thousands or millions of units in order to be profitable.

Fixed costs for an industry are the costs that have nothing to do with the number of units produced. The cost of the factory, the land that it is built on, and the cost of equipment, maintenance, and taxes are fixed costs.

Migration may also bring a country the following advantages: fresh ideas and enthusiasms; the possibility of growing international prestige because of larger size; and the increased probability of greater cultural, political, and economic independence. Immigrants bring fresh ideas and enthusiasm partly because they are usually young and hopeful, and partly because their life styles are interesting and exotic.

The source regions benefit from emigration because they gain relief from overpopulation. They may also benefit from the money that emigrants send back home to the old country. However, if migrants' remittances are large, and the source region's output of goods and services fails to match the increase in available money, then the source region will suffer from *inflation*, just as Europe did when Spanish explorers brought gold and silver back from South and Central America in the sixteenth century.

Inflation means an *increasing* amount of money in circulation in proportion to the quantity of goods and services available for purchase. Prices thus rise.

Both the destination and the source regions benefit from migration because the countries involved increase their contact with people from other parts of the world. As groups of people move from their homeland to new places, the countries become united by blood ties; these ties are to be encouraged as a general instrument of peace.

2. Problems

However, while migrations bring many advantages they also cause problems. For the source regions, emigrations often result in a loss of skills and enthusiasms which the countries can ill afford. England, which has lost doctors to North America, benefits when it admits doctors from Pakistan; Pakistan in turn suffers from the loss of its doctors. Some of the less developed countries are being drained of the small amounts of skilled talent they possess by the admission policies of the more developed countries. It is difficult for the less developed countries to provide work for their skilled labour; they may not be able to create enough job opportunities. As a result there is a tendency for skilled people to migrate upward through a perceived hierarchy of nations. The countries that lose most are precisely those that can least afford to lose anything.

This poses a basic dilemma; which are more important, the rights of the state or of the individual?

Countries may also lose the most active part of their labour force, namely the people from ages twenty to forty. This loss can be helpful if jobs are scarce; it can also be good if some of the migrants eventually return, bringing with them technical skills that they have acquired in the host country. For this reason, Algeria has gladly seen its young men leave for work in France. On the other hand, East Germany decided that it could not afford to keep on losing labour at the rate it had in the 1950s, so in 1961 it put up a guarded wall across the main escape route through Berlin. Other countries, such as the USSR and South Africa, also make it difficult for labour to leave. Military strength is also weakened when young people emigrate. Nevertheless, these persons may well emigrate in order to avoid being drafted, as happened in the USA, Italy, and Portugal throughout the 1960s. A country may also lose prestige when its people are persistently emigrating.

The receiving countries also face problems from immigration. If the economy is slow, the domestic population may resent the competition for jobs created by immigrants who may have been welcomed when the economy was booming. Immigrants may also be blamed for the competition they provide in the housing market, and for the rising costs of additional health care and educational facilities. Such costs are real, but must be offset against the benefits immigrants bring.

Receiving countries may also face the problem of ghettoes. Immigrants of a particular ethnic group tend to cluster together, and so the host society may eventually be composed of a number of such groups. The society can benefit from the variety of cultures if it accepts the different life styles of immigrants, and if the immigrants themselves seek to accept the life styles of the host country. However, the failure of each group to be open to the other causes ghetto isolation and ultimately, hostility and conflict. The hostility between the closed Hutterite colonies and the neighbouring farmers in Alberta is a case in point; so is the twin city of Johannesburg-Soweto, where blacks and whites live socially separate but economically intertwined lives.

When two different culture groups are brought into contact through migration, then the failure of *both* to adjust to the beliefs and life styles of the other inevitably produces tension. The more powerful group may end up ruling the other, but this relationship does not eliminate the problem of racial or cultural tension. The whites in North America are not immune to the tensions of living with native Indians, and, to a lesser extent, with the Inuit, even though whites are more numerous, and more powerful technically. Minor cultural differences can be ignored or simply regarded as interesting, but tensions are produced if basic values are different.

During the recession of the 1970s, many Canadians called for a reduction in immigration.

Discussion and Research

11. Europeans have been the world's major migrants. What benefits have they brought to areas they have colonized and settled?
12. What problems have Europeans caused by intruding into the realms of other culture groups?
13. What do you think are the most basic contrasts in values that may cause different cultures to exist in a state of mutual suspicion and hostility?
14. What are some examples of cultural traits that can be accepted by all groups as "interesting"?
15. Suggest some values that all culture groups hold strongly.

Section E
Urbanization

1. Characteristics

Migration patterns demonstrate two very human traits. One is the urge for *dispersal*, which is shown by the fact that migrants spread over wider and wider areas of the earth. The other is the drive for *agglomeration*, or gathering together; migrants seek to collect together at points that appear to offer the *maximum net benefit*, or the best opportunities for themselves.

Urbanization is one of the results of the drive for agglomeration; people seek a better life in the cities and towns than they expect to find in the countryside. The movement from country to city is undoubtedly the chief type of migration in the world today, and an important phenomenon that deserves close examination.

Statistical Interpretation

6-4 Using the data in column V of Appendix 2 and a world map similar to that in Appendix 1, construct a graded shading map to show the different levels of achieved urbanization in the world. Use four classes, as follows:

highly urbanized	75% and over	very bright red
moderately urbanized	60 – 74%	bright red
slightly urbanized	40 – 59%	pale red
not urbanized	0 – 39%	very pale red

Compare the map with others you have drawn for assignments in other chapters. How do the different maps compare?

6-5 Obtain a correlation coefficient (r) for the relationship that exists between the degree of urbanization (column V) and the annual percentage population increase (column H). Use the *standard deviation technique*, based on a sample, as shown in Appendix 3. Discuss the meaning of the value of r. You will probably find that the correlation is only moderately strong. There are reasons for this; what do you think they are?

2. Causes

The process of urbanization is tied to both an increase in population and a revolution in agricultural productivity. As the population of a region increases, the prime food-producing areas of land gradually get used up. New villages appear; marginal lands, previously thought unworthy of cultivation are brought into use; remoter areas are pioneered and settled. Eventually, under existing techniques, all the available land of the region is in use. The Indo-Gangetic Plain, lowland China, Guatemala, and Java are examples of areas with little unused land. As population continues to increase in size a land-hungry population surplus eventually develops. Where possible, this can be eased by emigration to other regions still relatively empty.

While international migration is now exceedingly difficult, internal movement is still a favoured solution. Brazil, for example, is encouraging more and more of its growing population to settle the less populated interior areas of the country. First, a new capital has been built at Brasilia, 1 000 km inland; second, a new road has been started across the Amazon basin; third, Amazon land grants are being made to willing farmers. Brazil faces a hard task because the various undertakings are expensive and the people are unused to pioneering. Some of the most important agricultural work in the Amazon has in fact been done by Japanese immigrants, but Brazil wants to move some of its own people inland as well. Similarly, Java would like to get people to move to Sumatra. Russia and China also seek to move people into relatively empty areas in central Asia, though only partly for farming reasons. In the past, Canada too, through government sponsorship, has encouraged pioneering in remote areas to ease the pressures on existing farmland; witness the Peace River District, the Ontario and Quebec clay belt, and the Lac St. Jean region of Quebec.

Brazil has been the main destination of Japanese migrants, and there are now more Japanese in Brazil than in any other country except Japan.

If population pressure cannot be eased by migration to remote areas, then the country faces a series of disasters, moving from hidden unemployment to per capita poverty, declining living standards, disease, and eventually, plague. This is clearly a Malthusian scenario. In the past this grim pattern resulted in a reduced population which permitted the cycle to start again. The pattern persisted until the technologies of farming began to change, first in eighteenth-century England, then throughout Europe, Australia, New Zealand, North America, and Japan; at present, farming techniques are changing throughout southern Asia, Latin America, and Africa. The immediate effect of this ongoing spread of improved agricultural technology is a reduction in the demand for farm labour.

The reduced demand for farm labour complicates the problem of rural overpopulation. When technology began to replace manual labour in eighteenth-century England, gangs of dispossessed and frustrated farm workers roamed the countryside. This unrest occurs today

These gangs were called *Luddites*, after one of their leaders, Ned Ludd. Their main purpose was the destruction of machinery, because they felt it deprived them of jobs.

in some countries of southern Asia, Latin America, and Africa. Occasionally the disturbances make newspaper headlines, as kidnappings or other terrorist acts are used to obtain food, jobs, money, or security.

3. Industrialization

The process of industrialization is a necessary corollary of agricultural revolution. Industry has to grow to provide jobs. It has to provide jobs on a massive scale, because it must absorb not only the excess numbers of rural people, but also the general increase in the population. Europe was fortunate when it went through the early phases of industrialization. Because it was the first to industrialize, there was little competition for its new technology; empires could be seized, and surplus people settled there. Countries that industrialized later could not do this so easily, as Japan found when it tried to expand first into Manchuria (now being filled with immigrants from China) and later into the Pacific Islands. It is hoped that the last violent attempt to occupy territory was made when the Nazi Government started World War II partly to gain "living room" (*Lebensraum*) for the Germans.

Unfortunately for most countries of the world, which only now are experiencing the agricultural revolution, there are few other lands to go to. The cities and towns, with their factories, are the chief hope of most rural unemployed. But there are not enough factories; the demands made on the cities and towns of the less developed countries today are too great to handle. This problem does not arise in the more developed countries. They are already highly urbanized, and the number of people moving to the cities there is accordingly small compared with the masses pouring into the cities of the less developed countries.

The cities and towns of the less developed countries are chiefly preindustrial settlements. These are towns that have developed to supply religious, administrative, marketing, transportation, and other urban services to their surrounding countrysides. They seldom contain factories. Preindustrial towns are service centres, part of the web of rural life rather than a component of the industrial-urban world.

Urbanization is the process whereby a country's population distribution shifts from rural to urban dominance. When a country is already highly urbanized it is not mathematically possible for startling increases to occur. For example, if a country is 85% urbanized, then even if *all* the rural dwellers left for the towns it would be possible to raise the level of urbanization by only 15 percentage points. This is clearly not the case when the starting percentage is much lower.

4. Central Places

Preindustrial towns tend to be fairly regularly distributed throughout farming areas, and are seldom more than a two-hour journey by foot or cart from even the remotest farm. The spacing of the towns varies with the type of transportation commonly used; people who walk require a closer spacing of urban areas than people who use cars or buses. The general density of population also affects the spacing of towns. The provision of any urban service requires a certain minimum number of people to make it worthwhile; such a minimum is called the *threshold*. If the rural population density is low, service centres must be spaced far apart in order to obtain a sufficient number of people (threshold) within their *urban fields*.

For these reasons—differences in transportation and in rural population density—the distribution of preindustrial towns and cities does not form a regular pattern, although it might approach this in places. Working on the assumption that a regular distribution will be formed wherever possible, Christaller developed the theory of *central places*, in which he saw a pattern of towns and cities developing in response to the varied threshold requirements of different urban services. For example, a bank requires a relatively low threshold population, so a small town may provide banking services. However, a university has a high threshold requirement, and therefore only a few towns will provide such a service. Christaller recognized the existence of a hierarchy of services, and accordingly assumed the existence of a hierarchy of service towns. His most famous model (there are others) is the *K3 Network*, in which towns are ideally grouped as shown in Fig. 6-6.

An *urban field* is the area of land around a town that is served by that town. In an analogy with electricity, the urban field is the area over which the town exerts a "magnetic" attraction.

Fig. 6-6
The principle of the K3 Network, idealized

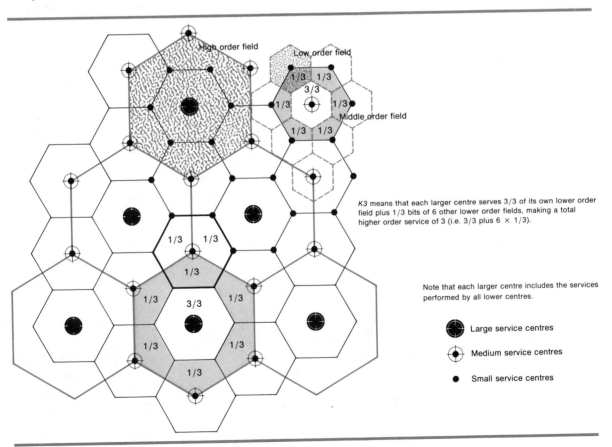

K3 means that each larger centre serves 3/3 of its own lower order field plus 1/3 bits of 6 other lower order fields, making a total higher order service of 3 (i.e. 3/3 plus 6 × 1/3).

Note that each larger centre includes the services performed by all lower centres.

⬤ Large service centres

⊕ Medium service centres

● Small service centres

5. Migration, Jobs, and Urban Hierarchies

When industrialization occurs, two things may happen. Industries may develop at points quite unrelated to the existing pattern of preindustrial towns, as at orebodies, or they may develop as part of the hierarchical pattern. The locations of industries are determined by their needs; some needs are input-loaded, such as the demand for power, raw materials, and labour; others are output-loaded, such as the need for good access to markets. Therefore the type of industry determines its location to a large extent.

Those industries most influenced by access to power and raw materials will locate close to them in order to obtain the greatest net advantage; such points may or may not coincide with the existing locations of preindustrial towns. On the other hand, industries which are labour-intensive or market-oriented will locate in the existing towns. In order to obtain the widest access to labour and maximum penetration of the market, which will give maximum economies of

Fig. 6-7
The percentage share of national manufacturing in some African capital cities

City	Percentage
Bathurst (Gambia)	100
Libreville (Gabon)	100
Monrovia (Liberia)	100
Bangui (Central African Rep.)	100
Bukavi (Rwanda)	100
Dakar (Senegal)	81
Bujumbura (Burundi)	80
Freetown (Sierra Leone)	75
Blantyre (Malawi)	73
Abidjan (Ivory Coast)	63
Dar es Salaam (Tanzania)	63
Khartoum (Sudan)	60
Conakry (Guinea)	50
Donala (Cameroon)	50
Addis Ababa (Ethiopia)	47
Nairobi (Kenya)	42
Lagos (Nigeria)	35
Lusaka (Zambia)	35
Brazzaville (Congo)	33
Accra (Ghana)	30
Kinshasa (Zaire)	30
Kampala (Uganda)	28

Source: *Economic Geography*, Vol. 49, p. 11.

scale, industries will choose the large service centres first. Only later will they filter down (expand) to the small service centres. The degree to which this filtering-down process has occurred is a measure of the extent of industrialization. In the more developed countries industries will be found in even the smallest service centres. In the less developed countries, on the other hand, the filtering-down process has barely started. In many areas only the largest service centres have any industry, and even then not enough to provide jobs for the people migrating from the countryside. Fig. 6-7 shows how far manufacturing industry has penetrated some of the national urban networks in Africa. In Gambia, for example, all the nation's manufacturing is concentrated in Bathurst. There has been no expansion into any lower order centres. Uganda, on the other hand, displays a high degree of industrial penetration down the urban hierarchy, with only 28% of its manufacturing located in Kampala.

Because industry and its accompanying jobs tend to filter *down* the hierarchy of service centres (i.e., from the largest to the smallest), job seekers tend to migrate *up* it. As the agricultural revolution occurs and rural population grows, people move to the towns. They may move first to the local service towns, but in time are likely to migrate to the highest service cities. On the way they may be joined by people from small towns seeking more opportunities in larger towns. Thus the largest cities in the less developed countries have become the major goal of rural-urban migrants.

Fig. 6-8
Populations of selected cities in 1950 and 1970, and estimated populations in 1985 (in millions)

	1950	1970	1985
Tokyo	8.2	14.9	25.2
New York	12.3	16.3	18.8
London	8.4	10.5	8.0
Shanghai	5.0	10.0	14.0
Mexico City	2.9	8.4	17.9
Buenos Aires	5.2	8.4	11.7
Sao Paulo	2.5	7.8	16.8
Calcutta	4.5	10.0	18.0
Peking	1.5	7.0	12.0
Bombay	2.7	5.8	12.1
Seoul	1.5	4.6	10.3
Karachi	1.0	3.5	9.2

Source: *UN Statistical Yearbook*, 1972.

Fig. 6-9
Population (in thousands) of the thirty largest urban areas in each of four countries (1975)

Rank	USA		Canada		USSR		India	
1	New York	16 037	Toronto	2 803	Moscow	7 172	Calcutta	7 031
2	Chicago	7 521	Montreal	2 802	Leningrad	4 002	Bombay	5 971
3	Los Angeles	7 032	Vancouver	1 166	Kiev	1 693	Delhi	3 647
4	Philadelphia	4 818	Ottawa-Hull	693	Tashkent	1 424	Madras	3 170
5	Detroit	4 200	Winnipeg	578	Baku	1 292	Hyderabad	1 796
6	San Francisco	3 110	Edmonton	554	Kharkov	1 248	Ahmadabad	1 742
7	Washington	2 861	Quebec City	542	Gorky	1 189	Bangalore	1 654
8	Boston	2 754	Hamilton	529	Novosibirsk	1 180	Kanpur	1 275
9	Pittsburgh	2 401	Calgary	470	Kuibyshev	1 069	Poona	1 135
10	St. Louis	2 363	St. Catherines	302	Sverdlovsk	1 048	Nagpur	930
11	Baltimore	2 071	Kitchener	272	Minsk	955	Lucknow	814
12	Cleveland	2 064	London	270	Odessa	913	Coimbatore	736
13	Houston	1 985	Halifax	268	Tbilisi	907	Madurai	712
14	Minneapolis	1 814	Windsor	248	Chelyabinsk	891	Jaipur	637
15	Dallas	1 556	Victoria	218	Donetsk	891	Agra	635
16	Seattle	1 422	Sudbury	157	Kazan	885	Varanasi	607
17	Anaheim	1 420	Regina	151	Dnepropetrovsk	882	Indore	561
18	Milwaukee	1 404	St. John's	143	Peru	863	Jabalpur	535
19	Atlanta	1 390	Saskatoon	134	Omsk	850	Allahabad	513
20	Cincinnati	1 385	Chicoutimi	129	Volgograd	834	Ernakulam	493
21	San Diego	1 358	Oshawa	120	Rostov on Don	808	Surat	493
22	Buffalo	1 349	Thunder Bay	119	Ufa	796	Patna	491
23	Miami	1 268	Saint John	113	Yerevan	791	Vadodara	467
24	Kansas City	1 254	Trois Rivières	98	Saratov	773	Tiruchirapalli	465
25	Denver	1 228	Sydney	91	Alma Ata	753	Amritsar	458
26	San Bernardino	1 143	Kingston	86	Riga	743	Jamshedpur	456
27	Indianapolis	1 110	Sherbrooke	85	Voronezh	676	Trivandrum	452
28	San José	1 065	Sault Ste. Marie	81	Zaporozhye	676	Dhanbad	434
29	New Orleans	1 046	Brantford	80	Krasnoyarsk	666	Salem	416
30	Portland Ore.	1 009	Sarnia	78	Krivoi Rog	581	Gwalior	406

Compiled from *The World Almanac*, 1976, and *Canada Year Book*, 1977-78.

Statistical Interpretation

6-6 Using the data in Fig. 6-8 and an appropriate log scale from Appendix 3, construct a semi-log time-series graph to show how the highest order urban centres have grown in population. Colour the cities of the developing countries in red, the others in blue. What do you notice?

6-7 One way of showing the hierarchical nature of urban centres is to apply the *rank-size rule* (see Appendix 3), which is based on simple observation. The rule states that the second city in a hierarchy will be approximately half the size of the first city, that the third city will be approximately one-third the size of the first city, the fourth one-quarter, and so on. We can best show the city rankings against size by drawing a log-log graph. Using the data in Fig. 6-9, and appropriate log scales from Appendix 3, construct a log-log graph to show size (population) on the vertical axis, and rank on the horizontal axis. Use differently coloured dots for each data set, and join the dots with a line.

a) What do you notice about the hierarchical pattern?

b) How does the data fit in with K3 theory?

The UN calculates that at the present rate of urbanization about half the world's population will be living in urban areas by the year 2000. It also calculates that the total population of the world may then be about 7 000 000 000. By 2000, then, the world's cities may have the huge task of providing housing and jobs for about 3.5 to 4 billion people. The bulk of the population increase will come in the towns and cities of the less developed countries—the same towns and cities that are having problems now. The existing situation is illustrated in the following articles.

A third of the world in shantytowns

by SAMUEL CHAMECKI

As incredible as it may seem, more than half the population of the globe will be city dwellers by the year 2000. According to a study just published by the United Nations entitled "World Housing Survey", 51 per cent of the world's population will be living in urban areas within the next two decades as opposed to 49 per cent living in rural areas.

Today, 39 per cent of the world's population live in towns and cities while in 1920 only 19 per cent lived in urban areas as compared to 81 per cent in rural zones.

More than one billion people, or nearly one third of the world population, now live in substandard housing conditions, and this situation is likely to worsen in the years to come. The problem has become increasingly acute in cities in the developing world, particularly capital cities, where slums and squatter settlements account for one third to half of the population.

Overcrowding and lack of basic sanitary facilities are the two most striking features of poor housing. These dwellings lack a water supply or a public service for waste collection. Already we find three and more persons to a room in many countries.

. . .

Migration from rural to urban areas accounts for most of the growth of cities, being responsible in many cities for more than 90 per cent of the total population increase.

Slums and squatter settlements bear the brunt of the accelerating rural-urban migration and city growth. In most cities of the developing world, slums and squatter settlements account for one third to a half of the population.

Africa has 44 cities with populations ranging between 100 000 and 500 000 inhabitants. Studies of 15 of these cities show that they have a consistently high percentage of slums and squatter settlements. In only two of the cities does the percentage of slums and squatter areas fall below 48 per cent and in one case it is actually seen to be as high as 90 per cent.

Precise data is available for only 6 of the 15 cities in Latin America with more than one million inhabitants. Of these, 3 each have more than one million slum and squatter dwellers. In Asia, 7 cities with a population surpassing one million each have squatter populations exceeding one million inhabitants. Three of these cities are found in India where 70 per cent of all families live in one room or less.

In fact slums and squatter settlements form only part of the desperate world housing situation. Deteriorating dwellings which are overcrowded and lacking in basic amenities produce squalid living conditions for another large portion of the world's population. Nor are these slums restricted to developing countries; they are traditional living quarters for the urban poor in many industrialized nations as well.

Over 730 million dwelling units need to be constructed by the end of the century in Africa, Asia and Latin America as compared to the 200 million dwelling units required in North America, Europe, the Soviet Union and Oceania.

Many countries are building only two or four dwelling units per one thousand population per year, whereas about eight to ten units per one thousand population per year are required to meet total housing needs.

This target, according to available information for the year 1970, is attained in most developed countries such as France with 9.3 units, Denmark, Finland and Switzerland 10.4 units, Japan 14.3, Czechoslovakia, Romania, Federal Republic of Germany 8.0, Spain 9.0, Sweden 13.6, Australia 11.3, and the Soviet Union 9.4.

However, enormous gaps between the mass housing needs and supply are to be found in most of the developing countries, a few examples on the poorer side being in Africa: Algeria 1.0 housing units, Egypt 1.5, Tunisia 1.5. In Latin America: Columbia 1.2, Dominican Republic 0.6, Trinidad and Tobago 2.0. In Asia: Iraq 1.8, Ceylon 0.8, Yemen 0.1.

As we have seen, one-third of the world's population is currently homeless or living in sub-standard housing. It has been estimated that with the present demographic growth, and doubling of the population every 30 years, the total number of people living today is greater than all the people who have lived and died in our entire past. Consequently humanity has to build, in less than 25 years, more dwelling units than mankind has produced until now, the developing countries bearing nearly 80 per cent of this immeasurable burden.

UNESCO Courier 1976 6

Slums of hope . . . slums of despair

by A. A. LAQUIAN

While slums in cities are as old as history, the dominance of squatter and slum communities over urban life now found in most developing countries is of relatively recent vintage. Most of the cities in the IDRC study started exploding after the Second World War, their populations rapidly expanding due to high natural growth rates and rural-urban migration. The immediate reaction of governments to the slum and squatter problem was punitive. This was especially true in Latin America, where "invasions" by hordes of squatters to occupy public parks or private subdivisions were met with police and military might. Squatting was seen as a basically legal problem. When migrants built their shanties on public or private domain without any permission, they were trespassing and were, therefore, prosecuted.

The sheer number of people involved in squatting and slum dwelling, however, soon proved exhausting to governments and those who would enforce law and order. Slowly, public policies started to become more "accommodating", especially in countries where the combined votes of those who lived in slum and squatter communities spelled the difference between political loss or victory for leaders. From being prosecuted and harassed, squatter and slum dwellers became ignored or unseen. However, when these policies of "benign neglect" also failed to solve the problem, more positive measures were instituted. Such measures as low cost housing, sites and services, urban community development, social welfare and others are now common in the cities of developing countries. Unable to lick the squatters and slum

Population, growth rates, and slum dwellers in the cities studied

Metropolitan Areas	Population 1970 (In '000)	Average Annual Growth Rate (%) 1961-1970	Population in slums and uncontrolled settlements ('000)	% of population in slums and uncontrolled settlements
Bandung	1 202	14.1	324	27
Caracas	1 937	4.6	814	42
Istanbul	2 247	3.3a	1 011	45
Kuala Lumpur	519	4.9a	156	30
Lagos	1 500	12.4	644b	43
Lima	2 800	7.0	1 000	36
Manila	3 200	4.9	1 103	34
Seoul	5 536	10.7	1 200	24

a—estimated growth rate for thirteen year period from 1957-1970.
b—estimated from the number of migrants in the total Lagos population.

dwellers, most governments are now joining them in common efforts to improve their lot.

In the early 1960s, a debate raged among those who were concerned with slums and squatters in cities of developing countries as to whether they were "slums of hope" or "slums of despair". Learned papers were written asking if such communities were "cancers or catalysts" to development. Those who held a dim view said that with high population growth rates in both rural and urban areas, the inclination of modern technology to use machines instead of human beings, and the inability of developing country governments to meet high levels of human expectations, the cities of developing countries were doomed. The spectre of Calcutta haunted the nightmares of these concerned people. With its population of 6.7 million, 700 000 of which knew only the city's pavements as home, this Indian metropolis has given strong support to the "despair" theorists.

Those who expressed hope, however, viewed the slum and squatter people as essentially in transition from a simpler rural to a more modern urban life. The communities were seen as "way stations" in this oldest of dramas involving social change. People who moved from villages to cities carried their dreams with their meagre belongings. They were willing to work, organize themselves, and fight, if necessary, to achieve their goals. From squatters and slum dwellers, they hoped to become skilled laborers and workers. Their children, perhaps, would be able to go to school and become professionals and technicians. Since most developing countries were short of material and physical resources but rich in people, the ambitious and driven rural-urban migrant adjusting to life

in the slum or squatter area seemed to be a symbol of hope rather than of despair.

The debates of the 1960s are only faint echoes now. In their place, a number of basic philosophical issues and program changes have occurred. Most countries have moved from debates to action. International agencies such as the United Nations, especially the World Bank, have launched positive programs that now recognize the squatter as signifying both hope *and* despair. More importantly, however, his role in development is now being recognized.

Cooperation Canada (CIDA) 1974 9

Urban explosion may never happen, Forum told

from the B.C. Bureau of The Globe and Mail

VANCOUVER—The predicted explosion of large cities, the projection of half the world's population living in urban areas by the year 2000, may never happen, according to the president of the Worldwatch Institute.

These projections assume food surpluses, cheap energy and jobs in cities, Lester Brown told an audience yesterday at Habitat Forum, the conference running parallel to the UN Conference on Human Settlements.

"There are three reasons why urbanization trends cannot continue as projected until the end of the century," Mr. Brown said.

"These are the inability of the countryside to produce sufficiently large food surpluses, the disappearance of cheap energy needed to underwrite the urbanization process, and the impossibility of creating enough jobs in urban settings."

Mr. Brown then analyzed the three interrelated essential elements for the growth of cities—food, energy and employment.

"In order for people to move from the countryside to the city there must be a surplus of food produced in the rural areas that can be used to feed the dependent urban populations," he said.

However, while 30 years ago Europe was the only continent that imported food, in 1976 North America is the only continent that does not have to import food.

"Virtually the entire world has come to depend on the North American food exports," he said. "Further analysis on a country-by-country basis shows that the world today consists almost entirely of food-deficit countries. Those remaining as important exporters at the global level can be numbered on the fingers of one hand."

Mr. Brown said that if these trends continue the needs of the more than 100 countries importing food will "greatly exceed" the capacity of North America to supply them.

"This is creating a politics of food, a type of food diplomacy," he said. "The hostages in this game are the cities of the world that are sustained with imported food. They are living quite literally 'from ship to mouth.' The trend of cities becoming more and more dependent on imported food is everywhere evident from Leningrad to Lagos, Cairo to Santiago, Tokyo to Bombay . . . inevitably harsh decisions will have to be made by the U.S. and Canadian governments on who gets food and who does not."

In such a situation he said countries should reconsider whether continued rapid urbanization and the resulting dependence on imported food was in their national interest.

Energy is equally closely related to

urbanization, he said. "The large-scale migration of people from countryside to city requires an abundance of energy."

Not only does urban living require more energy for housing and transportation, but as people leave the rural areas for big cities each person remaining in agriculture must produce a larger and larger surplus. To do this requires the use of energy-expensive machinery.

"The rapid urbanization characterizing so much of the world during the third quarter of this century occurred during an era of cheap energy, an era which may be historically unique," he said.

"Many planners and analysts believe that the tide from the countryside to the city cannot be slowed or stemmed, that it is inevitable. I am not among those," Mr. Brown said. "The most effective efforts to ameliorate the problems facing cities may well be those to improve living conditions and productivity in the countryside."

The Globe and Mail 1976 6 3

The crush of rural migration. The towns cannot cope.

UNHCR

Discussion and Research

16. How would you argue with the case presented by Lester Brown?
17. Can you suggest any actions that can be taken in the rural areas to ease the problems in the towns?
18. What measures can be taken in the towns themselves to help solve their accumulating problems?
19. It is estimated that by 2000 there will be many cities with populations over 10 000 000, some with populations over 20 000 000, and one or two with populations over 30 000 000 (perhaps Calcutta? Sao Paulo?).

   a) What are the problems of great size?
   b) What are the advantages of great size?
   c) Is there an ideal size for a highest order (*primate*) city?

6. The Future

When discussing the future of urbanization, people foresee the growth of *megalopolises* (super cities) and *conurbations* (chains of cities forming a single huge urban area). There are always pessimistic predictions of "concrete jungles" and polluted human anthills. However, these forecasts are based on present patterns of rural-urban migration. China and the USA provide examples of changes in migration patterns which may affect urbanization, and resolve some of the problems caused by migration.

China has most of its population in the countryside; its towns are essentially preindustrial, except for a few near the coast and along the major rivers. If normal migration patterns held true, China's rural population would now be migrating to the towns; but this is not happening on any large scale. The reason lies in the firm control that the totalitarian government has on the population. Migration to the cities is banned, and rural projects are designed to use as many people as possible in the rural areas. What the people of China lose in political and personal freedom they gain in freedom from hunger and poverty.

The USA, on the other hand, has experienced massive migrations into its cities and towns. Even as recently as 1950-70, New York gained 2 000 000 extra citizens by inward migration. But the situation is changing. Since 1970 the rural areas have been growing faster than the urban areas; the process of dispersal has taken over from that of agglomeration. Between 1970 and 1975, for instance, nearly 2 000 000 more Americans left the cities than moved into them. Inner New York had a net loss of 500 000, and Chicago of 250 000. Other large metro-

Not all major US cities are losing population. Houston, for example, is not. However, not *all* parts of a nation are expected to be at identical phases in economic, social, and political development.

politan areas that lost population include Los Angeles, Philadelphia, Detroit, St. Louis, Pittsburgh, Newark, Boston, and San Francisco. Among the various causes of this phenomenon is the growing desire of people to move into safer, sunnier, cheaper, quieter, or cleaner places. Arizona has in fact become the chief destination of many, and it is accordingly the fastest-growing state in the Union.

At one extreme, therefore, we see a government forcing people to stay on the land; at the other extreme we can see people voluntarily reacting against the problems of massive city growth.

What will happen in the less developed countries, where people are left in the middle, with few jobs in the cities and no way to return to rural self-sufficiency? Increasingly there are millions who can neither feed themselves from their land, nor find employment in the preindustrial cities. To many, it appears that social and economic forces are out of balance, and that political solutions must be found.

Rural-urban migration has occurred on a large scale in the USSR, putting great pressure on the cities. Housing is scarce. These are apartments in Moscow.

Novosti Press Agency

Case Study 6
Turkey: Migrations

Turkey's population is exploding. Its annual rate of natural increase is about 25/1 000, based on a birth rate of about 40/1 000 and a death rate of about 15/1 000. The country is situated demographically between phases 2 and 3. If present growth rates continue, its present population of about 40 000 000 will double by the year 2005.

The economy, despite impressive achievements, cannot create enough jobs. Thus, although many Turks have moved from rural to urban areas, they have found relatively little work. Indeed, urban unemployment simply replaces rural underemployment (the lack of steady or full-time jobs); estimates of up to 2 000 000 unemployed are common.

Meanwhile, except for economic problems in the late 1960s and mid-1970s, Western Europe has enjoyed much prosperity. Yet at the same time it has suffered from shortages of labour, due largely to a low rate of population increase. After World War II, refugees and displaced persons from the Eastern European countries formed a supply of cheap labour; however, the construction of the Berlin Wall virtually cut off that source at the start of the 1960s. For a while also, the improvements in farming techniques in Western Europe increased the drift of cheap-labour rural workers to the industrial towns. But by the 1960s this source too was drying up, especially as the Common Market's Common Agricultural Policy (CAP) was effectively keeping farmers in the countryside. The CAP's purpose of preserving a rural way of life, at the expense of vast subsidies to small farmers and huge food surpluses from efficient farmers, posed a threat to continued European economic prosperity. By the early 1960s there was a great need for labour, especially unskilled and semi-skilled labour.

West Germany, in particular, was desperately short of workers. These labour shortages did not suddenly appear in the early 1960s. They existed in the 1950s, partly as the flow of farm workers to cities gradually subsided and partly as iron curtain surveillance improved. In the 1950s, West Germany had managed to attract many migrants from southern Italy, especially after the formation of the Common Market. Equally, migrants from Spain, Portugal, and Greece were attracted to West Germany. The idea of immigrant *guest workers* was not new to the Germany of 1960. For the first time, however, Turkey became a source of immigrant labourers. During 1960, negotiations between West Germany and Turkey produced an international migrant worker agreement, which was signed at the start of 1961. The flow of Turks to West Germany began, and West Germany's continued economic growth came to be fed by an increasing and underemployed Turkish population. For many Turks, West Germany came to provide the opportunity of a lifetime; thus the agreement was beneficial to both countries.

In the first year of migration (1961) only about 2 000 Turks moved to West Germany, but by the end of the decade over 1 000 000 had done so. Most of them came from the areas shown in Fig. 6C-1. They were channelled to the industrial cities of West Germany largely through German and Turkish government agencies. There has been very little private or individual migration. Turks appear to leave Turkey only with the approval and organization of the Turkish government behind them. During the 1960s when over 1 000 000 Turks moved with government help to West Germany, fewer than 100 moved independently to the United States. In a report on this matter to the Council of Europe in 1970, it was noted that Turks are "very traditional and closely bound to their families," and it was assumed that migration within the same land mass, under government supervision, did not conflict with their basic values as much as independent migration across an ocean would.

Migration to West Germany proved so successful that Turkey negotiated similar deals with Belgium (1965 6), the Netherlands (1965 6), and France (1965 10), and eventually with Sweden (1967), Australia (1967), Denmark (1970), and the United Kingdom (1970). Turkey's high birth rate had become an exportable commodity, providing benefits not only to Western Europe but to Turkey itself.

Fig. 6C-1
Sources of Turkish migrants to West Germany

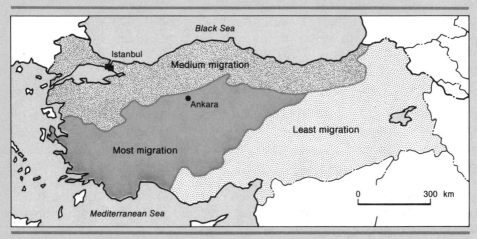

Source: *Migration News* 1976 12.

The purchasers of Turkish labour benefited greatly from the agreement. West Germans were able to avoid dirty, unskilled, and semi-skilled jobs. Also as a result of the agreement an exotic culture was admitted, and changes were introduced in the country. For instance, prior to 1961 West Germany had no mosques. After 1961 it gained three: one in Frankfurt, one in Cologne, and one, to serve migrant Turkish construction gangs, that folded down on a railway car in order to go through tunnels.

While Turkey paid a price, it also benefited. James Akré of Geneva, who worked on two separate occasions as a community development officer in Turkey, has these comments to make:

"I was attached to the village of Dag in west-central Turkey. In this brief account of that experience I shall try to outline my impressions concerning the migration of Turkish villagers to Western Europe for employment purposes.

"The village of Dag was a relatively prosperous farming community [in 1966], with approximately 1 300 people. The majority worked their own land, mainly for cash crops of wheat and sugar beet. These in turn provided a regular, if not always "adequate", source of income, through the services of government agents who bought at a fixed price. Indications of Dag's relative prominence among neighbouring villages were the size and quality of construction of its primary school, the importance of its mosque, the authority and influence of its mayor in area politics, the number of annual pilgrims to Mecca, and other similar factors.

"My first direct experience with Turks who had emigrated for employment came in 1966 with a more or less continuous flow of villagers returning for holidays. In some cases, as time passed, villagers would return permanently; likewise, others would receive the necessary clearance and depart for Western Europe. My impressions were that labour migration was a significant possibility for a large number of males aged 20-35 who were either employed but desired greater opportunities or underemployed due to either seasonal inactivity or overcrowding in relation to available arable land.

"A principal avenue of recruitment was the presence of a family member in an already secure position in Western Europe. Second to this was official recruitment through government or foreign-run offices in major cities.

"Migrants returning home on leave would invariably make highly visible displays of their new-found status and prosperity. Conspicuous consumption seemed to revolve around a fascination with a wide variety of gadgetry. A returning worker, in spite of the very unsuitable weather conditions, would never been seen without his "uniform"—the latest in western-style suit, shoes, etc. More noticeable, perhaps, were those migrants who returned on a final basis, yet failed to resume their previous occupations, usually farming. These persons would sit conspicuously in the coffee houses, still "in uniform", and recount their experiences abroad to a generally very attentive audience.

"Having lived with Turkish labour migration, and having seen first-hand such aspects of the movement as "fatherless" families, absentee landlords, completely idle land, and a gradual though entirely perceptible increase in disposable income, it was interesting to pay a second visit to this same village in the early 1970s.

"This is what I observed on my return:
— a departure of some of the brightest talent in the village.
— a general absence of men in the age group 20-40. An eerie sense of "disaster" in another time, when women, children, and old people seemed to be the only survivors.
— a drop in the overall population from 1300 to 1150.
— a rise in disposable income, obviously from sources external to the village.
— a most perceptible increase in consumer goods; for example, tape recorders, radios, gas stoves, and clothing of distinctively foreign style.
— the establishment of a Middle School (grades 6-8) which serves Dag and some surrounding villages.
— the advent of electricity and the high incidence of actual subscribers.
— the adoption of an air of general prosperity and active involvement in a dynamic process of change, and interest in affairs outside the village.
— returning migrant workers seen as predominant influences on all aspects of village social and economic life in their position as value transmitters.
— the appearance of extended-family relatives who were waiting to be "called". These did not wait until they were actually leaving for Europe to assume the external characteristics of the migrant. They too donned their best clothing and passed a good deal of their time in coffee houses while "preparing" in spirit to migrate. Such a situation is significant in that apart from land left idle by the absence of those willing to work it, those waiting to leave, now supported by remittances from their migrant relatives, were permitted a sort of "idle rich" inactivity, thereby causing a further reduction in agricultural output. The drop in numbers of the active population might serve to provide the unemployed and underemployed with a means for gainful activity. The opposite seems to be the case, however. Land is remaining unused, and formerly active males (farmers) have become inactive in anticipation of their eventual departure for work abroad.

"None of the above-mentioned effects on the village of Dag need necessarily be interpreted in a negative light. Change in traditional structures can be either reassuring or disturbing depending upon individual perspectives, and whether it refers to the shorter or longer term. These observations merit further study. The effect of labour migration on rural structures in the countries of migrant origin has been an area of inquiry badly neglected in the last two decades."

Adapted from an article in *Migration News* 1974 6 .

MIGRATIONS: Further Reading

The New Refugees, CHRISTY
The Black Experience, GROH
A Nation of Strangers, PACKARD
The Meeting Point, CLARKE
Storm of Fortune, CLARKE
A Bigger Light, CLARKE
Strangers Devour the Land, RICHARDSON
Exodus, URIS
The Immigrants, MONTERO
Exodus UK, ROHMER
Blue Mountains of China, WIEBE

Conclusion

From their origins, human beings have always migrated, and thus the earth's population has gradually spread over almost the entire globe. In this process, a great many benefits and problems have developed. Opportunities for a new life have been created, new lands opened up, and natural resources discovered. Different races have been brought into contact with one another, and some mixing has occurred. However in some areas migrations have also led to overcrowding, food scarcities, and unemployment. Different races have often clashed with each other.

As the earth's peoples have developed strong centralized governments, they have sought to reduce the problems caused by migration by controlling the flow of immigrants. Increasingly, migration has become subject to laws and regulations, and the flows are now more controlled than at any time in the past. Government action has in fact come to dominate much of what happens in the world. Governments generally try to act in the interests of their own countries, and so decisions about issues such as food supplies, natural resources, and migrations will be made according to these interests. In the next chapter, Geopolitics, we will closely examine the political aspects of geography.

Chapter 7
GEOPOLITICS

Introduction

Politics may be defined as the practice of decision-making by society as a whole, usually formalized at government level. Some political decisions have nothing to do with geography—the minimum age for voting, for example. Other political decisions, however, are very much concerned with geography; these include decisions on trade, military alliances, foreign aid, immigration and emigration, and territorial control. In some cases geographical facts cause political changes—as when Switzerland restricts immigration because it already has enough people. In other cases political facts cause geographical changes; for instance, the increase in oil prices by OPEC has led to an expanded search for oil in the Arctic and the North Sea.

We see that geography can affect or be affected by politics. *Geopolitics* is the study of the two-way relationship between political beliefs and actions on one side and any of the usual concerns of geography on the other.

Many political beliefs and actions arise out of certain aspects of the environment, such as the economic system, the distribution of wealth, the areas of land suitable for the support of society, and the possibilities of trade. As people look at their country, they develop political policies that are aimed at keeping the environmental characteristics they like, and changing those they do not. Indeed, politics may even be regarded as a means of decision-making whereby a society organizes its environment—both human and physical—either for change or for preservation. Geopolitics is therefore a key study in geography.

In this chapter geopolitics will be discussed with regard to the different countries of the world. In the first section we shall see that the earth's nations are often divided into three groups, or worlds. The following sections deal with first and second world relations, relations within the second world, and relations between the third world and the other two groups of nations. We shall then study the concept of national power, and attempt to assess the power of different countries. In the last two sections we will examine the clashes that inevitably occur in the world because of conflicting interests, as well as various movements for cooperation established to help maintain a certain degree of peace. The chapter ends with a case study of South Africa, a country whose political policies are causing many important geographical changes.

On trade

Freer trade felt aid to fishermen but deleterious to manufacturers

HALIFAX (CP)—Freer trade would help Atlantic Canada's fishing industry, but would hurt manufacturers, a Canadian Manufacturers Association seminar has been told.

The seminar is one of a series being held across the country to discuss the impact of the Economic Council of Canada's proposal that the country move toward eliminating tariffs.

Tom Stanfield, president of Stanfield's Ltd. of Truro, N.S., said Canada's textile industry is already withstanding "tremendous" pressure from imports and probably will be forced to reduce employment.

He said free trade could force Stanfield's to begin having its products manufactured abroad, "and this would disemploy 900 Canadians," or it could have to sell to a foreign company.

E. M. S. Fisher, president of Enterprise Foundry Co. Ltd. of Sackville, N.B., said Canadian appliance manufacturers agree that free trade could wipe out their industry, causing a loss of jobs in Ontario, Quebec and New Brunswick. Most of the current factories would become only distributors of products made by their U.S. parents.

The impact on Canadian suppliers of components would also be disastrous, he said.

. . .

H. P. Connor, chairman of the board of National Sea Products Ltd., Canada's largest fish processor, said the fishing industry would generally react favorably to free trade, and it would not face the same problems as other industries. . . .

The Globe and Mail 1975 10 3

On foreign aid

"Canadians should be concerned about world problems," says MP

by DOUGLAS ROCHE

Mr. Roche is Progressive Conservative MP for Edmonton-Strathcona.

Near the end of of our public meeting in Kelowna, B.C., a middle-aged man in a pink shirt and western tie rose to put a question to us which, he said, had been on his mind for several years.

"Does our aid to the developing nations really do any good? It seems to me the problem of world poverty is too complex for aid. Is there any hope for a solution?"

As three members of Parliament from three different parties—Andrew Brewin of the NDP (Greenwood), Irenee Pelletier of the Liberals (Sherbrooke) and myself from the Progressive Conservatives (Edmonton-Strathcona)—we travelled from Halifax to Vancouver for 10 days as a team.

"It's about time MPs started to work together," many callers said. But others rapped us for "not doing your job as MPs instead of running around the country worrying more about other people than Canadians."

The question of "putting our own house in order first" was a dominant reaction everywhere we went. We refused to allow the question to strain our unity, since it would inevitably lead us into domestic political delinquencies. But, more important, Canadians have to get away from the idea that we must solve all the problems of Canada before concentrating on international problems.

The world won't stand still. The World Food Council says 460 million people are either starving or malnourished. An estimated 75 000 people a day are migrating to overcrowded cities of the Third World already desperately short of physical and social services.

Shouldn't Canadians be concerned about this global crisis? Yes, most people responded, but how?

The Globe and Mail 1976 1 24

Reprinted by permission of the *Toronto Star.*

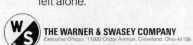
Courtesy of the Warner and Swasey Company

On migrations
Germany

The East Germans are still fighting the lure of the west; this was the central point of the past month's propaganda campaign surrounding the trials of numerous "human traffickers" who helped East Germans escape to the west. The statistics on escapes which the West German government released last week must have been an alarming reminder to East German leaders that all the sophisticated frontier barriers, minefields and hidden guns cannot close the border completely. In the first six months of this year, 442 East Germans managed to cross the border to West Germany and 1 216 escaped through eastern Europe or defected during trips to the west. A total of 155 147 people have left East Germany illegally since the building of the Berlin wall in August, 1961: 2 668 have been East German soldiers; 164 have died in the attempt.

The Economist 1974 8 24

Cyprus

Cyprus protest to UN at influx of Turks

From Our Correspondent
Nicosia, Dec 29

The Cyprus Government has protested once more to the United Nations over Turkey's intensified efforts to change the island's population structure by the colonization of the Turkish-occupied area with settlers from the Turkish mainland.

. . .

Turkey intended to settle another 20 000 mainland Turks in the northern part of the island "in a very short time", the spokesman said. These would be in addition to 20 000 already settled there earlier in the year.

The spokesman accused Turkey of planning to increase the Turkish Cypriot population from its pre-invasion figure of 120 000 (18 per cent of the total) to 160 000.

Turkey and the Turkish Cypriot leadership have denied earlier charges of large-scale colonization, while admitting that up to 5 000 mainland Turks—officially described as "seasonal workers"—have been brought to Cyprus for varying periods for temporary employment.

Despite the official denials, the settlement of mainland Turks has been verified both by neutral observers and Turkish Cypriots.

The new arrivals in some cases have been settled in empty villages abandoned by the 200 000 Greek Cypriot refugees who fled from the Turkish-occupied area at the time of the invasion in 1974.

The Times 1975 12 30

On frontiers

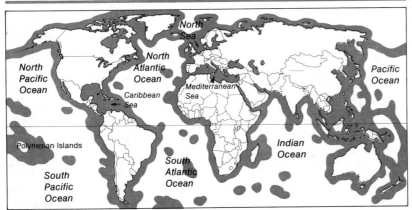

This map shows how an extension of national jurisdiction to 200 miles off all coasts, including those of islands, could affect as much as one third of the seas that cover 70% of the globe.

The Economist 1975 5 31

Here is a vision of the year 2000: The coastal nations have extended their sovereignty over the oceans; sea traffic is hampered by tolls and restrictions; tension flares constantly as nations seek to protect their share of the seabed's mineral wealth; the oceans' fish are in short supply as pollution spreads unchecked. . . .

Paul Lewis, *The Toronto Star* 1976 3 4

The dominion of the land ends where the power of its arms ends.

—Dutch Jurist Cornelius van Bynkershoek, 1703

Discussion and Research

1. Should the oceans be divided between nations?
2. The Warner & Swasey Company of Ohio asserts that "if Russia bought our system, they wouldn't have to buy our grain." Why does it say this, do you think?
3. What is the point of Macpherson's cartoon?
4. What are some of the conflicting views about aid to less developed countries?
5. Should politicians continue to protect Canada's manufacturing industry by tariffs?
6. What are some of the benefits and problems associated with the meeting of peoples with different values and beliefs?

Section A
Different Worlds

The chapters in this book demonstrate that the world is not the same throughout its whole extent. There are great variations in the rate of population growth (Chapter 1), amount and quality of food intake (Chapter 2), degree of industrialization (Chapter 3), production and use of energy (Chapter 4), quality of life (Chapter 5), migration patterns (Chapter 6), geopolitical interests (Chapter 7), and degree of change experienced (Chapter 8). Maps and exercises in the chapters reveal fairly strong, though far from perfect, correlations between many of these variables. For instance, a high rate of population growth tends to correlate well with a low level of food intake, a low degree of industrialization, and low production and use of energy.

On the basis of these correlations it is possible to divide the countries of the world into two groups: the more developed countries and the less developed ones. The differences between these two groups are many and include economy, life style, and outlook. There is a wide choice of criteria that can be used to determine whether any individual nation belongs to one group or the other; money is not used as a criterion, because some of the world's money-rich nations are the less developed oil-exporting countries. Key criteria are, instead, mostly infrastructural in nature (i.e., related to institutions or facilities that keep the country running smoothly). Examples include education, health, banking, and transportation and communication networks. Literacy is a useful criterion, for it reflects the penetration of the educational system, and helps to determine the potential for technological development. If literacy is low the achievements and potential of the country are likely to be low too, and the country can reasonably be classified as belonging to the less developed group.

This idea can be tested mathematically.

Statistical Interpretation

7-1 First we must check to see how *literacy* correlates with an important *economic* indicator of development, namely per capita energy consumption. The data in column X of Appendix 2 are for per capita energy consumption of all types of fuel in kilograms of coal equivalent. Standardization on coal equivalent makes it easier to compare the energy consumptions of those societies that rely largely on hydroelectricity or natural gas with those that rely largely on coal or oil.

a) Draw a scattergraph of the literacy data (column W) and the energy consumption data (column X). It is probably best to use a normal arithmetic scale for the literacy data and a log scale for the energy data. Insert a "line of best fit" and lightly shade a band along both sides of the line to include the majority of the nations.

b) What do you infer from the graph as a whole?

c) Which nations lie farthest from the line of best fit, and outside your shaded band? Can you suggest or find any explanations for this lack of fit?

d) Is literacy a reasonable criterion to use in assessing development achievements?

7-2 Second, we shall see if variations in literacy can be used to *explain* variations in the per capita value of manufactured output (column Q).

a) Perform calculations to establish the *coefficient of determination* (r^2) as shown in Appendix 3.

b) Variations in literacy are not alone in causing variations in the per capita value of manufactured output; there are other factors. What can you suggest?

7-3 Third, if you are satisfied that literacy is a useful criterion for separating the more developed countries from the less developed ones, draw a map to show the two groups. At what level of literacy should the division be made?

The concept of the three worlds, which is often used when it is desirable to group the world's nations into general categories, seems to have developed during the 1950s. The term *third world* was first used during the Bandung Conference of 77 Afro-Asian nations held in Indonesia in 1955. It appears to have evolved from political discussions starting in 1952 about the formation of a "third force" in the world, the other two forces being the Western and Communist worlds.

The countries of the more developed group are alike only in that they are developed, and even then the type and level of development vary, as shown in Chapter 5. In addition, the political ideologies of group members range from extremes of capitalism to communism. These differences in development and ideology cause basic contrasts to exist in the ways in which decisions are made and carried out. The profound ideological differences between the capitalist countries and the communist ones have caused the capitalist countries to be classified together into what is called the *first world*, a group led by the USA. The communist countries form the *second world*, and are led by the USSR.

For a long time all the less developed countries were categorized as the *third world*. Lack of development was generally seen as the main characteristic common to all these nations. The third world countries first organized themselves into a coherent political lobby in the mid-1950s at the Bandung Conference in Indonesia. The original *Group of 77* has grown since the creation of newly independent states

A coherent political lobby is a group organized to persuade others in government to pursue policies favourable to the group.

from former European colonies. There are now well over one hundred members of the third world group.

However, as time has passed, the third world has seen its members quarrel and fight, become richer and—in some cases—poorer, and either remain neutral with respect to the first and second worlds, or enter into alliances with either of the two groups. Their differences in ideology, history, and culture are proving to be more powerful than the common tie of lack of development. The most important differences have developed between the oil-exporting countries of the Middle East and the rest of the third world.

Some people have ranked the third world countries according to development potential, creating *third*, *fourth*, and *fifth* worlds in the process. In this classification, the *third world* consists of those countries capable of sustaining their own growth; they can earn their own way in the world. Resource-rich countries such as Iran and Zambia or incipiently productive countries such as Brazil and Mexico are included in the third world. The *fourth world* contains countries such as India and Egypt, which still need outside help to achieve self-sustaining growth, but which already have enough infrastructural development to survive. The *fifth world* comprises those countries such as Bangladesh and Mali which cannot survive without frequent outside help.

It is logical to divide these countries on the basis of their potential for development, since that is the criterion used to classify the nations in the first place. However, this type of categorization fails to take into account strong ties which bind the countries of the third world in other ways. For example, the Arab countries are fairly unified, since they have similar religious and ethnic origins; yet not all Arab nations are oil producers, nor are all found in the Middle East. Equally, the major oil exporters are not all Arab countries and in fact include nations as different as Iran, Indonesia, Nigeria, and Venezuela. Even the religion of the Arabs—Islam—is not confined to the Arab world; it exists in areas such as Indonesia and black Africa.

Third world countries therefore tend to have a wide range of interests and loyalties. Thus the oil exporters form one group, the Arab world another, Islam a third, black Africa a fourth, and so on. Venezuela, for example, is a member of the oil group but not of the others; Indonesia is a member of the oil and Islamic groups; Nigeria belongs to the oil, Islamic, and black African groups; and Saudi Arabia is part of the oil and Islamic groups and the Arab world. It is clear that the third world does not often speak with one voice.

China poses a special problem to those attempting to classify the world's countries. It is a centrally planned communist state, in many ways like the USSR, but it is also a third world country with relatively low literacy rates and little infrastructural development. The Chinese seem to prefer to think of themselves as leaders of the third world rather than as followers of the second.

There are many differences besides oil wealth. Some countries are military dictatorships, while others are democracies; some are lax on rules, while others are austere and tightly controlled; and some seek outside help, while others reject it.

The map in Fig. 7-1 shows you the possible geographical distribution of the three worlds. It should be remembered that some countries are on the borderline between the first and third worlds: Greece and Argentina are examples of this.

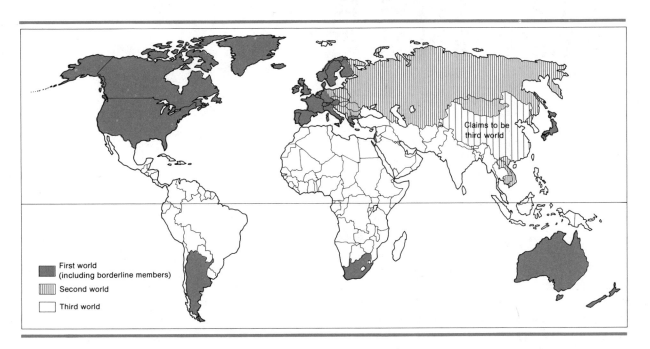

Fig. 7-1
The three worlds

Discussion and Research

7. What does China have in common with (a) the second world, and (b) the third world?

8. What steps have the countries of the third world taken to become organized as an effective lobby? What do you think they want?

Section B

First and Second World Relations

Although the first and second worlds broadly belong to the European culture realm, they represent opposed political and economic systems. These systems are a product of contrasted political ideologies, and their differences are reflected in the ways in which the societies make decisions about the geographical development of their environments.

1. The First World

The private enterprise, capitalist first world places priority on the private ownership of many different aspects of the economy. This is usually made possible in two ways: first, by means of stockholding, whereby many people own shares of the total stock of a company; and second, by direct ownership, whereby a person or a family owns an enterprise outright. In Canada, the Hudson's Bay Company is an example of a common stock enterprise, and Eaton's is an example of a family company.

In the private enterprise system, the market is the instrument used to determine what gets produced, how much gets produced, how much the product costs, and what resources are drawn into production. The market yields a compromise between the amount producers want to charge, and the price buyers are willing to pay. Wages and salaries are determined by a compromise between the amount of money the workers want, and the amount their employers want to pay. There is, in theory, a point at which an agreement is reached and all is in balance; the market is said to be in *equilibrium*. Such equilibrium is theoretical only; in practice adjustments are always being made. If a producer guesses wrongly and overproduces some item, then it will not sell until he lowers the price and attracts buyers. As the public buys the items, supply and demand for this particular commodity are brought back to equilibrium. Similarly, shortages will cause prices to rise. Because of a lack of a certain item, it is harder to get, and people are willing to pay more for it. Such price rises make production worthwhile, so producers produce more. Gradually the supply meets the demand and the market returns to equilibrium.

There are two main alternatives to price rises when there are shortages. One is rationing, whereby all buyers are permitted to receive only limited quantities of a product; the other is the line, whereby only the first few customers have the chance to buy an item. While these systems seem to be fair, they have the important long-term disadvantage that the producers of the goods are not encouraged to produce any more. Thus shortages tend to persist, along with rationing and lines. Price rises, on the other hand, yield higher profits, thus encouraging producers to produce more.

Whenever demand and supply get out of equilibrium, the utility principle will cause shifts to occur until equilibrium is restored. In practice, the world is dynamic, and supply and demand are rarely in precise equilibrium. The current situation therefore represents a search for a future equilibrium, and decisions about future levels of demand and supply must constantly be made. Chapter 4 illustrates part of the process with regard to the production of new energy supplies.

In the past the owners of the means of production, especially land and capital, came to wield most of the power; this power was often abused at the expense of labour. However, the same principle of market freedom that permitted the abuses to occur also allowed their removal. Democracy, the rise of labour-oriented political parties, and the growth of labour unions eventually combined to bring the situation back to equilibrium. Private enterprise production is accordingly guided by state regulations; in some fields it is directly subject to government control, and in a few instances it even has to compete with state-owned organizations. For example, Canada's energy production is controlled by the National Energy Board, radio and television by the CRTC, telephones by the CTC, and egg production and marketing by the CEMA. In addition, state airlines, railways, and broadcasting systems compete with privately owned companies.

CRTC = Canadian Radio-Television Commission
CTC = Canadian Transport Commission
CEMA = Canadian Egg Marketing Agency

Even in the USA, which is usually regarded as the best example of the private enterprise system, the federal government owns or controls large segments of the economy. For example, passenger railways are federally operated by AMTRAK; the automobile industry is subject to safety and environmental protection standards; the food industry is subject to health inspection; and the airline industry is subject to safety regulations and to route and fare licensing requirements. In most European first world countries the state plays an even bigger part than it does in North America. In the UK, for example, the government owns and controls all the railways, the coal industry, most of the airlines and steel industries, the main ports, and the facilities for the generation and distribution of power. Nowhere is the ideal free enterprise system in operation.

2. The Second World

The communist second world exists largely on a belief in state, or communal, ownership and control of the resources and means of production. The system developed partly as a reaction in the nineteenth century to the industrial revolution and the worst excesses of capitalism. But the idea of communal ownership and control was not new; Plato had recommended it in *The Republic* hundreds of years before urban slums and other signs of industrial exploitation became visible. Unrestricted private enterprise gave millions the choice of

Karl Marx wrote his chief book *Das Kapital* in England, after seeing some of the conditions brought about by early industrial exploitation of the workers.

starving or of working fourteen hours a day for a shilling or two. The concept of communal control had been part of European thought for hundreds of years, but it took the industrial revolution, the process of urbanization, and the European population explosion together to produce any action. The Paris Commune of 1870 pointed the way; the Russian revolution of 1905 provided a preliminary trial; World War I created the opportunity. And in 1917 the Russian revolution was taken over by the communists; the idea of communal control became reality.

The ideological basis for Marxist communism is that the workers are solely responsible for the production of wealth, and that the wealth ought to be given to the workers and not to an aristocratic elite. Communism was thus seen as the mechanism for securing greater equity in the distribution of wealth within a society. The pattern of inherited ownership, especially of land, was therefore broken, and the entrepreneurial class was almost eliminated. The state took over almost everything, setting up bureaucracies to supervise operations. Planning and decision-making were all done by central committees, called *soviets*, instead of by individuals. State ownership of all parts of the economy has not proved to be practical, however, and in consequence all communist governments permit a limited degree of private ownership. For example, most of Poland's farms are still privately owned, and even in the USSR and China there is some private ownership of land for small-scale farming. If, as we have seen, the ideal private enterprise system does not exist, neither does the ideal communist system.

3. Philosophic Differences

The first and second worlds therefore stand at philosophically opposed poles: in the first world the individual takes precedence over the state in all matters that are free from social regulation; in the second the state takes precedence over the individual in all matters that, according to the state, remain free to the individual. This philosophic contrast is not confined to the level of first world versus second world; it also exists within both separately. Just as the second world has its *revisionists*, so the first world has its socialists. It is interesting to note that the first world seems to be moving in the direction of greater state control; the second world tends to be moving away from full state control of all activities. It is also worth noting that in times of emergency, as in World War II, the first world has moved quickly to almost complete state control. On the other hand, as Russia rises above the problems of food production and job creation, there is more individual freedom.

Debate over the ideal system continues, at least in the first world. The following articles present different critical views of the free enterprise and socialist systems.

The question of the rights of the individual in relation to the rights of the state did not arise with the dispute between capitalists and communists. It began well before capitalism and communism were even talked about, and it will continue long after they are gone.

Courtesy of the Pennwalt Corporation

Counting Russia's camps

From our Israel correspondent

Zichron Yaacov, a quiet village set in the rolling hills of Mount Carmel, hardly looks like a target for the KGB, the Soviet secret police. But a month ago a tiny cottage there was broken into and documents and papers selectively rifled by trained hands. The cottage, the home and headquarters of Avraham and Elinora Shifrin, who used to live in Russia, is a vital centre in the worldwide system of gatherers of information on the prisons, forced labour camps and mental homes in which the Soviet regime deals with its dissidents.

The Shifrins' source material is obtained from émigrés as they reach the west. These people include former inmates as well as their families and other Soviet citizens whose day-to-day activities brought them into the prison camps or into contact with them: doctors, managers of industrial projects employing prison labour, former guards. Many run appalling risks to smuggle out maps, films, photographs and lists to fuel the human rights campaign in the west.

Hard evidence painstakingly pieced together so far has established the certain existence of 500 prisons, prison camps and "psychiatric" jails holding political dissidents—not only campaigners for democracy, nationalists, applicants for exit visas and Zionists, but also believers of many faiths: Jews, Buddhists, Pentecostalists, Adventists, Baptists, Methodists. The final figure may be much larger. Some researchers now put the Soviet Union's total of political prisoners at 1m-1½m.

There are prisons for every type of offender:

● "General regime" prisons, ostensibly for common criminals but containing "politicals" as well.

● "Strict regime" prisons for political prisoners.

● "Particularly strict regime" prisons for political prisoners.

● "Closed prisons" for political prisoners in isolation.

● Special camps for women.

● Special camps for children, including those separated from parents practising a religion. There are also the notorious psychiatric jails, investigation prisons and transit prison camps.

From the moment a "political" offender is arrested he is in the hands of the KGB, which runs the entire system, including fleets of specially designed prisoners' trucks, rail cars, barges, ships and aircraft. Each of the camps has its KGB commandant, armed sentries, dogs, electrified barbed wire fence and watchtowers.

The number of political prisoners in the Soviet Union is a closely guarded secret. One method of concealment, devised since Mr. Brezhnev became party leader, is to lock up dissidents together with common criminals after trying them on trumped-up criminal charges. Another is to pronounce men of strong convictions insane and commit them to psychiatric institutions. The various camps house anything from a few hundred prisoners in the smallest ones to 7 000 in the largest. The entire tally includes:

Moscow district: 14 prisons, some in the city itself, including Kryukovo, the show prison for foreign visitors.

Lvov district: Eight labour camps, of which six are inside the city, including one for women and another for children, and camps built around a huge furniture complex, an agricultural machine factory and an electro-mechanical factory.

Odessa: Four labour camps and two prisons. Two of the camps are for women, one of them "strict regime"; the inmates do manual work in metal production, building and agriculture. There is also a "strict regime" camp for men.

Leningrad: A large concentration of prisons, camps and "psychiatric prisons", including four mental prisons in the old Alexander Nevsky monastery and two more in the town.

Riga (Latvia): At least 25 labour camps and prisons, with closed prisons containing special cells for political prisoners in isolation.

Moldavia: Seven known labour camps.

Perm district (north Urals): 12 known labour camps, including one isolation jail—but estimates run to a total of 50-60 camps.

Archangel: 12 known labour camps.

Murmansk district: Seven labour camps known, many more suspected.

Kiev: Five known labour camps, prisons and psychiatric prisons.

Voroshilovka (Ukraine): Five known labour camps, and two specialised mental hospitals where political pris-

oners are said by ex-inmates to be receiving particularly harsh treatment.

Minsk district: Five known prison camps, one a jail in the city taking up three streets.

Azerbaijan: Seven known camps.

Tomsk district: 12 labour camps.

Dnepropetrovsk: Eight labour camps plus the Pridneprovskaya mental hospital.

Chernigov: Two labour camps.

Omsk: Seven large prison camps.

Krasnoyarsk territory (Crimea): 50 prison camps, many with "strict" and "particularly strict" regimes.

Krasnodar district: 16 known prisons and camps, including the general district investigation jail which has condemned cells from which men are sent to work in underground atomic plants in the Ukraine and allowed no contact with the outside world. Between 90 and 120 men are packed into cells for 30 or 40, without ventilation. There is also a psychiatric camp for 2000 men and women.

Sverdlovsk region: About 100 prison camps, of which 40 are "strict regime", including one for women felling timber.

Kola peninsula: A closed prison camp zone.

Vorkuta (Arctic circle): Four camps whose inmates work in the mines.

Chernovitsk region (Ukraine): One camp with 5 000 prisoners, mostly Baptists and Jews, doing hard labour in quarries.

Kaliningrad: One large camp whose inmates work on furniture manufacture.

Orlov: A specialised mental hospital.

Kishinev: One hard labour camp at a refrigeration plant.

Korkino, Chelyabinsk region: One strict regime camp for work in the gold mines.

Ionava (near Kaunas): One camp whose inmates do work hazardous to health at a chemical combine.

Khodyzhensk: One camp for 800 prisoners at an oilfield.

Since the beginning of this year, signals of a new wave of political persecutions and arrests have been flashing. People have recently been coming out of the Soviet Union with chilling tales of new conditions.

Inside the prison camps armed surveillance is constant. Each barrack is cordoned off with barbed-wire fencing and prisoners are marching everywhere under armed guard in platoons of 20-25—even to the camp doctor. Between 300 and 500 people may be packed into barracks of 2000-3000 square feet [about 200-300 m²] in area, in bunks made of planks. They are allowed no personal possessions in their barracks and are frequently searched to make sure. They may "visit" their belongings in the camp storehouse—with permission, again with their platoon. When not at work, they are locked in the barracks. Their average working day is 12 hours including travel, often on foot, sometimes more if the camp is behind its exhausting work quota. Outdoor work stops only when the temperature drops below 45 centigrade [Celsius] below zero. But extra hours are added in the "summer" months. Sick leave is awarded according to camp quotas.

Clothing is inadequate for the climate and often old. In the "particularly strict regime" camps, like the one in Sokal, Lvov district, prisoners are issued with concentration garb of rough sacking or tarpaulin for all seasons.

On many evenings political prisoners are forced to attend lectures by political instructors. If they do not show proper alertness, they are put into an isolated punishment cell for 10-12 days and lose their correspondence and visiting rights. With no blots on their record, they may receive and write two letters a month and have one visit a year from a very close relative. After completing half their term with a clean record, they are allowed one 9 lb [4 kg] parcel a year, but no meat or butter.

Prison labour has very probably become essential to the Soviet economy. The vast army of forced labour, including women, students and intellectuals, cuts timber, builds new towns, factories, power stations and railways, mans industries, particularly those that present health risks, works in mining and oil extraction and in manufacturing for military production and export, all with simple tools and often in dreadful weather conditions.

Safety precautions are rare. Even in the corrective camps for children, 14-year-olds put in a 6-hour working day in heavy industry. Prisoners quarry uranium at the Aksu mines in Kazakhstan and the Jolti Vadi mines in the Ukraine. From their camp near the secret naval base at Rakushka Bay near Vladivostok, they clean the waste outlets of the reactors in nuclear submarines. They burrow for gold in the far east, where women prisoners ruin their lungs by blowing at the gold as it runs along conveyor belts. At one camp a glass factory is under the same roof as the sleeping cells and the prisoners breathe glass dust 24 hours a day. Last year sailors brought news of a huge camp for women (with about 7000 inmates), previously unknown, at Shikotan on the Kurile islands in the Pacific, where women unload trawlers for the biggest canning centre in the country.

Colonies of former "politicals" are now springing up in the west. Regardless of why they were punished, they share the special bond of the one-time inmates. They remain amazingly buoyant, convinced that for every dissident suppressed two more will pop up. The indefatigable human rights campaigners among them say: publicity is our only weapon. *The Economist* 1977 4 2

A meeting of the Communist Party of the Soviet Union in Alma Alta, 1974.

Novosti Press Agency

The Soviet economy and its critics

While the highly developed capitalist countries cannot completely throw off the tenacious grip of economic crisis, under its Ninth Five-Year Plan (1971-1975) the Soviet Union registered larger increases in industrial output, capital investments and state allocations for undertakings to improve the people's living standard than in any previous five-year period. In the last ten years we added as much to our economic potential as we had in nearly half of a century before that. No wonder Soviet economic progress, the prospects for continued balanced growth and the steadily rising living standard attract keen attention everywhere.

The advantages of the planned socialist economy are admitted by many prominent bourgeois scholars and public leaders who take a realistic view of things. Professor Wassily W. Leontief of Harvard University

has noted that the Tenth Five-Year Plan targets point to a steady and uninterrupted Soviet economic upswing. In contrast to the fluctuating curve of America's annual industrial output, the corresponding figures of the planned socialist economy, he points out, climb persistently and steadily, without ever dropping.

Edward Lamb, an American industrialist and public leader, has called the Tenth Five-Year Plan a promising prospect for the Soviet people. The obvious lesson to be drawn from the contrast between the American and Soviet economies, he said, was that in the planned economy there is a rational distribution of manpower, raw materials, credits and output, and stable rates of research and overall economic growth are maintained. All this, he went on, was confirmed by the draft of the Tenth Five-Year Plan, which would lead to a further rise in the Soviet living standard.

Objective observers in capitalist countries note above all the stable and crisis-free growth of socialist pro-

duction and the rising living standards. D. Perton, a British economist, has pointed out that the guidelines for the current five-year period reflect the Soviet Union's outstanding successes in economic development and in improving the living standard. Such assessments are by no means isolated. They are shared by millions of progressive people abroad.

So much the worse for the truth

Confirming, as they do, the historical advantages of socialism, such opinions irritate and distress capitalist ideologists who are afraid to face up to the truth. The mass media controlled by Big Business, acting on the principle that if something does not conform to the truth so much the worse for the truth, are stepping up a campaign of misinformation to slander the socialist system.

In *The New York Times*, for instance, the steady economic growth and political stability in the Soviet Union are turned into a weakness, and the fact that socialism is a society without crisis is made to appear as proof that socialism is stagnating. These mass media have produced an amazing theoretical discovery: that crisis and stagnation are not a product of capitalism but are inevitable in any industrial economy, are "universal", so to say. But the figures relating to the Soviet economy make it clear that such "theorising" is both groundless and malicious. An economic crisis means, above all, a sharp cut-back in production, growing unemployment and a deterioration of the people's working and living conditions; stagnation means marking time, depression, hopelessness. All this refers to the Western economy. The Soviet economy follows fundamentally different laws; it is free from agonising fluctuations between periods of upswing and recession. "Speaking of the overall results of the Ninth Five-Year Plan," Leonid Brezhnev noted in the Central Committee's report to the 25th Congress of the Communist Party of the Soviet Union earlier this year, "the main thing is that the dedicated work of the Soviet people and the guiding, organising activity of the Party have ensured a steady growth of the economy. The principal socio-economic targets of that five-year plan have been achieved."

As provided for by the Directives of the 24th CPSU Congress, during the Ninth Five-Year Plan industrial output increased by 43 per cent and real incomes went up by nearly 25 per cent; 56 000 000 people moved into new or improved housing. The national income, which is used for consumption and accumulation, increased by 28 per cent. Each per cent of growth now stands for an immeasurably larger quantity of output than previously; it means the production of new commodities of a higher quality.

The American bourgeois press

claims that the Tenth Five-Year Plan will not be a period of growth for the Soviet Union but one of "stabilisation" or "consolidation" of the economy. The West German *Der Spiegel*, and *Die Welt*, and also some other bourgeois publications, speak about "stabilisation of the Soviet economy" and "pessimistic prospects". They fail to mention that the Tenth Five-Year Plan targets include a growth of industrial output by 35 to 39 per cent, with increases of 38 to 42 per cent in the production of means of production and 30 to 32 per cent in the manufacture of consumer goods. The West has not registered such growth figures for a long time. How can this be called "stabilisation"?

The relative reduction in our growth rate, compared to the previous period, has nothing in common with "stabilisation"—a steady rise in industrial production is planned. This is not connected with any change in the nature of our economic progress or with a re-evaluation of priorities but is a result of the aims of sharply improving the effectiveness of existing capacities and raising the quality of output. The Western economy cannot even dream of such a consistent and steady growth of industrial production.

Misinformation is the object
Bourgeois ideologists often claim that Soviet agriculture is in a "hopeless" state, collective farming has proved to be a failure compared with private capitalist farming and even with small-scale peasant farming.

Like the other myths, the "failure" of collective farming is refuted by the facts—but the bourgeois press ignores the facts. Between 1928 and the beginning of the Ninth Five-Year Plan in 1971 gross farm output in the Soviet Union nearly trebled, while the number of persons engaged in agriculture dropped by nearly 70 per cent. This progress couldn't have

been made without socialist collective farming.

. . .

Contempt for the facts
Some Western Sovietologists claim that by putting the accent on heavy industry the Soviet Union neglects the consumer goods industries or, in other words, the interests of the consumer. As evidence they point to the fact that between 1976 and 1980 an increase of 38 to 42 per cent is planned in the output of means of production, as compared to a 30 to 32 per cent increase in the manufacture of consumer goods.

It should be clear to any unbiased person, however, that in this age of scientific and technological revolution the development of consumer goods industries depends on how well heavy industry supplies them with up-to-date means of production. Under the Tenth Five-Year Plan there is to be a considerable increase in the quantity and a substantial improvement in the quality of goods in order to satisfy the growing demands of the public more fully as a result of retooling and modernisation, the application of new, highly productive processes, all-round mechanisation and automation. All this can be done only with help from the industry which produces means of production, and it calls for a gradual restructuring of production. On the whole, the output of light industry alone is to register a 26 to 28 per cent gain during the five years.

. . .

It is fashionable among Sovietologists to claim that the Soviet living standard is much lower than the American. They attempt to prove this by comparing average wages according to the official rate of exchange. But wages, as an economic category, differ fundamentally under capitalism and socialism.

Whereas wages in a capitalist society are the working people's only subsistence, under socialism king people receive, in addition their wages, a number of vital benefits at the expense of the state, through the social consumption funds, and these must absolutely be taken into account when comparing living standards. In the Soviet Union the prices of the main foods and services (bread, meat, milk, rent, electricity and gas, and so on) are maintained at a stable level by state subsidies. Education, from primary school through university, is free of charge. So is medical care. House rents in the Soviet Union are among the lowest in the world: between 10 and 15 rubles a month for a two- or three-room flat. Rents have not risen since 1928. Incidentally, rental proceeds cover only one-third of the housing maintenance expenses, the remaining expenditure being borne by the state. The Soviet citizen does not contribute a kopek to the pension scheme; the entire cost is borne by the state. Nobody in the Soviet Union can remember an increase in fares or in the electricity rates. To sum up, the picture is as follows: a growth and expansion of social benefits, a growth in payments, higher pensions for many categories of people, and stable prices.

In general, living standards cannot be compared by simply calculating wages and prices according to the official rate of exchange, which is designed only for international payments on foreign loans and trade and is based on world prices, not domestic prices. This is obvious, and when comparing living standards in capitalist countries, bourgeois economists use sensible arguments. For example, when it was reported that the living standard in Britain was lower than in France or in Federal Germany, *The Economist* made haste to declare that there was a big difference between the purchasing power of money at home and the exchange rates.

The living standard in the Soviet Union is not subject to fluctuations because of market factors. It is rising all the time. Over the past 15 years the real incomes per capita have approximately doubled, while the general volume of material benefits and services has increased by approximately 140 per cent. The average wages and salaries of factory, office and professional workers are to increase by another 16 to 18 per cent, and collective farmers' incomes by 24 to 27 per cent, under the current five-year plan, with stable prices. Payments and benefits to the population from the social consumption funds will grow by 28 to 30 per cent. These are the facts. . . .

Soviet Union 1976 8

Discussion and Research

9. How much freedom do you think an individual should have?
10. Is freedom a "right"?
11. Why do you think communist governments have found that state ownership of all parts of the economy is not practical?
12. Why have capitalist governments found that private ownership of all parts of the economy is not practical?
13. In your opinion, what are the duties and rights of the State?

4. Propaganda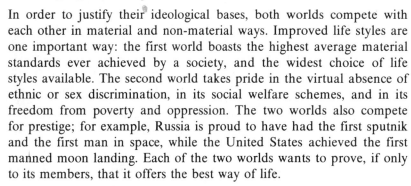

In order to justify their ideological bases, both worlds compete with each other in material and non-material ways. Improved life styles are one important way: the first world boasts the highest average material standards ever achieved by a society, and the widest choice of life styles available. The second world takes pride in the virtual absence of ethnic or sex discrimination, in its social welfare schemes, and in its freedom from poverty and oppression. The two worlds also compete for prestige; for example, Russia is proud to have had the first sputnik and the first man in space, while the United States achieved the first manned moon landing. Each of the two worlds wants to prove, if only to its members, that it offers the best way of life.

5. Heartland Theory

The two worlds also compete in the influence they try to exert on the rest of the world. The competition is keenest between the USA and the USSR, a fact that was foreseen by Halford Mackinder as early as the end of World War I. Mackinder's *Democratic Ideals and Reality* was a call to world statesmen to face up to certain geographical realities, notably those put forward in his *Heartland Theory*.

Heartland theory is summarized in the following statements: first, whoever controls Eastern Europe controls the Heartland; second, whoever controls the Heartland also controls the World Island; and third, whoever controls the World Island ultimately controls the world. *Eastern Europe* is loosely defined as the broad lowland area stretching from Germany to the Urals and from the Baltic/Arctic to the Carpathians/Black Sea. Within this area there are good sources of industrial energy, chiefly coal and hydroelectricity, as well as fertile farmlands. Internal transportation is excellent. Control of the vast resources of Eastern Europe more or less guarantees control of sparsely populated Siberia, because Siberia, with deserts and mountains to the south and east, and frozen seas to the north, is really only accessible from Eastern Europe.

In the past, many countries have fought to control this area. Throughout its history, from the Teutonic knights to Hitler, Germany has often pushed eastward; Russia has pushed westward from the time of Peter the Great to the present day. In consequence, border countries such as Poland have been invaded from both sides, and at times have even ceased to exist as separate states.

During World War II, Germany, in search of *Lebensraum* and eventual world control, failed to seize Europe and Siberia. Since that time, Russia has become a dominant power. With its control of both Eastern Europe and Siberia, Russia controls the Heartland. It is now pushing westward for several reasons; an important one is the country's need for access to "warm water", as postulated by the Heartland theory.

Russia's *warm water policy* means that it tries to obtain ice-free ports with access to the open ocean. In pursuit of this policy Russia has extended its control to the Baltic, which inconveniently freezes in winter. Another Russian target, the Black Sea, is not closed by ice, but it does not offer ready access to the oceans because it is almost landlocked, with its exit passing through Turkey. Russian fleets have thus gained only limited access to the Mediterranean by way of the Dardanelles-Bosporus channel. In addition, the northern fleet's base at Murmansk has opened up the North Atlantic to the Russians.

According to Heartland theory, once a country is secure in its resource-rich base of Eastern Europe and Siberia, it will seek access to the margins of the great land mass of Eurasia and Africa; such edges are termed the *Inner Crescent*. The theory predicts that a country

The Heartland is the area stretching from Germany into Siberia; the World Island is the whole of Europe and Asia, together with Africa.

Lebensraum = living room. The word was used by the Germans to refer to the territory needed for political and economic expansion. Germany used this concept to justify its conquest of Eastern Europe.

Novosti Press Agency

Russia has become the dominant power in central Asia. Here in Georgia, Russian tanks are on field exercises in February 1976.

Novosti Press Agency

One of the anti-submarine ships of the Russian Black Sea fleet.

seeking to penetrate the Inner Crescent will likely make its way first through Western Europe. This path is ideal for the following reasons: the North European Plain offers easy penetration from the Heartland right through to the Atlantic; the North Atlantic Drift creates year-round ice-free port facilities in Western Europe; and other directions are blocked by geographical features such as ice in the north, and deserts and mountains in the south. The theory asserts that in a struggle between the maritime regions of Western Europe and the country controlling the Heartland, the Heartland power will win, chiefly because of its superior internal transportation abilities and its ready access to vital resources. Once Western Europe has succumbed, the Heartland power will truly have access to the oceans. It can then try to bring all the isolated power centres around the rim of Afro-Asia into its orbit, by means of sea power based in Western Europe, and by land armies situated in the Heartland proper. Thus the *World Island* of Afro-Eurasia will be under the control of the Heartland power.

Due to its excellent transportation systems on land and sea, the Heartland power can extend its rule by pushing into the *Outer Crescent*, which consists of the Americas and Oceania. Mackinder believed that the countries of the Outer Crescent would be unable to resist penetrations from a central power; he forecast that the pressure would continue until the Heartland power ruled the world.

Presented at the end of World War I, Heartland theory did not foresee the use of aircraft and missiles, and it underestimated the growth of military and economic power in the USA. However it still

Russian tank crews being greeted as liberators in Czechoslovakia at the end of World War II (May, 1945).

Novosti Press Agency

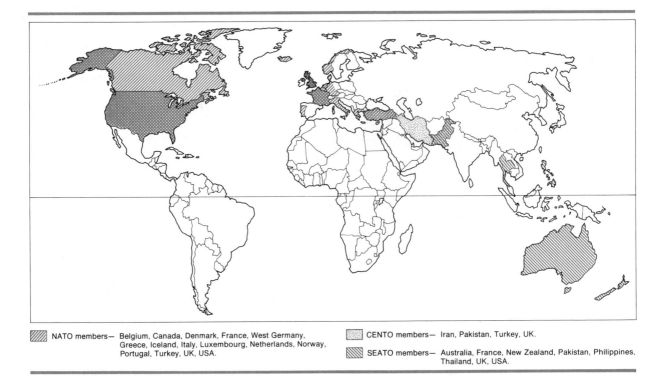

NATO members— Belgium, Canada, Denmark, France, West Germany, Greece, Iceland, Italy, Luxembourg, Netherlands, Norway, Portugal, Turkey, UK, USA.

CENTO members— Iran, Pakistan, Turkey, UK.

SEATO members— Australia, France, New Zealand, Pakistan, Philippines, Thailand, UK, USA.

offers valuable insights into many aspects of Russian and American foreign policy. For example, Russia has ruthlessly held on to its European satellites. The economies of Poland, East Germany, Czechoslovakia, Hungary, the Ukraine, Romania, and Bulgaria have been linked to the mother economy in Russia; it would be very hard to break up COMECON (Council for Mutual Economic Assistance). Political separation is also nearly impossible, as events in Hungary (1956) and Czechoslovakia (1968) have shown. Russia is still attempting to turn the other European countries communist. It tried for example during the 1974-75 revolution in Portugal, but failed; current efforts are concentrated in warm-water areas such as Italy and France. Even Angola is seen as a potential Russian naval base in the South Atlantic.

6. Containment

In defence, the USA has sponsored the creation of NATO (North Atlantic Treaty Organization). The organization maintains forces in Europe, for Europe is regarded as the first bulwark against communism. The US strongly feels the need to maintain defensive posts in Europe, as required for the Berlin Air Lift of 1948. The US has

Fig. 7-2
Member countries in alliances developed as part of the policy of containment

Russian attempts to gain influence in Africa are almost continuous. The Russians send advisers, technicians, and aid frequently. Their efforts are not always permanently successful; for example, they had influence in Egypt for many years after the Americans refused to build the Aswan Dam, but their influence there is now disappearing.

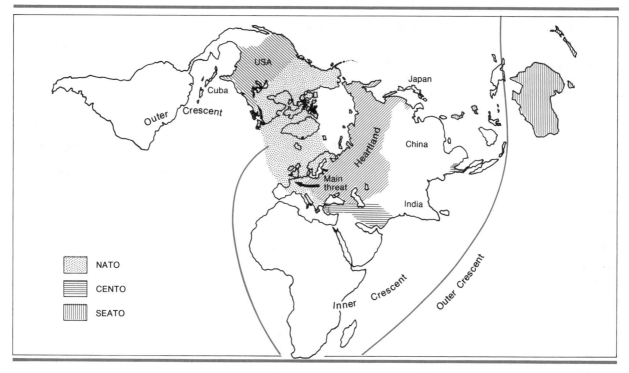

Source: *Geographical Magazine* 1970 6.

Fig. 7-3
Salient aspects of US containment policy and Heartland theory

developed its European interests as part of a general *policy of containment*, which is designed to stop the Russians from extending their influence beyond the Heartland. The US has therefore formed several defensive alliances with the countries of the Inner Crescent; two such alliances are SEATO (South East Asian Treaty Organization) and CENTO (Central Treaty Organization). The map in Fig. 7-2 shows the member countries of these defensive alliances; Fig. 7-3 shows the application of the containment policy schematically. On this second map, notice the importance of the Arctic and Canada to the US containment policy.

Since the US, with its containment policy, has a hold on Europe, the Russians must leapfrog this area to extend their influence. In the past, Russia has attempted to generate support in Africa, chiefly by sponsoring various anti-colonialist movements; efforts will likely continue. Russian influence is also strong in Vietnam, where the American response was long and unsuccessful despite the appeal to arms of the US domino theory (if Vietnam falls, so will Laos, then Cambodia, Thailand, etc.). The penetration of Cuba is probably Russia's greatest success, as Fig. 7-3 confirms, for it represents a toehold in the Outer Crescent. Chile, by contrast, is a country that the Russians failed to take over.

Fig 7-4
Distances of capital cities from Washington and Moscow

The world's thirty most populous countries, excluding the USA and the USSR	Approximate distance from Washington (km)	Approximate distance from Moscow (km)
China[1]	10 900	6 200
India[2]	13 000	4 600
Indonesia	18 400	9 600
Japan	10 600	7 800
Brazil	7 600	11 500
Bangladesh	14 700	5 700
Pakistan	11 400	3 800
Nigeria	8 500	6 400
West Germany	5 800	2 100
Mexico	3 400	10 200
UK[2]	5 500	2 400
Italy[2]	6 600	2 400
France	5 700	2 600
Vietnam[1]	16 800	7 200
Philippines	16 000	8 500
Thailand[2]	17 000	7 000
Turkey	8 200	2 000
Egypt[2]	9 100	3 000
Spain	5 400	3 400
Poland[1]	6 600	1 200
South Korea	10 800	7 200
Iran	10 300	2 600
Burma	16 500	6 700
Ethiopia[2]	12 500	5 300
South Africa	13 100	9 000
Argentina	8 500	13 800
Zaire	10 600	7 300
Colombia	3 900	11 200
Canada	700	7 200
Yugoslavia[1]	7 900	1 700

[1] = communist (bright red)

[2] = socialist (pale red)

No number = capitalist (blue)

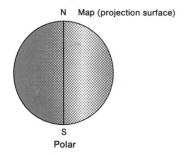

N Map (projection surface)

S
Polar

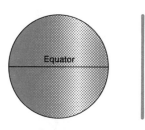

Equator

Equatorial

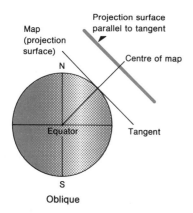

Oblique

An oblique projection is one in which the plane of projection is neither polar nor equatorial, but somewhere in between. A zenithal projection is one in which the plane of projection is parallel to a tangent at the earth's surface at the centre of the projection. An equidistant projection is one in which distances are correct from the centre of the projection only. Oblique zenithal equidistant projections are widely used for all target maps, as on radar screens.

Statistical Interpretation

7-4 **a)** On a world outline map draw lines at 2 500 km and 5 000 km parallel to the frontiers of the USA and the USSR; remember that Alaska and Hawaii are part of the USA. Since this is a very difficult thing to do solely on a flat map, you should refer to a globe to do it properly.

b) What contrasts strike you when you compare the two sets of lines?

c) Which areas of the world are largely beyond the high intensity spheres of influence of both the USA and the USSR?

d) Which areas, if any, exhibit any marked degree of overlap?

7-5 Construct a scattergraph for the data in Fig. 7-4, and draw in an equal distance line. Name and colour the dots as indicated. How far does the graph fit in with Mackinder's Heartland theory?

7. Hemispheres of Influence

Another way of examining the significance of Heartland theory is to see how the world looks when a particular region is placed at the centre of a map. The maps used are based on *oblique zenithal equidistant projections*, which give a good indication of the territories that a powerful nation may see as being within its sphere of interest. Any areas not shown on a particular map are literally on the other side of the world (see Fig. 7-5).

The USSR map clearly shows that the Afro-Asian World Island is well within the USSR's sphere of interest. Compare it with the map of the USA's hemisphere, which includes the Americas, Europe, North Africa, and northern Asia. This hemisphere contains much less land than that of the USSR; there is a great deal of ocean in the USA's hemisphere, which suggests the need for extensive shipping links to other areas. The European hemisphere, which would be inherited by the Heartland power if the theory has validity, contains an even greater proportion of land to sea than does the USSR's own hemisphere. We can therefore understand the importance of Europe to world migrations and world empires. Europe is the key access point to more of the world than is any other area.

The other maps illustrate various points: China, with a great deal of land in its hemisphere, is in a good position to assume a fairly important world role; Australia is isolated from other Outer Crescent areas, and seems to be vulnerable to any power controlling the World Island. The maps also show that South America is really only in North

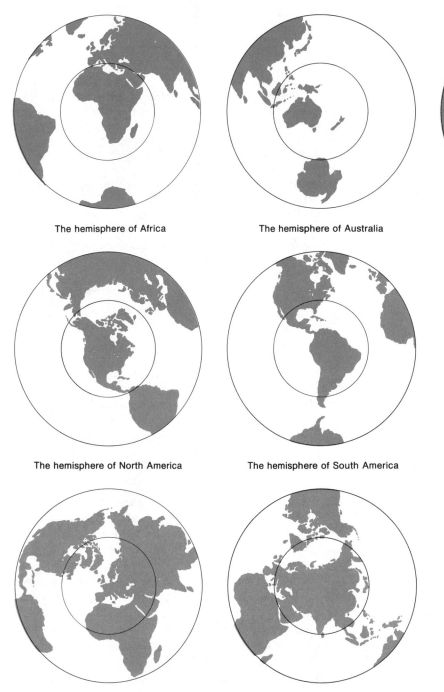

The hemisphere of Africa

The hemisphere of Australia

The hemisphere of China

The hemisphere of North America

The hemisphere of South America

The hemisphere of Europe

The hemisphere of the USSR

Based on J. P. Cole, *Geography of World Affairs*, 1972.

Fig. 7-5
Selected hemispheres

Circles at 5 000 km and 10 000 km on all maps

Sea links are a necessary part of US containment strategy. Here are two of the more than fifty nuclear-powered naval vessels operated by the US: The aircraft carrier in the foreground is the *Enterprise.*

US Information Service

Russia shipped missiles to Cuba by disguising them as ordinary freight and sending them on freighters. From the North America hemisphere map, can you suggest which Russian port would have been used for the shipments, and what route the freighters would have taken?

America's sphere of influence (though note which European countries have the easiest access), and that Africa is most likely to be influenced by Europe, and possibly the USSR. (Where does North America lie in Africa's world?)

From an examination of these maps can you see why the Cuban revolution was such a spectacular success for Russia? Cuba is not even in the USSR's hemisphere; Russia was able to penetrate an area far outside its immediate sphere of interest. Control of Cuba was an advantage for Russia because North America had set up its entire defence network in the 1950s and early 1960s on the basis that attack would come from over the North Pole or across Greenland. The Distant Early Warning (DEW) line, the Strategic Air Command (SAC) bases at Goose Bay in Labrador and Thule in Greenland, and the entire North American Air Defence (NORAD) organization were all predicated on an attack across the North Pole. The takeover of Cuba by the communists came as a major setback. Russia's act of installing missiles on the island (1962) was a definite and unexpected threat, countered only by an American blockade of all Russian shipping to Cuba which lasted until the missiles were withdrawn. The Cuban missile crisis is of significance because it looked for a while as if the incident would spark off a major war between the US and Russia.

Discussion and Research

14. If you were the chief Russian strategist, where would you contemplate making the next Russian probe? Why?

15. If you were in charge of American defence strategy how would you react to Heartland theory?

16. At one time the maritime powers of Western Europe virtually ruled the world. Why do they not do so now?

On the deck of a US Navy missile-carrying nuclear submarine shortly before it submerges for a two-month patrol of the oceans.

US Information Service

Section C
Relations within the Second World

The philosophy of communism does not actually bind as tightly as military domination does. Even within Eastern Europe there is no strong common purpose; Moscow directs and the other countries more or less follow. The Russian army is an ever-present threat that encourages the satellite nations to obey.

China is different from both Eastern Europe and Russia; it is populous, its army is well versed in guerilla activity, and it has a distinct culture. Thus its communism is different. When China became communist in 1949 after 22 years of civil war, the Russians were overjoyed, since the gain of 500 000 000 people (as it then was) to "the cause" was a major victory. The Russians accordingly tried to win the friendship of the Chinese, but without success.

While Russian communism had developed in an urban-industrial environment, with goals for standards of living similar to those of the first world, the Chinese revolution occurred in an essentially rural-agricultural environment. Its priorities and day-to-day goals were unlike Russia's. Russian help in great power and industrial projects was neither wanted nor needed. Differences of opinion between the two countries became quarrels, and then open hostility. Nowadays the Chinese revile the Russians, accusing them of being in league with the Americans to dominate the world. Naturally the Americans have come to see the Chinese as a potential ally against the Russians, as well as a barrier against Russian expansion in eastern Asia. The Russians, in search of support, have developed strong ties with Vietnam.

Vietnam is not friendly toward China, in spite of the two countries' geographic proximity. It was therefore fairly easy for the USSR to help North Vietnam in its struggle to unify the country under communism. Vietnam, successful in its unification and friendly with the USSR, now poses the same threat to China as Cuba did to the USA in the 1960s.

There has even been fighting between Russia and China, along the Siberian frontier. Both sides see the inner Asian frontier from Manchuria to Kashmir as a relatively weak link in their defences. The region is largely desert (Gobi, Mongolian) and mountains (Pamirs, Tienshan, Altai), and is inhabited chiefly by scattered tribes of nomadic herdsmen. Both sides have pushed for development of the inhospitable terrain; Russia has settled at least 20 000 000 people along the line of the Trans-Siberian Railway, while China has sent even more millions into Manchuria, Tibet, and Sinkiang. When China tests nuclear weapons, it uses Sinkiang, its emptiest land, as its test area. Russia similarly uses the eastern steppes. What reasons can you suggest for this? In a sense it is fortunate that the frontier runs through such inhospitable land; there is little population pressure against it.

Some of the tensions between Russia and China are illustrated in the following articles.

Sinkiang: Where it could begin

If full-scale war ever erupts between the Soviet Union and China, a likely location for the opening battle is the Chinese region of Sinkiang. Occupying almost one-sixth of China's area, Sinkiang contains several volatile ingredients. Unlike other disputed border areas farther east, where the Amur and Ussuri rivers create a natural boundary, the 1 500-mile [2 400 km] Sinkiang-Soviet frontier in many stretches is only vaguely demarcated. In addition, the area is the site of one of the most tempting targets in all of China: the nuclear testing grounds at Lop Nor.

Sinkiang is accustomed to trouble. A sparsely populated land of towering, snow-capped peaks and arid deserts, it is the fought-over gateway between Central Asia and the east. Marco Polo passed through Sinkiang on his way to China. So did other traders who carried Asia's luxuries to Europe. Chinese, Tibetans, Mongols and Turks have all left their mark.

Only 3 000 000 of Sinkiang's 8 000 000 people are Chinese, many of them recent settlers imported to strengthen Peking's ethnic hold. The others come from at least 14 minority nationalities. Some 4 000 000 are Uighurs, descendants of the 9th century Turkic invaders, and 600 000 are Kazakhs, Kirghiz and Tadjiks.

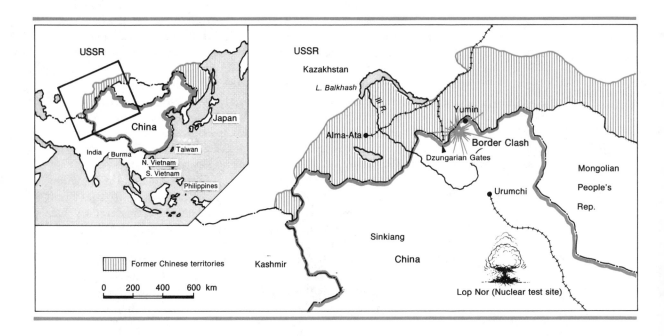

Divided by customs and heritage, the various minorities nonetheless are united in their hate of their present masters, who first penetrated Sinkiang under the Han Dynasty (206 B.C.- A.D. 220).

Russian involvement in Sinkiang dates to the Czars. In the mid-19th century, Alexander II sent troops into northwestern Sinkiang to quell a Moslem revolt. An 1881 treaty restored part of the area to China, but Russia retained a large hunk. Stalin expanded Soviet influence in Sinkiang by using Soviet consulates and cultural centers for propaganda. In 1944, Moslem rebels financed by Moscow set up the East Turkestan Republic in Sinkiang. Up to the time Mao Tse-tung won control of China, the Russians were trying to establish Sinkiang as an independent republic.

In a sense, the Chinese Communists might be better off if Stalin had succeeded. Sinkiang has meant mostly trouble for them. The proud, independent tribesmen have resisted Communist indoctrination efforts. They resent attempts to collectivize their herds of goats and cattle. Playing on these resentments, the Soviets in 1961 encouraged Sinkiang's Moslems to stir up the native groups by comparing their bad treatment under the Chinese with better conditions in the Soviet Union. When the snows melted in the spring, some 60 000 Uighurs and Kazakhs fled across the border. Soviet trucks picked up the refugees, while Russian troops sometimes covered their escape.

Since then, the situation has grown increasingly serious. Soviet radio stations beam programs into Sinkiang exhorting the minority groups to rise up in a war of liberation against the Maoists. The Chinese, badly outgunned along the entire Sino-Soviet border, are at a special disadvantage in Sinkiang. Against some 150 000 to

200 000 troops across the Soviet border the Chinese have only 85 000 to 100 000. The Soviet troops, moreover, are backed up by medium-range missiles.

Despite their military superiority, the Soviets so far have carefully avoided even mentioning the possibility of a preventive strike against the Chinese nuclear test site in Sinkiang. At present, the Chinese lack an effective missile for their nuclear bombs. In four or five years, however, they may develop a delivery system that could establish a balance of terror between the two nervous neighbors. So far, Soviet policy has been to confine the fighting strictly to limited border areas. Still, the increasing gravity of the Sino-Soviet dispute— and the relative weakness of China's defenses—must present a certain temptation to Soviet military planners.

Time 1969 8 22

China accuses USSR

by JACK CAHILL
Star staff writer

HONG KONG—China has begun to unleash a barrage of abuse at the Soviet Union, bringing relations between the two Communist superpowers to their lowest ebb in years.

The attack became almost personal today when the New China News Agency claimed that Soviet society is rife with graft, embezzlement, widespread prostitution, venereal disease, drunkenness and divorce.

Other hard-hitting articles in Chinese newspapers and magazines in the last few days have accused the Soviet Union of nuclear arms expansion and have bitterly attacked what they describe as Soviet leader Leonid Brezhnev's policies of "guns instead of butter."

And in speeches in Peking Chinese leaders have been sternly warning the 900 million Chinese people of the imminent dangers of a Soviet-inspired third world war.

· · ·

In simultaneous attacks on the Soviet Union, the Peking People's Daily and Red Flag, the official organ of the Chinese Communist party, pulled no punches.

In an editorial, the People's Daily compared Soviet policy with that of Nazi Germany and accused Moscow of deploying most of its forces "in a presumptuous attempt to devour Europe—a juicy piece of meat in the eyes of the Soviet gluttons."

Red Flag described Brezhnev's 10 years in power as "years of frantic pursuit of expansionism abroad and years of setbacks and internal difficulties for the Soviet revisionists at home."

The article said that despite Soviet lip service to nuclear disarmament, the number of Soviet intercontinental ballistic missiles had multiplied 15 times within the 10 years.

At the same time, it said, the tonnage of Soviet naval craft had nearly doubled while the tonnage of the country's nuclear submarines increased 5.5 times in the last four years.

"In the past 10 years or more, the total expenditure for nuclear armament alone amounted to over $100 000 million U.S.," the article said.

The Toronto Star 1975 10 8

Film as a weapon in the Sino-Soviet feud

If you are in Moscow this week, and you want to see villainy pitted against virtue, then hurry, hurry to see Alexander Medvedkin's film, The Truth and The Lie.

The villains, of course, are those men in Peking. The selfless heroes—you guessed it—are the Russians.

On the face of it, Medvedkin's masterpiece is a documentary. It is made up of newsreels, 30-year-old film clips, and segments from Chinese movies. But the documentary flavor evaporates in the narrator's biting anti-Chinese commentary.

Mao Tse-tung is shown in 1945, praising the Soviet Union—and then, in recent years, denouncing it. Other clips show Chinese multitudes "joyously welcoming their liberators" 30 years ago and, more recently, joining in anti-Soviet demonstrations.

This is how Moscow's Literary Gazette describes a scene in the movie: "A sunbathed field. The peasants are harvesting. Suddenly, from beyond the horizon, missiles roar in. The 'enemy' has invaded the land. With his tanks he wants to destroy the crops. He burns down the villages and kills everyone within sight.

"To arms! The peasants pick up their rifles—these are always within reach—and counter-attack. Faces distorted with fury, heavy gunfire, explosions. A girl's pretty smile is replaced with the horrifying mask of hatred. . . .

Who is the enemy?
"Who is this 'enemy' who must be destroyed with animal ferocity? He is, to use Peking's terminology, the 'Soviet revisionists'. . . . "

This scene, lifted bodily from a made-in-China anti-Soviet film, miraculously becomes part of an anti-Chinese film made in Moscow. In Medvedkin's hands, it serves to demonstrate to the Russian viewer the fury and fanaticism of the Chinese, as well as Peking's efforts to poison the minds of its people against Soviet friends and liberators.

The film is part of the Sino-Soviet feud, as intense today as it has ever been since the dramatic break in July, 1960.

Mark Gayn, *The Toronto Star* 1975 10 29

Section D
Relations with the Third World

The third world tends to have a sort of love-hate relationship with the first world. The advanced technology, investment funds, markets, and business expertise of the first world promote admiration; the history of colonialism and the exploitation of resources provoke hate. The people of the third world have mixed feelings about first world medicine, in particular. They welcome the relief from disease and early death, yet at the same time they blame their hunger and malnutrition on their increased numbers caused by death control.

To further complicate matters, the second world insists that the first world is an exploiter, and points out the advantages of the second world view of the future. In the third world, then, the first world is condemned as a colonialist exploiter, yet welcomed as a beacon to the future. The complex relationship that exists between the three worlds is best reflected in their aid and trade patterns.

1. Aid

Nearly 90% of the world's aid is given by the first world to the third world, for humanitarian reasons as well as the strategic desire to win friends. The second world supplies relatively little aid since it believes that the first world has caused most of the third world's problems. It does, however, supply *some* aid, because it too has the desire to win friends. The second world also helps third world countries to rebel against colonial and economic domination.

Propaganda is very important in the entire aid situation. The donors, from either the first or second worlds, believe that their prestige rises among the recipients, and that the recipients will favour the donors' politico-economic system. The sources of aid therefore are usually made known.

Apart from the desire to win the third world's favour and political support, aid is given for reasons of conscience and humanity (have a look, for instance, at Terry Leonard's experiences, described in Chap-

"The sources of aid are usually made known. . . . " These are books donated by Canada to a vocational training institute in Lebanon.

UNRWA

ter 2). Many people in the first world think that they themselves are selfishly using up more than their share of the world's resources, while the third world peoples are poor and starving. The clipping in Chapter 5 that presents the views of Bruce McLeod is worth reading in this context.

On the other hand there are many first world people who think that aid to the third world is a waste of time. They claim that the aid provided simply prolongs the third world's problems, and that the third world ought to be encouraged to solve its own problems. Such people deny any responsibility for third world problems, and claim that in return for resources the first world has built railways, towns, and ports, and has introduced modern technology, medicine, and education. They assert that the third world's problems are the product of uncontrolled birth rates as well as of an unwillingness to organize production efficiently. Many say that the first world should give aid only to those third world countries that have introduced birth control practices. Others go farther, and say that no aid should be given at all. These opinions clearly differ from Bruce McLeod's view. The following articles discuss the problem of aid from three different viewpoints.

The case for helping the poor

Remember you don't live here all alone. Your brothers are here too.
Albert Schweitzer

We the North Atlantic Community of Nations represent 16% of the world's population but we control 65% of the world's wealth and 75% of the world's trade. An equitable distribution?—hardly. One which we should consider as lasting?—again, hardly. For as Pope Paul has pointed out in his encyclical *On the Development of People*: "Excessive economic, social, and cultural inequalities arouse tensions and conflicts and are a danger to peace".

Can this dichotomy between 'us' and 'them', the 'rich' and the 'poor', the 'haves' and the 'have nots' continue? As the hungry, the diseased, the illiterate watch us eating cake, how will they respond when we throw them some crumbs? How will they respond when they learn that we eat 4½ pounds [2 kg] of food a day and then throw away enough to feed a family of six in India? How will they respond when they learn that the average dog in North America has a higher protein diet than millions of their children? How would you respond?

The problem in North America of course is that we're not aware of the problem; or more precisely we're (vaguely) aware that it exists but we're already tired of hearing about it. Prime Minister Pearson has said, "We are living on a powder-keg of anger and revolt. We are living in a world so small that the violence affects us all. We are confronted with the risk of international class war. The curious fact today is not that we do not know those things but that a great many people are bored with them and feel less and less obligation to do anything about them." (The Dilemmas of Development, A Policy Paper of the U.N.A. in Canada, Toronto, P. 8)
Extracted from *Oxfam of Canada* Sheet 1.01

The case against helping the poor

The less provident and able will multiply at the expense of the abler and more provident, bringing eventual ruin upon all.

by GARRETT HARDIN

If we divide the world crudely into rich nations and poor nations, two thirds of them are desperately poor, and only one third comparatively rich.

Metaphorically each rich nation can be seen as a lifeboat full of comparatively rich people. In the ocean outside each lifeboat swim the poor of the world, who would like to get in, or at least to share some of the wealth. What should the lifeboat passengers do?

We have several options: we may be tempted to try to live by the Christian ideal of being "our brother's keeper," or by the Marxist ideal of "to each according to his needs." Since the needs of all in the water are the same, and since they can all be seen as "our brothers," we could take them all into our boat making a total of 150 in a boat designed for 60. The boat swamps, everyone drowns. Complete justice, complete catastrophe.

Suppose we decide to preserve our small safety factor and admit no more to the lifeboat. Our survival is then possible, although we shall have to be constantly on guard against boarding parties.

The harsh ethics of the lifeboat become even harsher when we consider the reproductive differences between the rich nations and the poor nations. The people inside the lifeboats are doubling in numbers every 87 years, those swimming around outside are doubling, on the average, every 35 years, more than twice as fast as the rich. And since the world's resources are dwindling, the difference in prosperity between the rich and the poor can only increase.

As of 1973, the U.S. had a population of 210 million people, who were increasing by 0.8 per cent per year. Outside our lifeboat, let us imagine another 210 million people, (say the combined populations of Colombia, Ecuador, Venezuela, Morocco, Pakistan, Thailand and the Philippines) who are increasing at a rate of 3.3 percent per year. Put differently, the doubling time for this aggregate population is 21 years, compared to 87 years for the U.S.

Multiplying the Rich and the Poor

Now suppose the U.S. agreed to pool its resources with those seven countries, with everyone receiving an equal share. Initially the ratio of Americans to non-Americans in this model would be one-to-one. But consider what the ratio would be after 87 years, by which time the Americans would have doubled to a population of 420 million. By then, doubling every 21 years, the other group would have swollen to 354 billion. Each American would have to share the available resources with more than eight people.

The Tragedy of the Commons

The fundamental error of spaceship ethics, and the sharing it requires, is that it leads to what I call "the tragedy of the commons." Under a system of private property, the men who own property recognize their responsibility to care for it, for if they don't they will eventually suffer. A farmer, for instance, will allow no more cattle in a pasture than its carrying capacity justifies. If he overloads it, erosion sets in, weeds take over, and he loses the use of the pasture.

If a pasture becomes a commons open to all, the right of each to use it may not be matched by a corresponding responsibility to protect it. Asking everyone to use it with discretion will hardly do, for the considerate herdsman who refrains from overloading the commons suffers more than a selfish one who says his needs are greater. If everyone would restrain himself, all would be well; but it takes only one less than everyone to ruin a system of voluntary restraint. In a crowded world of less than perfect human beings, mutual ruin is inevitable if there are no controls. This is the tragedy of the commons.

Learning the Hard Way

What happens if some organizations or countries budget for accidents and others do not? If each country is solely responsible for its own well-being, poorly managed ones will suffer. But they can learn from experience. They may mend their ways, and learn to budget for infrequent but certain emergencies. For example, the weather varies from year to year, and periodic crop failures are certain. A wise and competent government saves out of the production of the good years in anticipation of bad years to come. Joseph taught this policy to Pharaoh in Egypt more than 2 000 years ago. Yet the great majority of the governments in the world today do not follow such a policy. They lack either the wisdom or the competence, or both. Should those nations that do manage to put something aside be forced to come to the rescue each time an emergency occurs among the poor nations?

Population Control the Crude Way

On the average, poor countries undergo a 2.5 percent increase in population each year; rich countries, about 0.8 percent. Only rich countries have anything in the way of food reserves set aside, and even they do not have as much as they should. Poor countries have none. If poor countries received no food from the outside the rate of their population growth would be periodically checked by crop failures and famines. But if they can always draw on a world food bank in time of need, their population can continue to grow unchecked, and so will their "need" for aid. In the short run, a world food bank may diminish that need, but in the long run it actually increases the need without limit.

Besides, any system of "sharing" that amounts to foreign aid from the rich nations to the poor nations will carry the taint of charity, which will contribute little to the world peace so devoutly desired by those who support the idea of a world food bank.

Every one of the 15 million new lives added to India's population puts an additional burden on the environment, and increases the economic and social costs of crowding. However humanitarian our intent, every Indian life saved through medical or nutritional assistance from abroad diminishes the quality of life for those who remain and for subsequent generations. If rich countries make it possible, through foreign aid, for 600 million Indians to swell to 1.2 billion in a mere 28 years, as their current growth rate threatens, will future generations of Indians thank us for hastening the destruction of their environment? Will our good intentions be sufficient excuse for the consequences of our actions?

Extracted from *Psychology Today* 1974 9

Another case against helping the poor

The guilt and the gingerbread

by RICHARD J. NEEDHAM

I've never persecuted Jews, or held blacks in slavery, or taken anything from Canada's Indians (they, through taxes, have taken a great deal from me), so I don't feel guilt towards any of these people. To put it bluntly, I don't feel guilt towards any race or nation, including those which, so we are told, are at or over the brink of mass starvation. They're there, I'm here, we're separated by some 10 000 miles [16 000 km], and there's not much I can or intend to do about it.

It's true that I eat little, and what I do eat is mainly vegetable, thus saving grain which otherwise would go into meat. Maybe that grain will get to some Asian who needs it, more likely not. The point is that I feel no duty to "help" anybody in this respect, I'm just suiting my own peculiar tastes and lifestyle. Accordingly, I was bemused to read in the New York Times (Nov. 24) about Maya Pines who serves her family meals that are "meatless, guiltless"—her own expression.

Mrs. Pines says, "I can no longer eat a bite of beef without feeling guilty at the thought that 20 pounds [9 kg], of vegetable protein are lost in producing one pound [0.45 kg] of beef protein, and that in a world of food shortages, I have just robbed 20 persons of their fair share." Well, I don't know. If, as sometimes happens, I feel like gnawing a chunk of salami, it goes down okay; I'm not choked up with remorse.

There's another way of expressing this guilt, what you might call the National Policy—"We must feed the hungry people of Outer Fluoristan!" Who, in this context, is "we"? It practically always means the central government—Canadian, American, whatever. But as Earl Butz likes to point out, governments don't produce food, only farmers do that; and they'll only do it with the encouragement of good prices—good for them, that is, probably bad for Outer Fluoristan, unless Canadian and American taxpayers are willing to put up the necessary.

Even at that, there's no assurance the hungry people will get the food. My observation of this world is that politicians and bureaucrats are incompetent to do or manage or arrange or transfer or distribute anything. As Wacky Bennett once expressed it, "Those people in Ottawa couldn't even run a peanut stand." It seems to me that if anyone in North America feels guilt about starvation in Asia or Africa, and if he really wants something done about it, he should have the guts to do it himself, immediately, and with his own money.

There are all sorts of private, voluntary organizations working in this field, and I suspect that a dollar given to them goes further than any $10 exacted by politicians. There's Oxfam, CARE, the Catholics, Lutherans, Unitarians and all such. According to CARE officials, a $2 donation will serve 12 children a daily bowl of high-protein porridge for a month. I don't contribute to these agencies, because like Rhett Butler, I don't give a damn; but if I did, I'd want to put my money where my mouth was.

This brings me around to Prof. John Crispo of the University of Toronto, who will likely get barbecued by many people for his proposal (Globe and Mail, Nov. 27) that Canada should "concentrate all of its foreign aid on birth-control measures of every conceivable type". I'm disposed to agree with him after reading Peter Kann's series on Bangladesh in last week's Wall Street Journal.

Bangladesh is slightly larger than the island of Newfoundland. On this small area, it has 75 million people, who in 20 years will number 150 million, and in 30 years 230 million. There's no birth-control program and no prospect there ever will be any. Mr. Kann says Bangladesh "may well be the world's poorest, most hopeless nation, an international basket case". He tells this story:

"An Irish nun is visiting Bangladesh, staying at a Christian hostel in Dacca. On her second evening in the city, she finds an emaciated baby deserted on the doorstep. She takes the baby in, feeds it, doctors it, bathes it, and then goes out searching for the mother, who is nowhere to be found. The next morning the nun finds a second starving baby lying in the street in front of the hostel. So she takes the second baby in. Then she goes off to the local police station to report the missing babies and to seek advice. That advice is to put the babies back in the street or, the police officer says, you will find four more babies tomorrow."

To close, here's the scenario envisaged by a Bangladesh business man: "The bankrupt country will be unable to obtain fertilizer for crops, and the countryside will get hungrier. The transportation system will break down for lack of petrol. Famine will prevail. Landless agricultural laborers and subsistence farmers will flock to the cities seeking food. Finding none, they will loot and burn and return to the villages along with many of the urban unemployed. Government services, such as they are, will collapse. Whether some government continues to sit in Dacca won't make any difference in the rest of the country. Each village will survive—or disintegrate—on its own. Bands of brigands will roam the countryside. Naked men will fight with sticks and stones." *The Globe and Mail* 1974 12 2

Discussion and Research

17. How would you argue with Garrett Hardin? And with Richard Needham?

18. What great flaw exists in the arguments of both Bruce McLeod and Garrett Hardin?

19. Do you agree with the idea of "lifeboat ethics"?

20. Another idea concerning aid sometimes suggested is *triage*. In wars, the wounded used to be sorted into three groups: those who would likely survive whether they got medical help or not; those who would probably die with or without medical aid; and those who would die without help but survive with it. Medical scarcities on battlefields were taken into consideration, and so existing supplies and help were concentrated on the third group; the other two were left to survive or die. It is now sometimes suggested, in the light of world food scarcities and inadequate distribution facilities, that aid ought to be given only to those countries that are equivalent to the third group. Countries that will "die" anyway should be left to do so. What do you think?

Canada is a middle-rank first world country in terms of the amount of aid it can give. It does not have the population and national wealth of countries such as the USA, France, West Germany, and the UK, nor does it have the conscience and ties of a former imperial power. In consequence, Canada ranks midway in the list of seventeen aid-giving countries that belong to the Development Assistance Committee (DAC) of the Organization for Economic Cooperation and Development (OECD).

Canadian aid originates from many sources; some organizations are private, such as CARE, Oxfam, Foster Parents Plan, and the Red Cross, while others such as the Canadian International Development Agency (CIDA), Canadian University Students Overseas (CUSO), and the Canadian Executive Service Overseas (CESO) are government-sponsored. Private and public sources provide approximately equal funds. As an indication of where the aid, in the form of both money and food, goes, the Official Development Assistance (ODA) appropriations are listed in Figs. 7-6, 7-7, and 7-8.

Statistical Interpretation

7-6 Construct a *compound line graph* (see Appendix 3) to illustrate the main points only of Fig. 7-6.
   a) Which sector has grown the fastest?
   b) Why do you think this is so?

7-7 Using the data in Fig. 7-7, shade on a world map all the countries that received direct Canadian bilateral aid in 1973-74. How does the map compare with your answer to assignment 7-3?

7-8 Can you calculate which country's people received the highest per capita bilateral aid from Canada in 1973-74?

Fig. 7-6
Official development assistance appropriations (Allocation of appropriations by programs, in millions of Cdn. dollars)

	1970-71	1971-72	1972-73	1973-74	Proposed 1974-75	Percentage of 1974-75 program	Average annual growth rate 1970-71 to 1974-75 %
Total	383.71	431.21	491.00	565.03	638.11	100	13.6
Multilateral	83.21	110.55	147.34	172.32	206.22	32.3	25.5
International Development Association grants	3.51	.83	2.13	6.45	7.00		
Food aid	14.21	14.35	13.55	13.02	14.24		
Multilateral International Assistance Program	23.88	29.85	33.05	36.50	42.41		
Loans and advances	41.61	65.52	98.61	116.35	142.57		
Bilateral	289.49	306.20	319.15	357.67	388.53	60.9	7.6
Food aid	81.29	70.65	76.95	54.98	80.76		
Other grants	65.48	77.13	98.84	137.89	143.63		
Loans	139.37	135.82	141.76	164.20	163.54		
International Emergency Relief	3.35	22.60	1.60	.60	.60		
Other	11.01	14.46	24.51	35.04	43.36	6.8	40.9
Non-governmental organizations	8.50	11.93	16.13	20.77	23.66		
International Development Research Centre	2.51	2.47	8.00	14.00	19.00		
Miscellaneous	—	.06	.38	.27	.70		

Source: CIDA

Fig. 7-7
Bilateral (country to country) disbursements, by countries and areas, 1970-71 to 1973-74 ($ millions)

	1970-1971	1971-1972	1972-1973	1973-1974
Asia				
India	103.14	101.50	78.26	69.28
Pakistan	47.50	24.32	9.41	38.51
Indonesia	3.57	3.95	14.47	21.64
Malaysia	2.36	3.59	2.84	2.31
Sri Lanka	5.18	6.41	7.53	5.65
Thailand	.98	.58	.32	.42
South Vietnam	.77	2.38	1.90	2.76
Laos	.23	.20	.16	.28
Khmer Republic	.03	.03	.05	.10
Bangladesh	—	—	48.29	58.27
Other countries	8.82	4.74	5.64	4.56
Sub-total	172.58	147.70	169.14	203.78
Francophone Africa				
Tunisia	5.49	5.93	13.58	13.06
Cameroon	3.27	4.51	4.58	3.92
Senegal	3.18	5.38	4.85	5.62
Algeria	4.01	4.24	4.96	5.06
Zaire	.95	.59	1.08	3.54
Ivory Coast	1.39	2.88	6.54	4.23
Morocco	4.77	4.46	4.31	5.55
Niger	2.47	7.19	8.59	8.40
Rwanda	1.29	1.47	1.66	1.55
Other countries	2.88	8.48	8.93	15.73
Sub-total	29.70	45.13	59.08	66.65
Commonwealth Africa				
Nigeria	6.63	12.13	12.61	11.98
Ghana	7.01	10.01	9.21	9.66
Tanzania	3.12	6.02	6.22	17.67
Kenya	2.07	2.53	2.25	6.19
Uganda	1.84	1.53	1.66	1.15
East African Community	3.14	11.27	1.87	2.50
Zambia	—	—	2.10	2.35
Other countries	1.27	6.34	17.52	11.17
Sub-total	25.08	49.83	53.44	62.87
Commonwealth Caribbean				
Jamaica	2.53	3.91	4.75	3.24
Trinidad and Tobago	1.72	.63	.65	.90
Guyana	4.18	2.37	1.54	2.85
Barbados	1.05	.77	1.74	2.93
Belize	.24	.49	.80	.41
Leeward and Windward Islands	7.32	4.89	.83	.36
University of the West Indies	1.85	.58	1.19	.99
Other		1.26	4.04	3.83
Sub-total	18.89	13.64	15.54	15.51
Latin America				
Brazil	1.28	2.42	3.41	1.03
Chile	2.36	.75	2.11	2.15
Colombia	4.05	4.36	5.28	3.71
Ecuador	0.11	1.33	.56	1.07
Nicaragua	—	—	—	1.41
Other countries	0.77	1.56	1.71	3.35
Sub-total	8.57	10.42	13.07	12.72
Other countries and programs				
Turkey	8.00	.70	5.51	.03
Ethiopia	.06	.10	.51	1.51
International Emergency Relief	3.33	13.79	10.40	.60
Other programs	2.70	1.97	3.32	4.47
Sub-total	14.09	16.56	19.74	6.61
Grand Total	268.91	203.28	330.01	367.94

Note: Part of the 1971-72 disbursements listed under Pakistan were for Bangladesh. In addition, a portion of the disbursements for relief in Bangladesh amounting to over $13 million is included under the International Emergency Relief sub-vote.

Source: CIDA

Fig. 7-8
Multilateral (to international agency) disbursements, 1970-71 to 1973-74
($ millions)

	1970-1971	1971-1972	1972-1973	1973-1974
Economic assistance				
United Nations Development Programs	15.27	16.23	17.70	20.28
Indus Basin Fund	.40	3.75	3.39	1.00
Commonwealth Fund for Technical Cooperation	.22	—	.72	1.00
Sub-total	15.89	19.98	21.81	22.28
Population and health				
UN Fund for Population Activities	1.02	2.01	1.99	1.94
Int'l. Planned Parenthood Federation	.51	.77	.99	1.50
World Health Organization	.20	.14	.15	1.15
Sub-total	1.73	2.92	3.13	4.59
Relief and welfare programs				
UN Children's Fund	1.20	1.50	1.70	1.90
UN High Commissioner for Refugees	.40	.40	.49	.95
Sub-total	1.60	1.90	2.19	2.85
Agricultural programs				
Int'l. Institute for Tropical Agriculture	.57	.76	.74	.75
Int'l. Centre for Tropical Agriculture	—	—	—	.78
Int'l. Maize Research Institute	—	—	—	.33
Int'l. Crop Research Institute for the Semi-Arid Tropics	—	—	—	.80
Int'l. Potato Centre	—	—	—	.20
Sub-total	.57	.76	.74	2.86
Food aid				
World Food Program				
-cash	4.02	3.32	3.28	3.74
-food	12.29	11.62	12.20	15.79
UN Relief and Works Agency				
-cash	.65	.65	.65	1.15
-food	.70	.70	.90	.88
Sub-total	17.66	16.29	17.03	21.56
Other	.43	2.03	1.11	5.28
Sub-total	.43	2.03	1.11	5.28
Loans and advances to international financial institutions				
Int'l. Bank for Reconstruction and Development	—	—	16.06	—
International Development Association	24.91	49.92	53.94	59.55
Asian Development Bank	2.73	.32	.27	4.43
African Development Bank	—	—	—	5.60
Caribbean Development Bank	.74	1.90	1.08	5.64
Caribbean Agricultural Development Fund	—	1.25	—	—
Central American Bank of Economic Integration	—	.11	—	—
Inter-American Development Bank	—	—	35.77	42.44
Andean Development Corporation	—	—	—	5.00
Sub-total	28.38	53.50	107.12	122.66
Grand total	66.26	97.38	153.13	132.08

Source: CIDA

2. Trade

Increasing numbers of third world countries have recently been asking for beneficial trade rather than more aid. Periodically they combine voices at the continual UN Conference on Trade and Development (UNCTAD). These countries are looking for markets for their manufactured goods, and so they want first world countries to reduce their tariffs on such goods. (See the article in Chapter 3 entitled "Again we're asked 'want to pay extra for a Canadian shirt?'") They also want higher prices for their raw materials. Over the years the third world countries have felt themselves at a disadvantage; the first world countries have protected their own domestic industries by tariff barriers, and the international prices of many third world commodities have tended to be low. Now, however, *trade not aid* has become a common cry.

To improve trade with the first world, third world countries must get some kind of advantage. They must either be able to persuade a first world country to reduce tariff barriers, or else be able to manufacture cheaply enough to sell at a profit despite tariff barriers. Another option is to control a major part of the world supply of some important commodity. These courses are not easy to pursue. First, if first world countries decide to reduce their tariffs, they will want something in exchange, like access to raw materials. Second, manufacturing at costs low enough to leap tariff barriers is difficult unless wages are extremely low. Finally, control of a major world commodity has been possible so far only for the major oil exporters. Attempts by copper producers, and banana and coffee growers have failed. Cornering the market can only work if the commodity possessed by a country is unavailable elsewhere, or if there are no acceptable substitutes for it. Nevertheless the third world countries are determined to keep on trying for beneficial trade. They want what is called a *New Economic Order*. The following CIDA reading gives you some views on the proposal.

Some countries manufacture cheaply enough to sell over tariff barriers, notably Taiwan, Korea, Hong Kong, and Singapore.

Through 1976 and 1977 Brazil was busy buying up as much coffee as it could on the world markets. Brazil is in any event the world's largest coffee producer, and it did not intend to use or sell the bought-up coffee; it merely stockpiled the coffee to keep it off world markets and thus keep the price up.

Canada and the New Economic Order

by A.E.D. MACKENZIE

What will be the nature and dimensions of the New Economic Order? And if the Third World Countries want a larger slice of the world's pie —assuming for a moment that this is needed—how are they preparing to win the battle, and how will their resolve affect Canadians?

The Asians, Africans and Latin Americans have, of course, been inspired by the success of the Organization of Petroleum Exporting Countries (OPEC) cartel in securing what they feel is a more just price from the industrialized west. In 1970, Iran and the seven Arab OPEC countries received $5.8 billion; in 1971, $12 billion; by 1980 possibly $30 billion. In that year, Saudi Arabia alone may have currency reserves exceeding those of the U.S. and West Germany combined. But the developing countries themselves were seriously hurt by the rise in the price of oil, and while the Persian Gulf States and the multinational oil companies reaped tremendous profits, countries like India and Bangladesh were brought almost to their knees. In the fight for the New Economic Order, in breaking the political and economic stranglehold of the developed nations, the Third World Countries will likely receive support from the coffers of OPEC.

How just is the cause of the Third World commodity exporting countries, ignoring for a moment our own prejudices in favor of getting the best deal for ourselves? And what is the best deal for us in the long run, as citizens of a small planet? A few statistics may help put the situation in some perspective: for example, the percentage change in real purchasing power of the Canadian exports, nickel and wheat, increased 70.3 per cent and 28.3 per cent respectively while developing nations' exports of cotton and tea dropped—28.6 per cent and 63.3 per cent—over the same time period (1950-1973).

In response to these glaring inequities, the UNCTAD secretariat is presently proposing establishment of an $11 billion commodities fund, so that the economies of the developing countries will be insulated against too great or swift variations in world commodity prices. Price supports for corn, wheat, coffee, cocoa, tea, cotton, jute, wool, rubber, copper, lead, zinc, tin, bauxite, alumina and iron ore—the 16 commodities accounting for 60 per cent of world trade in non-oil raw materials—will ensure a more orderly development of the Third World, and hopefully, should prevent the possibility of a massive world trade war, or even the formation of OPEC-style cartels in which everyone eventually comes out a loser.

Where does Canada—no mean commodity exporter herself—stand in relation to these new trade patterns and agreements? Is she willing to support UNCTAD's buffer stock program in corn, wheat, copper, lead, zinc and iron ore, or go against the developing countries and plump for a free market? Or is there a middle way? Will Canada opt for a buffered international price for her own commodities in exchange for a controlled rise in the price of her imported sugar, coffee, tea or bauxite?

In 1973 the United Nations symposium on Population, Resources and Environment attempted to deal with the inter-relationships of these global concerns, and provided excellent background material for the World Population Conference held in Bucharest in late August, where the developing countries avowed clearly and forcefully that population control was linked to economic well being. In other words, in most developing countries security is provided by the family. An acceptable world population growth rate in their terms will only be achieved if there is a more equitable distribution of resources, income and power. They realize that the population growth rate must be curbed, particularly in many of the more populous countries. Most of the developing countries have launched family planning programs with China, Taiwan and South Korea making rapid gains in controlling their growth rate while recognizing that standard family planning programs alone will not work.

In 1970 the U.S. contributed $74.5 million to family planning programs and escalated this amount to $125 million in 1973 while the Canadian International Development Agency doubled its contribution from $1.02 million in 1970/71 to $2.44 million in 1973/74. At the Bucharest conference the donor countries finally grasped the significance of the relationship between population and income, resources and the distribution of power. John Rockefeller, Chairman of the U.S. Commission on Population Growth and the American Future and a strong proponent of population control for more than 40 years, had always believed that traditional family planning programs appeared to be the simplest and most direct route. However, he reassessed

EVOLUTION OF COMMODITY PRICES
(1950-73—4th Qtr.)

Canadian exports	Percentage change in price	Percentage change in real purchasing power in terms of manufactured goods
Zinc ore	348.9	119.0
Copper ore	326.0	107.8
Fish	291.9	91.2
Nickel	249.1	70.3
Lumber	214.1	53.2
Wheat	163.0	28.3
Crude petroleum	163.0	28.3
Developing country exports		
Bauxite	76.5	4.6
Sugar	73.4	−15.4
Cotton	46.3	−28.6
Coffee	44.2	−29.7
Jute	20.7	−41.1
Tea	−24.8	−63.3

(Source: United Nations Document A-9544, 2 April, 1974. Note by the Secretary General to 6th Special General Assembly on the study of the problems of raw materials and development.)

his stand at the conference and strongly urged that the "only viable course is to place population policy solidly within the context of general economic and social development in such manner that it will be accepted at the highest levels of government and adequately supported".

At the Rome World Food Conference, November 1974, the Third World Countries, supported by the OPEC nations and China, forcefully articulated the connection between famine and poverty, and the unequal distribution of the world resources and power. Attempts were made at the Conference to deal with these matters in relation to trade. However, the developed nations including Canada attempted to stall these meetings and deal simply with food and agricultural matters in isolation. Many of the developed nations viewed the Conference as a vehicle for dealing with a short-term or emergency relief operation, but Third World countries viewed the Conference as the beginning point of a New Economic Order. Sayed Marei, Conference Secretary, summed up the mood of the Third World when he suggested that the world needed "a new level of political will and planning for human needs".

The decision by the United States to expend 4 billion dollars in 1968 to take 35 million acres of good soil out of production and a similar decision in 1970 by Canada although on a smaller scale to avoid a glut on the market and thus lower prices, did not sit well on an international stage when hundreds of thousands of people were starving. This move by Canada and the United States ended in disaster with the now famous 1972 sale whereby the USSR purchased approximately 1.2 billion dollars of grain or almost one quarter of the total U.S. wheat supply. The once

full grain bins of Saskatchewan and the American mid-west shrunk to a 29 day supply. The serious droughts which affected the Russian crop as well as India and other countries led in part to this increase demand for cereal grains. The USSR which in previous times would have disposed of their livestock and eaten bread, chose to purchase large supplies of grain as feed for their livestock to enjoy the luxury of beef. The short supply and strong demand pushed the price of wheat from $2 per bushel to $5 per bushel. India, herself suffering a shortfall in cereal grain could not compete financially on the international market and suffered the consequences. The USSR eventually sold at a profit some of her American purchases to India. The wheat sale heightened the awareness of many countries that no matter whether the country concerned is Communist or Capitalist the unequal distribution of wealth and political power assured the developed nations a far greater control of the world market place. That the developed nations were not loathe to use this control to enrich themselves at the expense of poorer and weaker nations did not escape Third World attention.

The appearance of the petro-dollar on the world market has provided much needed economic muscle to support the developing nations call for a revision of the economic order. The Persian Gulf States have well over half the world's proven resources of liquid crude oil. In 1973 OPEC asked for and got a four fold increase in price. From January to December 1973 the price of oil rose from $2.59 per barrel to $11.65 per barrel. The majority of mankind lives in the Third World and the 400 per cent increase in oil prices coupled with 150 per cent increase in cost of grains and an even higher price for

rice has had a devastating impact. India provides a prime example of the real cost of importing crude oil, since oil is one of the prime sources of fertilizer particularly when converted into ammonia. The price of ammonia has more than tripled and a 1 million ton shortfall in fertilizer could account for a decline of some 10 million tons of grain harvest. Although India, Bangladesh and other developing nations have been seriously affected by the oil price hike, they unanimously supported the OPEC cartel at the recent special United Nations General Assembly meeting on Raw Materials and Development. They see the OPEC position as a leverage to obtain a realignment in the world economy and hopefully the opportunity to usher in a new economic order.

The OPEC nations have responded to this support with massive aid commitments to Third World Countries which in 1974 nearly matched all the aid provided by the Organization for Economic Cooperation and Development (OECD) countries, including the U.S., Canada and all of Western Europe. According to the Far Eastern Economic Review major commitments were made to many of the nations hardest hit by the increase in oil prices. Total OPEC aid in 1974 to Pakistan amounted to $957 million, to India $945 million; to Sri Lanka $86 million; to Bangladesh $82 million. Iran has committed $2.1 billion in loans to a number of developing countries.

The foregoing is illustrative of some of the issues which brought about the endorsement of the United Nations for a Special Session this fall on the New Economic Order. Undoubtedly most nations will support the concept of greater international cooperation and planning. The greater challenge however will be to build and develop an awareness and participation in a global culture while retaining pride and joy in national or ethnic cultural roots. If this can be accomplished then the political will may exist to carry out some of the following tasks which many perceive to be the necessary roots of a New Economic Order:

a) to assist developing countries in the export of agricultural, processed mineral, and labor-intensive products which will ensure a more just relationship between the price of exports and imports. This will require a reduction in current trade barriers, and more planned pricing of commodities;

b) to support countries with a one or two cash crop economy and to assist them in diversifying their agricultural base and processing more of their own raw materials for export. This will be a difficult choice for many nations as development plans should be indigenous and based on their physical and human resources;

c) to allow greater participation by developing countries in the management of international monetary reforms;

d) to develop an international mechanism to monitor and control Multinational Corporations and to allow greater participation of host countries in MNC decision making processes;

e) to give Third World countries greater access to technology appropriate to the needs and resources of their country;

f) to develop land reform policies which will bring about a more just distribution of the rewards of labor throughout society;

g) to create favorable conditions for the transfer of financial resources;

h) to ensure that women are not forced to seek economic security and social status solely as mothers but have access to other career opportunities;

i) to recognize that while people will continue to consume and acquire material goods, a system of global resource management, conservation and environmental protection is vital for human survival. Therefore our concept of economic growth must be reassessed in human rather than material terms.

Extracted from an article in *Cooperation Canada,* *(CIDA)* 1975 7-8

Discussion and Research

21. How should the prices of international commodities be determined?

22. What differences exist between first and second world reasons for giving aid to the third world?

23. How could the third world help itself?

24. Research the aid activities of one of the organizations listed in Fig. 7-8 as a recipient of Canadian ODA.

Section E
National Power

Only to a certain extent can disputes between nations be resolved by appeals to reason, logic, or humanity. Eventually a nation may choose to ignore such appeals, and act in its own interests.

The level at which the decision to ignore appeals is made depends on the relative strengths of the countries concerned. For example, when France and the UK invaded the Suez Canal Zone in 1956 they were persuaded to withdraw by the United Nations; but when the USSR invaded Hungary in that same year, it chose to ignore all appeals. The more powerful a country is, then, the more independence of action it has, and the more it can influence other countries. It is the weaker countries that have little influence and relatively little freedom of action.

What makes a country powerful? And how can we measure its power? Power can be found in several areas. It can exist in strength of purpose, or *national will*, as exemplified by the North Vietnamese throughout the 1950s and 1960s. It can originate in a country's *technology* and *industrial capacity*. It can be found in the size of *armed forces* and stores of weapons, as well as in a country's ability to produce arms, as shown by the USA. Power can be based in the strength of *moral beliefs* and the extent to which these beliefs can influence people's minds; communism and religions are examples of influential tenets. Power can exist in the supply of *natural resources*, including population, food supplies, minerals, and energy; the USA and USSR possess such power. One of the main strategic aims of the Germans in World War II, for instance, was to starve the British into submission by sinking food convoys from Canada. The Allies, on the other hand, tried to destroy Germany's energy sources, especially oil. The Germans countered with technology, developing large-scale coal-to-oil conversion plants. It is probable that in the end, the European war became largely a matter of manpower (the Germans were greatly outnumbered by the British, French, Russians, and Americans) and industrial capacity.

Column headings for accompanying table Fig. 7-9

Industrial capacity	Technology
A Steel output in thousands of t **B** Electricity output in mkW·h **C** Commercial vehicles in use	**E** Research and development funds in dollars

Armed forces	Natural resources
D Number of men in army, navy, and air force	**F** Total population **G** Area in km² **H** Iron ore in t **I** Agricultural GNP per person in dollars

Fig. 7-9
National power criteria

	Country	A	B	C	D	E	F	G	H	I
1	China	25 600	50 000	1 000 000	2 990 000	500 000	831 300 000	9 596 961	39 000 000	1
2	India	6 915	70 516	463 900	936 000	228 841	598 100 000	3 280 483	22 175 000	61
3	USSR	131 481	914 700	10 000 000	2 900 000	17 382 388	254 380 000	22 402 200	118 151 000	3 314
4	USA	136 803	1 947 079	22 307 900	2 500 000	27 327 600	213 630 000	9 363 123	53 236 000	3 551
5	Indonesia	—	2 932	173 300	239 000	250 000	127 590 000	1 491 564	—	1
6	Japan	119 322	470 082	10 157 000	206 300	4 868 000	110 950 000	372 313	588 000	642
7	Brazil	7 150	61 381	809 300	214 600	250 000	107 140 000	8 511 965	39 380 000	110
8	Bangladesh	68	1 172	23 300	26 000	5 000	76 820 000	143 998	—	1
9	Pakistan	—	7 449	79 100	422 000	10 929	70 260 000	803 943	—	79
10	Nigeria	—	2 625	69 000	202 860	33 355	62 930 000	923 768	—	89
11	W. Germany	49 521	298 995	1 104 200	482 000	5 017 000	61 830 000	248 577	162 000	1 581
12	Mexico	4 652	37 084	632 000	83 000	82 796	60 150 000	1 972 547	3 113 000	158
13	UK	26 649	282 128	1 820 000	361 000	2 589 466	55 960 000	244 046	1 926 000	2 312
14	Italy	20 995	145 518	1 508 200	422 000	1 048 000	55 810 000	301 225	220 000	857
15	France	25 264	174 080	3 272 000	502 000	2 650 000	52 910 000	547 026	15 671 000	1 218
16	Vietnam	—	3 250	195 400	1 147 000	100 000	44 000 000	329 556	—	79
17	Philippines	—	10 398	252 500	62 000	50 000	42 510 000	300 000	1 414 000	157
18	Thailand	40	6 209	191 300	190 000	15 073	42 280 000	514 000	21 000	73
19	Turkey	1 163	12 289	210 800	602 000	44 457	39 180 000	780 576	1 455 000	141
20	Egypt	290	8 104	48 000	323 000	50 000	37 230 000	1 001 449	320 000	110
21	Spain	10 490	75 765	923 900	293 000	79 575	35 470 000	504 782	3 495 000	347
22	Poland	14 000	84 302	346 200	300 000	5 598 000	34 020 000	312 677	432 000	1 440
23	S. Korea	1 157	15 234	83 500	635 000	28 052	33 950 000	98 484	233 000	133
24	Iran	2 000	12 093	87 600	238 000	63 578	33 020 000	1 648 000	294 000	163
25	Burma	—	633	34 300	141 000	10 000	31 240 000	672 552	—	46
26	Ethiopia	—	585	12 700	44 000	5 000	27 950 000	1 221 900	—	40
27	S. Africa	5 630	64 857	620 800	17 000	1 000 000	25 470 000	1 221 037	6 910 000	262
28	Argentina	1 995	26 737	850 900	134 000	51 875	25 380 000	2 766 889	96 000	675
29	Zaire	—	3 884	59 600	60 000	25 000	24 900 000	2 345 409	—	13
30	Colombia	266	9 721	107 000	63 000	1 018	24 720 000	1 138 914	439 000	242
31	Canada	13 386	262 272	2 211 800	82 000	1 157 000	22 830 000	9 976 139	30 744 000	2 298

Source: *Statesman's Yearbook*, 1974-75; also *UN Statistical Yearbook*, 1975.

It is impossible to say which of these sources of national power is the most important; the relative importance of the sources will be different in each case. For example, what have Israel's sources of power been in its several wars with the neighbouring Arab states? What are the Palestine Liberation Organization's (PLO) sources of power? Why did the USA fail in Vietnam despite its technological superiority?

How do we assess national power? How can we assert that one nation is more or less powerful than another? There is of course no perfect method of assessing power. Nevertheless strategists try it, because choices over proposed courses of action need to be made as reasonably as possible. The entire business of planning for defence or attack rests upon many assumptions, most of which are impossible to predict accurately. It is often a case of asking "what would happen if...?" Strategists are forced to use complex computer programs to analyze possible actions and consequences; trials of computer-run actions and consequences are called *war games*.

What criteria should we use to assess national power? While national will and strength of moral beliefs are important, they cannot be expressed in quantitative terms. We will therefore use industrial capacity, armed forces, technology, and natural resources in order to obtain our "best estimate". The individual criteria for the world's 31 most populous countries are listed in Fig. 7-9.

Statistical Interpretation

7-9 **a)** Calculate the mean value for each criterion.

b) Calculate each value as a percentage of the mean for that criterion.

c) Add the percentages for each country across the columns to arrive at an *aggregate relative power index*.

d) Rank the nations according to their aggregate relative power indices.

e) What differences do you think the omission of *national will* and *moral beliefs* makes to your final ranking?

A Russian submarine with its mother ship. Both are part of the Red Banner fleet in the Pacific Ocean.

A US nuclear submarine of the Ethan Allen class being launched at the General Dynamics yard in Croton, Connecticut.

US Information Service

Novosti Press Agency

Section F
Clashes

The interests of the three worlds are obviously different; so are the interests of individual nations, and even of groups within nations. Whenever the interests of groups differ strongly there is a risk of friction, and the possibility of war.

War is fairly easy to define: it is more or less all-out continuous fighting. However, friction may take many forms. What can you suggest?

1. Clashes within Nations

Clashes caused by strong differences may occur within a nation or between nations. Those within a nation are usually racial (hereditary) or cultural (environmental) in origin. Examples of racial troubles with overtones of cultural tension are the problems between the native whites and the immigrant blacks and browns in England, and the potentially explosive black-white situation in South Africa. Cultural conflicts with overtones of racial differences include the anti-Chinese movement in Malaysia, the anti-Jewish feeling in the Middle East, and the anti-Spanish actions of the Basques.

Frequently one of the groups involved in such disputes is stronger than the other. Because the weaker side has insufficient weapons, it often resorts to terrorism. Terrorism may take several forms: random *guerrilla* (literally "little war") raids on property and people, as in Rhodesia; kidnapping, as done by the urban Tupamaros guerrillas of Uruguay; or aircraft hijackings, as by the PLO. The stronger side may negotiate and make some concessions to secure temporary relief from terrorism, or it may retaliate with force. Three classic examples of forceful and successful retaliation are the French raid near Djibouti in 1974 to free 25 kidnapped French schoolchildren, the Israeli raid on Entebbe airport to free 100 Jewish hostages of the PLO in 1976, and the raid by Dutch commandos in June, 1977 to rescue 51 hostages from a train hijacked by nine South Moluccan terrorists.

Terrorism within a country also occurs when a majority group suppresses the rights of a minority. The minority, feeling oppressed, usually seeks to separate from the main body. These separatists may lose material advantages by doing so, but for many of them a sense of

The extinction of minority rights may readily provoke terrorism, but it may also display terrorism in itself. For example, the extinction of the rights of the Jewish minority in Nazi Germany was accompanied by extraordinary terrorism on the part of the Nazis. Equally, the rights of the entrepreneurial minority in Russia under Lenin (the *kulaks*) were crushed with great terrorism.

identity is more important than material success; examples of groups who feel this way are found among the Basques, the Bretons, the Québécois, the South Moluccans, and the Scots. However, not all separatists are driven by their idealism; some are motivated by what they regard as economic oppression, and seek to establish better conditions under their own management. Thus East Pakistan became Bangladesh, Biafra tried to separate from Nigeria, and Irish Catholics are trying to get Northern Ireland out of the UK. Do you think that Quebec separatists are idealists, or are they reacting against economic oppression?

2. International Conflict: Frontiers

It goes without saying that just as there are clashes between groups within a single nation, so also is there conflict between countries. Any discussion of international conflict requires a study of frontiers. Frontiers develop in response to the vague emotional need for some sort of national identity or consciousness. On a more practical level, they mark the limits of a state, and the limits of its laws, privileges, and security. There are two main types of frontiers: *natural* and *artificial*.

a) *Natural frontiers*

Natural frontiers formed the earliest boundaries between countries, because natural features are generally highly visible and easily recognizable by both sides, and they require no exact surveying or mapmaking skills. Natural frontiers therefore are common in older settled lands, especially in Eurasia.

Why are mountains generally (not always) regions of low population density? Why are there exceptions?

Mountain ranges are among the most common natural frontiers. They are easy to see and few people live on them. Also, when mountains are taken as frontiers, natural communities are not split down the middle, since different communities usually develop on each side of the mountains. However, the effectiveness of mountain ranges in separating people depends to some degree upon their height and the number of passes they contain. The Pyrenees, for example, with few passes, are more effective at separating people than are the Alps. The effectiveness of separation also depends upon the width of the mountain barrier. For example, even though they are not high, the Appalachians proved to be a considerable barrier in the early days of European settlement in North America, simply because of their great width and numerous ridges. If the mountains are wide enough they may even be permitted by powerful neighbours to house independent buffer states such as Switzerland and Austria.

The advantages of mountains as frontiers are to some extent offset by certain disadvantages. There may be disagreements over summer grazing rights, mineral rights, trade routes, water control rights, and both summer and winter tourist revenues.

Deserts also have the advantages of low population density and easy recognizability. For many years they were left as uncharted wildernesses and used as natural boundaries. However, the development of underground resources, chiefly oil and water, has created friction among neighbouring nations and thus the need for more exact demarcation.

Rivers are often used as frontiers because they are narrow and easily recognizable. They do present problems, however. Their valleys are usually areas of high population density, often peopled by a single ethnic group; thus frontiers established along rivers may divide the community. Rivers are important for navigation if they are wide, and they are easily crossed if they are narrow; thus it is desirable that both sides be under a single authority. They can be the source of disputes over fishing rights, effluent disposal, hydroelectricity generation, removal of water for irrigation, silting, bank maintenance, bridge construction, flood control, meander migration, thermal pollution, and so on. These problems may occur between nations that are situated upstream or downstream from one another as well as those that face each other on opposite banks. For example, West Germany and the Netherlands quibble over the Rhine waters, and Egypt and the Sudan over the Nile waters, just as much as the USA and Mexico argue over the Rio Grande, and China and the USSR over the Amur. Indeed, rivers usually make poor frontiers; they should be integrative rather than divisive forces.

Swamps and marshes are areas of low population density as a rule, but they may create conflict because they are a valuable source of rushes, eels, fish, and birds. Marshes therefore tend to be shared by different countries, except where they are very wide and therefore more effective as a barrier (e.g., the Pripet marshes). In addition, marshes that have been drained can provide fertile soil which neighbouring countries may want to claim. Few large swamps remain in the world today, since most have been drained. However, the Chad Basin swamps and the Mato Grosso are worthy of note. Both of these areas have low population densities so there is as yet little pressure for drainage and reclamation; conflict is thereby minimized.

Which countries have frontiers in the Chad Basin swamps? And in the Mato Grosso?

Lakes may be used as boundaries, but very often both sides of the lake have been settled at the same time and by people of the same ethnic group. This is the case of the Indians living around Lake Titicaca, which divides Bolivia and Peru. Numerous problems occur when a lake divides communities. There are frequent border crossings, for the purpose of work or family reunions; the possibility of smuggling increases because of the frequency of border crossings; workplaces and labour supplies are occasionally separated; people may become unhappy because of unequal taxation and benefit policies; and national identities become confused.

The International Joint Commission governs not only the Great Lakes but also all the other waters along the Canada-United States border. It has no power to order either government to act in a particular way, but its recommendations have never yet been ignored.

Lakes whose shores are shared by two or more nations also give rise to problems of effluent disposal, navigation control, water level, removal of water for irrigation, fishing rights, and so on. The International Joint Commission governing the Great Lakes deals with problems like these that arise between Canada and the US.

Seas and oceans are highly visible, but are ineffective as barriers; in fact, for the last thousand years or more they have been of more use as routeways than as barriers. They also present the problems of demarcation and delimitation. Demarcation involves the actual surveying of a boundary line at a certain distance from the coast; problems arise over the definition of "coast", and exactly how the line along such a coast should run (e.g., headland to headland? parallel to the water line? including or excluding islands?). The chief problems, however, are with delimitation; it is difficult to know just how far out from the coast the demarcation line should be drawn.

This problem is more serious nowadays because countries are becoming aware of the resource potential of sea and oceans. In recent years large factory fleets (fishing fleets with a factory ship that fully processes the fish out at sea) have moved into fishing grounds that bordering countries regard as their own. Iceland has had several encounters with the British over this matter, as has Canada with Russia, Korea with Japan, and Ecuador with the US. In order to protect "their" fisheries, the bordering states have pushed their territorial limits from the traditional cannon-shot distance of 4.8 km to 19.2 km, 80 km, and even 320 km. Such moves are naturally resisted by the states that own the factory fleets.

The countries with the chief merchant marine interests are the United States, Japan, Norway, Greece, Panama, and Liberia.

The extension of territorial claims is also resisted by countries that operate large merchant fleets. They prefer to maintain the traditional freedom of passage on the high seas, and are concerned about the possible closure of several strategically located straits.

Maritime frontiers are also becoming more important today because of the fossil fuels and minerals found underwater. The oceans cover about 70% of the earth's surface, and contain vast fuel and mineral wealth. This wealth is present not only in the rocks under the seabed, but also *on* the seabed and *in* the water. Although fishing rights may not yet have been settled, countries have already agreed to divide up the continental shelves for mining operations. There have been experiments in deep-sea mining by Inco and the Howard Hughes Corporation in the mid-Pacific. As deep-sea mining becomes more efficient, there will likely be further agreements to divide up the oceans. The entire globe is being claimed and divided up; states are pushing their frontiers into the oceans in the hope of benefiting from the tremendous potential. In this new scramble for resources, land-locked states, together with the less developed third world, feel that the wealth of the oceans should be put into trust for all people to share.

b) Artificial Frontiers

Artificial frontiers were the result of European map-making and surveying skills, developed during and after the Age of Discovery. Most early European exploration was done by sea, and so the coastlines of newly explored lands came to be known first. Interior areas, on the other hand, were largely unknown. Faced with large blank spaces on maps of newly discovered lands, European nations often drew lines of latitude and longitude on the maps. Boundaries thus determined were then agreed to by treaty. Many of the frontiers in Africa and the Middle East, as well as the western part of the Canada-US border, were established in this way.

These artificial frontiers presented problems when the ground was actually surveyed. It was found that native tribes had been cut in two, and natural boundaries such as rivers and hills ignored. Also, peculiar pieces of political property had been created; an example is Point Roberts, a little tip of land south of Vancouver that is bisected by the 49th Parallel. The southern tip belongs to the US, while the rest of the land is Canadian. The only land access the US has to the American piece is through Canada.

Artificial frontiers do offer certain advantages. They can be clearly indicated by a line of boundary markers, a fence or wall, or a minefield with gun towers. Stretches of such frontiers are often straight.

Statistical Interpretation

7-10 A crude measure of the amount of conflict that may arise because of frontiers can be obtained by ascertaining the number of states crowded into a given area of land. Obviously, for a given area, if only one state has control there will be no frontier conflict; but when two states share the land, conflict is possible. The more states there are sharing the land, the greater the risk of conflict. Bearing in mind that the sizes of the different continents are as follows, count the number of nations in each continent and calculate the average size of a country for each continent.

Areas, km²:	Africa	30 044 000
	Asia, including USSR east of Urals	44 030 000
	Europe, including USSR west of Urals	10 101 000
	North America, excluding Mexico	19 166 000
	South and Central America	20 461 000

a) Is conflict more likely with a small figure or a large figure?
b) Does population density play a part in the conflict?
c) Where should we look for future conflicts?

Fig. 7-10
Frontiers of achievement

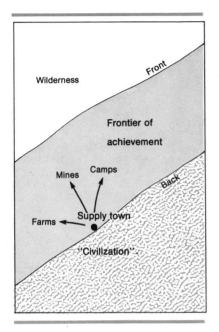

The Inuit of the Canadian Arctic did not initially live as far north as many of them do now. They used to live mostly on the northern edges of the mainland, but Canadian government officials persuaded large numbers of them to move into the islands of the High Arctic.

Paraguay is also permitted to exist as a buffer state between Brazil and Argentina. At one time, when Paraguay wanted to have its own access to the Atlantic Ocean, both Brazil and Argentina refused to allow this. Half of Paraguay's young men were killed in the ensuing war.

c) Phases of Frontier Development

Generally, the development of a frontier follows a certain sequence. First, an isolated but growing group of people pushes a frontier into a sparsely settled territory, forming a *frontier of achievement*. This boundary marks the edge of the *ecumene*, the settled area, and is still typical of pioneer districts in areas like the Australian outback, the Canadian north, southern Siberia, and western China. The frontier of achievement is usually very ragged and discontinuous; scattered and more or less isolated settlements such as farms, mines, lumber camps, research stations, and military bases are backed by sporadic supply towns. This boundary may exist on a natural frontier. For example, the American frontier of achievement existed successively along the Appalachian Mountains, the Mississippi River, the Western Deserts, and the Pacific Ocean. Where do you think it is now?

Beyond the frontier of achievement may lie the *frontier of hope*, the political frontier claimed by the state, and often extending well beyond the limits of settlement. The frontiers of the middle of South America – Western Brazil, eastern Bolivia, and eastern Peru, for example – are of this type. In all these cases the frontiers of hope run through virtually unknown land; they represent the edges of territorial claims that the governments hope to take up in the future. Such frontiers of hope have more chance of being recognized by other countries if the home country occasionally "shows the flag" in the unsettled areas. Thus Canada has planned to build roads and pipelines into the Arctic, and has encouraged the Inuit to occupy some of the previously barren islands in the High Arctic. If a country fails to exercise its interest in an area the land may be claimed by someone else.

In the second stage of frontier development, expanding states will often come into contact with one another, usually giving rise to a *frontier of conflict*. It is unlikely that languages and customs will be similar, or even compatible, and it is even more unlikely that a tradition of expansion will be given up by both groups at the same time.

A prolonged period of conflict brings about a third stage of frontier development, the phase of *shifting frontiers*. For example, the boundary between France and Germany has been shifting throughout history. The movements of the frontier depend on the relative strengths of the states. Fig. 7-11 shows how the western frontiers of Russian influence have shifted during the twentieth century. It is quite possible that two major combatants will agree to set up *buffer states* in order to minimize conflict. Uruguay was set up as a buffer state between Argentina and Brazil; Belgium and the Netherlands were allowed to exist by France and Germany; and Poland separates Germany and Russia.

The fourth phase, eventual *stability of frontiers*, may occur as the neighbouring states become less aggressive, or when the more powerful neighbour decides to end its aggression. The US-Canada frontier is the classic example; it is known as the "longest undefended border in the world".

After a time, neighbouring states may decide to merge their territories, thus producing *relic frontiers*, the fifth and last stage of frontier development. In the past, political unification of tiny, separate kingdoms has produced present-day Germany, Italy, Spain, and the UK. In somewhat the same manner the unification of the USA proceeded through the nineteenth century, as did that of Canada. At the present time, the same process is starting again in western Europe where economic union is hoped by many to be a precursor of political union. Many of the traditional frontier controls (e.g., passports and work permits) have already disappeared, although others, such as currency controls, still remain.

The national flag of the UK is called the *Union* flag (or, usually, the Union Jack). It is a combination of the flags of England, Wales, and Scotland. The flag of the United States is also similar in principle, in that the number of stars on it has varied throughout history according to the number of states in the union.

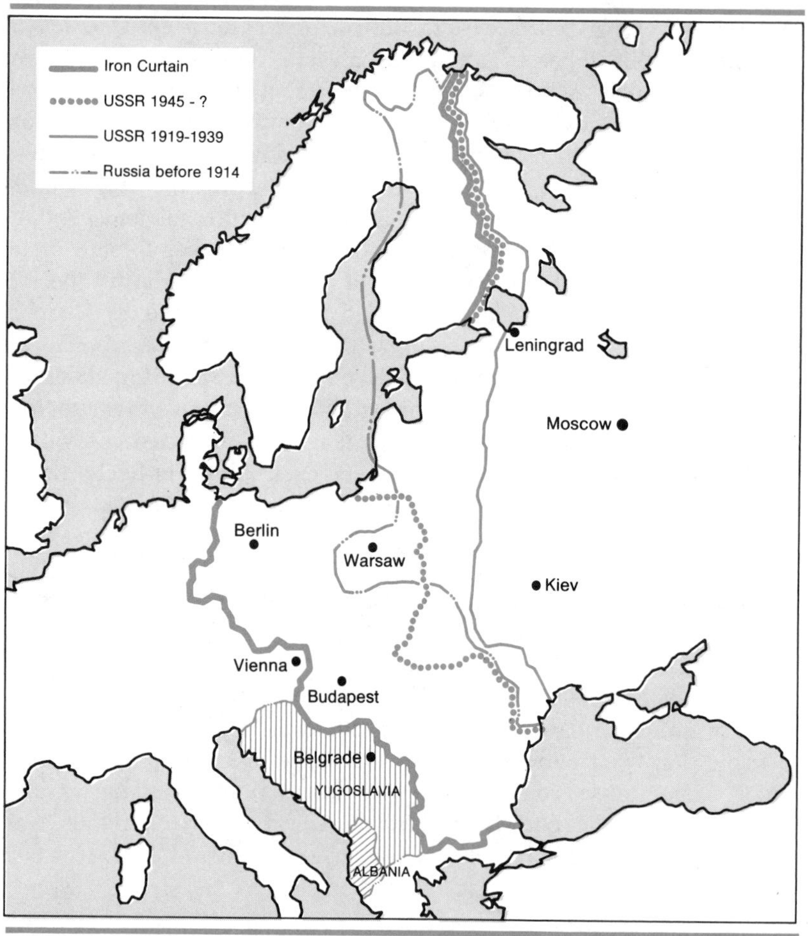

Fig. 7-11
Changes in the western frontier of Russian influence during the twentieth century

Based on J. P. Cole, *Geography of World Affairs, 1972.*

Section G
Cooperation

Gunboat diplomacy still occurs. Powerful nations still send battleships or aircraft carriers to lie at anchor off the shore of a weaker, stubborn nation in the hope of persuading it to follow the more powerful nation's wishes. A milder form is called "sabre rattling", where politicians make threatening speeches and armies are mobilized.

The geopolitical picture is not completely one of trouble or potential trouble. There appears to be a growing realization that cooperation and interdependence may be more helpful to all people than selfishness, military conquest, and gunboat diplomacy. There are still troubles, of course; the world is far from perfect. But there is also hope.

There is an increasing number of movements for cooperation among groups of countries, such as the DAC, the European Community, the Organization for African Unity (OAU), the Organization of American States (OAS), the Latin American Free Trade Association (LAFTA), and the Pacific Basin Economic Community (PBEC). In addition, the various branches of the UN are powerful instruments for putting the world in a war-resistant, if not entirely peaceful, state.

The UN is an association of states that have agreed to maintain international peace and security, and to promote political, economic, and social conditions that favour this purpose. The member states have no power or authority under the UN to interfere in the internal affairs of any other state. But a protest by a majority of nations may bring about a positive response from a troublesome nation; it was a UN appeal that prevented the Anglo-French invasion of Suez in 1956. On the other hand, the UN's protest over Russian interference in Hungary in 1956 and Czechoslovakia in 1968 had no effect. The UN has little real power; in too many cases nations simply put their own interests first. South Africa is an example of this.

The UN is not truly representative of the peoples of the world, either. In the UN General Assembly, each nation gets one vote; this ensures that even tiny nations can be heard. It also means that large nations such as China and India have no more say than small nations like Guatemala and Chad. Is this fair? Another point is that most small nations are often newly independent third world countries, and so the third world has a majority in the Assembly. Again the fairness of the system can be questioned.

Much of the best work of the UN is done by its associated agencies. These form a network for international help and improvement, and are either widely used or supported by almost all nations. The fourteen agencies are: the International Atomic Energy Agency (IAEA), Vienna; the International Labour Organization (ILO), Geneva; the Food and Agriculture Organization (FAO), Rome; the UN Educational, Scientific, and Cultural Organization (UNESCO), Paris; the World Health Organization (WHO), Geneva; the International Monetary Fund (IMF), Washington; the International Bank for Reconstruction and Development (IBRD, World Bank), Washington; the International Finance Corporations (IFC), Washington; the International Civil Aviation Organization (ICAO), Montreal; the International Maritime Consultative Organization (IMCO), London; the World Meteorological Organization (WMO), Geneva; the General Agreement on Tariffs and Trade (GATT), Geneva; and the International Telecommunications Union (ITU), Geneva.

In addition to the agencies there are a few organs of the UN itself whose main job is decision-making. The two chief organs outside the General Assembly are the International Court of Justice located in The Hague, and the Security Council in New York. These agencies and organs of the UN provide hope for the future of the world.

Discussion and Research

25. What are the different sorts of problems that could face minority groups?
26. What have been the causes of recent acts of terrorism?
27. Canada's frontier of hope stretches to the North Pole. If Canada didn't claim this land, who would? How does Canada try to exercise sovereignty in the Arctic? Is it challenged at all?
28. What were the origins of the black-white frontier in southern Africa?
29. Can you identify those areas of the world that experience (a) frontier tension (phases 2 and 3), and (b) frontier stability (phase 4)?
30. Why do you think the western frontiers of Russian hegemony have fluctuated more in southern and central Europe than in northern Europe, as shown in Fig. 7-11?
31. What do you think ought to happen to ocean resources?
32. What are the properties of an ideal frontier, assuming that frontiers are needed?
33. Frontiers are the scenes of many problems. Why then do nations have them?
34. For frontiers to disappear, what would have to happen? Is this realistic?
35. Investigate the development of the Canada-US frontier. How far does it fit into the evolutionary phases described in the text?
36. What and where are some of the disputes over water along the Canada-US border?

37. Is the Tennessee Valley Authority a good model to follow for river basin management?
38. What are the components of a national identity?
39. What are the disadvantages of nationalism, once described as the "greatest curse in history"?
40. Does nationalism serve a useful purpose?
41. Because the third world has majority voting strength in the UN General Assembly, and often uses it to pass anti-first world resolutions, some of the first world countries that pay most of the money for running the UN have felt that continued support of the UN is a waste of both time and money. Is it?

Case Study 7

South Africa: Apartheid and Multinationalism

South Africa used to be legally called a Union; it is now trying hard to cease to be one. Government policy is to partition the country. The inspiration for this policy is partly *political*, based on the "divide and rule" philosophy. To some extent it is also *religious*, because of the Dutch Reformed Church's dogmas that God created people separately black, white, and brown, and therefore we should not alter that divine separation. Some of the government's reasons are *economic*, based on the perceived benefits to the whites of a large supply of cheap black labour. There are also *historical* reasons, based on the more or less simultaneous original settlement by both blacks and whites in that part of southern Africa. Another reason is the desire for a *peaceful solution* to the problems caused when several ethnic groups occupy the same land. South Africans justify their policy of separateness by pointing to the problems in other parts of the world where the peoples of two or more nations are citizens of the same state. They point to Belgium with its Flemings and Walloons, Northern Ireland with its Catholics and Protestants or Irish and English, Malaysia with its Malays and Chinese, and Cyprus with its Greeks and Turks. They say that a multinational state is not workable; they want each nation to have its own state.

The policy of separate development for the different national groups within South Africa is called apartheid. The word means "separateness". According to this policy South Africa is to be divided into a number of different and independent nation-states. The history and ethnic structure of the population lend themselves to this idea. The first European settlers were the Dutch (1652) who pioneered the land from Cape Town. There were no other people in the area at that time. As the Dutch made the land productive, they needed more people; additional settlers from Holland, Germany, and France arrived, and slaves were brought in from Malaya, Mozambique, and East and West Africa. The people prospered and sought new land beyond the Cape. Close to 1800 they encountered the nomadic Xhosa Bantu migrating southward along the coastal plain. Fighting over land was inconclusive, and both sides came to a halt, the Dutch near the Great Fish River, the Xhosa to the north.

In the early 1800s the British absorbed these regions into their growing empire. They made English the official language instead of Dutch, and in 1834 abolished slavery. Both of these acts greatly upset the Dutch, who relied on slaves to support their own hard-working life style. Accordingly, many Dutch moved into the interior, to get away from the English. The Great Trek of 1836 took them into a region that became the Orange Free State and Transvaal; here they encountered only small groups of nomadic herdsmen who were migrating at about the same time from the north. The Dutch settled in the empty areas, far from the English on the coast. Their language developed into Afrikaans and they called themselves the Boer (farmer) people. They largely ignored the British around the coast.

In 1867 British explorers discovered diamonds at Kimberley, and in 1886 gold at Johannesburg. Boer isolation was ended as British industrialism pushed into the interior. In 1899 the Boers fought back, but ultimately had to sign a peace treaty in 1902. The entire region came under British control, much to the disgust of the Boers.

Meanwhile the British brought in thousands of Indians as indentured labour to work in the sugar plantations of the east coast. Most refused to return to India when their term of labour was over, despite intense repatriation propaganda by the British.

Thus by the early years of this century the varied ethnic mixture of South Africa was basically set, and the attitudes of one group to another firmly established. The first census (1904) showed a total population of 5 174 827, consisting of whites (1 117 234) and non-whites (4 057 593). But these were not, nor are they yet, homogeneous groups. The whites were and still are divided into mutually hostile groups of Afrikaners (60%) and English (40%). The non-whites are split into several groups: *coloureds*, the products of multiracial breeding by the early Dutch, Germans, French, Malays, immigrant blacks, and imported black slaves (11%); *Asians*, mostly the descendants of indentured Indians (4%); and *blacks* (85%). The black segment itself consists of several tribes, chiefly the Nguni-speaking Xhosa, Zula, Ndebele, and Swazi, the Sotho-speaking Tswana, Northern Sotho, and Southern Sotho, the Venda-speaking Venda, and the Shangana-Tsonga-speaking Tsonga.

Through the years the internal proportions of whites (60% Afrikaner, 40% English) and non-whites (85% black, 11% coloured, 4% Asian) have remained relatively constant; but the proportions of these two major populations altered considerably. In 1904 the proportion was 1 white to 3.63 non-whites; by 1974 it was 1 white to 4.85 non-whites. The whites are becoming increasingly outnumbered, which may to some extent explain their developing fortress mentality.

What is perhaps more important, though, is the resumption of political power by the Boer Afrikaners. Since its election in 1948 on a platform of *Save White South Africa*, the Afrikaner-supported Nationalist Party has set out to give legal precedence to the traditional Dutch Reformed Church beliefs of white superiority. For example, it is now illegal as well as sinful for whites and blacks to marry each other, or even to go out together. The English-supported opposition United Party has not won an election since the Nationalists came to power; however it still contains many white people who speak out, albeit without much effect, against the apartheid policies of the Nationalists.

Successive Nationalist governments have enacted apartheid legislation designed to keep the blacks and whites apart and to legalize the Afrikaner feelings of superiority over the blacks. Much of the legislation concerns what is called "petty apartheid"; for example, blacks cannot use the same restaurants, hotels, or park benches as whites. But some laws are much more fundamental. For example, one of the major grievances of black workers has been that they cannot gain promotion to positions that

An apartheid sign near the beaches of Simonstown.

UNESCO/Roger Carrington

involve directing or teaching whites. This situation has been worsened in the last few years by South Africa's great economic growth, because it has put strains on white labour's ability to cope. There are not enough skilled whites to manage the growing economy.

Another major grievance has been the inferior education that is given to the blacks; for example, in 1974, the educational expenditures per child were about $600 for a white and $35 for a black. Education for blacks is not compulsory, and only about 3% get to secondary school, compared with about 35% of the whites.

A further grievance has been the implementation of a police state. The Nationalists have passed various laws, chiefly the Pass Laws and the Terrorism Act, that in effect harass the blacks. The Pass Laws require the blacks at all times to carry passbooks showing their identity and racial group; failure to produce it immediately upon request is a cause for arrest. Since 1965 there have been over 15 000 000 such arrests. People have even been killed in riots over the passbooks, as at Sharpville in 1960. As a result of the Terrorism Act, *habeas corpus* has been removed from the lawbooks. Therefore, people arrested under the Act can disappear without a trace for years at a time; some never reappear.

There is evidence of a police state at work in South Africa. For example, in June 1976, a black journalist for the Johannesburg Star wrote an article about life in Soweto which was published in the *Toronto Star*; in July he was arrested under the Terrorism Act. Other examples include arrests of English clergymen who speak out against apartheid, and the censorship of news and opinion in the Rand Daily Mail.

The goal of the various policies of apartheid is, however, the partition of South Africa itself. The entire land area is being apportioned to the different major "nations", so that the various groups get rights to the regions they originally settled. Thus the white "nation" acquires rights to 87% of South Africa, including all the arid and semi-arid interior as well as the south coast. The numerous black "nations" acquire the remaining 13%. The coloureds and Asians get nothing, but will be permitted, unlike the blacks, to reside in white South Africa.

The black "nations" are identified and divided on the basis of differences in language (Nguni, Sotho, Venda, Tsonga), customs, physical appearance, modes of dress and ornamentation, and so on. To the outside observer, some of the characteristics used to distinguish the groups may appear trivial. For example, in the South African government's advertising supplement in the *Globe Magazine*, 1969 6 7, it is stated that "the traditional Zulu leopard skin and beadwork are quite different from the red ochre dyed blanket of the Xhosa or the multicoloured woven blanket of the South Sotho;" and "The North Sotho still love their own make of sour porridge and beer, while the South Sotho cheerfully eat horse and donkey flesh." Nevertheless, on the basis of such "nationhood" the different tribes of Bantu have been allocated their own *homelands* (see Fig. 7C-1) in the same way that the people of Swaziland and Lesotho previously gained independence from the British. The blacks have citizenship and full voting rights in their own homelands, but nowhere else. Thus South Africa legally has no black citizens; it is entirely a "white" area that permits Asian and coloured residents. The blacks are thereby encouraged to leave South Africa and return to their original homelands.

Fig. 7C-1
South African homelands

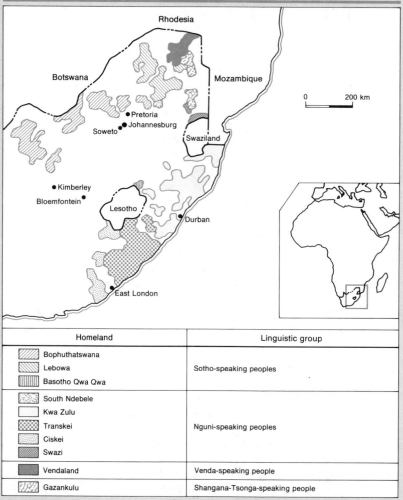

Homeland	Linguistic group
▨ Bophuthatswana	
▨ Lebowa	Sotho-speaking peoples
▥ Basotho Qwa Qwa	
▨ South Ndebele	
☐ Kwa Zulu	
▨ Transkei	Nguni-speaking peoples
▨ Ciskei	
▨ Swazi	
▨ Vendaland	Venda-speaking people
▨ Gazankulu	Shangana-Tsonga-speaking people

Note 1) In order to consolidate the pieces, blacks and whites are both being moved. So far, about 2 000 000 people have been moved.
2) The blacks with 70% of the total population have been given rights to 13% of the land. They prefer to have either **a)** *all* the land under their control, with the whites as a minority in a black state, or **b)** independence in the homelands, but with much bigger and more consolidated homelands reflecting their 70% of the population.

Source: *The Economist* 1977 1 1.

Nationalists argue that the blacks outside their homelands are really in a foreign country, and that they should not expect to have the privileges of citizenship. Indeed, there are various "influx control" laws that prevent blacks from just walking into South Africa from a homeland, even though the blacks still regard it all as a single country. The blacks living in white South Africa are therefore regarded by the whites as "temporary sojourners" who will one day leave. However, many of these blacks were born in white South Africa, and have never seen the homelands given to them.

The nationalists see the blacks as visitors because the towns and cities now occupied by white South Africans were initially founded by the Dutch or British; the blacks on the other hand migrated to the towns in search of jobs many years ago. According to the Nationalists, the drift to the cities has continued because of high rates of population growth in the homelands, and jobs provided in the cities are often the major source of livelihood for the people of the homelands, most of whom still follow traditional preindustrial customs. Only workers are permitted to come to the cities because Afrikaners fear that if whole families came then the workers would probably not return to their homelands.

The black workers are not too happy with these arguments and the resulting working conditions. They contend that even though the salary is welcome, it is only 10% of the money earned by whites doing similar work. They also complain bitterly about the "contract" nature of the work, whereby they sign a contract agreeing to work for a certain length of time without striking for more than the original wage. The effect of this is to hold wages down and render strikes illegal.

While blacks and Nationalists argue strongly over the economic aspects of the homeland policy, they differ even more widely over the political aspects. The Nationalist government is pushing ahead with the policy despite severe objections from the blacks. The blacks themselves are also divided on the issue; some are prepared to take independence now, even if it comes a bit at a time, while others want nothing to do with the homelands, preferring to lay claim as a majority of the population to the whole of South Africa.

The first homelands to be given almost full independence are the Xhosa "nation" of the Transkei and the Sotho "nation" of Bophuthat-swana. Their leaders, together with those of Kwa Zulu, Lebowa, and Basotho Qwa Qwa, while accepting the privileges that go with independence, argue strongly for an integrated South Africa. They do not regard the formation of politically independent homelands as acceptable. They want a fully integrated majority-rule single nation South Africa.

The Afrikaners do not agree at all. They see 87% of the land as rightfully theirs, and they regard the blacks as temporary but useful occupants. They even regard their aid to the black homelands as aid to the third world! What do you think?

GEOPOLITICS: Further Reading

The Odessa File, FORSYTH
Z, VASSILIKOS
World Without Borders, BROWN
Farewell, Babylon, KATTAN
Exodus, URIS
Atlas Shrugged, RAND
We the Living, RAND
Anthem, RAND
Topaz, URIS
The Day of the Jackal, FORSYTH
The Dogs of War, FORSYTH
The New Industrial State, GALBRAITH
Spy Story, DEIGHTON
One Day in the Life of Ivan Denisovitch, SOLZHENITSYN
Oil Spill, SLATER
Separation, ROHMER
It Couldn't Happen Here, LEWIS
Trinity, URIS
1984, ORWELL
Animal Farm, ORWELL

Conclusion

In this chapter, we have seen that the countries of the world are often roughly divided into three groups, or "worlds", according to variations in population growth, food production, industrialization, energy production, and quality of life. The third world appears to be the poorest of the three; it experiences most of the problems we have discussed in previous chapters.

There is no doubt that the contrasts between these worlds exist to some extent because of ideological differences. Every nation has its own beliefs, and acts according to them; this ideology will help to determine the type of life experienced in a country. Because of their different beliefs, nations often disagree, and clashes occur. Yet in this chapter we have also looked at the forms of cooperation that nations are developing in the world. We have seen the move toward a New International Economic Order.

The differences in ideologies and development, the clashes, and the projects based on international cooperation are all components of a dynamic situation. The world is unlikely to remain as it is. As nations become more developed, for example, ideologies may change; new goals may be established, and conflicts with other nations may occur as a result of the new policies. Change is indeed a fundamental characteristic of life. Our concluding chapter is therefore an analysis of change.

Introduction

In previous chapters we have examined problems and phenomena occurring in various countries throughout the world. Although they are at different stages of development and have their own problems to deal with, all nations share one characteristic—they are all subject to change.

Today's world is not the same as yesterday's, and tomorrow's will be different again. Change is a feature of life. Fast or slow, localized or universal, progressive or regressive, it is inevitable. Changes occur not only in the physical environment, but also in human values and beliefs. Each change that occurs affects the world and causes new alterations; change, therefore, is a continuous process.

In this chapter, we will examine the ever-present phenomenon of change. Section A presents a general discussion of the topic; in it we

All nations share the characteristic of change. This is part of the Asian Highway between India and Afghanistan.

United Nations

will study basic changes that occur in the world, ways of predicting change, theories, and rates of change. In subsequent sections we will look at specific changes that take place in the third world and the more developed world, and at the possibilities of the development of One World. We will conclude the chapter with a case study of Brazil, an important nation that has recently undergone a great deal of change, and promises much in the way of future development.

To begin, the following items present an idea of the number and variety of changes taking place in the world today.

Population

Where is Japan heading?

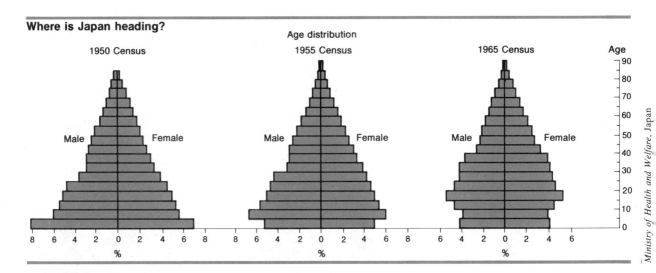

Age distribution

Ministry of Health and Welfare, Japan

The position of women in society

Since March 8, 1975, a law adopted in Cuba obliges husbands to help their wives with housework

Today in Cuba women are "in transition" on the road to equality. By 1970, girls accounted for 49 per cent of children in elementary schools, 55 per cent of those in secondary schools, and 40.6 per cent of students in higher education.

Prior to 1959 Cuba's 194 000 women workers—70 000 of them domestic servants—represented only 9 per cent of the country's total labour force. By 1974 the figure had reached 590 000, or more than 25 per cent of all workers, thereby freeing a large segment of manpower for other occupations, such as sugar-cane harvesting.

Cuban women considered they had won a victory when a provision stating that every business enterprise should reserve a certain number of posts "for women" was removed from the Labour Code. Today women are even working in the docks and on building sites, doing jobs which were traditionally men's.

Whereas scarcely 20 per cent of Cuban women could afford hospital and clinical services before 1959, today 95 per cent benefit from them. This has reduced the death-rates of babies and deaths in childbirth in Cuba to the lowest levels in Latin America. Death-rates of babies in other Latin American countries are sometimes as high as 150 or 200 per 1 000, but in Cuba only 26 babies died for every 1 000 births in 1973 and fewer than six mothers out of every 10 000 died in childbirth.

Nevertheless, just as everywhere else in the world, Cuban women have been, as it were, an *occupied territory*, and liberation has not brought instant emancipation from the colonized mentality, and still less from the *occupying power*, the male.

Male supremacy in its extreme form is known as "machismo" and is attributed to Latin Americans as if it were an exclusive legacy from ancient times, or something inherited from Hispanic tradition. Its remote origins are surely to be found in the economic dependence that has always been woman's lot, first under her father (who at least considers it a moral and legal duty to provide for her), and subsequently under her husband (who often hands her money as if he were giving alms, disdainfully like a millionaire or grudgingly like a poor man).

But when women are economically independent, as they are in Cuba, the die-hards who still defend the old way of life turn to biological arguments, such as the weakness and timidity of women (even though they serve as soldiers and paratroopers), or to historical arguments, such as their supposedly greater aptitude for housework than for creative activities (though it now appears that both sexes are equally capable of both types of work), or even to some distant justification taken from the Bible to the effect that woman was created to be man's companion (in which case man should automatically become woman's companion).

From an article by Jorge Enrique Adoum in the *UNESCO Courier*, 1975 9.

Incomes

The top 25 countries compared (GNP in US dollars per person)

1965		1975	
Kuwait	3 257	Kuwait	11 510
USA	3 221	United Arab Emirates	10 480
Canada	2 284	Qatar	8 320
Switzerland	2 213	Switzerland	8 050
Sweden	2 163	Sweden	7 880
Norway	1 830	USA	7 060
New Zealand	1 818	Denmark	6 920
Iceland	1 787	Canada	6 650
West Germany	1 774	Brunei	6 630
Australia	1 731	West Germany	6 610
UK	1 688	Norway	6 540
Denmark	1 659	Belgium	6 070
Belgium	1 623	Luxembourg	6 050
France	1 490	France	5 760
Finland	1 298	Australia	5 640
USSR	1 253	Iceland	5 620
Netherlands	1 246	Netherlands	5 590
Israel	1 184	Finland	5 100
Austria	1 139	Libya	5 080
Italy	927	Austria	4 720
Ireland	918	New Zealand	4 680
South Africa	846	Japan	4 460
Venezuela	759	East Germany	4 230
Japan	725	UK	3 840
Greece	531	Czechoslovakia	3 710

Source: *World Bank Atlas*, 1976

The environment

The Yellow River produces happiness

by JOHN BURNS

Special to *The Christian Science Monitor*© 1972 *Toronto Globe and Mail*

CHENGCHOW, CHINA Ma Yinting is an engineer, by all accounts one of the best men in his field. But more than that, he is that rare thing, an engineer who talks laymen's language.

It is in such terms that he describes the progress that has been made by the Communists in harnessing the Yellow River, once known as China's Sorrow, for its history of catastrophic floods.

"For more than 2 000 years," he says, his small voice rising for emphasis, "the people thought of the river as a scourge. They feared it, they hated it, and if they could, they left it.

"Today, thanks to the work that has been done, their attitude is completely changed. There is no longer any fear or hate. Instead, the people love the river, they rely on it, and they use it."

It does not look like a killer, but it has been. Since the earliest records were taken, 2 000 years ago, it has overflowed its banks more than 1 500 times in the lower reaches alone, with 26 major changes of course.

The first priority was the strengthening of the dikes throughout its 450-mile run [720 km] through Honan, and beyond that to the sea. Altogether, more than 1 100 miles [1 760 km] of dikes were reinforced, involving more than 9 billion cubic feet [250 million cubic metres] of earthwork and 243 million cubic feet [7 million cubic metres] of stone.

But ending the floods required more than better dikes, for the root cause remained. That was silt, 1.6 billions tons [1.4 billion tonnes] of it a year, carried down from the mountains and deposited on the river bed in the plains.

Year by year, the silt raises the level of the river. It now averages a height of between 10 and 35 feet [3 and 11 m] above the level of the surrounding countryside throughout Honan. Left to itself, it would surmount any dike.

Dredging has helped, but the only long-term solution is to halt the soil erosion upstream that gives rise to the silt in the first place. Thousands of acres [hectares] of river bank have been terraced and sown with grass, and millions of trees have been planted.

"Life is so much better than before," says Mr. Shao, leaning on the railing of the barge and looking out across the dike to the new site of the village of Huayuankou. "We really do have a good life now."

The Globe and Mail 1972 7 8

Quality of life

In the decade 1941-51 the expectation of life at birth in India was only 33.50 years. In 1971, this had already risen to 48.75 years and was expected to rise further to 51.75 years in 1976. This has become possible because of a reduction in the death rate in the country from 29.2 per thousand in the decade 1941-51 to 16.2 per thousand in 1971 and to an expected 15.1 per thousand in 1976.

Hannan Ezekiel, in *The Toronto Star* 1976 8 5

Discussion and Research

1. What aspects of change are illustrated (a) directly, and (b) indirectly in the introductory items?
2. Some people are opposed to what they call "change for the sake of change".
   a) What do you think they mean?
   b) Do you agree with them?
3. Suggest some cultural traits or values that might stand in the way of change.
4. Is change desirable?

Section A
A Changing World

1. Basic Changes

a) Physical change

From its origins the earth has been in a constant state of change. Our planet is believed to have been formed when clouds of space dust were amassed into a coherent body. It eventually developed a relatively solid skin. Tectonic plates have caused ocean basins to open or close, and continents to move; mountains have been formed from sea floor deposits; landscapes have been eroded to peneplains; life has started and spread over the earth; human beings have emerged. During the time of humans, glaciers have advanced and melted away; sea levels have risen and fallen; climates have varied between warm and cold and between dry and humid; plant life has spread over most of the earth, producing dense forests in many places. Other regions have become deserts. Geologic and climatic change continues.

b) Human change

People themselves have changed throughout time. Cranial capacities have increased; modern skulls show almost three times the brain capacity of early skulls, mainly because of a thinner skull bone. Humanity has become diversified through the development of hereditary racial characteristics such as hair shape, eyelid folds, skin colour, and lip shape.

Human society has also undergone change. From an early universal pattern of hunting and food-gathering there appeared pockets of cultivation in certain suitable locations. The areas were characterized by natural warmth, year-round water availability, and fertile lowland soil. Cultivation practices were slowly diffused from these source regions, or *hearths*, as they are called. Thus, carbon dating shows us that from a hearth in the Tigris-Euphrates region around 6000 BC cultivation slowly spread to Turkey and Greece by 5000 BC, to Lower Egypt and the central Danube lands by 4000 BC, to Upper Egypt, Italy, southern France, and the North European Plain by 3000 BC, and to the Atlantic fringes and Alpine mountain districts of Europe by

2000 BC. Some groups of people have not yet settled as cultivators; a few food-gathering tribes still exist.

For example, food-gathering and hunting are environmental necessities for the Kalahari Bushmen or the traditional Inuit, while the Semang and Sakai tribes of Malaysia and the Pygmies of Zaire continue to follow this ancient pattern for other reasons.

Another important stage of human development was marked by industrialization. In the eighteenth century, the hearth regions were located in Western Europe, but aided by vast numbers of migrants industrialization spread quickly to North America. Subsequent diffusion was slower; industrialization occurred first throughout Europe, then in Japan, and now in relatively isolated pockets such as Hong Kong and Singapore. Industrial diffusion is currently occurring from three hearths: Europe, Japan, and North America. The main agents of diffusion are multinational corporations; the main destinations are those third world countries that have a desire to industrialize. Meanwhile, the industrial hearth regions themselves are changing into service-oriented post-industrial societies.

Other social changes include the rise of organized religion, the growth of government, the development of towns and cities, and the creation of communication and transportation networks.

Organized religion was a strong element in early government, and both were important in early city growth. All three were partly the product of the rise of cultivation in lands where strong seasonality was imposed by rains and floods, and where efficient organization was necessary to manage irrigation schemes.

Novosti Press Agency

As communication and transportation systems expand over the globe, the pace of change quickens. Information spreads more quickly, and the adoption of exotic ideas is made easier. The pressures of change put a strain on existing social structures. Social hierarchies, customs, values, and beliefs, all developed to suit one particular community life style, are subjected to great stresses. There are arguments between groups in a country that want change and those that do not. Some of these arguments flare into revolutions.

◄ Social changes include, among other things, the growth of cities. This is part of the southern suburbs of Moscow.

The business centre of Kuwait.

UNESCO

UNESCO/P.A. Pitter

2. Predicting Change

At one time, in most societies, the future was expected to be much the same as the past because things did not change very quickly. Today, however, the world is becoming a "global village"; news travels around the world rapidly, and each nation is aware of the others. Every country realizes that change is possible and that choices have to be made. In order to try to control change, the world looks to the science of futurology, the study of the choice of futures.

Demonstrating this interest in the future, some of the more developed countries have set up "think tanks" to analyze trends and developments. Three important examples in the USA are the Hudson Institute, the Rand Corporation, and the Stanford Research Institute; in the USSR there is the Section for Social Forecasting of the Academy of Sciences. Techniques of analysis vary, but broadly fall into four patterns: first there is *brainstorming*, in which a group is asked to "invent the future" in some particular field. The members of the group then react to each other's suggestions and reasons, debating over them until a consensus is reached. In the *Delphi technique*, forty to sixty specialists are questioned individually about the likely or desired future in some field. The minority views in each round are eliminated until a consensus is reached. In a third technique, *contextual mapping*, trends are projected forward in the light of expected changes. One of the best known examples of this method is the computer study called *The Limits to Growth*. Lastly, there is *normative forecasting*, in which norms, or targets, are set and plans made to implement them in the society.

In the Delphi technique, the experts are not allowed to know what the others are thinking. They are given only the more popular thoughts of the group, and asked to respond to them individually. In each round (there may be several) the least common responses are deleted, and the more common ones are re-presented to the experts for further thought.

Statistical Interpretation

8-1 Construct a compound line graph to illustrate the changing pattern of employment in the Canadian labour force, using the data in Fig. 8-1.

8-2 Construct a compound line graph to illustrate the changing pattern of rural-urban occupancy in Canada, using the data in Fig. 8-2.

8-3 On a 3 cycle semi-log graph (see Appendix 3), plot the primary data from Fig. 8-1 and the rural data from Fig. 8-2. What do you notice about the nature and rate of change of both lines? Can you explain the changes? What is likely to happen in the future?

8-4 On the same graph used for assignment 8-3, but with an additional scale, plot in the line for the data in Fig. 8-3. How do you explain the slope of this line in view of your answers to assignments 8-1, 8-2, and 8-3? What do you think it means in practical day-to-day terms?

Fig. 8-1
Distribution of employment in the Canadian labour force, by major category, percentages, 1881-1971

Employment category		1881	1901	1921	1941	1951	1961	1971
Primary	Agriculture Forestry Fishing Mining	51.2	44.3	36.6	29.3	20.7	16.8	8.4
Secondary	Manufacturing Construction	29.4	27.8	26.5	26.3	32.6	31.7	26.8
Tertiary	Services	19.4	27.9	36.9	44.4	46.9	51.3	64.8

Source: Urquhart and Buckley, *Historical Statistics*; also *Canada Year Book*, 1968 and 1973.

Fig. 8-2
Rural-urban distribution of Canada's population, percentages, 1871-1971

	1871	1881	1891	1901	1911	1921	1931	1941	1951	1961	1971
Rural	80.4	74.3	68.2	65.2	58.3	54.7	50.3	49.1	37.1	28.9	23.9
Urban	19.6	25.7	31.8	34.8	41.7	45.3	49.7	50.9	62.9	71.1	76.1

Source: Urquhart and Buckley, *Historical Statistics of Canada*; also *Canada Year Book*, 1968 and 1976-77.

Fig. 8-3
Canada's GNP in current dollars

1922	4 672 000 000	1950	18 491 000 000
1923	4 947 000 000	1951	21 640 000 000
1924	na	1952	24 588 000 000
1925	na	1953	25 833 000 000
1926	5 146 000 000	1954	25 918 000 000
1927	5 561 000 000	1955	28 528 000 000
1928	6 050 000 000	1956	32 058 000 000
1929	6 139 000 000	1957	33 513 000 000
1930	5 720 000 000	1958	34 777 000 000
1931	4 693 000 000	1959	36 846 000 000
1932	3 814 000 000	1960	38 359 000 000
1933	3 492 000 000	1961	39 646 000 000
1934	3 969 000 000	1962	42 927 000 000
1935	4 301 000 000	1963	45 978 000 000
1936	4 634 000 000	1964	50 280 000 000
1937	5 241 000 000	1965	55 364 000 000
1938	5 272 000 000	1966	61 828 000 000
1939	5 621 000 000	1967	66 409 000 000
1940	6 713 000 000	1968	72 586 000 000
1941	8 282 000 000	1969	79 815 000 000
1942	10 265 000 000	1970	85 610 000 000
1943	11 053 000 000	1971	93 402 000 000
1944	11 848 000 000	1972	103 407 000 000
1945	11 863 000 000	1973	112 584 000 000
1946	11 885 000 000	1974	144 616 000 000
1947	13 473 000 000	1975	165 445 000 000
1948	15 509 000 000	1976	190 027 000 000
1949	16 800 000 000	1977	207 714 000 000

Source: *Canada Year Book*, 1922-77.

Discussion and Research

5. Why would a greater awareness of the world lead countries to show an interest in the future?
6. Be a futurologist. A hundred years from now, what will housing be like? Food? Transportation? Education?

3. A Theory of Change

A theory of change is an attempt to develop a series of explanations that help us to understand the forces and changes that are observably at work in the world. One of the best known theories of change is that proposed by Walter Rostow. Rostow's theory was presented in a book *Stages of Economic Growth*, which set out to do for capitalism what Marx's *Das Kapital* had done for communism. Rostow identifies five stages of social and economic development: the traditional society, the phase which sets up the preconditions for take-off, the take-off, the drive to maturity, and the age of high mass consumption.

The *traditional society* has a small range of *production functions*. A production function is any combination of the factors of production necessary to obtain a desired output. For example, 10 t rice may be produced by a combination of 1 ha land, 0.1 t IR8 rice seed, 1 t chemical fertilizer, 2 t insecticide, 1 worker, 1 *cultivator*, and 1 controlled irrigation system. It may also be produced by a combination of 1 t traditional rice seed, 0.5 t human fertilizer, 40 workers, and whatever flood irrigation waters are available. Both combinations are production functions, or combinations necessary to secure output. Both functions are of equal value, for both give the same output, 10 t rice. A more developed society can use varying quantities of individual factors, (i.e., it can vary the proportions of fertilizer, land, labour, etc.) but a traditional or less developed society cannot. It lacks the knowledge, the techniques, and the variety of inputs. It has to use the traditional combination of factors or it may get no output at all. A society tied to traditional production patterns is usually hierarchical; the number of people in the upper echelon is small, while there are large numbers in the lower levels. There is little upward mobility, and power is usually concentrated in the hands of the landowners. Family and inheritance are highly valued, and a rigorous social and religious code is followed. Medieval Europe, Shogunate Japan, and pre-revolutionary Russia are good examples.

The next phase sets up the *preconditions for take-off*. According to Rostow, it takes time to alter a traditional society so that a variety of production functions can be introduced. Old beliefs and the security of traditional ways are difficult to challenge. The viewpoints of powerful and established people have to be altered. Sometimes these people come to see that change is in their own interests, but other times it must be forced upon them by revolution. With the exception of the West European hearth, where the transition occurred more or less spontaneously, the preconditions for take-off have usually been quickened by the intrusion of a more fully developed society. The entry of Commodore Perry's ships into Tokyo harbour in 1853 is a good example of such an intrusion.

The chief signs that the preconditions for take-off are being developed include the following: the growth of education; the rise of banks; the building of transportation and communication systems; the development of effective centralized government; the shifting of spending power from those who prefer to act in their own interests to those who give priority to public interest; and the growing efficiency of farming, so that yields per unit of input are greatly increased. Farming changes are crucial; the diminishing numbers of farmers must be able to feed the growing urban population, and in addition, prevent unemployment in the towns by demanding industrial products.

Cultivators are small hand-pushed power sources, widely used for tilling small fields in eastern Asia. They were invented in Japan and are now being sold abroad in increasing quantities.

Shogunate Japan was replaced in 1868 by the open-minded government of the Emperor Meiji. The so-called Meiji Restoration was a crucial step in Japan's development into a modern industrial state.

Farming input factors are such things as land, labour, and capital equipment. Increasing yields may accordingly be measured in relation to land (so much per hectare), to labour (so much per farm worker), and to capital equipment (so much per tonne of fertilizer, etc.).

The *take-off* occurs when the bulk of society favours growth and change. Change now becomes steady and self-sustaining rather than erratic. Take-off may be stimulated by a number of factors, but war and socio-political revolution such as the American Civil War and the Austro-Prussian War are two of the most important. Output per person increases enormously during take-off. The country as a whole benefits greatly from advances in a few leading industries. For example, in Britain the cotton industry led the take-off phase; in the USA it was the railways, in Germany, armaments, and in Sweden, the industries exploiting raw materials. After take-off such leading industries are usually replaced by domestic consumer goods industries, such as car and radio manufacturing.

Another characteristic of take-off is the widespread acceptance of literacy, which usually results from compulsory education. Mass circulation newspapers then become established. According to Rostow, democracy becomes the preferred system of government. Health care improves and life expectancy increases. Because populations explode, urban areas grow and emigration is encouraged to relieve crowding and unsynchronized job creation. Trade is increased and empires may be built in other countries.

The *drive to maturity* is a long period of sustained change. Modern technology gradually spreads throughout all areas of economic activity. Society adapts to the changes; rural-urban migration continues and service activities create universal educational and medical facilities.

An adult literacy class in Iran, taught by a member of the "Army of Knowledge."

UNESCO/Dominique Roger

Since people become better off individually in all material ways, travel and a variety of recreational activities become common. Democracy becomes firmly established and governments begin to appropriate and apportion ever-larger parts of the national wealth. As the old ways gradually die, people begin to feel free in their choice of beliefs. The society comes to assume that it can do almost anything it wants.

During the *age of high mass consumption*, Rostow notes that the leading sectors shift more toward services, especially those of finance, information, and government. Material production continues to grow through the application of such refined inputs as automation. Social welfare becomes a major concern, first at the local level and eventually throughout the society. People talk of the quality of life and question even those values most recently established. There is a tremendous range of choices, not only for the individual but also for the whole society. Should the society increase its leisure? Explore space? Develop the ocean beds? Clean up the environment after the drive to maturity? Give aid to the less developed parts of the world? Establish world government?

4. Rates of Change

The process of change may indeed be constant, but the rate of change is by no means the same all over. Some parts of the world began the process of rapid change envisioned by Rostow many decades ago; others started a few years ago; some others are just starting. The societies that started first are accustomed to change by now, but in some societies even the coming of piped water to the village is a major breakthrough. The *types* of change are also different; the more developed societies worry more about the action of a remote-controlled sensor on Mars than about the availability of piped water. The changes sought vary from one society to the next because needs are hierarchical in nature, and a society will welcome change that fulfils its particular basic needs. In the case of a less developed society this need may be piped water, but in a more developed society the need will be less basic.

There is no single index that can be used to measure either the amount or rate of change in the world. However, we do have *indicators*, items for which data are available, and which can be used to interpret change. Assignments 8-1, 8-2, and 8-4, which dealt specifically with Canada, involved some of the possible indicators: employment categories, rural-urban ratios, and GNP. In each case you used the statistics to show the degree and rate of change in a particular area, and then tried to relate these processes to other areas of change. Thus a fall in the rural percentage of the total population from 80.4 to

UNICEF / Sennett

In some societies the coming of piped water to the village is a major breakthrough. UNICEF is assisting ten Indian states to extend their piped water supply.

23.9 suggests more than just the degree to which the rural percentage of the total population has changed. The correlations of this fall indicate that the society has changed from an agriculture-forestry-mining base to an industry-service base and that it has become much richer in the process. In addition, by interpretation, the figures suggest that as a result of urban growth, literacy has increased and health care has improved. They suggest that in the demographic transition model the society has passed into phase 4; the statistics tell of rising living standards, improved economic efficiency, changing social structures, greater individual freedom, and the rise of democracy. Indicators may be used—with care—to make inferences in other areas.

It is possible to "read into" data a whole series of related items. First you must know the related items; the more you know the more, obviously, you can "read into" other statistics.

Good indicators correlate well, though not perfectly, with other possible indicators, and they permit fairly easy, though not perfect, interpretation. In assignment 8-3 we saw how well the rural component of total population correlated with the proportion of the labour force in primary activity for Canada. This was a dynamic correlation, because it was shown to exist over time as both data sets changed. The strength of this dynamic correlation permits us to assume that a significant correlation may also be established for a single moment of time. In other words, a rural percentage of say, 50, indicates that primary employment also falls into a certain range and that other associated variables show expected correlations. We can test this assumption by establishing the strength of the *worldwide* correlation between rural percentages and primary employment.

Statistical Interpretation

8-5 Using the data for rural percentages (column Y) and primary activity percentages (column Z_1), either calculate a correlation coefficient, using the grouped data technique described in Appendix 3,

OR

construct a scattergraph to illustrate the strength of the relationship.

---

5. Employment Patterns: A Useful Indicator of Change

Your answer to assignment 8-5 suggests that employment classification of the labour force is probably quite useful as an indicator. We will therefore use it.

Countries that have not yet undergone much change, and whose people live much as their ancestors did one hundred or one thousand years ago, are found to concentrate on *primary* activities, chiefly farming and fishing. If a high percentage of the population is employed in the primary sector then it is almost certain that the society's technology will be primitive and its way of life materially poor. A high percentage of people in primary activities indicates that people themselves must still do most of the work needed to grow food; machinery, chemical fertilizers, and other modern aids will be scarce, and yields will be low in relation to labour input. In such societies, hunger will be a common condition, and starvation frequent. Children will tend to have expectations about life that are no higher than their parents'; their view of the environment will be, in Rostow's sense, traditional. They will probably expect to live in the same community and perhaps even in the same house as their parents; they will expect to do the same work their parents do, marry within the community, and have the same expectations of their own children as their parents have of them. Change is so slow that it is hardly noticeable within the span of a single lifetime.

In a geographical sense, their actions and beliefs are largely *determined* by their environment.

"Change is so slow that it is hardly noticeable within the span of a single lifetime. . . . " This is a scene in Kabul, Afghanistan.

United Nations

By contrast, a high proportion of the labour force in the *secondary* category indicates a factory society that will be producing goods in large quantities. As a result, its material standard of living will rise fairly rapidly. The primary area becomes smaller as workers move to the growing secondary category. In Rostow's system, this provides the preconditions for take-off. Farming output per unit of labour input must be greatly improved so that there is surplus labour for the expanding urban-industrial sectors. As long as rural labour is moving to the towns, wages will nearly always be low because few rural workers have the industrial skills to command good wages. In addition, supply often exceeds demand, a situation that puts downward pressure on wage rates. Thus for factory owners, labour is cheaper than labour-saving equipment. For these reasons countries such as Taiwan, Hong Kong, and Korea can offer cheap labour to prospective industrialists. Under such conditions there will generally be more urban poverty than usual; a high proportion of labour input per unit of output almost guarantees low wages.

A large section of the labour force in the *tertiary* sector indicates a service-oriented society. The quantity of goods a society has depends upon the way it reached the tertiary phase. It is quite possible for a country to bypass the secondary phase, and enter the tertiary phase with wealth derived from a primary source. Such a country will have few, if any, factories. Examples of countries that have passed directly from the primary to the tertiary category include most OPEC members, and countries dependent on tourism. More usually, however, a country in the tertiary stage will have gone through the secondary phase of development. Its factories will be efficient, usually automated, and highly productive per unit of labour input; wages will be high. This largely service-oriented post-industrial society will have the characteristics of Rostow's age of high mass consumption.

There are many complaints about the "sweatshop" wages paid to workers in newly industrializing countries. What would be likely to happen if they were paid markedly higher wages?

Statistical Interpretation

8-6 In accordance with the concept of using labour force categories as an indicator of change, construct a map showing the degree of change achieved by different countries around the world. Use the data in columns Z_1 and Z_3 in the following manner: first, calculate the ratio of tertiary to primary; for example, Canada's ratio is 65.7:7.5, reducible to 8.76:1. Second, group the countries as indicated below, and draw a graded shading map showing them; third, make up a title.

ratios:	10.0 and over	very strong orange
	5.00-9.99	strong orange
	1.00-4.99	medium orange
	below 1.00	pale orange

a) Comment on the main aspects of the pattern.

b) Are there any unexpected plots? Can you explain these apparent anomalies?

c) Which country still has the greatest degree of change to come, assuming it follows the pattern?

d) Suggest some of the associated pressures of change likely to affect those areas of the world that still have the greatest changes to come, according to the pattern established so far.

8-7 The map in assignment 8-6 has the disadvantage that it does not take into account all three employment categories. To do this we need to use a triangular graph such as the one illustrated in Appendix 3. To avoid cluttering the graph, plot only the following countries:

Algeria	China	Greece
Angola	Czechoslovakia	Hungary
Australia	France	India
Brazil	West Germany	Israel
Canada	Ghana	Italy

Ivory Coast	Portugal
Jamaica	Sweden
Japan	UK
Mexico	USA
Poland	USSR

a) Can you identify any groupings in the plotted distribution?

b) Insert an arrow on the graph to indicate the main direction of change.

c) Can you explain any major anomalies?

Discussion and Research

7. What kinds of societies suffer the greatest stresses from change? What are the characteristics of these societies?

8. Many multinational companies are criticized because they pay low wages to labourers in less developed countries. What would happen if they paid significantly higher wages?

6. The Challenge of Change

In June 1973 the Chairman of the Canadian Imperial Bank of Commerce delivered an address at a University of Toronto Convocation. He spoke about the characteristics of change and the challenges presented by it. Excerpts from the address are given below.

The challenge of change

As one who has been caught in the buffets and pressures of change during the past half century, I have something of a fellow-feeling with you who are about to enter a similar world. At no time in history has the pace of change been so rapid; in transportation, communications, production and distribution of goods and services of all kinds and mobility of people. All of these changes have altered the nature of society and enhanced the material well-being of people in the developed countries on an unparalleled scale.

During the past quarter century, newly independent nations have gradually been emerging, also seeking higher standards of living. More recently, the conquest of space has impressed the world and provided still more amazing communication systems. For example, last week I dialed directly by telephone from Athens to Toronto and received an answer as quickly and clearly as in one's own city. This was by way of Tel-Star.

For the years to come, the harnessing of nuclear energy (following the creation of its companion source, the nuclear bomb) offers another source of energy, in addition to coal, hydro electric power, petroleum and natural gas, that will diminish still further the necessity for using human labour.

All this has taken place during a century which has seen the greatest slaughter of humanity the world has known. And, sadly, in the world today, at least one-third of the population live under authoritarian systems which deny intellectual and other freedoms to the majority of the people.

The rapidity of change in one lifetime has been, to many, bewildering and confusing. Younger people take for granted and are rather blasé about the striking scientific and technological advances the world has known. Others find adjustment to this new environment more difficult.

The world has been greatly compressed in many ways. We are all told by the press, radio and television what is going on all over the world but few of us are able to evaluate the information in terms of perspective and relevance.

Meanwhile, personal standards of behaviour and inter-personal relations have altered in many ways. The old rules of society are less respected now and give the outward appearance of change. Whether this is true in substance or mainly in appearance may be argued, but at any rate there is less hypocrisy today and more candour. For many people, the old terms of reference have gone but dependable new ones have yet to be determined and accepted.

It is to be expected that a society uprooted from its relatively placid past should resort, in disillusionment, to different ways of behaviour. And this reaction is not confined only to the younger generation. Morality in its broadest sense, ethics and principles, is under test.

Much of all this changing pattern of behaviour represents symptoms of a deeper problem, the struggle to find a sense of values in life more enduring and more satisfying than those that guided society in the past.

Complex Man

The nature of man has been the subject of thought and discussion by philosophers for centuries—mankind at once so creative and so destructive, so aggressive and so peace-loving, so self-seeking and so generous, with so many noble aspirations but also at times so base in behaviour. Because the nature of man is so complex, and varies so much between different societies at any given time, universal conclusions about the nature of man are not to be found. Perhaps the only common denominator in man's behaviour down through the ages has been the combination of continuous struggle, continuous restlessness, continuous dissatisfaction with his lot, whatever that lot may be. Probably the struggle, the restlessness and the dissatisfaction which have characterized societies from the beginning of recorded history will continue; perhaps if these characteristics should ever cease to prevail, mankind will gradually disappear from this earth.

Our Physical Resources

Now let us look briefly at our immediate physical surroundings. This globe has been a great storehouse of riches which lay beyond the control and use by mankind for many centuries. During the past two centuries, and particularly since the beginning of the twentieth century, there has been tremendous progress in bringing these resources into use for the material well-being of man. Standards of living have risen to undreamt of levels, particularly in the western world.

Now there are concerns that the human race with its rapidly increasing population may overtax the productivity of the globe, eventually bringing about a prolonged decline in living standards and an enforced shrinkage of population. Although these fears may underestimate the ingenuity of man in discovering or creating substitutes, they are valid fears and lend emphasis to the necessity for eliminating waste of all kinds. A major aspect of the problem is world population growth. Although progress in limitation of population growth may seem to be slow in many parts of the world, increasing recognition of the problem is gradually taking place and improving levels of education are having an increasing influence on the solution.

It is useful to recall just how and where the striking progress in harnessing the earth's resources for human benefit took place. It occurred mainly in the free nations of Europe and America and the driving force was the encouragement of men, by liberal incentives in free societies, to bend their energies to filling the needs and wants of the people.

As each need was filled, new wants were created, and perhaps the most important of these was the desire for steadily improving levels of education. The process of raising the levels of education, particularly in the sciences, led to more sophisticated ways of developing our natural resources and the discovery of new materials, both natural and synthetic. While the most vital source of energy for increasing production in primitive times was human labour, in contemporary times it is the intellectual resources of an educated people and a highly educated elite. New materials and new sources of energy are developed that diminish the requirements for manual labour, increase productivity and enhance still further the material well-being of the people.

Economics and Politics

It is also useful to remember the nature of the economic and political structure which unleashed all this human energy to such productive ends. Politically, it was in an ordered society in which peaceful years predominated over war-torn periods. Economically, it was a society which provided material incentives to maximize human ingenuity, inventiveness and effort. It was a society which recognized the need for individual freedom and the right to self-determination within reasonable limits. It was a society that expected its leaders in every aspect of its social structure, political, financial, industrial, educational and scientific, to follow high principles of integrity, dedication to duty and obligation to society at large. Such high standards were not always maintained but back-sliding was not tolerated for long. Abuses had to be eradicated, often by government intervention.

It was also a society that needed accumulations of capital because capital was essential in greatly increasing amounts to finance the harnessing of power potentials, transportation and communication systems of all kinds, manufacturing plants and distribution systems. Capital was also necessary to finance housing, schools, universities and the myriad of amenities which have become a part of contemporary life.

The capitalist system, as we know it in the free world, has become greatly modified to serve the common good of all people and not solely to provide benefits for the owners of capital. At the same time, there has been increased government intervention in our free enterprise system, to provide a broad base of social insurance; pensions, unemployment insurance and medical care for individuals, and also protection for the physical environment.

Within the economic and social structure of our society, centres of power and influence have altered. Labour unions have grown to tremendous power, objectives of governments have broadened in their attempts to achieve a managed economy. There has been a vast increase in the number of government employees and the volume of spending by all levels of government. Now expenditures by our three levels of government in Canada account for 24% of the Gross National Expenditure compared with 18% twenty years ago, and government transfer payments to individuals now account for 18% of personal income compared with 12% in 1952.

Over the years, of course, there have been striking increases in taxation. The exercise of imagination and ingenuity in creating taxes of all kinds has been truly remarkable; to mention only a few, excise and sales taxes concealed from the consumer, direct sales taxes clearly exposed to him and taxes on incomes and capital of individuals. And there has also come into being, a system of imposed partnership of government with business, under which the government takes about one-half of business profits in taxes but of course does not share in business losses. Taxes, however dressed up, ultimately all fall on the individual consumer.

Questions for the future

The economic system which has provided the affluence of today still functions. But it is showing strains and cracks. Will the system gradually erode and become a less productive system? If so, what will replace it? Knowing that prolonged experiments elsewhere with socialism and communism have not been successful in terms of greatly improved standards of living, we may well question whether a more efficient and effective system than the one we now have can be devised? If not, can this existing system be effectively maintained to serve the needs and wants of the people?

Let us consider the nature of government under our system. I think it was Sir Winston Churchill who said that contemporary democracy is the worst form of government except all those other forms that have been tried from time to time. But with full recognition of the large number of honest, sincere and dedicated people who serve the nation, does democracy now produce leaders who study deeply the means to serve the long-range interests of the people, or does it mainly produce followers of public opinion polls who promise the people what they seek for their immediate wants, perhaps to the detriment of their long-run needs? Has the drive for power in government become an end in itself instead of a means to serve worthier ends?

Let us also think about the universities. Can they be centres of wisdom and judgment to which the people may turn for guidance in improving the quality of life? Or should their role be mainly to instill knowledge? I suggest that if the universities succeed in training students to think clearly, logically, and objectively, to avoid dogmatism and preserve a healthy skepticism, and to tackle questions for which there are no pat or easy answers, they will have gone a long way in fulfilling their role in our society. If, as well, they instill within each student a desire for excellence in his or her individual approach to the problems of life and a deep sense of obligation to society, they will have discharged the major part of their responsibilities. From my experience here as a former governor, I am sure that these high objectives are being constantly pursued at this great university.

I have touched on a few of the problems you will face in taking up where the older generation, with its many accomplishments and many failures, is leaving off. On the happier side, there seems at the moment to be little likelihood of another major world war among the great powers. But there will be continuous international frictions with tensions that sometimes may be minimized but often will be exaggerated and always will be a test of composure.

In this unpredictable world, both domestically and internationally, if there is any certainty at all, it is that the pace of change will accelerate with all its pressures and stresses and anxieties. But it is a challenging and exciting world. It is a world in which you will have disappointments and failures at times but these are merely to steel you for the effort and accomplishments which each of you has within yourself to achieve. The opportunities are great; the challenge is greater.

Discussion and Research

9. What are the changes noted by the speaker?
10. What changes did he not mention?
11. Why should change be regarded as "bewildering and confusing"?
12. Can you suggest any values that have disappeared? Or others that have come in?
13. What changes have occurred since 1900? And in the last fifteen to twenty years?
14. What do old people think of the modern world?

Section B
The Third World

1. Diffusion

Think of progressive change as the abandonment of old ways and skills and the adoption of new ideas and techniques. New ideas and techniques do not arise everywhere in a spontaneous fashion. As we have noted, they originate in *hearths*, and spread out gradually. The means of diffusion are chiefly trade and travel. For centuries, many areas of the world remained isolated from trade and travel routes; they gained no benefits from the diffusion of ideas and techniques. As transportation and communication media developed in the hearths, however, the frontiers of trade and travel were pushed outward; Alexander the Great, the Romans, Marco Polo, and the Portuguese navigators are among the people who contributed to the diffusion of knowledge. Eventually, almost the whole world came to lie within the trade and travel range of the hearths. The accumulating impact of the hearths upon the formerly isolated areas of the world, an impact that was at first missionary and imperial in character, was spurred by World War II. The war took technology into areas that had never before been exposed to it; native people were curious and imitative. One of the strangest examples of this technological impact was the Cargo Cult incident of the South Pacific, where some local people found a crashed American supply plane and treated it as a gift from the gods. After World War II the numerous agencies of the UN, accompanied by several multinational companies, spread hearth values and techniques to many countries.

Within present-day China, people are increasingly being collected into closed compounds called *units*. What do you think this does for the diffusion of ideas? Who stands to gain from this arrangement? And who to lose? Which workers will be the freest?

There are still some areas where modern technology has not penetrated. Where are they? Why have they been left alone?

2. Change

The greatest impact of modern technology so far has been in population growth. The populations of areas newly exposed to change have increased strongly. Infant mortality has been dramatically reduced, life expectancy greatly increased, and the death rate significantly lowered. Generally, however, for a variety of cultural reasons, the birth rate remains high. In consequence there has been a population explosion.

Other changes have been slower to come, and slower still to be adopted. It is easier and cheaper to persuade someone who is sick to take medication than it is to persuade someone who is hungry to try new farming methods. A medical squad can travel the countryside giving inoculations much more easily than an agricultural squad can train people in new farming methods, and supply them with new seeds, fertilizers, and insecticides until they can buy their own. As a result, populations have often grown faster than food supplies have.

The hearths have tried to remedy this imbalance by producing new high yielding varieties (HYVs) of seeds, chiefly wheat and rice. This agricultural advance, nicknamed the *Green Revolution*, has met with some success, but it has also caused problems. To succeed, the new seeds require hearth technology such as reliable irrigation, chemical fertilizers, and insecticides. These are scarce in newly changing areas so only the wealthier farmers can afford to use them. The higher yields obtained by the farmers give them greater profits on the harvest, and often permit them to buy out the poorer farmers and put them off the land altogether. Fig. 8-4 shows the areas in India first selected for the introduction of HYVs. These were designated under the Intensive Agricultural District Program (IADP), and were selected

Farming experiments are not readily done because of the problem of future security; why alter techniques that you know will produce food, albeit barely enough? Many third world farmers feel that they cannot afford to take the chance.

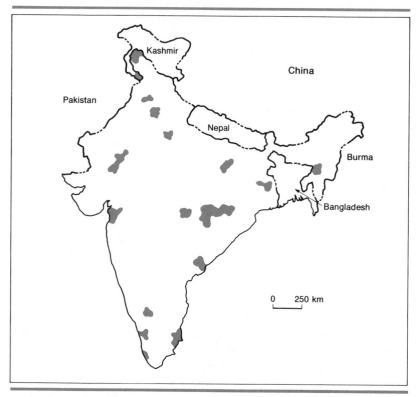

Fig. 8-4
Districts where HYVs were first introduced, 1965

Source: *Canadian Geographer*, No. 2, 1976, p. 199.

as the areas most suitable for rapidly increased agricultural production. Thus they acted as local hearths. HYVs were first introduced in the chosen districts in 1964-65. By 1966-67 their use had been diffused to 11 500 000 ha, or 2.2% of India's cropland; by 1972-73 the area had increased to 137 530 000 ha, or 28% of the cropland. Fig. 8-5 illustrates the 1972 situation, as the new methods spread. Clearly, not all hearths were equally efficient in diffusing the use of HYVs.

Urbanization is a further aspect of the chain of change. Dispossessed rural people migrate to the towns to find work, but there is often not enough. Urban slums, often called shanty towns, bustees, favelas, or barrios, have therefore come to characterize the major cities of the third world. Some third world countries have attracted enough industry to provide jobs for most urban dwellers; among the successful countries are Brazil, Taiwan, Korea, Singapore, Hong Kong, and Barbados. But on a world scale, jobs are extremely scarce.

Job creation, now one of the world's major tasks, is restricted by infrastructural weaknesses throughout much of the third world. Illiteracy is a major problem; so are deficiencies in road and rail construction, dock and airport building, telephone installation, power development, and banking and financial services.

Fig. 8-5
The extent of diffusion of HYVs of rice and wheat by 1972

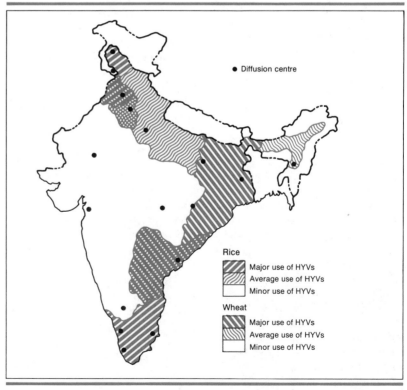

Source: *Canadian Geographer*, No. 2, 1976, p. 199.

Those countries that can afford the cost of *infrastructural development* are rapidly going ahead with it. Mostly these are countries, like the members of OPEC, that are rich in resources. Nigeria is a good example: its rapid rise of income from oil in 1973 and 1974 permitted a huge burst of spending in 1975 for roads, docks, airports, etc. Unfortunately, like all newly developing countries, it lacked the facilities to handle the material it ordered. Over five hundred cement-carrying ships were tied up outside Lagos waiting to unload, many remaining there for over a year. Other oil-rich countries face similar opportunities and problems, as the following article illustrates.

The United Arab Emirates—a maturity beyond its six years

Six years ago, on December 2, 1971, the United Arab Emirates was established as a single sovereign state. In that relatively short time vast and varied problems have been tackled and overcome. Each year has brought new achievements in industrial development, agriculture, housing, education and social services. The UAE has emerged as a progressive and confident state.

Partners for Progress

The Federal government embraces the seven emirates of Abu Dhabi, Dubai, Sharjah, Ajman Umm, al Quirain, Ras-al-Khaima and Fujairah. Success in political and economic unity, bringing together scattered and distant populations, is rare. It is testimony to the wisdom of those who inspired the concept of union that the UAE economic and social successes are evident throughout this unified country.

The leader of the country in its embryo years, Sheik Sultan bin Zaid al Nahyan, re-elected President in November 1976, was one of the chief architects of the moves toward federation that was to bring the United Arab Emirates into being.

Industry and Agriculture

The UAE's oil resources are being responsibly developed and diversified to ensure a strong alternative industrial base for the future. The first oil refinery in the United Arab Emirates was inaugurated on April 28, 1976. Situated on the Island of Umm al-Nar, the refinery can process 15 000 barrels per day. It is estimated that later development plans will increase dramatically so that production will cover the whole UAE market. Additionally, a second refinery is to be built near Jebel al Dhanna producing 120 000 barrels per day. But possibly more significant still is the policy of the UAE towards natural gas. New technologies will enable enormous natural gas reserves to be exploited from the four inland oil fields at Asab, Bu Hassa, Sahil and Bab, whose reserves are considered possibly the largest in the Middle East, second in the world only to those of the Soviet Union.

Other industrial projects include an aluminium plant in Dubai, and cement factories in Ras-al-Khaima, Al-Ain and Dubai, while factories under construction include a tile and marble factory, brick factory and industrial pipe factories. Moreover, the industrial zone city at Jebel Ali will include a steel plant, an aluminium smelter, oil refinery and liquefied petroleum gas plant. And, to meet the country's need for water and irrigation projects, in June of last year the UAE's first plastic pipes factory was completed in Masfah, 20 kilometres south of Abu Dhabi city. Over the next five years the United Arab Emirates will be investing $1 000 million for the development of petro-chemical industries.

It is the UAE's government policy to make the country as self-sufficient as possible, therefore the development of agriculture is encouraged at all levels. The combination of modern technology and determination now seem likely to turn the dream of making the desert bloom into a reality. The planting of trees has already helped to reduce soil erosion and provide a barrier from the desert winds and sand storms which destroy valuable crops. Of the 50 635 acres of land in the UAE considered suitable for agricultural development more than half—28 000 acres—has already been reclaimed. The most widespread and successful system of irrigation being used in the UAE is the ingenious "trickle irrigation system". This system controls the amount of water fed to each tree and overcomes the problems of evaporation and salt concentration experienced with conventional methods. The agricultural trials station at Digdagga leads the field in intensive agrarian research and provides one of the most advanced study units in the UAE. A total of almost 400 acres [160 ha] of land is under intensive experimental cultivation.

The complex also includes an agricultural school which acts as a training centre for students from all over the Arab world as well as from within the UAE. Crops produced at Digdagga range from luxury strawberries to the simple radish.

Cattle and other meat producing farms are also being established as consumer demand continues to rise. The poultry farm at Umm al Quwain is one such example.

With the Arabian Gulf rich also as a source of food, the fishing industry is being rapidly developed. Government financial contribution to port facilities and fish market construction and the purchase of large modern fishing vessels has resulted in a sixfold increase in catch size in 10 years.

Overseas Aid – A World Leader

The United Arab Emirates has created new dimensions in economic aid with upwards of 30 per cent of the country's GNP being channelled into projects spanning not only Arab countries, but countries in Africa and Asia.

The important administration for these funds is the Abu Dhabi Fund for Arab Economic Development (ADFAED) established in 1971. After six years its scope is dramatically broadened and countries as diverse as India, Bangladesh, Sri Lanka, Mali, Somalia and Egypt are among those now receiving development aid.

Central to this aid programme is the belief that development of the Third World should embrace cooperation with the industrial nations. Technology and equipment from the West, coupled with the monetary resources of the oil-producing states, is seen as benefiting not only the developing nations but also helping to boost export trade revenues for the industrialised world.

As a director of ADFAED, Dr Hassan Abbas Zaki, puts it: "We are not interested in a simple transfer of money, but in the real transfer of technology and natural resources".

Among those major projects towards which ADFAED contributed during 1976 are a power and water station in Bahrain, a hydro power station in India, a business centre and two cotton mills in Morocco, a dam construction in Mali and a machine tools factory in Bangladesh.

The UAE can be expected to continue its new role as a major aid donor. As the late Minister of State for Foreign Affairs Mr Saif bin Ghobash said in an address to the UN General Assembly: "We will continue in future to provide aid to our brethren with all the limited means available to us as a developing country".

Tourism

To encourage visitors from all parts of the world, the United Arab Emirates has constructed first-class hotels in Abu Dhabi, Dubai, Sharjah and Ras-al-Khaima (the latter with its own casino).

There are also museums and many places of historical interest to be seen, particularly those at Al-Ain and Fujairah, and the old fort in Dubai. Furthermore, a new airport is to be built six kilometres from Abu Dhabi town on the road to Al-Ain, due for completion in 1979.

Present-day industrial development and the rapid changes in life-style make the UAE exciting enough, but the country's archaeological heritage and historic past combine with the modern bustle to present an intriguing balance of interests for the visitor.

After six years of uninterrupted progress through partnership the UAE is able not only to look back on past achievements but to prepare with confidence for the challenges of the future.

THE UNITED ARAB EMIRATES – PARTNERS FOR PROGRESS

Courtesy of the United Arab Emirates

3. No Change

While the OPEC members raise their own standards of living quite dramatically, and in most cases help their neighbours too, the rest of the third world changes very little. Standards of living, as shown by food supplies (columns I, J, and K), proportion of people still in agriculture (column L), extent of industrialization (column Q), general material wealth (column U), literacy (column W), and energy consumption (column X), remain relatively low. Changes have yet to come in these fields. Life continues to be hard and survival is usually the most urgent concern. Cultural values tend to reflect the poverty of life; slavery exists, women continue to be oppressed, executions may be held in public; the state is paternalistic, and democracy does not flourish.

It is difficult to know just how much these cultural values, which are rejected by the first world, are *caused by* lack of development and how much they help to *cause* it. For example, is it poverty that causes women to be oppressed, or does the oppression contribute to the traditional poverty? What is your opinion?

Discussion and Research

15. Where does the allegiance of the UAE lie?
16. What is the quality in the Islamic religion that promotes the concept of aid? How does this compare with Christianity? Is aid given for other reasons?
17. What are the infrastructural developments sought by the UAE? Are these the ones you would rate as high priority items? Is anything omitted?

In many parts of the world, literacy is still not widespread. Here is a public letter writer in Morocco. His job is to fill out forms and write letters for people who cannot do so themselves.

UNESCO/Dominique Roger

Section C
The More Developed World

1. Hearths

The more developed countries support the world's major industrial hearths. It is in these regions that ideas and techniques originate, to be diffused to other areas later. The developed world has gone through the changes that the third world countries are just now experiencing, or still awaiting. The changes that are now taking place in the third world are almost ancient history to the more developed world: the population explosion is past; industrialization is almost completed; urbanization has now even begun to reverse itself slightly.

This is not to say that the third world countries will *necessarily* experience the same sorts of changes that have already occurred in the first and second worlds. They *may*, if past experience is any guide; but the changes may also be different.

None of this means that change has ceased in the more developed world. Populations continue to evolve, but no longer explosively, farming is increasingly productive, food supplies are becoming more varied, and industry continues to develop. However, there are now other major areas of change.

2. Major Areas Of Change

a) Information and Technology

Technology is becoming concerned more with the processing and transmission of information than with the production of goods. Computers and satellites are examples of information-processing technology. Improvements in transportation systems, particularly in sea and air modes, have increased communications. As a result of these improved intercontinental transportation systems, the world has become a smaller place, a "global village". Work is also progressing on road and rail transportation: electric cars, magnetic suspension for railways, turbine-powered motors, and linear induction motors.

People in developed countries have had access to most parts of the globe for a long time; improvements in transportation and communication systems have therefore increased this accessibility and made the world a smaller place for them. On the other hand, such improvements have made the world a larger place for persons in the undeveloped world, because for the first time these people have access to areas beyond their towns and villages. This is one of the ironies of differential change.

Statistical Interpretation

8-8 The world has become smaller as a result of shortened travel times. About 400 years ago it took 40 days to cross the Atlantic from New York to London; about 75 years ago it took 10 days; 40 years ago 6 days; 25 years ago 10 hours; 10 years ago 7 hours; now it takes 3 hours. Draw a series of straight lines to a time scale, with hours and days along the horizontal axis and past time in years along the vertical axis, to illustrate the above information. Is there a period of time when progress seemed to lag?

Experiments are taking place in the transmission of messages by laser beams. This beam could carry 100 000 000 messages.

Bell Telephone Laboratories

b) Trade and Travel

The areas of trade and travel are also experiencing change. Both are growing fast, partly because nations seek to broaden their consumption and experience patterns, and partly because the international movement of people and goods is made easier by improved transportation systems. Travel is also increasing because production is becoming more and more automated, giving people more leisure time. For this reason the number of recreational activities is growing, too. As technology advances and their horizons broaden, most people in the developed world expect more. The more products and opportunities people have, the more they want. Some individuals are critical of the economic growth made necessary by this "tide of rising expectations", but there is little doubt that the majority of the people want more than they already have. In the developed world they expect to obtain it.

3. Environmental Modification

The Snowy River Scheme transfers water from the rainy eastern side of the Snowy Mountains in Australia to the drier Murray Basin in the interior. The Dutch Delta Plan controls sea and river flooding in the Rhine Delta, and is part of continuing Dutch efforts to reclaim land from the North Sea.

Earthquake prediction may be done successfully, but not every time. In 1975 the Chinese evacuated a million people from Haicheng before the earthquake struck, but they failed to predict the 1976 Peking earthquake. In the United States, earthquake prediction is officially forbidden, because of the risk of lawsuits if the warnings should prove false.

Most people believe that society can accomplish what it wants given sufficient mobilization of resources. Thus they believe that the physical environment can be modified to a considerable degree. Some passive aspects of the physical environment have long been changed to suit society's wishes; witness the Dutch Delta Plan, the James Bay Project, the California Water Plan, the Snowy River Scheme, and many others. Now researchers are trying to find ways of controlling the more violent manifestations of the environment too. Thus earthquake prediction by means of measurements of radon gas in groundwater, the timing of P and S waves, the dilation of surface rocks, and the behaviour of animals has become an experimentally successful activity. Reliable earthquake *control* is some distance away yet, although successful experiments have been carried out in Nevada. Researchers at the US earthquake centre at Menlo Park in California hope that some control can be exerted by pumping water into a locked pressure fault, thus permitting controlled slippage rather than allowing the build-up of catastrophic pressure.

Similarly, hurricane prediction and necessary safety adjustments are now quite common; meanwhile work continues on methods of preventing or controlling hurricanes. Floods also create the need for warning and safety programs, and on all major rivers there are extensive control systems. However, disaster can still strike whenever normally small streams flood, as did the Thompson River in Colorado, August 1976, when eighty people were killed. There are many other examples of environmental control by the more developed world; rain may be made by cloud seeding, fogs dispersed with smoke pots and chemical precipitation, frosts avoided with fans and heating systems, droughts resisted by planned sprinkler irrigation, and avalanches controlled by gunfire.

One of the few major environmental worries left is the possible cooling of the world's climate. While present evidence is contradictory and inconclusive, some people nevertheless worry that the climate is going to become much cooler. The following items discuss this issue.

Major change in climate predicted

CIA sees risk of international conflict
WASHINGTON (Reuter)—Major changes in climate will bring about global unrest of a proportion almost beyond comprehension, heightening the risk of international conflict, according to a Central Intelligence Agency report released yesterday.

The report said world climate changes would sharply reduce crop production and spread drought, famine and political unrest throughout the world.

The adverse weather is likely to last for at least 40 years and possibly for centuries, the report said.

The report was based on a working paper prepared by the CIA's Office of Research and Development from a study by Reid Bryson of the University of Wisconsin, an expert on climatology.

The report said the change in climate began in 1960 but no one recognized it.

It said the crop failures in the Soviet Union and India during the first part of the 1960s were attributed to the natural fluctuation of the weather, but were actually the result of the change in climate.

The report said the adverse climate, according to the University of Wisconsin study, would mean that India will suffer a major drought every four years, resulting in the starvation of 150 million people.

Crop failures predicted
China will suffer a major famine every five years and the Soviet Union will lose its wheat fields in Kazakhstan, the report said.

The Soviet Union will thus show a yearly loss of 48 million metric tons of grain and China will require a supply of 50 million metric tons of grain to feed its population.

Canada, a major exporter, would lose more than 54 per cent in production capability and 75 per cent of its exporting capabilities.

Northern Europe would lose 25 to 30 per cent of its present production capability while exports from countries of the European Economic Community would be cut to nothing, the report added.

Warning that a major shift in the earth's climate already is under way, the report said: "The economic and political impact of a major climatic shift is almost beyond comprehension.

"Any nation with scientific knowledge of the atmospheric sciences will challenge this natural climatic change. The potential for international conflict due to controlled climate modification can be a reality in the 1970s."

The report was prepared in August, 1974. The CIA said its views and conclusions did not necessarily represent the agency's official position.

A copy of the report containing some deletions was released by Representative Fred Richmond (D, N.Y.).

Mr. Richmond also released segments of another CIA report prepared in August, 1974, which said grave food shortages would tempt powerful but hungry countries to obtain grain by any means they could.

Massive migrations from one country to another, sometimes backed by force, would be possible and political and economic instability would be widespread as a result, the report said.

Global cooling trend
The report said the changes in climate had been caused by a global cooling trend similar to one that brought about the downfall of a number of ancient civilizations.

Changes in high-altitude wind patterns kept high-pressure zones further south "blocking the monsoons out of regions where they are vital to the survival of hundreds of millions of people," the report said.

It added that other wind changes had affected the rainfall patterns in temperate regions and made the climate more variable.

The Globe and Mail 1976 5 4

Baffin Island research

Recent research in Baffin Island indicates that the earth was in the threshold to a glacial period between 1600 and 1900. Around 1900 the climate began to get warmer, but since about 1945 it has been getting slightly colder once more. Around 1960 it also began to snow more in winter in the Arctic. The evidence of ice behaviour on Baffin Island is apparently contradictory: small ice masses have expanded in the last 10-15 years, but large ones have continued to diminish. Researchers assume that this anomaly is caused by the more immediate reaction of small ice masses to minor fluctuations, whereas large ice masses react to long term trends only. Thus the question, are we now in a minor cooling fluctuation or the start of a long term cooling trend? Based on reports in the *Canadian Geographical Journal* 1976

Case Stu
Brazil:
Change

Many Brazilians
land of tomorro
always be a lar
The poten
problems. Br
bauxite, tin,
and a weak
There a
northeast,
pioneer la
are the re
one milli
relations
ight

p
pr
for
feeble
tries, a

Mar
future sho
danger of
government
systems perm

ch
mputer

these questions, ...y praise ... ...es such as Charlie
Chaplin's *Modern Times* and George Orwell's *1984*, and seek comfort
from E. F. Schumacher's *Small is Beautiful*. Other people see few
risks. As always, they expect to retain their freedom and their rights,
although knowing that they must pay the price of "eternal vigilance".

Discussion and Research

21. Where are the processes of change taking us?
22. Discuss the proposition that change is inevitable.

Development and

claim they are the people of the future, inhabiting the
w; but there are sceptics among them who say that it will
d of tomorrow.

ial for development is undoubtedly great, but so are the
zil has some of the world's largest supplies of iron ore,
manganese, and hydro power, but it also has mass illiteracy
national infrastructure.

e, in fact, three separate Brazils. One is the old and decaying
nother is the modern and dynamic south, and the third is the
d of Amazonia (see Fig. 8C-1). The differences in the regions
sult of Brazil's previous development. Initially there were about
on people of Amerindian descent in the area, living in a close
ip with their environment. The arrival of the Portuguese in 1500
brou changes.

At first (1500-1550) the Portuguese relied on simple trade with the
Indians of the interior, bartering axes and other objects for brazilwood
which they used for dye. There were no permanent settlements. Around
1500 sugarcane was introduced along the moist tropical coast from Rio
Grande do Norte to Bahia. African slaves were brought in to provide the
necessary labour. The sugar planters—the *coronels*—grew rich by selling
sugarcane to Portugal. These people, with their grand houses and numerous servants, more or less ran Brazil. But most of their money accumulated merely as private wealth; little was spent on development. Vast
estates, called *latifundia*, were created to provide employment and food
for the bulk of the population. These estates also created rental income
for the owners, or *latifundistas*, who were already earning money from the
sugar they planted. Society in the northeast became extremely hierarchical, with a small rich elite group at the top of the scale, followed by a
large tenant peasantry, and with a mass of slaves at the bottom.

The northeastern sugar plantations continued to dominate the economy, even when gold and diamonds were discovered in Minas Gerais
around 1700. In fact, sugar remained the dominant commodity until the
nineteenth century, when coffee began to gain importance. (see Fig. 8C-2).

Fig. 8C-1
The three Brazils

Source: *Quarterly Journal of Economics* 1972 5, p. 246.

Fig. 8C-2
Percentage share of sugar and coffee in Brazil's total exports, by value

	1821	1871	1912
Sugar	23.1	12.3	0.3
Coffee	18.7	50.2	60.4

Coffee fortunes were made by *fazendeiros* in the plantations of Sao Paulo and Parana, but unlike the fortunes of the northeastern sugar families, this wealth was put into industrial investment. Sao Paulo City became the hub of this development. Thus, over one hundred years ago, the south of Brazil began a separate development, and a southward migration of people began.

Over the years, Sao Paulo City has become one of the fastest-growing cities in the world, receiving about 1 000 rural migrants *every day*. Its population is now about 10 000 000, and its municipal facilities are overloaded. *Favelas*, or shanty towns, fringe the built-up areas, both public and private transportation is difficult because of crowding, sewerage and water facilities serve only half the homes, and infant mortality has started to rise (84/1 000 in 1974 compared with 63/1 000 in 1961).

Sao Paulo, the country's primate (highest order) city, is the goal of all upwardly mobile migrants, as well as the diffusion centre for all downwardly mobile industries. Thus its problems exist on a larger scale than elsewhere. However all cities in Brazil have the same problems, even Brasilia in the interior and Recife in the northeast.

Two views of Sao Paulo, Brazil's largest city.

Embassy of Brazil, Ottawa

In the northeast, Recife acts as the first urban stop for the constant flow of rural migrants in the area. Apart from the faded gentility of the still-existing sugar plantations, the area is desperately poor; the people often call each other *flagelados*—beaten ones. In the interior, called the *sertao*, drought often triggers migration, but rural poverty is the root cause. At one time, buses from Sao Paulo drove up to collect loads of workers for southern factories, but this service is now unnecessary because the flagelados make their own way south. In an attempt to remedy some of the worst aspects of northeastern poverty the government has set up the Superintendency for the Development of the North East (SUDENE), which is active in setting up local industry. This is not enough; people still drift south.

Because of the population pressures building up in the eastern parts of the country (in the northeast as a result of impoverished peasant farming, and in the south because of urban overcrowding) the government has made determined efforts to persuade people to move to the interior. The interior offers the last refuge for the native Indians, but it is the last frontier for the new Brazilians. It is mostly tropical swamp and rain forest, with a variety of environmental characteristics that the eastern people see as hostile. This has not stopped them from moving in when the chance to make money has presented itself, as during the Amazon rubber boom of 1880 to 1912. The invention of bicycles and cars had led to a huge demand for rubber, which grew only in the Amazon region. Indians were hunted and trapped for slave labour; many tribes were all but wiped out. During this period fortunes were made, and an opera house flourished at Manaus. The market collapsed after an Englishmen smuggled rubber plants out of the country and got them into plantations in Malaya.

The government wants the interior opened up again. To this end it moved the capital from Rio de Janeiro to Brasilia in 1960. Brasilia, despite the evidence of its satellite favelas, has not proved very popular. It is a city of wide avenues and open spaces, lacking the *movimento* of normal Brazilian city life.

In addition the government arranged the construction of the Trans-Amazon Highway, from which run a number of tributary highways. Roadside farms are available to people from the east, especially from the sertao—the northeast interior. But people do not adjust easily from a crowded drought-prone environment to an isolated humid one. As some people say about Amazonia, in summer it rains every day, but in winter it rains all day. The Superintendency for the Development of Amazonia (SUDAM) is disappointed with the number of migrants to the area—only about one million to date. To add to the problems, some of the Amazon land has been taken up by Sao Paulo cattle breeders, who have been known to dispossess peasants who have come from the northeast.

There are also cultural clashes between the Brazilians and the Indians. The former Indian Protection Service (before 1967) was not a great success, and the new service, the National Indian Foundation (FUNAI) is little better. For example, the impressive reserves that were promised to the natives have not materialized, and slow acculturation of the Indians has been abandoned as a policy. As the Minister of the Interior said in 1974, "We are going to create a policy of integrating the Indian population into Brazilian society as rapidly as possible. We think that the ideals of preserving the Indian population within its own habitat are very beautiful ideas, but unrealistic."

Brazil is plagued by the problems of all phases of development. It has its pioneer frontier, its clash of cultures; it has its old colonial heritage, its hierarchical society, its land-hungry peasants; it has its burgeoning industries and cities that nevertheless cannot cope with the rural flood.

Brazil also has additional problems. Not only is its regional development lopsided, but it also has inequitable personal rewards. One of the recent presidents once commented that "Brazil has gained but not Brazilians." Generally the few rich have become even richer, while the many poor workers have become poorer. Top Brazilian business executives, who are regarded by the government as the generators of development, may earn anything over $100 000 a year; a middle manager may earn $30 000 – $40 000, and a white collar office worker $10 000. An assembly line worker in one of the car factories may receive $4 000, an unskilled worker perhaps $2 000, and a maid possibly $750. The situation does not appear to be improving for those at the bottom of the wage scale, as Fig. 8C-3 shows.

Fig. 8C-3
Income distribution curves, showing a more unequal distribution in 1970 than in 1960

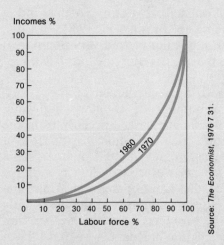

It should be noted that only 30% of Brazil's potential labour force earns any money at all; the remaining people—the marginals—try to scrape a living as best they can. If they beg or steal, it is for food; some say that they do not know what money is for. These are the millions who scrape a subsistence living off the soil, or eke out an existence in or near the forests, or live on the edge of survival in the *favelas* and *mocambos* of the big cities.

Previous governments tried to spread the rewards more equitably throughout society. In the 1930s President Vargas took power away from the *coronels* and *fazendeiros*, and permitted more money to filter down to the workers. In order to do this he strengthened the central government and the federal army. Later, after gross mismanagement in the 1950s and 1960s by popular presidents, the army took control of Brazil. Running the country as a ruthless military dictatorship, the army brought stability and economic growth to Brazil. They saw the benefits of foreign technology, and accordingly opened Brazil to foreign investment. American, German, Japanese, and Canadian investment poured in; Brazil started to grow as an industrial power.

Under the military dictatorship, the people are not free to dissent. The government first broke the strength of the labour unions, and crushed revolt by the intelligentsia. The National Information Service (SNI) now keeps a watchful eye on security matters. Only left-wing churchmen are free to disagree; among them is Dom Helder Camara of Recife, whose name is forbidden mention in Brazilian newspapers, and who argues for global revolution. Most Brazilians do not listen. They appear to prefer the real prospects of economic growth offered by the military, backed by a proved yearly 10 – 11% growth rate over the last few years. They hope the rewards will eventually filter down, and so do not risk changing the promising economic situation.

A high economic growth rate is necessary for Brazil because of its high rate of population increase, 2.8% a year. Brazil has no official population policy, so nature takes its course—one of rapid growth (see Fig. 8C-4).

Fig. 8C-4
Brazil's population growth

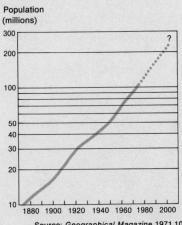

Source: *Geographical Magazine* 1971 10.

Recently, however, *birth* rates have been falling (43.4/1 000 in 1960; 37.8/1 000 in 1975) and it looks as though demographic phase 3 has come into existence. Even so, projections show a population of over 200 000 000 by 2000. Both the military and the church oppose birth control, but for different reasons: the military would like to see a more powerful Brazil, with a well-populated interior; the church would like to see more Brazilians born freely. Neither the military nor the church believes that a high rate of population increase inhibits growth or wealth distribution; they point to the fact that existing breakneck growth makes only a slight impact on the marginals, and that there is therefore no need to worry about an additional 2.8% a year.

Both the people and the military take pride in the country's accomplishments, even though it has a long way yet to go. As a government official said, "the statistics of human poverty in Brazil are appalling. But other developing countries don't even have statistics." Or, as most people said after Brazil had won the World Cup of soccer in 1970, "*ninguem segura esse pais*"—"no one can hold back this country".

CHANGE: Further Reading

Future Shock, TOFFLER
Z for Zachariah, O'BRIEN
Memoirs of a Survivor, LESSING
The Intruders, GARNER
The Next 200 Years, KAHN
Shogun, CLAVELL
The Cooling, PONTE
Utopia or Oblivion, FULLER
The Future of Canadian Cities, RICHARDSON
Thirty Acres, RINGUET
Where Late the Sweet Birds Sang, WILHELM
Five Ideas that Changed the World, WARD
The Coming of Post-Industrial Society, BELL
Profiles of the Future, CLARKE
A Study of Future Worlds, FALK
Mankind 2000, JUNGK & GALTUNG
Things to Come, KAHN & BRUCE-BRIGGS
Grow or Die, LOCKLAND
World Facts and Trends, McHALE
The Next 10 000 Years, BERRY
Ragtime, DOCTOROW
1984, ORWELL

Conclusion

In this chapter we have attempted to put the various changes that take place in this world into focus. We now have a general knowledge of change, and some understanding of the changes occurring in the developed and less developed worlds. The case study has provided a sample of the range of problems and characteristics associated with change; Brazil's population growth, industrialization, regional variations, contrasts of cultures, migrations, and urbanization are typical of the experiences of much of the world. Brazil's future is therefore of great interest to other nations.

This entire book has in fact been about change; throughout the text we have looked at the forces of change at work in several major fields of concern. We have examined the factors involved in the world's great population growth, and we have developed, through the demographic transition model, some awareness of the dynamic aspects of the issue. All the other issues discussed are also dynamic. Food production and consumption, industrialization, energy production and consumption patterns, quality of life, migration patterns, and geopolitics are all in a constant state of change. As these aspects change, they bring about modifications in other areas.

We should also note that these components of life and livelihood have developed at different speeds in various parts of the world, so that some countries have experienced great change while others have experienced little. As a result, the world is enormously varied. Can we reasonably expect that cultural and economic differences will remain, or will they diminish? Is it likely that the numerous countries of the world will eventually develop into a more or less homogeneous group with similar social characteristics and standards of living? Or will differences continue to exist? Will the differences be regarded as culturally enriching, or will they produce hostility and war?

These questions, while easy to raise, are difficult to answer. In 1977 10 the World Bank released information that suggested that *One World*, on the economic level, was an unattainable ideal. Figures indicated that even if the third world countries double their annual growth rates, while already industrialized countries remain unchanged, only eight will be able to close the gap within the next hundred years, and only another sixteen within the next thousand years. The President of the World Bank stated that policies to close the gap were unrealistic and that the World Bank should plan instead to "narrow the gap", not in monetary terms, but in terms of quality of life, nutrition, literacy, life expectancy, and so on.

Thus it appears that the world's countries will always differ in many basic respects, and the resulting problems and advantages will demand our greatest attention. There is no doubt that we should occupy ourselves with the world we live in; its development to its present condition and its prospects are probably our most vital concern.

The earth as seen from the moon.
What are our planet's prospects?

Appendix 1
Sample World Map

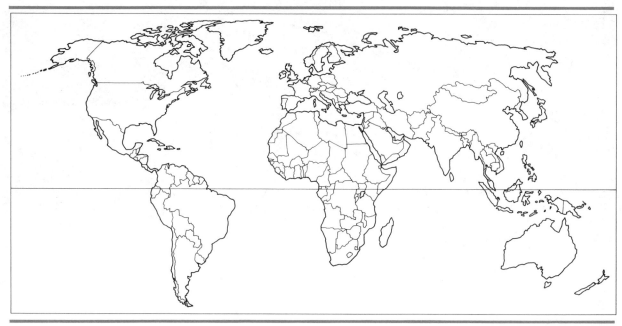

Modified Robinson Projection

Appendix 2
Statistical Data

COLUMN HEADINGS

A   Population

B   Area, km²

C   Population density, people/km²

D   Birth rate, births/1 000 people/yr

E   Death rate, deaths/1 000 people/yr

F   Natural increase rate, birth rate minus death rate

G   Life expectancy, yr

H   Annual rate of natural increase, % of total population

I   Average daily food intake, kJ

J   Average daily food intake, g

K   Average daily intake of proteins, g

L   Agricultural population, % of total population

M   Value of international reserves, $ millions

N   Average daily food requirements, kJ

O   Average daily food intake, kJ (I) as a percentage of average daily food requirements, kJ (N)

P   Electricity production, kW·h/person

Q   Value of manufacturing output, $/person

R   Food production, 1974 index numbers (1961 = 100)

S   Population growth, 1974 index numbers (1961 = 100)

T   Per capita food production, 1974 index numbers (1961 = 100)

U   GNP, $/person

V   Urban population, % of total population

W   Literacy rate, % of total population

X   Energy consumption, kg/person

Y   Rural population, % of total population

Z_1   Primary activity, % of the labour force

Z_2   Secondary activity, % of the labour force

Z_3   Tertiary activity, % of the labour force

Note: 1) All data from UN sources (*UN Statistical Yearbook*, 1971-75; *UNESCO Statistical Yearbook*, 1974; *FAO Production Yearbook*, 1974; and *UN Demographic Yearbook*, 1974).

2) na = not available

COUNTRY	A	B	C	D	E	F	G	H	I	J	K
Afghanistan	19 280 000	647 497	29.8	50.5	26.5	24.0	37.5	2.4	8 274	842	58
Albania	2 480 000	28 748	86.2	33.3	8.1	25.2	66.0	2.5	10 038	1 085	74
* Algeria	16 780 000	2 381 741 √	7.0	49.1	16.9	32.2	50.7	3.2	7 266	806	46
Angola	5 800 000	1 246 700 √	4.7	50.1	30.2	19.9	33.5	2.0	8 400	1 324	42
Argentina	25 380 000	2 766 700 √	9.1	22.9	9.4	13.5	67.4	1.4	12 852	1 892	100
Australia	13 510 000	7 686 848 √	1.8	18.9	8.4	10.5	70.9	1.1	13 766	2 017	108
Austria	7 520 000	83 849	89.7	12.8	12.5	0.3	71.1	—	13 902	1 898	90
Bangladesh	76 820 000	143 998	533.5	na	na	na	na	na	7 728	na	40
Belgium	9 790 000	30 513	320.8	12.6	11.9	0.7	71.0	0.1	14 196	2 031	95
Belize	140 000	22 965	6.1	39.0	5.3	33.7	47.0	3.4	na	na	na
Benin (Dahomey)	3 110 000	112 622	27.6	50.9	25.5	25.4	38.5	2.5	9 492	1 254	56
Bolivia	5 630 000	1 098 581	5.1	44.0	19.1	24.9	49.7	2.5	7 980	1 104	46
Botswana	690 000	600 372	1.1	44.2	22.6	21.6	41.0	2.2	8 568	na	65
* Brazil	107 140 000	8 511 965 √	12.6	37.8	9.5	28.3	59.4	2.8	11 004	1 523	65
Bulgaria	8 720 000	110 912	78.6	17.2	9.8	7.4	71.3	0.7	13 818	1 475	100
Burma	31 240 000	676 552	46.2	40.3	17.4	22.9	47.5	2.3	9 282	790	50
Burundi	3 760 000	27 834	135.1	48.1	25.2	22.9	36.8	2.3	8 568	na	62
Cameroon	6 230 000	475 442	13.1	43.1	22.8	20.3	41.0	2.0	10 122	na	64
* Canada	22 830 000	9 976 139 √	2.3	15.5	7.4	8.1	72.9	0.8	13 356	1 969	101
Central African Republic	2 610 000	622 984	4.2	46.1	25.1	21.0	34.5	2.1	9 240	na	49
Chad	4 030 000	1 284 000 √	3.1	47.7	25.0	22.7	32.0	2.3	8 862	na	75
Chile	10 250 000	756 945	13.5	27.6	8.5	19.1	63.2	1.9	11 214	1 425	77
China	831 300 000	9 596 961 √	86.6	33.1	15.3	17.8	50.0	1.8	9 114	927	60
* Colombia	24 270 000	1 138 914 √	21.7	44.6	10.6	34.0	45.1	3.4	9 240	1 307	51
Congo	1 350 000	342 000	3.9	44.4	22.8	21.6	41.0	2.2	9 492	1 944	44
Costa Rica	1 970 000	50 700	38.9	28.3	5.1	23.2	63.4	2.3	10 962	1 272	66
Cuba	9 090 000	114 524	79.4	25.4	5.8	19.6	66.8	2.0	11 340	1 237	63
Cyprus	640 000	9 251	69.2	23.3	7.8	15.5	66.2	1.6	11 214	1 429	6
* Czechoslovakia	14 800 000	127 869	115.7	19.8	11.7	8.1	70.2	0.8	13 356	1 734	94
Denmark	5 060 000	43 069	117.5	14.2	10.2	4.0	73.4	0.4	13 608	1 940	93
Dominican Republic	4 700 000	48 734	96.4	48.5	14.7	33.8	57.9	3.4	8 904	1 374	48
* Ecuador	6 730 000	283 561	23.7	44.9	11.4	33.5	52.4	3.4	8 442	1 354	47
* Egypt	37 230 000	1 001 449 √	37.2	35.4	12.9	22.5	52.7	2.3	10 500	1 341	69
El Salvador	4 010 000	21 393	187.4	40.3	8.3	32.0	58.5	3.2	8 106	881	52
Equatorial Guinea	310 000	28 051	11.1	35.0	22.1	12.9	41.0	1.3	na	na	na
Ethiopia	27 950 000	1 221 900 √	22.9	45.6	25.0	20.6	38.5	2.1	9 072	739	72
Fiji	580 000	18 272	31.7	28.2	5.0	23.2	68.1	2.3	na	na	na
Finland	4 710 000	337 009	14.0	13.3	9.6	3.7	70.0	0.4	12 810	1 872	93
* France	52 910 000	547 026	96.7	15.2	10.4	4.8	71.5	0.5	13 482	2 206	105
French Guiana	60 000	91 000	0.7	28.3	7.7	20.6	na	2.1	na	na	na
Gabon	530 000	267 667	2.0	32.5	25.0	7.5	35.0	0.8	9 324	2 254	57
Gambia	520 000	11 295	46.0	42.5	23.1	19.4	41.0	1.9	10 458	768	64
* Germany, East	16 850 000	108 178	55.8	10.4	13.3	−2.9	71.5	−0.3	13 818	1 711	87
Germany, West	61 830 000	248 577	248.7	10.1	11.7	−1.6	70.5	−0.2	13 524	2 033	89
* Ghana	9 870 000	238 537	41.4	46.6	17.8	28.8	46.0	2.9	9 744	1 475	49
* Greece	9 050 000	131 944	68.6	16.1	8.5	7.6	72.4	0.8	13 398	2 041	113
Greenland	50 000	2 175 600 √	0.02	19.6	5.8	13.8	62.4	1.4	na	na	na
* Guatemala	5 540 000	108 889	50.8	43.4	15.4	28.0	49.0	2.8	8 946	851	59
Guinea	4 420 000	245 957	18.0	47.2	25.1	22.1	27.0	2.2	8 484	1 070	45
Guinea-Bissau	53 000	36 125	14.7	40.7	29.9	10.8	33.5	1.1	8 484	na	45

L	M	N	O	P	Q	R	S	T	U	V	W	X	Y	Z$_1$	Z$_2$	Z$_3$
82	61	10 215	81	25	na	126	130	97	100	15.0	8	30	85.0	na	na	na
62	na	10 139	99	547	na	156	135	116	530	33.8	94	656	66.2	na	na	na
56	1 143	10 092	72	150	88	101	141	72	650	52.0	20	628	48.0	57.3	12.8	29.9
64	na	9 882	85	169	na	126	125	101	580	na	15	203	na	70.9	10.0	19.1
15	1 323	11 176	115	1 101	na	118	118	100	1 900	na	91	1 908	na	17.0	30.2	52.8
8	5 697	11 200	123	4 935	2 336	143	121	118	4 760	85.6	98	5 956	14.4	8.3	33.8	57.9
16	2 873	11 034	126	4 161	1 587	119	105	113	4 050	51.9	98	3 952	48.1	14.0	39.6	46.4
71	na	9 660	80	17	7	117	146	80	100	7.0	22	29	93.0	85.9	4.8	9.3
5	5 100	11 091	128	4 209	884	128	105	121	5 210	87.1	98	6 253	12.9	4.6	38.5	56.9
na	na	na	na	219	na	na	143	na	660	53.9	89	606	46.1	39.1	21.0	39.9
52	33	9 686	98	17	na	140	132	106	120	13.1	na	31	86.9	na	na	na
58	72	10 101	79	169	23	152	130	117	250	na	40	214	na	67.5	12.5	20.0
87	na	9 848	87	47	56	175	127	138	270	12.3	na	na	87.7	91.6	2.1	6.3
44	6 417	10 004	110	605	176	151	137	111	900	60.0	67	566	40.0	44.4	17.9	37.7
42	na	10 468	132	2 547	na	137	107	128	1 770	57.3	94	4 145	42.7	52.1	8.6	39.3
64	100	9 100	102	22	na	116	129	90	90	na	60	64	na	72.0	7.9	20.1
86	22	9 736	88	7	na	233	129	181	80	2.2	10	11	97.8	na	na	na
82	51	9 733	104	184	47	152	126	121	260	20.3	15	97	79.7	na	na	na
8	5 768	10 353	129	11 854	2 685	108	119	92	6 080	76.1	97	11 237	23.9	7.5	26.8	65.7
87	2	9 429	98	22	31	117	127	92	200	26.6	10	53	73.4	na	na	na
91	1.5	9 957	89	15	na	74	129	58	90	13.9	10	na	86.1	na	na	na
25	na	10 288	109	857	223	120	126	96	820	76.0	87	1 458	24.0	21.5	31.9	46.6
67	na	10 015	91	na	na	133	121	110	300	na	25	594	na	na	na	na
45	534	9 726	95	419	151	142	145	98	510	64.3	73	601	35.7	39.1	19.6	41.3
45	8	9 306	102	93	84	103	127	81	390	na	20	219	na	na	na	na
45	42	9 450	116	719	143	175	140	125	790	40.6	89	450	59.4	39.2	19.1	41.7
33	na	9 692	117	481	na	120	123	97	640	60.5	78	1 145	39.5	30.2	26.5	43.3
35	307	10 384	108	1 200	308	181	110	165	1 310	42.2	na	1 810	57.8	29.5	19.7	50.8
16	na	10 353	129	3 672	1 730	144	105	138	3 220	55.5	94	na	44.5	19.3	43.9	36.8
12	1 324	11 340	120	3 585	1 752	108	108	100	5 820	79.9	98	5 547	20.1	9.5	31.9	58.6
61	88	9 472	94	279	153	151	145	104	590	42.1	64	253	57.9	52.3	14.3	33.4
54	241	9 593	88	166	72	119	144	83	460	41.3	67	321	58.7	57.5	17.2	25.3
55	391	10 500	100	228	77	136	136	100	280	44.3	26	294	55.7	53.5	15.4	31.1
57	62	9 650	84	222	133	147	144	102	390	38.5	60	210	61.5	57.8	12.7	29.5
79	na	na	na	na	na	66	116	57	260	na	na	168	na	na	na	na
85	177	9 755	93	23	7	113	126	90	90	11.3	5	35	88.7	na	na	na
49	na	na	na	395	173	106	140	77	720	33.4	na	508	66.6	64.7	15.0	20.3
25	644	11 336	113	5 283	1 797	111	104	107	4 130	57.1	99	4 899	42.9	16.7	34.9	48.4
14	8 529	10 616	127	3 339	2 191	133	110	120	5 190	70.0	98	4 389	30.0	12.3	36.5	51.2
28	na	na	na	1 000	na	na	138	na	1 360	66.5	na	962	33.5	20.0	27.0	53.0
na	48	9 815	95	320	na	132	109	121	1 560	32.0	12	913	68.0	87.5	3.6	8.9
72	20	10 056	104	na	na	147	125	118	170	14.2	10	61	85.8	na	na	na
12	na	10 967	126	4 529	3 447	141	100	141	3 430	74.3	94	6 233	25.7	14.1	45.1	40.8
9	33 147	11 177	121	4 825	2 722	122	108	113	5 890	na	98	5 692	na	7.3	46.9	45.8
55	189	9 648	101	357	35	142	140	101	350	31.4	25	155	68.6	62.9	12.4	24.7
47	1 047	10 467	128	1 651	426	165	105	152	1 970	53.2	80	1 828	46.8	41.8	24.7	33.5
na	na	na	na	2 157	na	na	158	na	2 780	66.8	na	4 314	33.2	19.7	27.8	52.5
63	212	9 223	97	168	98	144	137	105	570	33.8	38	267	66.2	58.7	18.1	23.2
84	na	9 641	88	112	na	118	128	92	120	na	10	95	na	na	na	na
86	na	9 641	88	27	na	na	113	na	330	na	na	79	na	na	na	na

COUNTRY	A	B	C	D	E	F	G	H	I	J	K
Guyana	790 000	214 969	3.7	36.3	7.6	28.7	61.0	2.9	10 038	988	58
Haiti	4 580 000	27 750	165.0	43.9	19.7	24.2	44.5	2.4	7 266	1 064	39
Honduras	3 040 000	112 088	27.1	49.0	17.1	31.9	49.0	3.2	8 988	1 041	56
Hong Kong	4 370 000	1 045	4 181.8	19.3	5.2	14.1	71.2	1.4	9 971	1 035	65
Hungary	10 540 000	93 030	113.3	17.8	12.0	5.8	69.8	0.6	13 776	1 658	100
Iceland	220 000	103 000	2.1	20.4	7.0	13.4	73.5	1.3	12 176	1 650	99
* India	598 100 000	3 280 483	182.3	42.8	16.7	26.1	41.2	2.6	8 694	720	52
* Indonesia	127 590 000	1 491 564	85.5	48.3	19.4	28.9	47.5	2.9	7 518	789	38
* Iran	33 020 000	1 648 000	20.0	45.4	16.6	28.8	50.0	2.9	9 660	928	60
Iraq	11 120 000	434 924	25.6	49.3	15.5	33.8	51.6	3.4	9 072	1 137	60
Ireland	3 130 000	70 283	44.5	22.5	11.0	11.5	70.7	1.2	14 322	2 156	103
* Israel	3 370 000	20 700	162.8	27.6	7.2	20.4	71.5	2.0	12 432	1 979	93
Italy	55 810 000	301 225	185.3	15.7	9.6	6.1	72.0	0.6	13 356	1 976	100
Ivory Coast	4 890 000	322 463	15.2	46.0	22.7	23.3	41.0	2.3	10 206	1 548	56
* Jamaica	2 030 000	10 962	185.2	30.4	7.1	23.3	64.6	2.3	9 912	1 361	63
* Japan	110 950 000	372 313	298.0	19.4	6.6	12.8	73.2	1.3	10 542	1 478	79
Jordan	2 690 000	97 740	27.5	49.1	16.0	33.1	52.3	3.3	10 206	1 474	65
Kampuchea (Cambodia)	8 110 000	181 035	44.8	44.6	15.6	29.0	43.7	2.9	10 206	995	55
* Kenya	13 400 000	582 646	23.0	47.8	17.5	30.3	49.1	3.0	9 912	1 053	67
Korea, North	15 850 000	120 538	131.5	38.8	11.2	27.6	57.7	2.8	9 408	1 083	73
Korea, South	33 950 000	98 484	344.7	35.6	11.0	24.6	65.0	2.5	10 584	1 046	68
Kuwait	1 000 000	17 818	56.1	43.3	7.4	35.9	68.9	3.6	na	na	na
Lao (Laos)	3 300 000	236 800	13.9	42.1	17.2	24.9	47.5	2.5	8 862	779	49
Lebanon	2 870 000	10 400	276.0	24.5	4.3	20.2	na	2.0	9 576	1 472	63
Lesotho	1 040 000	30 355	34.3	38.8	21.0	17.8	43.5	1.8	na	na	na
Liberia	1 710 000	111 369	15.4	49.8	20.9	28.9	54.1	2.9	9 114	1 311	39
Libya	2 440 000	1 759 540	3.2	45.9	15.8	30.1	52.1	3.0	10 794	1 181	62
Luxembourg	360 000	2 586	139.2	11.5	12.6	−1.1	63.7	−0.1	14 196	2 031	95
Malagasy (Madagascar)	6 750 000	587 041	11.5	46.0	25.0	21.0	37.9	2.1	10 626	1 096	58
Malawi	5 040 000	118 484	42.5	49.0	25.0	24.0	38.5	2.4	9 282	802	63
Malaysia	11 650 000	329 749	35.3	33.3	6.9	26.4	65.6	2.6	10 332	925	54
Mali	5 700 000	1 240 000	4.6	49.8	26.6	23.2	37.2	2.3	8 652	806	64
Malta	330 000	316	1 044.3	16.8	8.5	8.3	70.0	0.8	11 844	1 272	89
Mauritania	1 320 000	1 030 700	1.3	44.4	22.7	21.7	41.0	2.2	8 274	1 039	68
Mauritius	860 000	2 045	420.5	27.1	7.3	19.8	60.3	2.0	9 912	902	48
Mexico	60 150 000	1 972 547	30.5	43.2	8.9	34.3	62.4	3.4	10 836	1 092	62
Mongolia	1 440 000	1 565 000	0.9	41.5	11.2	30.3	57.7	3.0	9 996	1 063	106
Morocco	17 310 000	446 550	38.8	49.5	16.5	33.0	50.5	3.3	9 324	837	62
Mozambique	9 240 000	783 030	11.8	43.3	22.9	20.4	41.0	2.0	8 610	1 331	41
Namibia	890 000	824 292	1.1	44.4	25.0	19.4	38.5	1.9	na	na	na
Nepal	12 570 000	140 797	89.3	44.6	22.9	21.7	40.6	2.2	8 736	744	49
Netherlands	13 650 000	40 844	334.2	13.8	8.0	5.8	74.2	0.6	13 994	2 051	87
*New Zealand	3 090 000	268 676	11.5	20.5	8.5	12.0	71.2	1.2	13 440	2 043	109
Nicaragua	2 160 000	130 000	16.6	46.0	16.5	29.5	49.9	3.0	10 290	1 152	71
Niger	4 600 000	1 267 000	3.6	52.2	23.3	28.9	41.0	3.0	8 736	855	74
Nigeria	62 930 000	923 768	68.1	49.6	24.9	24.7	37.0	2.5	9 534	1 362	63
Norway	4 010 000	324 219	12.4	14.9	9.9	5.0	74.3	0.5	12 432	1 853	90
Oman	770 000	212 457	3.6	na	na	na	na	na	na	na	na
* Pakistan	70 260 000	803 943	87.4	36.0	12.0	24.0	51.3	2.4	9 072	979	56
Panama	1 670 000	75 650	22.1	41.1	8.8	32.3	65.9	3.2	10 836	1 320	61

L	M	N	O	P	Q	R	S	T	U	V	W	X	Y	Z_1	Z_2	Z_3
2	14	9 560	105	504	na	143	135	105	470	40.0	80	950	60.0	36.6	23.0	40.4
7	17	9 436	77	32	na	122	131	93	140	19.4	10	27	80.6	83.2	5.5	11.3
7	42	9 562	94	15	100	156	145	108	340	31.1	45	241	68.9	57.1	14.6	28.3
5	na	na	na	1 637	na	107	133	80	1 540	na	na	998	na	4.6	53.5	41.9
25	na	11 020	125	1 691	1 262	157	103	152	2 140	49.8	94	3 461	50.2	23.3	44.0	32.7
17	100	na	na	10 802	na	115	115	100	5 550	86.4	98	5 439	13.6	24.1	35.8	40.1
8	1 142	9 249	94	123	27	121	127	96	130	20.6	34	188	79.4	72.5	10.7	16.8
0	807	9 058	83	24	9	147	136	108	150	18.2	43	146	81.8	na	na	na
6	1 237	10 063	96	386	143	145	138	105	1 060	43.3	23	1 086	56.7	na	na	na
7	1 553	10 080	90	234	67	153	146	105	970	62.6	24	724	37.4	48.1	14.0	37.9
7	1 025	10 531	136	2 426	1 071	133	105	124	2 370	52.2	98	3 569	47.8	26.6	29.2	44.2
1	1 815	10 810	115	2 740	1 061	180	134	135	3 380	82.0	84	2 868	18.0	6.4	33.5	60.1
1	6 434	10 600	126	2 651	1 040	122	109	112	2 770	na	98	2 737	na	17.6	41.9	40.5
1	88	9 720	105	171	na	157	130	121	420	na	20	325	na	86.6	1.7	11.7
7	128	9 440	105	1 080	329	114	126	90	1 140	37.1	82	1 680	62.9	29.4	20.0	50.6
1	12 246	9 852	107	4 339	2 242	122	112	109	3 880	72.1	98	3 601	27.9	13.4	35.9	50.7
9	312	10 309	99	111	35	77	142	54	400	43.0	31	339	57.0	46.2	22.9	30.9
6	na	9 363	109	20	na	49	137	36	70	na	41	24	na	80.4	3.6	16.0
0	233	9 718	102	58	51	135	140	96	200	9.9	25	180	90.1	na	na	na
3	na	10 571	89	na	na	138	135	102	390	na	na	2 470	na	na	na	na
8	1 094	9 892	107	463	141	134	131	102	470	41.2	71	908	58.8	48.6	21.4	30.0
1	501	na	na	4 219	399	na	251	na	11 640✳	na	55	10 849	na	2.0	28.0	70.0
8	na	9 328	95	77	na	159	132	121	70	14.7	25	75	85.3	na	na	na
7	862	10 409	92	586	na	170	138	123	1 080	60.1	86	848	39.9	19.1	24.1	56.8
9	na	na	na	na	179	117	122	96	120	na	na	na	na	na	na	na
4	na	9 696	94	546	na	124	122	102	330	27.6	9	338	72.4	84.4	5.0	10.6
3	2 127	9 903	109	309	60	203	140	145	3 360	29.8	27	5 724	70.2	42.1	15.5	42.4
9	na	11 091	128	na	na	115	108	106	5 690	68.9	98	na	31.1	7.5	42.7	49.8
7	68	9 573	111	42	23	125	135	93	170	14.1	39	79	85.9	na	na	na
8	67	9 771	95	40	25	161	132	122	130	5.0	22	50	95.0	na	na	na
7	1 342	9 393	110	412	145	200	140	140	660	26.9	43	1 356	73.1	51.7	12.5	35.8
1	42	9 832	88	11	7	93	129	72	70	na	5	22	na	na	na	na
8	325	10 389	114	1 081	334	151	98	150	1 063	94.3	na	1 304	5.7	6.5	36.8	56.7
5	42	9 734	85	75	na	81	128	63	230	21.7	5	95	78.3	na	na	na
2	67	9 531	104	215	146	119	122	98	480	43.9	na	157	56.1	32.9	23.0	44.1
7	1 356	9 762	111	683	na	143	146	98	1 000	61.9	76	1 355	38.1	42.0	22.9	35.1
9	na	9 430	106	492	na	109	140	78	620	46.3	na	957	53.7	na	na	na
1	267	10 135	92	162	na	151	143	106	430	37.9	14	235	62.1	56.4	16.4	27.2
2	na	9 784	88	88	83	131	126	104	420	na	7	156	na	77.7	8.2	14.1
5	na	na	na	na	na	162	124	131	na	na	na	na	na	58.5	10.2	31.3
2	121	9 196	95	9	na	109	127	86	110	4.0	9	14	96.0	94.4	1.2	4.4
6	6 547	11 377	123	3 916	2 458	147	113	130	4 880	77.1	98	6 090	22.9	12.2	39.6	48.2
12	893	11 107	121	6 113	1 658	119	119	100	4 100	81.4	98	3 225	18.6	13.7	32.9	53.4
6	117	9 440	109	439	na	142	140	102	650	48.6	58	456	51.4	47.5	12.8	39.7
1	51	9 816	89	13	na	96	138	70	100	na	5	28	na	96.9	0.1	3.0
7	592	9 931	96	44	26	104	132	79	240	na	25	67	na	na	na	na
4	1 575	11 302	110	18 365	2 127	124	109	114	5 280	44.7	99	4 979	55.3	10.4	33.6	56.0
na	na	na	na	237	na	na	135	na	1 250	na	na	180	na	na	na	na
1	479	9 755	93	116	38	157	140	113	130	26.8	16	149	73.2	59.3	15.3	25.4
3	2 303	9 675	112	755	298	160	144	111	1 010	49.5	79	860	50.5	41.4	8.8	49.8

COUNTRY	A	B	C	D	E	F	G	H	I	J	K
Papua New Guinea	2 760 000	461 691	6.0	45.0	20.0	25.0	46.8	2.5	na	na	na
Paraguay	2 650 000	406 752	6.5	44.6	10.8	33.8	59.4	3.4	11 508	1 810	73
* Peru	15 870 000	1 285 216	12.3	41.8	11.1	30.7	54.0	3.1	9 744	1 400	60
* Philippines	42 510 000	300 000	141.7	44.7	12.0	32.7	51.1	3.3	8 148	898	47
Poland	34 020 000	312 677	108.8	18.4	8.5	10.2	70.3	1.0	13 776	na	101
* Portugal	8 760 000	92 082	95.1	19.3	11.1	8.2	68.0	0.8	12 180	1 799	85
Puerto Rico	3 090 000	8 897	347.3	23.3	6.5	16.8	72.4	1.7	10 630	1 567	67
Rhodesia	6 420 000	390 580	16.4	48.4	14.4	34.0	51.4	3.4	11 172	893	76
Romania	21 180 000	237 500	89.2	20.3	9.1	11.2	69.0	1.2	13 188	1 483	90
Rwanda	4 200 000	26 338	159.5	51.8	23.3	28.5	41.0	2.9	8 232	1 560	58
Saudi Arabia	8 700 000	2 149 690	4.0	50.0	22.7	27.3	42.3	2.7	9 534	985	62
Senegal	4 140 000	196 192	21.1	46.3	22.8	23.5	41.0	2.4	9 954	882	65
Sierra Leone	2 710 000	71 740	37.8	44.8	22.7	22.1	41.0	2.2	9 576	1 016	51
Singapore	2 250 000	581	3 872.6	19.9	5.3	14.6	67.5	1.5	10 261	1 183	63
Somalia	3 170 000	637 657	5.0	45.9	24.0	21.9	38.5	2.2	7 686	876	56
* South Africa	25 470 000	1 221 037	20.9	40.3	16.6	23.7	49.0	2.4	11 508	1 126	78
Spain	35 470 000	504 782	70.3	19.3	8.4	10.9	70.4	1.1	10 920	1 838	81
Sri Lanka	13 990 000	65 610	213.2	29.5	7.7	21.8	65.9	2.2	9 114	868	48
* Sudan	17 760 000	2 505 813	7.1	48.9	18.4	30.5	47.5	3.1	9 072	1 275	63
Surinam	420 000	163 265	2.6	40.9	7.2	33.7	64.6	3.4	10 290	908	59
Swaziland	490 000	17 363	28.2	52.3	23.5	28.8	41.0	2.9	na	na	na
Sweden	8 200 000	449 964	18.2	13.4	10.6	2.8	75.0	0.3	11 802	1 910	86
Switzerland	6 400 000	41 288	155.0	12.9	8.5	4.4	73.2	2.1	13 398	2 124	91
Syria	7 350 000	185 180	39.7	47.5	15.3	32.2	56.6	3.2	11 130	1 286	75
Taiwan	7 600 000	35 759	212.5	na	na	na	na	na	na	1 108	na
* Tanzania	14 760 000	945 087	15.6	47.0	22.0	25.0	40.5	2.5	9 492	1 349	63
* Thailand	42 280 000	514 000	82.3	42.8	10.4	32.4	56.3	3.2	10 752	918	56
Togo	2 220 000	56 000	39.6	50.9	25.5	25.4	35.1	2.5	9 786	1 452	56
Trinidad & Tobago	1 070 000	5 128	208.7	26.5	6.7	19.8	66.1	2.0	9 996	1 176	64
* Tunisia	5 770 000	163 610	35.3	46.3	16.0	30.3	51.7	3.0	9 450	1 004	67
Turkey	39 180 000	780 576	50.2	39.6	14.6	25.0	53.7	2.5	13 650	1 562	91
Uganda	11 550 000	236 036	48.9	43.2	17.6	25.6	47.5	2.6	8 946	1 570	61
* UK	55 960 000	244 046	229.3	13.1	12.1	1.0	70.8	0.1	13 398	1 888	92
* USA	213 630 000	9 363 123	22.8	15.0	9.1	5.9	71.3	0.6	13 986	2 216	106
* USSR	254 380 000	22 402 200	11.4	18.2	8.7	9.5	69.0	1.0	13 776	1 837	101
United Arab Emirates	220 000	83 600	2.6	na	na	na	na	na	na	na	na
Upper Volta	6 030 000	274 200	22.0	49.4	29.1	20.3	31.6	2.0	7 182	691	59
Uruguay	3 060 000	177 508	17.2	20.9	9.6	11.3	68.5	1.1	12 096	1 645	100
* Venezuela	11 990 000	912 050	13.1	40.9	7.8	33.1	66.4	3.3	10 206	1 313	63
Vietnam	44 000 000	329 556	133.5	37.5	16.1	21.4	50.0	2.1	9 807	924	53
Western Sahara	100 000	266 000	0.4	20.9	4.5	16.4	na	1.6	na	na	na
Yemen	6 670 000	195 000	34.2	50.0	22.7	27.3	42.3	2.7	8 568	697	61
Yemen, Democratic	1 690 000	332 968	5.1	50.0	22.7	27.3	42.3	2.7	8 694	816	57
Yugoslavia	21 330 000	255 804	83.4	17.9	8.5	9.4	68.0	0.9	13 398	1 543	94
* Zaire	24 900 000	2 345 409	10.6	44.4	22.7	21.7	38.8	2.2	8 652	1 744	33
* Zambia	4 900 000	752 614	6.5	49.8	20.7	29.1	43.5	2.9	10 878	808	68

L	M	N	O	P	Q	R	S	T	U	V	W	X	Y	Z_1	Z_2	Z_3
82	na	na	na	184	na	139	131	107	440	11.1	32	195	88.9	na	na	na
53	57	9 671	119	142	na	133	145	91	480	35.7	74	142	64.3	50.5	19.0	30.5
46	551	9 842	99	438	179	125	140	89	710	55.3	61	641	44.7	42.0	19.2	38.8
70	1 038	9 474	86	266	81	144	144	100	310	31.7	72	291	68.3	55.6	14.3	30.1
38	na	11 021	125	2 527	865	139	110	126	2 450	54.4	94	4 575	45.6	40.8	31.5	27.7
37	2 839	10 322	118	1 147	370	107	110	na	1 540	26.4	65	898	73.6	32.7	30.9	36.4
14	na	na	na	3 814	na	79	120	66	2 400	58.1	na	3 614	41.9	8.4	30.5	61.1
63	na	10 065	111	1 233	na	161	145	111	480	19.4	30	597	80.6	11.9	22.7	65.4
52	na	11 176	118	2 246	na	151	112	135	na	42.1	94	3 429	57.9	57.2	24.6	18.2
91	16	9 800	84	8	6	131	137	96	80	3.4	10	12	96.6	na	na	na
61	3 877	10 143	94	na	na	155	135	115	2 080	na	15	1 023	na	na	na	na
76	12	9 954	100	4	na	98	130	75	320	na	10	154	na	na	na	na
73	50	9 673	99	na	na	137	128	107	180	na	10	135	na	79.9	6.1	14.0
8	1 237	na	na	1 702	865	271	130	208	2 120	na	na	874	na	2.7	33.3	64.0
82	35	9 729	79	13	11	139	129	108	80	na	5	33	na	na	na	na
30	1 234	10 275	112	2 734	480	173	130	133	1 200	47.9	35	2 815	52.1	39.5	18.9	41.6
34	6 772	10 302	106	2 174	716	151	112	135	1 960	na	86	1 993	na	23.8	35.8	40.4
52	87	9 300	98	76	27	126	130	97	130	22.4	76	117	77.6	54.7	13.6	31.7
80	61	9 861	92	16	23	170	140	121	150	13.2	15	124	86.8	85.8	5.6	8.6
27	na	9 440	109	na	na	188	140	135	870	na	84	2 130	na	35.8	13.7	50.5
82	na	na	na	261	146	181	138	132	400	7.9	na	na	92.1	na	na	na
9	2 528	11 348	104	9 596	2 756	124	107	116	6 720	81.4	99	6 110	18.6	7.2	35.7	57.1
7	8 078	11 259	119	5 682	na	123	114	108	6 650	54.6	98	3 752	45.4	7.6	48.3	44.1
49	481	10 402	107	167	120	132	143	93	490	45.9	31	469	54.1	52.0	15.5	32.5
na	na	na	na	na	na	na	na	na	720	na	85	na	na	na	na	na
86	145	9 686	98	36	21	144	133	109	140	7.3	20	75	92.7	−90.2	3.1	6.7
77	1 296	9 350	115	171	27	140	142	99	300	13.2	68	303	86.8	72.4	8.5	19.1
75	38	9 689	101	42	33	115	132	87	210	15.2	10	61	84.8	na	na	na
17	49	10 200	98	1 228	185	129	116	112	1 490	12.4	89	3 891	87.6	14.9	18.9	66.2
46	307	10 053	94	205	105	149	140	107	550	40.1	30	365	59.9	44.2	14.9	40.9
69	2 120	10 581	129	324	136	143	134	107	690	42.6	51	625	57.4	67.6	11.2	21.2
86	na	9 831	91	74	35	125	133	94	160	7.1	20	64	92.9	na	na	na
3	6 476	10 634	126	5 044	2 687	131	105	125	3 360	76.4	98	5 778	23.6	4.2	40.8	55.0
4	14 378	11 100	126	9 254	3 265	126	112	112	6 640	73.5	98	11 960	26.5	4.7	30.1	65.2
32	na	10 516	131	3 662	1 733	147	112	132	2 330	60.1	99	4 937	39.9	25.2	45.1	29.7
na	na	na	na	na	na	na	139	na	13 500	na	20	13 510	na	na	na	na
89	63	9 975	72	7	na	75	126	60	80	na	10	12	na	na	na	na
17	232	11 200	108	812	na	111	115	97	1 060	na	90	969	na	20.0	27.1	52.9
26	2 420	10 414	98	1 452	550	176	144	122	1 710	75.7	77	2 818	24.3	21.9	25.1	53.0
76	375	8 835	111	84	na	127	128	99	150	30.4	67	420	69.6	na	na	na
na	na	na	na	na	na	na	144	na	na	45.1	na	na	54.9	na	na	na
73	na	10 200	84	na	na	110	135	81	120	na	10	13	na	na	na	na
62	76	10 109	86	112	66	132	135	97	120	33.3	10	405	66.7	na	na	na
53	1 484	10 718	125	1 673	476	149	111	134	1 200	38.6	80	1 709	61.4	48.1	18.7	33.2
78	235	9 303	93	165	19	162	128	127	150	26.4	20	79	73.6	87.6	5.6	6.8
69	193	9 713	112	738	122	143	138	103	480	34.3	20	415	65.7	na	na	na

Appendix 3
Statistical Techniques

Most of the statistical techniques explained here may be examined in Arkin and Colton, *Statistical Methods*, 1968.

A. Arithmetic and Logarithmic Scales

For all practical purposes the scales used in graphing may be classified into two groups: arithmetic and logarithmic.

Arithmetic scales are the most generally used of the two types. They are employed whenever there is a need to represent on a map or graph a certain distance or quantity in the real world. For example, a map with a scale of 1 cm = 1 km (1:100 000) has an arithmetic scale; so also does a graph with a vertical scale of 1 cm = 1 000 000 t of product. Arithmetic scales, whether on maps or graphs, always have consistently equal divisions. Thus, if 1 cm = 10 years is the scale along the horizontal axis of a graph, then 1 cm always represents 10 years along that same axis; it does not suddenly equal 5 years or 20 years.

Logarithmic scales are more unusual. They are used whenever there is a need to show *rates of change* accurately. Arithmetic scales are unable to do this; they yield a false visual impression. For example, in Graph A3-1, it appears that line C represents the slowest-growing quantity, while line A represents the fastest-growing quantity. Furthermore, in Graph A3-2 it looks as though there is a sharp change in the rate of increase at point X.

Graph A3-1

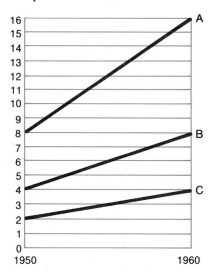

Graph A3-2

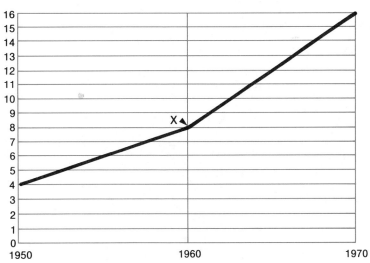

Graphs A3-1 and A3-2 are plotted on arithmetic scales, and as a result they convey incorrect impressions of rates of change. If we examine the figures being plotted we see that in *all* cases there is a doubling of the data between the beginning and end of each time period. All the *rates* of change shown in the two graphs are in fact identical. If we are to give the correct visual impression we cannot therefore use arithmetic scales. We must use logarithmic scales, which have diminishing distances between scale lines as quantities increase, as shown in Graph A3-3.

Graph A3-3

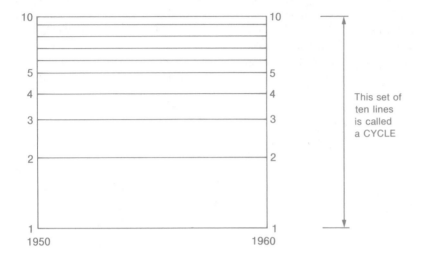

Graph A3-4

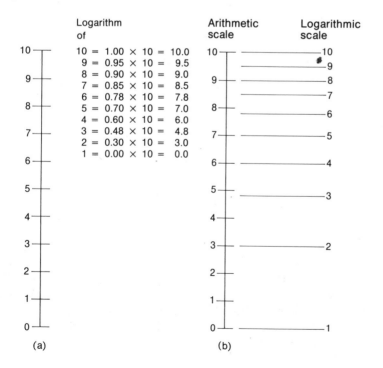

(a)   (b)

The spacing and value of the lines in a cycle are determined by plotting the logarithms (multiplied by ten) of the numbers from one to ten on a standard arithmetic scale. In Graph A3-4, (a) is an arithmetic scale set up to represent numbers from zero to ten. If the logarithms of the numbers from one to ten are multiplied by ten and plotted against the arithmetic scale, they will appear as in (b); these numbers determine the basic spacing of the lines in a cycle.

Notice that there is no zero on a logarithm (log) scale. The reason for this is that there is no logarithm for zero. This means that the scale may be extended to infinity, both upward and downward, simply by inserting more cycles as needed. (Each set of ten lines is called a cycle.) Graph A3-5 shows just two cycles, along with lines A, B, and C from Graph A3-1. Notice that the lines are now all parallel, indicating identical rates of change. Graph A3-6 shows the data of Graph A3-2 on a 2 cycle log scale; note that the line is completely straight, indicating no change in the rate of increase from one time period to the next.

Graph A3-5   **Graph A3-6**

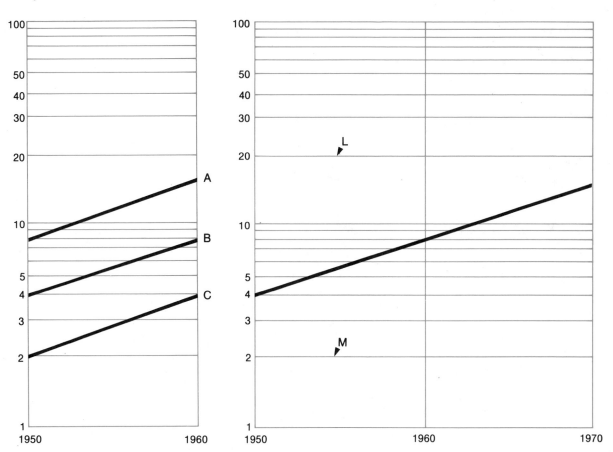

The numbering of the vertical axis on a log scale graph is done according to powers of ten. The bottom line of a cycle is *always* some power of ten, such as

$$10^9 \quad (= 1\ 000\ 000\ 000)$$
$$10^6 \quad (= 1\ 000\ 000)$$
$$10^3 \quad (= 1\ 000)$$
$$10^2 \quad (= 100)$$
$$10^1 \quad (= 10)$$
$$10^0 \quad (= 1)$$
$$10^{-1} \quad (= 0.1)$$

Graph A3-7   Log scales : sample cycle frequencies and sizes

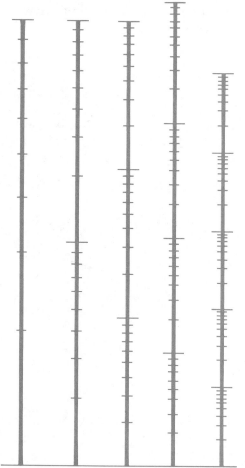

1 cycle   2 cycles   3 cycles   4 cycles   5 cycles

According to this system of numbering, each cycle has a value ten times as large as that of the cycle below it, and each line in a cycle is ten times larger than the equivalent line in the next cycle below. Thus in Graph A3-6 line L has a value ten times that of line M.

Log scales can be of any actual size. Thus a single cycle (representing quantities as diverse as, say, 1 to 10 or 1 000 000 to 10 000 000) can be the size shown in Graph A3-3, or it can be as large as a football field. Graph A3-7 gives you a selection of cycle frequencies (1 cycle to 5 cycles) as well as a choice of cycle sizes (a single cycle being progressively smaller in the sequence of 1 cycle to 5 cycle log scales). Notice that all these log scales fit neatly on a normal page.

Notice that Graphs A3-3, A3-5, and A3-6 have log scales on the vertical axis only. They have a normal arithmetic scale representing quantities of time along the horizontal axis. Such graphs, with a log scale on the vertical axis and an arithmetic scale on the horizontal axis, are called *semi-log graphs*. They are used whenever time is plotted on the horizontal axis and a log scale is required for the vertical axis. Time, in other words, is always plotted on an arithmetic scale. It is worth noting that any graph with time plotted along the horizontal axis is called a *time-series graph*, because it shows a series of plots over a period of time.

B. Multiple and Compound Line Graphs

These graphs offer two different methods of presenting information. The multiple line graph is more versatile in that it can accommodate either related or unrelated material, either to the same scale or to different scales, including log scales. The compound line graph is restricted to showing variations in the components of a total, always on an arithmetic scale. The following table, which shows the numbers of passengers carried by different Leningrad City Transportation modes, 1950–1973, may be illustrated by either type of graph, as shown in Graph A3-8.

Mode	1950	1960	1965	1970	1973
Streetcar	860	909	790	783	786
Trolley bus	112	238	249	332	393
Bus	182	565	738	810	959
Subway	—	106	263	418	503

Numbers of passengers (thousands) carried by different Leningrad City Transportation modes, 1950-1973

Source: *Geographical Review* 1978 4, p. 192

Graph A3-8   Multiple and compound line graphs of the same information

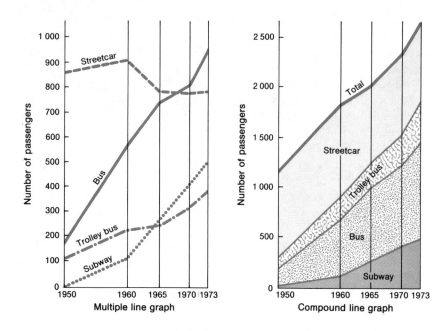

Multiple line graph

Compound line graph

C. Linear Dispersion Diagrams

These diagrams are a simple way of showing the distribution of data along a continuum. For example, in a geography class in Edmonton a few years ago, the final marks for thirty students were 27, 48, 76, 94, 72, 68, 57, 59, 63, 82, 45, 53, 61, 64, 74, 43, 54, 62, 60, 59, 38, 70, 62, 87, 51, 78, 80, 67, 58, 70. Graph A3-9 is a linear dispersion diagram showing the distribution, or dispersion, of the marks on a scale of 0–100.

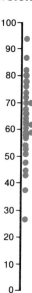

D. Proportional Circles

A circle is the most compact means of enclosing an area, and thus on maps, where space is scarce, it is often desirable to use circles to represent data. Proportional circles provide two important pieces of information.

First, the *position* of the circle on the map indicates geographical location. Second, the *size* of the circle shows the quantity found in a particular area.

Since different quantities are represented by different circle sizes (e.g., large quantities are represented by large circles), it is essential to calculate the circle sizes carefully. In order to make the sizes proportional to the quantities being mapped, we must first obtain the square roots of these quantities. Square roots are required because it is the *area* of the circle that represents the quantity, and the area of a circle is given by the formula πr^2. In all cases π is constant, and can be ignored when comparing circle sizes. Variations in circle sizes are therefore caused by variations in r^2. Since r^2 thus represents the quantity to be mapped it is possible to find r (the radius of the circle) by obtaining the square root of the quantity to be mapped.

North America, for example, produces 32.4%, or 2 774 020 000 tce, of the world's energy. If we are going to plot the latter quantity on a world map, then we need to know the square root of 2 774 020 000. It is 52 669 (i.e., $r = \sqrt{2\ 774\ 020\ 000} = 52\ 669$). This particular figure is, however, much too big to use as the radius of a circle; we must divide it by a number that will bring it down to a useful size. By *useful size* we mean a figure that, in appropriate units, can be used as the radius of a circle on a map. For assignments in the text, the map we will likely use is the world map in Appendix 1; thus we need to find a radius for a circle that will fit well over North America on a map of similar size. If we divide 52 669 by 2 000 we get a figure of 26.33, which we can round to 26. A radius of 26 mm would be suitable. Of course, in order to keep the comparisons valid, we must divide the square roots of all the other data in the same set by 2 000.

Each data set will have to be processed differently. It may be necessary to divide the square roots of the data in some sets by only two or three; in other sets, the square roots may have to be multiplied by a common number to become a useful size. Sometimes we may be able to use the square roots of the figures in the data set just as they are. It is always up to us to decide the best radius sizes for the proportional circles.

E. Triangular Graphs

These graphs are used for showing patterns in data whenever three components of a whole are given in percentage terms. For example, the employment categories for Canada are: primary (8.4%); secondary (26.8%); and tertiary (64.8%). These figures may be plotted on a triangular graph in the manner shown in Graph A3-10.

Graph A3-10   A triangular graph

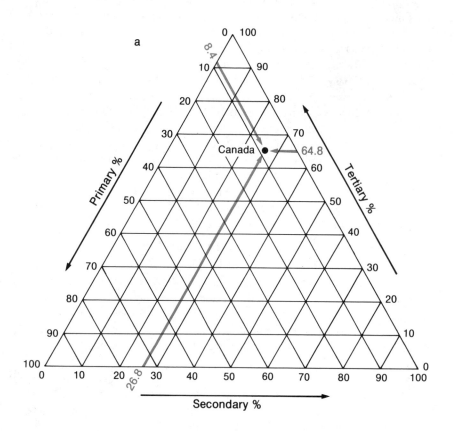

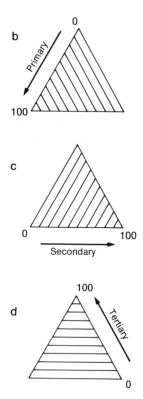

The location of plotted data on the triangular graph is important. A position close to the centre of the triangle indicates that all three components are more or less equal, whereas a position near one of the sides means that one of the components makes up only a small portion of the whole in relation to the other two components. A position close to two of the sides (i.e., near a corner) indicates that two components constitute a small part of the whole, while the remaining component makes up a large part.

Triangular graphs are used chiefly for plotting data for several countries. The resulting groupings or clusters are then analyzed; deviations must also be accounted for.

F. Correlations: Scattergraphs

A scattergraph shows the correlation between two variables. It is often impossible to tell from a mass of data whether or not two variables go well together; we can find this information quickly on a scattergraph. For example, if we wish to discover the extent of relationship between the two hypothetical data sets shown below, then we can construct a scattergraph like Graph A3-11, which clearly provides the information.

Student #	Data set x Final mark %	Data set y Initial job earnings $K (K = thousands)
1	68	15.3
2	54	13.2
3	38	9.3
4	55	16.2
5	68	19.4
6	84	27.3
7	46	10.2
8	34	9.3
9	62	18.5
10	35	17.0
11	67	21.5
12	98	24.3
13	82	18.7
14	27	9.2
15	63	18.2
16	71	12.7
17	65	21.0
18	78	25.2
19	59	12.2
20	16	14.3

We can tell from the graph that a relationship exists, because there is a pattern made by the plotted data. We observe that the relationship is fairly strong, but not perfect, because the data fall into a fairly narrow band. If the relationship were perfect then the dots would form a line rather than a band.

The line that can be drawn through the middle of the plotted data, so that distances between the line and data are minimized, is known as the *line of best fit*. It is a representative of the data being plotted. The farther any dots are from the line of best fit, the less typical they are of the displayed correlation. We should always try to discover reasons for such deviations. The line of best fit also clearly shows whether the relationship is positive or negative. The relationship in Graph A3-11 is positive (i.e., one variable rises as the other one does), because the line of best fit slopes up to the right.

Graph A3-11   A scattergraph

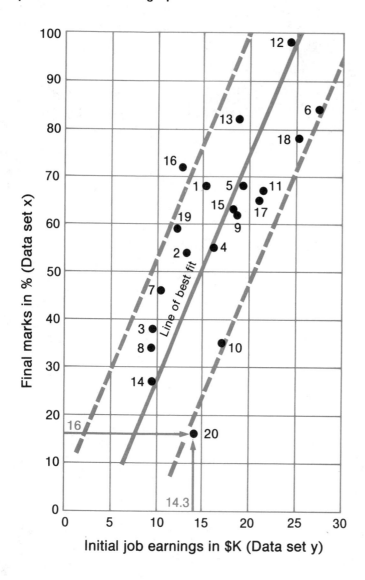

Occasionally the range of data is so great that a normal arithmetic scale cannot accommodate it. At such times it is customary to use appropriate log scales along one axis or both. Graph A3-12 illustrates a scattergraph that has log scales along both axes; in this case each axis has a 3 cycle log scale. It is possible to construct *log-log graphs* like this one with as many cycles as desired along either axis. Thus there can be three or four cycles along the vertical axis if needed, with one or two along the horizontal axis. The number of cycles used depends upon the range of data being plotted.

Graph A3-12   A 3 x 3 log-log graph

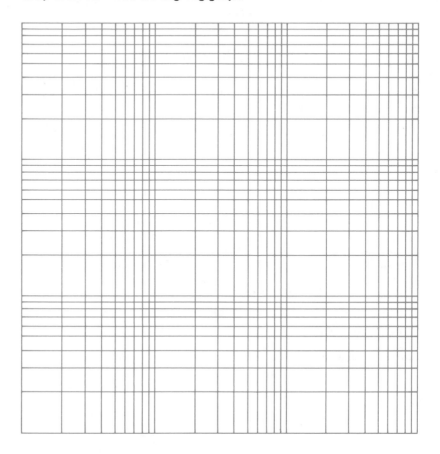

G. Correlations: The Phi (ϕ) Coefficient

The phi coefficient gives us a mathematical indication of the nature and degree of correlation between two variables. This indication is not difficult to obtain. For example, we can examine the correlation between average daily food intake and agricultural population (columns I and L of Appendix 2). First we divide the data in column I into two groups; daily per capita food availability of 10 000 kJ and under, and food availability of over 10 000 kJ. We then merely count the number of countries in each group. The next step is to divide the countries in each of these groups into two further groups: the first group consists of those countries with 50% or less of the population engaged in agriculture, and the second, of those nations with over 50% of the people in agriculture. Again, we simply count the number of countries in each category. We then set up a two by two table as shown below, and insert the numbers we have counted in the appropriate boxes.

Daily per capita food availability (column I)

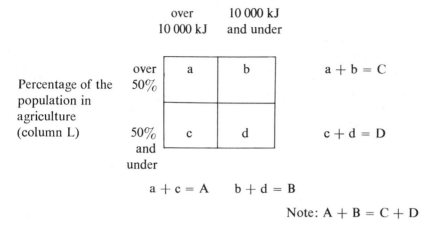

$$\phi = \frac{(a \times d) - (b \times c)}{\sqrt{A \times B \times C \times D}}$$

Add the numbers across and down, as shown by the letters, and then apply the formula:

For example, if we had thirty countries distributed as follows,

a 5	b 8	5 + 8 = 13 (C)
c 10	d 7	10 + 7 = 17 (D)

5 + 10 = 15 (A)   8 + 7 = 15 (B)

then the formula would read:

$$\phi = \frac{(5 \times 7) - (8 \times 10)}{\sqrt{15 \times 15 \times 13 \times 17}}$$

$$= \frac{35 - 80}{\sqrt{49725}}$$

$$= \frac{-45}{223}$$

$$= -0.2$$

In this example the coefficient is negative, indicating an *inverse* relationship. It is also quite small, indicating a weak relationship. The maximum range of coefficients is from +1.0 to −1.0; the first value reveals a perfect positive relationship, and the second, a perfect negative (inverse) relationship. A coefficient of zero (0.0) indicates no relationship at all.

$$+1.0 \quad \text{perfect positive relationship}$$

+1.0 ↑	perfect positive relationship
	strong positive relationship
	weak positive relationship
0.0	zero relationship
	weak negative relationship
	strong negative relationship
−1.0 ↓	perfect negative relationship

Since a correlation may never be more than perfect, it is impossible to obtain correlation coefficients that fall outside the designated range.

H. Correlations: Rank Correlation

The rank correlation technique is an attempt to obtain a correlation coefficient through a comparison of the rank positions of any item (such as a country) in two different data sets. Actual quantities are not involved. The technique involves arranging the items in each data set in order from highest to lowest. Because of the large number of countries in the world we recommend that you use only those marked with an asterisk (*) in Appendix 2. If you had to find the rank correlation coefficient for the relationship between, say, average daily food intake and electricity production (columns I and P in Appendix 2), then you would proceed as follows:

Step 1. Rank the sample countries (*) according to their per capita food value in column I; the country with the largest value will be first. Write in the countries' rank order (1, 2, 3, etc.) in the first column, and then set up another three columns.

Step 2. Assess their rank (1, 2, 3, etc., the largest first) in the matter of electricity generation (column P), and write the appropriate rank for each country in the second column.

Step 3. Find the difference d in each pair of ranks. For example, if a country ranks 3 in the first column and 8 in the second, then the difference d is 5. If another country ranks 12 in the first column and 3 in the second, then the difference d is 9. Write the difference in the third column.

Step 4. Square the difference d, producing d^2. Write the answer in the fourth column, and then add ($\sum$) all these d^2 answers to produce the sum of d^2 ($\sum d^2$) at the bottom of the fourth column.

Step 5. Apply the rank correlation formula

$$\rho = 1 - \frac{6(\sum d^2)}{n(n^2 - 1)}$$

where ρ (rho) is the *rank correlation coefficient*, whose range of values and method of interpretation are identical with those of the ϕ (phi) coefficient explained in Section G of Appendix 3. The number $6(\sum d^2)$ is $\sum d^2$ multiplied by 6, and n is the number of countries in the sample.

Step 6. Analyze the value of ρ. This means that you must explain why the two variables exhibit the degree of relationship shown.

I. Correlations: Grouped Data Technique

The calculation of a correlation coefficient can be laborious if we do it for 150 or so countries individually; this is why we often restrict our examination to a sample of countries. As an alternative to taking a sample, we can use the *grouped data technique*, in which we study countries by groups rather than individually. The steps are as follows:

Step 1. Set up a correlation table, as in Graph A3-13.

Step 2. Examine the data and decide on appropriate *class intervals* for

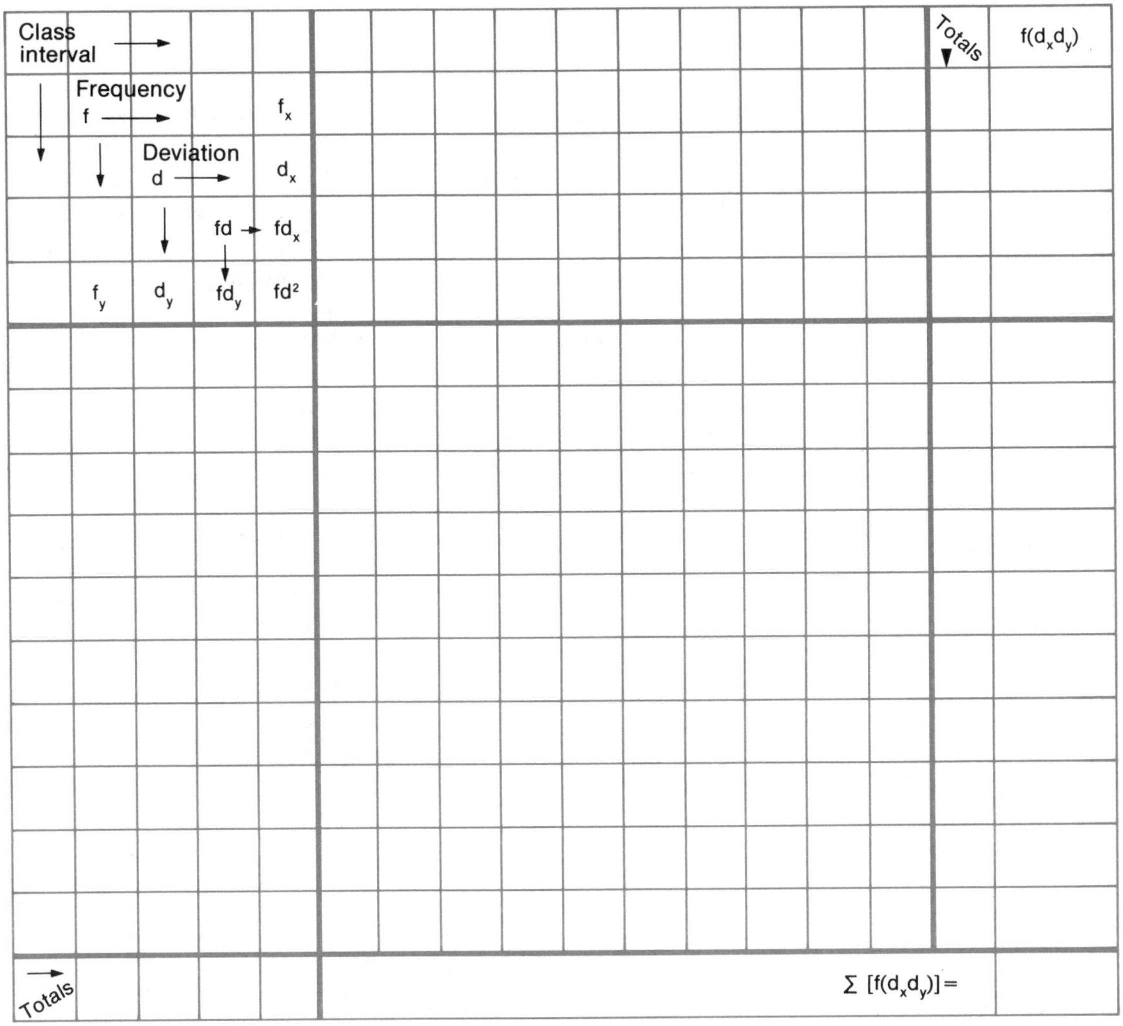

Graph A3-13 A correlation table for data grouped into ten classes

both sets. Classification is the arranging of large amounts of data into groups. Incomes, for example, may be arranged in groups of $5 000: $0 to $4 999, $5 000 to $9 999, $10 000 to $14 999, and so on. The size of the group selected is called the class interval. For our example we will use the hypothetical data in Fig. A3-1, and group both sets into ten classes.

Step 3. Write in the class intervals that have been decided upon, in the manner shown in Graph A3-14.

Graph A3-14 A completed correlation table for the data in Fig. A3-1

Variable x: Final marks of 58 students

Variable y: Initial earnings in $K of 58 students

Class intervals →				0-9	10-19	20-29	30-39	40-49	50-59	60-69	70-79	80-89	90-99	Totals ▼	$f(d_x d_y)$
Frequency f →		f_x		1	3	2	8	4	11	17	6	4	2	58	
Deviation d →		d_x		0	1	2	3	4	5	6	7	8	9		
fd → fd_x				0	3	4	24	16	55	102	42	32	18	296	
f_y	d_y	fd_y	fd^2	0	3	8	72	64	275	612	294	256	162	1 746	
26-27.9 3	9	27	243								$_{72}2^{144}$	$_{81}1^{81}$			225
24-25.9 2	8	16	128							$_{56}1^{56}$		$_{72}1^{72}$			128
22-23.9 3	7	21	147							$_{42}1^{42}$	$_{49}2^{98}$				140
20-21.9 4	6	24	144							$_{36}3^{108}$	$_{48}1^{48}$				156
18-19.9 11	5	55	275						$_{25}2^{50}$	$_{30}7^{210}$	$_{35}1^{35}$	$_{40}1^{40}$			335
16-17.9 6	4	24	96				$_{12}1^{12}$			$_{20}1^{20}$	$_{24}3^{72}$	$_{28}1^{28}$			132
14-15.9 7	3	21	63		$_31^3$				$_{12}2^{24}$	$_{15}1^{15}$	$_{18}3^{54}$				96
12-13.9 6	2	12	24				$_61^6$		$_{10}4^{40}$		$_{14}1^{14}$				60
10-11.9 7	1	7	7		$_11^1$		$_31^3$	$_42^8$	$_53^{15}$						27
8-9.9 9	0	0	0	$_01^0$	$_01^0$	$_02^0$	$_05^0$								0
Totals 58		207	1 127										$\Sigma [f(d_x d_y)] =$		1 299

← 10 spaces for 10 classes →

Variable y: Initial earnings in $K of 58 students ← 10 spaces for 10 classes →

Step 4. In the boxes of the f rank, insert the number of students classified in each marks category. In the f column, insert the number of students grouped into each earnings class. Now, enter in the central boxes the number of times a given combination of variables occurs. Consider, for example, the students whose earnings fall into the $8-9.9K category. There are nine students in this class; of the nine, only one has final marks in the 0-9% class. Thus a combination of a final mark between 0 and 9% and an initial income of $8-9.9K occurs only once, so 1 is entered in the appropriate central box, as shown in Graph A3-14. From the graph we also see that an income of $8-9.9K combines with a final mark of 10-19% once, with a mark of 20-29% twice, and with a mark of 30-39% five times. The double classification right through two data sets that is required in this step must be completed with care.

Step 5. Add all the numbers in the f rank (f_x) to obtain the frequency total for data set x. Similarly, add the numbers in the f column (f_y) to get the frequency total for data set y. Make sure that the sum of f ($\sum f$) equals the number (n) of items in your data, and that $\sum f_x = \sum f_y$.

Step 6. For deviations, count the lowest class in each data set as zero and insert the value (0) in the d space opposite the lowest class. Count each class above the lowest as one deviation, and insert those values (1, 2, 3, etc.) in the appropriate d spaces (d_x and d_y).

Step 7. Multiply the d_x and d_y values by the corresponding f value; i.e., d_x by f_x and d_y by f_y. Enter your answers in the fd rank (fd_x) and column (fd_y).

Step 8. Add ($\sum$) the fd_x figures and enter the answer ($\sum fd_x$) to the right in the totals box, where the figure of 296 is entered in Graph A3-14.

Step 9. Add ($\sum$) the fd_y figures and enter the answer ($\sum fd_y$) below the column in the totals box, where 207 is located in Graph A3-14.

Step 10. Square all individual d values (d_x and d_y) and multiply the squares by the appropriate f value (d_x^2 by f_x and d_y^2 by f_y). Enter the answers in the fd² rank (fd_x^2) and column (fd_y^2). Sum ($\sum$) the fd_x^2 figures and enter the answer to the right, where 1 746 is entered; then sum the fd_y^2 figures and enter the answer under the column where 1 127 is shown.

Step 11. For each central box of the correlation table in which data are classified, multiply the appropriate d numbers; i.e., d_x multiplied by d_y. Enter the answer in the lower left corner of each box.

Step 12. Multiply the $d_x d_y$ values just obtained by the frequency (f) figures already inserted in the central boxes. Enter the answer, $f(d_x d_y)$, in the upper right corner of each box. For example, in Graph A3-14 for the combination of marks in the class 60-69% and earnings in the class $18-19.9K, the frequency (f) is 7; the class deviation

Fig. A3-1

Final marks and initial job earnings of 58 students, hypothetical data

	Data set x	Data set y
Student #	Final mark %	Initial job earnings $K
1	68	15.3
2	54	13.2
3	38	9.3
4	55	16.2
5	68	19.4
6	84	27.3
7	46	10.2
8	34	9.3
9	62	18.5
10	35	17.0
11	67	21.5
12	98	24.3
13	82	18.7
14	27	9.2
15	63	18.2
16	71	12.7
17	65	21.0
18	78	25.2
19	59	12.2
20	16	14.3
21	68	15.7
22	73	22.1
23	64	20.0
24	23	8.0
25	58	19.2
26	66	18.9
27	77	22.0
28	46	15.0
29	63	18.3
30	68	23.9
31	30	13.2
32	45	15.2
33	47	11.1
34	71	18.2
35	60	18.7
36	81	21.4
37	55	12.4
38	63	15.2
39	57	14.3
40	59	10.2
41	50	18.7
42	82	26.1
43	63	16.7
44	16	8.2
45	51	10.4
46	33	9.0
47	57	10.5
48	35	11.1
49	58	13.7
50	18	10.0
51	63	16.2
52	8	8.2
53	68	16.7
54	93	27.5
55	72	16.6
56	33	9.1
57	61	18.0
58	31	9.5

of marks (d_x) is 6 and the class deviation of earnings (d_y) is 5, so $d_x d_y = 30$. This figure can be seen in the lower left corner of the box. The frequency (7) multiplied by the $d_x d_y$ figure of 30 produces an $f(d_x d_y)$ figure of 210, which can be seen in the upper right corner of the box.

Step 13. Add the $f(d_x d_y)$ figures across, and put each rank's total in the extreme right hand column. Thus 144 and 81 add up to 225, and so on.

Step 14. Add ($\sum$) the figures in the right hand column. Enter the answer, $\sum f(d_x d_y)$, at the foot of the column.

Step 15. Apply the formula for the *coefficient of correlation* (r):

$$r = \frac{\theta}{\sigma_x \sigma_y}$$

where

$$\theta = \frac{\sum[f(d_x d_y)]}{n} - \left(\frac{\sum(f d_x)}{n}\right)\left(\frac{\sum(f d_y)}{n}\right)$$

$$\sigma_x = \sqrt{\frac{\sum(f d_x{}^2)}{n} - \left(\frac{\sum f d_x}{n}\right)^2}$$

$$\sigma_y = \sqrt{\frac{\sum(f d_y{}^2)}{n} - \left(\frac{\sum f d_y}{n}\right)^2}$$

In the case of our example in Graph A3-14 the appropriate values are

$$\theta = \frac{1\ 299}{58} - \left(\frac{296}{58}\right)\left(\frac{207}{58}\right)$$

$$= 22.3966 - (5.1034)(3.5690)$$

$$= 22.3966 - 18.2140$$

$$= 4.1826$$

$$\sigma_x = \sqrt{\frac{1\ 746}{58} - \left(\frac{296}{58}\right)^2}$$

$$= \sqrt{30.1034 - 26.0447}$$

$$= 2.0146$$

$$\sigma_y = \sqrt{\frac{1\ 127}{58} - \left(\frac{207}{58}\right)^2}$$

$$= \sqrt{19.4310 - 12.7378}$$

$$= 2.5871$$

Substitution of these values in the formula indicates that

$$r = \frac{4.1826}{2.0146 \times 2.5871}$$

$$= \frac{4.1826}{5.2120}$$

$$= 0.8025$$

Our example therefore yields a correlation coefficient of 0.8025. This is high. The full range of possibilities for this coefficient is the same as that for the coefficient described in Section G of Appendix 3.

J. Correlations: Standard Deviation Technique

Most plotted data tend to be distributed in such a way that the majority cluster around a middle point; this tendency is illustrated in the linear dispersion diagram in Graph A3-9. There is also, of course, a range of deviation from this central point. In statistics there are various methods of measuring the extent of such deviation; one of the most commonly used is the *standard deviation* (σ) *technique*. A comparison of standard deviations between two sets of data enables us to arrive at a widely used measure of correlation. In order to determine such a correlation between, for example, data sets in columns H and V of Appendix 2 (annual rate of natural increase and percentage of population that is urban), we would proceed as follows:

Step 1. Select the sample. These are the countries marked with an asterisk (*) in Appendix 2.

Step 2. Set up a table with five empty columns. Write the names of the selected countries down the left side, outside the five columns. Alphabetical order will do.

Step 3. Write the appropriate data from column H of Appendix 2 in the first column of your table; call them data set x.

Step 4. Square these data and write the answers (x^2) in the second column.

Step 5. Write the appropriate data from column V in the third column; call them data set y.

Step 6. Square these data and write the answers (y^2) in the fourth column.

Step 7. Multiply the x data by the y data, and write the answer (xy) in the fifth column.

Step 8. Calculate the mean ($\bar{x}$) of the x data.

Step 9. Calculate the mean ($\bar{y}$) of the y data.

Step 10. Add the figures in the second column to give a total, $\sum x^2$.

Step 11. Add the figures in the fourth column to give a total, $\sum y^2$.

Step 12. Add the figures in the fifth column to give a total, $\sum xy$.

Step 13. Apply the standard deviation correlation formula

$$r = \frac{\theta}{\sigma_x \sigma_y}$$

where

r = standard deviation correlation coefficient

σ_x (standard deviation of x data) $= \sqrt{\dfrac{\sum x^2}{n} - \bar{x}^2}$

σ_y (standard deviation of y data) $= \sqrt{\dfrac{\sum y^2}{n} - \bar{y}^2}$

$\theta = \dfrac{\sum xy}{n} - \bar{x}\bar{y}$

Step 14. Interpret the result in the manner shown at the end of Section G of Appendix 3.

K. Percentage Deviation from the Group Mean

A fairly simple way of determining the extent of variation within a group of data is to calculate the mean of the data and then see how far each item deviates from the group mean. When different magnitudes of data are being compared it is better to use proportions rather than absolute quantities; hence percentage deviations are a useful tool. Consider, for example, the following values for one criterion (x) for twenty sample countries (n = 20):

162
173
98
42
263
117
84
37
427
349
150
226
191
175
138
104
88
209
191
112

Total ($\sum$x) 3 336

These values yield a mean ($\bar{x}$) of 166.8 ($\bar{x} = \dfrac{\sum x}{n} = \dfrac{3\,336}{20} = 166.8$).

Each individual item *deviates* from the mean, and we can assess the degree of such deviation by a simple percentage calculation, giving the mean a value of 100 in all cases. Thus the item 98 deviates from the mean of 166.8 to the degree of 41 percentage points, rounded to the nearest whole number (98 is 58.75% of 166.8; 58.75 subtracted from 100 is 41.25; 41.25 rounded to the nearest whole number is 41). Therefore the percentage deviation of the item 98 from the group mean of 166.8 is 41.

L. Coefficient of Determination

There is often a need to ascertain the extent to which variations in one variable may cause (or determine) variations in another. For example, to what degree does a high rate of population increase cause starvation? We can obtain some idea by calculating the coefficient of determination (r^2) as follows. We will use the sample countries marked by an asterisk (*) in Appendix 2, because the calculations would be laborious if we were to perform them for all countries listed. The number of countries in the sample $= n$.

Step 1. Set out columns as shown below.

Country	F (Column F data — Natural increase rate)	$F - \bar{F} = f$	f^2	I (Column I data — Average daily food intake)	$I - \bar{I} = i$	i^2	fi
Algeria Brazil Canada etc.							
	$\bar{F} = \dfrac{\sum F}{n}$		$\sum f^2 =$	$\bar{I} = \dfrac{\sum I}{n}$		$\sum i^2 =$	$\sum fi =$ $(\sum fi)^2 =$

Step 2. Add ($\sum$) the data for the sample in column F and calculate the mean ($\bar{F}$).

Step 3. Add ($\sum$) the data for the sample in column I and calculate the mean ($\bar{I}$).

Step 4. Subtract the mean $\bar{F}$ from each actual item of F data, to give f. Some answers will be negative; mark them so.

Step 5. Subtract the mean $\bar{I}$ from each actual item of I data, to give i. Again, be sure to show negative values.

Step 6. Square the f answers and the i answers to give f^2 and i^2 respectively.

Step 7. Add the f^2 column ($\sum f^2$).

Step 8. Add the i^2 column ($\sum i^2$).

Step 9. Multiply f (not f^2) by i (not i^2), to give fi in the last column. Some of these figures may be negative.

Step 10. Add ($\sum$) the fi figures ($\sum fi$), remembering to subtract any negative values, and square the result to give $\sum fi^2$. You now have all the information you need to obtain the coefficient of determination, also known as r^2. Do it by applying the following formula:

$$r^2 = \frac{(\sum fi)^2 / \sum f^2}{\sum i^2}$$

Step 11. Interpret your result. The answer should be between 0 and 1. The closer it is to 1, the stronger the causality. In our example, for instance, a result of 0.8314 indicates that 83.14% of starvation is caused by the high rate of population increase. On the other hand, a result of merely 0.1796 indicates that 17.96% of starvation is caused by high rates of population increase. The answer, as with many statistical answers, is likely to be more precise than the truth warrants. Such accuracy is often called *spurious accuracy*; an example of this is a statistical item showing an average family size of 2.483 children. While statistics accurate to two or three decimal places are too precise to be truthful, they nevertheless help to quantify phenomena and causes that may otherwise exist only as vague ideas and statements.

M. Moving Averages

These are a way of looking at a set of data over a long period of time and obtaining the long-term trends by eliminating all the minor fluctuations. Moving averages are frequently used for unemployment statistics; people often speak of these figures as being "seasonally adjusted".

The technique is very simple, and can be easily illustrated with unemployment data. Let us assume that the unemployment rates for each month in the past year were as follows:

Jan. 9.7%
Feb. 9.9%
Mar. 9.8%
Apr. 9.3%
May 8.7%
June 8.1%

July 7.2%
Aug. 6.3%
Sept. 7.4%
Oct. 8.0%
Nov. 8.6%
Dec. 8.9%

In such a case the average for the whole year may be obtained by adding all the rates and dividing by 12. The annual average is thus 8.5%. We may therefore say that 8.5% unemployment was the norm for the year, and that some months were above the norm and some below. When the unemployment figure for the following January comes in, a figure of 9.5%, we again perform the calculations, replacing the first January figure with the most recent one.

The twelve month sequence now reads:

Feb. 9.9%
Mar. 9.8%
Apr. 9.3%
May 8.7%
June 8.1%
July 7.2%
Aug. 6.3%
Sept. 7.4%
Oct. 8.0%
Nov. 8.6%
Dec. 8.9%
Jan. 9.5%

The average for this new sequence is just under 8.5%; consequently there arises the situation in which some people say that unemployment is 9.5% while others say that it is only 8.5% "seasonally adjusted". If moving average calculations are performed for a long period of time, they effectively eliminate all minor fluctuations. Long-term trends may thereby be established.

N. Index Numbers

Index numbers are a device for measuring changes in data over a period of time. They are based on a percentage system, so that comparisons are possible between data of different magnitudes. The calculation of an index number proceeds as follows:

Step 1. Examine the information at the start of the period of time for which the index number is to be calculated. Consider, for example, the data series below:

1970	1971	1972	1973	1974	1975	1976	
1 350	1 225	1 150	1 125	980	1 000	1 120	Canada's fishery catch, t
205	210	240	320	285	290	390	Landed value of fishery catch, $ millions

(Source: Fisheries and Environment Canada)

If we wish to compare both sets of data from the period 1970 to 1976, then 1970 becomes what is called the *base year* and its data are assigned an index value of 100 (1970 = 100).

Step 2. To find the index numbers for the data in 1976, divide them by the appropriate 1970 data and multiply the answer by 100. For instance, 1 120 divided by 1 350 is 0.83, and 0.83 multiplied by 100 is 83. Similarly, 390 divided by 205 is 1.90, and 1.90 multiplied by 100 is 190. Thus the 1976 index numbers for Canada's fishery catch in tonnes and landed value in dollars are, respectively, 83 and 190 (1970 = 100).

Step 3. Interpret the results. The 1976 index numbers indicate that, as compared with those of 1970, the catch had gone down a little and the value had risen considerably. What could the reasons be for this situation?

O. Rank-Size Rule

The rank-size rule is based on generally observed phenomena. It states essentially that the size of a city (in population) is the reciprocal of its rank. Thus the population of the second-ranked city would be about half that of the first-ranked city, the population of the third-ranked city one third the size of the first-ranked city, and so on.

It is a general rule that if the rank (first, second, etc.) of cities is plotted against their size on a log-log graph, the pattern will appear as a fairly straight line. Rank is measured along the horizontal axis, so that up to one hundred cities can be accommodated on a 2 cycle log scale. Size is measured along the vertical axis in appropriate units (thousands, millions, etc.).

Index